THE PROPHECY COLLECTION

WHAT DOES THE BIBLE SAY ABOUT OUR TROUBLING TIMES— AND THOSE TO COME?

MARK HITCHCOCK

TYNDALE
MOMENTUM®

A Tyndale nonfiction imprint

Visit Tyndale online at tyndale.com.

Visit Tyndale Momentum online at tyndalemomentum.com.

Tyndale, Tyndale's quill logo, *Tyndale Momentum*, and the Tyndale Momentum logo are registered trademarks of Tyndale House Ministries. Tyndale Momentum is a nonfiction imprint of Tyndale House Publishers, Carol Stream, Illinois.

The Prophecy Collection: The End Times Survival Guide, The Coming Apostasy, Russia Rising

Designed by Faceout Studios, Lindy Martin

Published in association with the literary agency of William K. Jensen Literary Agency, 119 Bampton Court, Eugene, Oregon 97404.

For information about special discounts for bulk purchases, please contact Tyndale House Publishers at csresponse@tyndale.com, or call 1-855-277-9400.

Library of Congress Cataloging-in-Publication Data
A catalog record for this book is available from the Library of Congress.

ISBN 978-1-4964-5736-3

Printed in the United States of America

27   26   25   24   23   22   21
7   6   5   4   3   2   1

CONTENTS

THE END TIMES
SURVIVAL GUIDE

MARK HITCHCOCK

INTRODUCTION

ULTIMATE SURVIVOR

The future, like everything else, is not what it used to be.
PAUL VALÉRY

Survival is big business. Everywhere you look these days, someone is talking about survival. Entertainment outlets and the media have seized the survival craze.

The initial offering in the new survival genre, and reality TV, was the series *Survivor*, which premiered in the United States in 2000. The series features a group of strangers marooned at an isolated location where they have to scrounge for food, water, shelter, and fire. The show completed its thirty-fifth season in 2017. *Survivor* is the quintessential survivor in the media industry. Since *Survivor*, a steady stream of movies and series has focused on surviving in almost every possible predicament, including in a postapocalyptic world.

A spate of survival reality TV shows has also erupted. Consider these:

> *Out of the Wild: The Alaska Experiment*
> *Extreme Survival*
> *Man vs. Wild*
> *Survive This*
> *Fat Guys in the Woods*
> *Survivorman*
> *Surviving Disaster*
> *Dual Survival*
> *The Wheel*

Doomsday Preppers is another offering that demonstrates how to survive various doomsday scenarios. The survival business is booming online with all kinds of products designed to enhance a person's ability to endure any conceivable disruption, from living off the grid to all-out apocalypse. You can learn survival tips and buy survival gear for any eventuality. Online you can find all kinds of survival gurus touting their tips for surviving everything from school shootings to nuclear holocaust.

What's behind the survival obsession? Why are these programs, products, and pointers so successful? Because the future has never been more uncertain. Never more unknown. Never more unpredictable. We live in a world that seems to be on the verge of coming apart.

In 2017, a Las Vegas shooting spree at an outdoor concert left dozens massacred, a terrorist plowed through innocent pedestrians in New York City, and a gunman opened fire on a church service in a small Texas town, all in a little over a month. Evil is intensifying.

Political rancor and polarization in American politics has shifted to another gear. Both sides are so entrenched that for someone to give any ground or to compromise in the least is viewed as total capitulation, making that person an outcast from all groups. Even commonsense solutions seem unachievable. The anger and outright malice on cable news and social media is over the top. Increasingly, protests fill the streets. Violence and racial tension are boiling over. Anarchy threatens. The family is in dire trouble. Deadly diseases and viruses like Ebola and Zika erupt with frightening regularity and can spread globally very quickly. Cataclysmic weather events seem to be escalating in frequency and intensity.

Beyond these things, the once faraway threat of a terrorist attack has jumped into everyone's life—the World Trade Center, the Pentagon, a subway in London, a train in Spain, a convention in California, a tourist hot spot in France, a nightclub in Orlando, a Christmas market in Berlin. No one seems safe anywhere. Millions of displaced, devastated people are fleeing their homelands, potentially giving terrorists cover to blend into and infiltrate Western nations.

Rogue regimes such as North Korea already have the bomb, and other nations like Iran are on the threshold. Barbaric terrorists threaten our safety and very way of life. Even as the caliphate is crumbling and ISIS is on the run, fleeing ISIS fighters are exporting their savagery to more locations. ISIS-inspired killers are hiding among us. There seems to be a collective, growing sense that things can't go on this way much longer.

And then there's the world economy, which, while doing well on many fronts, seems increasingly fragile, susceptible at any time to a geopolitical crisis. The United States is twenty trillion dollars in debt, and that number is climbing. The debt bomb must explode at some point, triggering financial Armageddon.

In addition to all these things, there's an increasing indifference and malaise—and sometimes outright militancy—toward the central truths of the Christian faith and practice. Anti-Christian momentum is palpable. Hate and hostility toward Bible-believing Christians is on the rise. Christians are taking fire. Believers who dare even to question the legitimacy of same-sex marriage and gender fluidity are labeled "haters" and "homophobes." Believers in Jesus Christ now find themselves playing in enemy territory in American culture, and the crowd is getting more and more hostile.

Pornography is metastasizing like a deadly cancer and infecting an entire generation of young men and women. The young are swallowing a deadly cocktail of toxic ideas in the name of love and tolerance. We have front-row seats to a moral freefall. We're waiting for the other shoe to drop. Time seems to be running out.

What can we do?

ARE WE LIVING IN THE LAST DAYS?

Many of us have probably asked ourselves at some point whether we're living in the last days. Maybe we've asked it more often in recent times. When we ask about living in the last days, what we're really asking is "Are we living in the final days before the apocalypse? Is this the end of the age predicted in the Bible?"

In the New Testament, the term "last days" (or "last times") refers most often to the last days of the church on earth or this current age (see 1 Timothy 4:1; 2 Timothy 3:1; James 5:3; 1 Peter 1:20; 2 Peter 3:3).

All the way back in the first century, the apostle Peter said, "The end of the world is coming soon" (1 Peter 4:7). Even in New Testament times the apostles "sensed that they had moved dramatically closer to the consummation of God's plan for this world."[1] The Old Testament age had ended; they were now living in a brand-new era. For the apostles, the end of the age was already a present reality. The Scriptures indicate that the first coming of Jesus Christ inaugurated the "last days" for the church. According to the New Testament, we are living right now in these last days: "Now in these final [last] days, he has spoken to us through his Son. God promised everything to the Son as an inheritance, and through the Son he created the universe" (Hebrews 1:2).

The apostle John even calls this present age "the last hour": "Dear children, the last hour is here. You have heard that the Antichrist is coming, and already many such antichrists have appeared. From this we know that the last hour has come" (1 John 2:18). According to the New Testament, the last days commenced with Christ's first advent and will close with the return of the Lord to catch his bride—the church—away to heaven. Therefore, the entire current age, commonly known as the church age, is known as the last days.

Labeling this age as the "last days" is a vivid reminder that Christ could come at any time. Every generation since the death and resurrection of Christ has lived with the hope that it might be the final generation and that Christ could return at any moment. There are no prophecies that must be fulfilled before Christ can come. We are living in the last days and may be living in the last days of the last days before Christ's coming. As the end approaches, the enemy is ramping up the attacks in a final onslaught.

THE ULTIMATE SURVIVOR

Jesus, Paul, Peter, John, and others warn of an unprecedented increase in demonic deception, moral corruption, doctrinal error, and spiritual lethargy in the last days. Believers today face unparalleled spiritual danger. These are treacherous times. As Erwin Lutzer notes, "The day of the casual Christian is over. No longer is it possible to drift along, hoping that no tough choices will have to be made. At this point in American history, any moral and spiritual progress will have to be won at great cost. The darker the night, the more important every candle becomes."[2] We need to stand firm and shine brightly in the darkness.

In August 1990, Saddam Hussein invaded Kuwait, triggering the Gulf War. When she heard of the invasion, British Prime Minister Margaret Thatcher was in the United States. She described her initial thoughts in an interview with PBS's *Frontline*: "I went out for a walk, always lovely in the mountains, and got things worked out in my mind, but it was perfectly clear, aggression must be stopped. That is the lesson of this century. And if an aggressor gets away with it, others will want to get away with it too, so he must be stopped, and turned back. You cannot gain from your aggression."[3]

Toward the end of her tenure as prime minister, Thatcher helped spur President George H. W. Bush to intervene militarily in the Persian Gulf after the Iraqi invasion. Urging President Bush to join the fight against Saddam, Thatcher famously declared that "this is no time to go wobbly."[4] The same is true for us—this is no time to go wobbly.

But how can we stand strong in perilous times? How can we shine brightly in the darkness? How can we keep from "going wobbly" as the end of the age draws near?

GIVE ME THE TOOLS

Winston Churchill was prime minister of Great Britain during the trying days of World War II. Despite his massive influence, he often downplayed his own part in winning the war. He gave credit to the people, saying after the war had ended that they "had the lion's heart," and he merely "had the luck to be called upon to give the roar." In February 1941, Churchill delivered one of his most lauded wartime speeches. He claimed that in wartime, what mattered was "deeds, not words." After walking listeners through what had already transpired in the war, he urged US President Franklin Roosevelt to get involved in the fight rather than sitting on the sidelines. He said, "We shall not fail or falter; we shall not weaken or tire. Neither the sudden shock of battle, nor the long-drawn trials of vigilance and exertion will wear us down. Give us the tools, and we will finish the job."[5]

There's no doubt the church of Jesus Christ is locked in a deadly spiritual war. Sitting on the sidelines is not an option. The war is multiplying on numerous fronts. The good news is that God has given us the tools, or maybe it would be better to call them the truths, that we need to finish the job as we await Christ's coming. God has given us sufficient resources to effectively encounter and engage the world we're facing.

Many have wondered in recent years why the apocalypse craze in movies and video games appeals to people so strongly. One answer is "because they show people returning to the fundamentals of existence."[6] In the same way, I believe what's happening in our world today is moving believers to return to the foundations of our spiritual existence. Believers everywhere must get back to what matters most. We must always remember that our battle "at the most basic level is spiritual, not political or even moral."[7]

Some Christians today are carefully preparing *physically* for the apocalypse—hoarding cash, gold, weapons, and food. To one degree or another they're the ultimate "doomsday preppers."[8] There's nothing wrong with reasonable preparation for disruptions in basic services that could occur in our complex world; however, the most important "prepping" for every believer should be *spiritual*. Whatever view we may hold concerning the apocalypse or the end times, our focus should be on spiritual survival. That's the consistent focus of Scripture.

So, what are the spiritual tools, the spiritual truths, Scripture tells us we must understand and use as the end draws near? How can we be spiritually prepared for today and for what lies ahead?

In the pages that follow, you will discover ten spiritual tools the Bible relates directly to our spiritual preparation for the Lord's coming—ten biblical survival strategies to live out these last days so you and your family can prosper in an increasingly decaying, darkening world.

These strategies won't guarantee your physical or financial well-being, but they are guaranteed to bring life and vitality to your spiritual health and welfare as you cling to the immovable rock of God's Word. The truth is that even if you survive physically and prosper financially, your deepest need—and mine—is spiritual survival and stability. When life is whittled down to its essence, the real issue is our spiritual condition before God.

My prayer is that God can use these basic, biblical tools and strategies to help you survive and thrive as you await Christ's coming.

Mark Hitchcock
JANUARY 2018

CHAPTER 1

USE THE 46 DEFENSE

Most news . . . could carry a universal headline to get our attention:
YOU SHOULD BE WORRIED.

GARY STOKES

One of the greatest defenses in NFL history was that of the 1985 Chicago Bears. They employed a defensive scheme known as the "46 defense," developed in 1981 by defensive coordinator Buddy Ryan. Armed with this scheme and some great talent, they throttled and terrorized offenses across the league, reaching their zenith in 1985. The pressure they applied, led by middle linebacker Mike Singletary, was reckless and relentless. The '85 Bears struck fear into the hearts of opposing quarterbacks, blazing a trail of devastation through the NFL. Their domination was so overwhelming that "during one three-game stretch, the Bears scored more points on defense than they allowed, and they're the only team in history to post back-to-back shutouts in the playoffs."[1]

The 46 defense is legendary. None has ever been better.

As our world becomes more volatile and uncertain, wouldn't it be nice to have that kind of spiritual defense against the mounting cares, stresses, and worries of life? Wouldn't it be comforting to have an impenetrable wall that holds back the fear and fretting that floods our minds with anxious thoughts?

The truth is that God *has* given his people a "46 defense" against the cares, worries, and anxieties we face. It's a 46 defense that's better known even than that of the '85 Bears. It's Philippians 4:6. (We'll look at another famous 46 defense—Psalm 46—in chapter 7.)

The "Philippians 4:6" defense is renowned. It shuts down opposing offenses. They have no chance against it. It's a fail-safe formula against worry and stress:

> Don't worry about anything; instead, pray about everything. Tell God what you need, and thank him for all he has done. Then you will experience God's peace, which exceeds anything we can understand. His peace will guard your hearts and minds as you live in Christ Jesus.
>
> PHILIPPIANS 4:6-7

In anxious times, with worry on the offensive, more and more people are using it. Amazon tracks information about the most highlighted passages in their e-books. This list of what people highlight or annotate sheds light on what people find interesting, important, or valuable. According to Amazon, the verse in the Bible that is most frequently highlighted is not a traditionally familiar one like Psalm 23, John 3:16, or the Lord's Prayer—it is Philippians 4:6-7.[2] Apparently, it has become "America's go-to passage of Scripture."[3]

This shouldn't surprise us, because by all accounts, the United States is the most anxious nation in the world. Ironically, one of the world's wealthiest nations is also the most worried.

We live in a world of cascading crises. The world and its troubles and trials seem to be getting worse.

Jesus told us this would happen. In his famous sermon about the end times, just a few days before his death, Jesus outlined the signs of his coming and concluded by warning about the worries of life that can overwhelm us. Jesus said, "Watch out! Don't let your hearts be dulled by carousing and drunkenness, and by *the worries of this life*. Don't let that day catch you unaware, like a trap. For that day will come upon everyone living on the earth" (Luke 21:34-35, emphasis added).

Jesus said that the "worries of this life" in the final days will get so strong and will dull our hearts to such an extent that we might lose our hope and expectation of his coming if we allow them to go unchecked.

The worries of this life produce anxious days and sleepless nights. They distract us. They threaten our spiritual survival in these last days. Jesus said they're traps that dull our hearts and leave us unprepared for his coming. We can't thrive spiritually at the same time our hearts are weighed down with worry. But let's face it: maybe only a few of us worry none of the time, most of us worry some of the time, and some of us worry all the time.

Worry is a national addiction. You could even call it a plague. "Anxiety has become the number one mental health issue in North America. It's estimated that one third of the North American adult population experiences anxiety unwellness issues."[4]

Part of the explanation for the surge of worry is our constant connection to everything that's going on all over the world. Through 24-7 cable news, the Internet, and smartphones, we instantly know about nuclear threats, child kidnappings, famines, disasters, riots, economic problems, and on and on and on. The daily load of bad news can overwhelm us. Before means of mass communication, people lived mostly secluded lives. News traveled slowly, and sometimes not at all. How things have changed. Immediate access to world news threatens to crush us with stress and worry.

When Jesus spoke of the end times and the worries of this life, he knew that these worries would grow to the point that people are paralyzed and trapped. We all sense that anxiety is increasing and intensifying as the end draws near. We're anxious about all kinds of things:

> World problems and politics
> Our health
> Our finances and the economy
> Our children or grandchildren
> Our marriages
> Our choices
> Retirement
> Death
> What has happened
> What could happen

Sometimes we even get worried that we don't have anything to worry about.

We hear more and more about anxiety attacks, panic attacks, and people just generally being stressed out. Anti-anxiety drugs regularly appear on the top ten list of prescription medications in the United States. Many people have turned worry into a lifestyle, a full-time job. Life is consumed with worry and fear.

This reminds me of a story I heard about a woman who for many years had trouble sleeping because she worried about burglars. One night her husband heard a noise in the house, so he went downstairs to investigate. When he got there, he found a burglar and said, "I'm pleased to see you. Will you please come upstairs? My wife has been waiting ten years to meet you."

It's far too easy for worry to become a way of life and for us even to find ourselves worrying about the same things for years. But for God's people, life shouldn't be that way. A real burglar can steal from you once, but worry can steal from you night after night for years.

As the stresses of life multiply in these last days, how can we win over worry? How can we bury worry before worry buries us? What's the spiritual survival strategy?

We have to employ the Philippians 4:6 defense.

And this defense is strikingly simple. The antidote to anxiety is thankful prayer. To state it more fully: *we experience God's peace instead of worry when we pray with thankfulness.*

We can't worry and pray at the same time.

The three simple parts of this strategy come from the three key words in this passage.

> The Problem: Worry
> The Prescription: Prayer
> The Promise: Peace

THE PROBLEM: WORRY

Philippians 4:6 begins with four sweeping words: "Don't worry about anything," or as some translations say, "Be anxious for nothing."

It doesn't say,

> "Be anxious for less"
> "Be anxious for a few things"
> "Be anxious for only one hour a day"
> "Be anxious for only the big things"

It says, "Be anxious for *nothing*." "Don't worry about *anything*." It's categorical. God's people are never to worry—period. About anything.

The word *worry* in the original Greek (*merimnao*) literally means "to be divided into parts." To worry or be anxious is to have a distracted, divided mind—a mind torn down the middle and pulled in different directions. The worried mind is restless, filled with tension, and unsettled, like a flag twisting in the wind. It's a mind fighting on two fronts. The English word *worry* comes from an old English word that means "to strangle." This is a fitting image, because we all know how worry strangles and squeezes the peace and enjoyment out of life. Sometimes anxiety can get to the point that the worrier actually feels short of breath.

Worrying is having your mind torn between the real and the possible. Worry feeds on the what-ifs of life. It's a stream of thoughts focused on fear of what might happen. I once heard someone say that worry pulls tomorrow's cloud over today's sunshine. The worrier lives in the past and the future, spending life crucified between two thieves that rob the present of its joy and vitality. Helmut Thielicke aptly describes worry as "*wandering in times not our own.*"

ANXIETY ATTACKED

Jesus confronted worry in his Sermon on the Mount in Matthew 5–7. Interestingly, one-seventh of Jesus' famous sermon is about worry. That's fascinating and instructive. Here is the Master's wisdom on worry:

> That is why I tell you not to worry about everyday life—
> whether you have enough food and drink, or enough clothes
> to wear. Isn't life more than food, and your body more than
> clothing? Look at the birds. They don't plant or harvest or

store food in barns, for your heavenly Father feeds them. And aren't you far more valuable to him than they are? Can all your worries add a single moment to your life?

And why worry about your clothing? Look at the lilies of the field and how they grow. They don't work or make their clothing, yet Solomon in all his glory was not dressed as beautifully as they are. And if God cares so wonderfully for wildflowers that are here today and thrown into the fire tomorrow, he will certainly care for you. Why do you have so little faith?

So don't worry about these things, saying, "What will we eat? What will we drink? What will we wear?" These things dominate the thoughts of unbelievers, but your heavenly Father already knows all your needs. Seek the Kingdom of God above all else, and live righteously, and he will give you everything you need.

So don't worry about tomorrow, for tomorrow will bring its own worries. Today's trouble is enough for today.

MATTHEW 6:25-34

There's a lot here to unpack, but we'll just look at this passage briefly. Jesus uses the word *worry* five times (verses 25, 27, 28, 31, 34). He tells us three simple things about worry. First, worry is *fruitless*. It doesn't do any good. As Jesus said, "Can all your worries add a single moment to your life?" We see the worthlessness of worry in that most of the things we worry about never happen. We expend countless hours exhausting our emotions on events that never materialize.

Sometimes people will say or think something like "I know worry works because when I worry about something, it doesn't happen." But that doesn't mean the worry worked. It simply proves that most things we worry about never happen. Like Vance Havner once said, "Worry is like sitting in a rocking chair. It will give you something to do, but it won't get you anywhere." It doesn't produce a thing. Fretting is a lot of work for nothing.

A recent study discovered that "85 percent of what subjects worried about never happened, and with the 15 percent that did happen, 79 percent of subjects discovered either they could handle the difficulty better than expected, or the difficulty taught them a lesson worth learning. This means that 97 percent of what you worry over is not much more than a fearful mind punishing you with exaggerations and misperceptions."[5]

Worry doesn't do any good—and results in a great deal of bad.

Second, worry is *faithless*. Jesus put his finger on the core issue when he said, "Why do you have so little faith?" Worry brings our weak faith to the surface. Many of us believe God can take care of the "Sweet By and By," but we have trouble trusting him with the "Nasty Now and Now." We trust him for heaven but not for earth.

Worry is the opposite of trust. It's a failure to trust God to take care of us. Worry has been described as the stepchild of unbelief. We can dress it up and disguise it however we want to, but worry is nothing but lack of trust in God to meet our needs in his perfect time.

Third, Jesus says worry is *fatherless*. When we worry, we act as if we have no Father who cares for our needs and yearns to meet them. Jesus says, "Your heavenly Father already knows all your needs." Worry diminishes our heavenly Father's loving care for us. Think of how our worry must make God feel. When he sees us worried and afraid, we aren't trusting him. He is our Father, but we choose to live like we're orphans when we worry and fret.

We live under the canopy of God's fatherly care. In Matthew 6:26-30, there's an argument from the lesser to the greater. God loves his children more than his pets. If God cares for birds, he will care for us.

We are his children through faith in Jesus Christ. God is our Father—and he's a *perfect* father. We can trust him to care for us at all times, even during these dark days.

WORRY WEARY

With worry comes a host of unwanted results. Robert J. Morgan vividly outlines some of the consequences of an anxious outlook: "When worry barges into our brains, it brings along a gang of accomplices—discouragement, fear, exhaustion, despair, anguish, hopelessness, pain, obsession, distraction, foreboding, irritation, impatience—none of which are friends of the Holy Spirit."[6]

Anxiety saps your strength, leaving you spent and stressed out. Worry slowly drains our strength and focus. As the old saying goes, "Worry doesn't empty tomorrow of its sorrows, but it empties today of its strength."

It's not wrong to think about the future and to make plans. The book of Proverbs tells us in various ways that planning is wise. I love to plan and think about the future. It's fine and even faithful to *think* about tomorrow, as long as we submit our plans to the Lord, but it's never right to *worry* about the future.

At one point during his presidency, the people around Abraham Lincoln were anxious about coming events. In response to their worries, Lincoln told this story:

> Many years ago, when I was a young lawyer, and Illinois was little settled, except on her southern border, I, with other lawyers, used to ride the circuit; journeying with the judge from county-seat to county-seat in quest of business. Once, after a long spell of pouring rain, which had flooded

the whole country, transforming small creeks into rivers, we were often stopped by these swollen streams, which we with difficulty crossed. Still ahead of us was Fox River, larger than all the rest; and we could not help saying to each other, "If these streams give us so much trouble, how shall we get over Fox River?" Darkness fell before we had reached that stream; and we all stopped at a log tavern, had our horses put out, and resolved to pass the night. Here we were right glad to fall in with the Methodist Presiding Elder of the circuit, who rode it in all weather, knew all its ways, and could tell us all about Fox River. So we all gathered around him, and asked him if he knew about the crossing of Fox River. "O yes," he replied, "I know all about Fox River. I have crossed it often, and understand it well; but I have one fixed rule with regard to Fox River: I never cross it till I reach it."[7]

Far too many believers are wearing themselves out crossing the Fox River long before they reach it. Wait until you get there.

GOOD WORRY?

The Bible makes an important distinction between what we might call "good worry" and "bad worry."

Philippians 4:6 says, "Don't worry about anything." Clearly this is sinful worry. But in Philippians 2:20, the apostle Paul lauds his friend Timothy when he says, "I have no one else like Timothy, who genuinely cares about your welfare." The phrase "genuinely cares" translates the same Greek word used for "worry" in Philippians 4:6. So there is a kind of care that's applauded and appropriate that we could call "concern" and another inappropriate form we could call "anxiety."

There are many good things to be concerned about. Our marriages. Our children. Our aged parents. Our own spiritual lives. The spiritual condition of our family and friends. The future and welfare of our nation. We all have genuine, legitimate concerns. There are many good things that should burden us—things we should care about. But genuine concern can quickly degenerate into godless worry or what Jesus called the "worries of this life."

We all know what it feels like to be concerned about something and suddenly feel our mind being pulled in different directions. Our thoughts become restless and distracted, and sleep evades us. We're tense and unsettled and feel like we're being pulled apart. We can feel the surge of uneasiness. We're moving from concern to worry—from "good" worry to "godless" worry.

The Bible is clear that we aren't to worry about anything. But how do we shake the worries of life?

THE PRESCRIPTION: PRAYER

In Philippians 4:6, the word "instead" (or "but" in some translations) appears right after the words "Don't worry about anything," drawing a sharp contrast. After the word "instead" we have God's prescription for worry: "Pray about everything. Tell God what you need, and thank him for all he has done." The antidote to anxiety is to pray about everything.

Three different Greek words for "prayer" are found in this verse. The first one is a general word for prayer in which we give adoration, worship, and devotion to God. The second term focuses on our needs and connotes the idea of dependence or a desperate cry arising from need. The third word refers to precise petitions or specific requests.

Jesus highlighted prayer as the antidote to anxiety in his sermon about the end times:

Watch out! Don't let your hearts be dulled by carousing and drunkenness, and by the *worries of this life*. Don't let that day catch you unaware, like a trap. For that day will come upon everyone living on the earth. Keep alert at all times. And *pray* that you might be strong enough to escape these coming horrors and stand before the Son of Man.

LUKE 21:34-36, EMPHASIS ADDED

Jesus says prayer is our defense against the worries of life.

Robert J. Morgan vividly highlights the connection between prayer and overcoming the trap of worry:

> Prayer is the closet where we change clothes and replace
> a spirit of despair with a garment of praise. It's the bank
> where we present the promissory notes of God's promises
> and withdraw endless deposits of grace. It's the darkroom
> of the soul where negatives become positives. It's the transfer
> station where the pulse of fear is exchanged for the impulse
> of faith. It's a currency exchange where we trade in our
> liabilities for God's abundant life.[8]

Prayer is our defense against the worries of life, but not just any prayer—*thankful* prayer. Philippians 4:6 includes the all-important words "and thank him for all he has done." Recalling God's blessings must accompany our prayers. When we give thanks, we're recognizing and remembering God's good gifts to us. This intentional recounting of God's blessings creates faith and trust. Grateful prayer builds our faith, pushing worry out of our hearts. Praying with an attitude of gratitude wipes out worry. Thankful prayer is the fail-safe formula that transfers our cares to God and taps into his peace.

As Charles Spurgeon once said, "No care but all prayer. No anxiety but much joyful communion with God. Carry your desires to the Lord of your life, the guardian of your soul. Go to Him with two portions of prayer and one of fragrant praise. Do not pray doubtfully but thankfully."[9]

As we plunge deeper into the end times, the worries of life will increase and intensify. We see it already. To survive and stand, we must run the 46 defense every day, every moment in our lives. You may have to use the 46 defense over and over again every day as worry tries to worm its way into your heart and mind. Every time worry knocks, immediately use the 46 defense. It will work every time.

THE PROMISE: PEACE

Few promises in the Bible are more comforting than Philippians 4:7: "Then you will experience God's peace, which exceeds anything we can understand. His peace will guard your hearts and minds as you live in Christ Jesus."

Did you catch those words? "God's peace." This is stunning. When a believer humbly approaches the throne of God in thankful prayer, the serenity of the Trinity is unleashed in that believer's heart. God has never experienced one worried moment. Nothing disturbs him. He's never shaken. He's perpetually at peace. There's never panic in heaven. The Trinity never meets in emergency session. God has an infinite, measureless supply of peace, and he makes that peace available to us by means of prayer.

There are two beautiful things in Philippians 4:7 about God's peace. First, it's *unexplainable*. The peace of God infinitely surpasses the ability of the human mind to perceive or understand how it works. It "defies all attempts to describe, analyze, explain, or comprehend it."[10] Charles Spurgeon says, "This shall bring you God's own peace. You shall not be able to understand the peace which you shall enjoy. It will enfold you in its infinite embrace. Heart and mind through Christ Jesus shall be steeped in a sea of rest. Come life or death, poverty, pain, slander, you shall dwell in Jesus above every rolling wind or darkening cloud."[11] I hope you've experienced this peace.

Our first son, Justin, was born while Cheryl and I lived in Dallas during my first semester at Dallas Theological Seminary. Cheryl was in the hospital for a month before he was born. He was born very prematurely and had a cleft lip and palate. He spent his first six weeks in the neonatal intensive care unit at Baylor Hospital. During those dark days, I used the 46 defense over and over again. Every time, my cries to God were met with his supernatural calm. I still can't explain it. God's peace is unexplainable.

Second, the peace of God is *unassailable*. The word "guard" is a military term for a contingent of soldiers assigned to protect someone. The peace of God acts as a guard at the door of your heart and mind to provide security against the assaults of worry, confusion, tension, and uncertainty.

At the time Paul wrote the epistle to the Philippians, he was eight hundred miles away from them in Rome under house arrest, guarded 24-7 by the Roman Praetorian Guard, the most elite force in the Roman Empire. But as Steven J. Lawson points out, "He was also being guarded in a far more secure way—God was protecting his heart so that anxiety and fear would not enter it. Fear was being denied entrance into his heart. . . . anxiety cannot crack the divine defense."[12] The believer who prays with thanksgiving is guarded against the assault of anxiety.

As we're hurtling toward the end of days and the worries-of-life mushroom, God's peace is like a spiritual "SEAL Team Six" stationed at the entrance of your thoughts and emotions to protect and keep you, giving you mental and emotional stability and tranquility.

Philippians 4:7 ends with the comforting words "in Christ Jesus."

In Jesus we have nothing to fear; without him we have everything to fear. Jesus is our peace.

Joseph Scriven said it well in the hymn "What a Friend We Have in Jesus":

What a friend we have in Jesus,
all our sins and griefs to bear!
What a privilege to carry
everything to God in prayer!
O what peace we often forfeit,
O what needless pain we bear,
all because we do not carry
everything to God in prayer.

Don't forfeit God's peace. Don't go on bearing needless pain. Carry everything to God in grateful prayer. Use the 46 defense. Claim God's fathomless, unshakable peace.

NO WORRIES

An early Greek manuscript bears the name of a man called Titedios Amerimnos. The first name is a proper name—like the name Titus. The second name is like a nickname, and it is made up of the word that means "to worry" (*merimnos*) prefixed by the Greek letter alpha, which negates the meaning of the word. *Amerimnos* means "not to worry." Based on this nickname, many believe this man was a Greek who constantly worried but who stopped worrying once he was saved. Thereafter he was known as Titedios Amerimnos—"Titedio, the man who never worries."[13]

The question for us is, can we write our name and add to it, "The One Who Never Worries"? This will only be true if we learn the spiritual survival strategy of thankful prayer.

We must use the prescription in Philippians 4:6 and claim the promise in Philippians 4:7. There's no need to have any more anxious days and sleepless nights.

Some days and nights you may have to use the 46 defense over and over again. You may have to go to the Lord in thankful prayer again and again. But you can rest assured it will work every time. God's perpetual peace is available if we will humbly lift our hearts to him in grateful prayer. The only question is, will we obey this clear command? If we will, our days and nights of worry are over.

In my early twenties I spent two to three hours every Friday night studying the Bible with an elderly friend. He was a faithful, loving Bible teacher who helped me a great deal. He had several adages he liked to repeat, but there was one saying he repeated most often—"When in a fix, go to Philippians 4:6." I know it's a bit corny, but I've never forgotten it. I still apply it often today. I hope you will too.

"When in a fix, go to Philippians 4:6."

This world is not becoming a safer, more stable, or more secure place. As technology explodes and threats expand, the potential for worry widens. Stress surges. Jesus lovingly warned us about the prevalence and peril of the "worries of this life" that threaten our spiritual strength, stamina, and stability as this age draws to a close, and through the pen of the apostle Paul, he graciously gave us a fail-safe defense that will work every time—the 46 defense:

Don't worry about anything; instead, pray about everything. Tell God what you need, and thank him for all he has done. Then you will experience God's peace, which exceeds anything we can understand. His peace will guard your hearts and minds as you live in Christ Jesus.

CHAPTER 2

RUN FOR YOUR LIFE

We ain't gonna have no sport where you sit down and go backwards.

CLEMSON ATHLETIC DIRECTOR FRANK HOWARD,
IN RESPONSE TO A SUGGESTION THAT
CLEMSON FIELD A ROWING TEAM

In a devotion titled "Run for Your Life," Philip De Courcy references Christopher McDougall's *Born to Run*: "Every morning in Africa, a gazelle wakes up, it knows it must outrun the fastest lion or it will be killed. Every morning in Africa, a lion wakes up, it knows it must run faster than the slowest gazelle, or it will starve. It doesn't matter whether you're the lion or the gazelle, when the sun comes up, you'd better be running."[1]

De Courcy writes, "Not to do something is to have something done to you. If the gazelle fails to run it gets eaten, if the lion fails to run it has nothing to eat. Both the gazelle and lion must run for their life. And so it is with the Christian."[2]

When I look around today, I believe more strongly than ever that the end of days is near. On every front, world events bear a remarkable correspondence to ancient prophecies in Scripture. As time runs out, we need to run as never before—we need to run for our lives. Our enemy, Satan, is on the prowl. He knows his time is short. The "lion" wakes up every day and never stops roaming, searching for prey (see 1 Peter 5:8). Standing still is not an option. If you stand still, you'll get swallowed up. We must run and keep running, which requires spiritual stamina and endurance.

The disappointments and discouragements of life can sap our strength and will. And underneath the bigger struggles of life is the daily grind and routine that can slowly wear us down. As I once heard someone say, "The problem with life is that it's so daily." We need to run with endurance.

Christians should not be strangers to running. Athletic metaphors are liberally sprinkled throughout the New Testament, especially in the writings of the apostle Paul, who must have witnessed the games many times in his day. He often compares the Christian life to a race.

> Don't you realize that in a race everyone runs, but only
> one person gets the prize? So run to win! All athletes are
> disciplined in their training. They do it to win a prize that
> will fade away, but we do it for an eternal prize. So I run
> with purpose in every step. I am not just shadowboxing.
> I discipline my body like an athlete, training it to do what
> it should. Otherwise, I fear that after preaching to others
> I myself might be disqualified.
> I CORINTHIANS 9:24-27

I don't mean to say that I have already achieved these things or that I have already reached perfection. But I press on to possess that perfection for which Christ Jesus first possessed me. No, dear brothers and sisters, I have not achieved it, but I focus on this one thing: Forgetting the past and looking forward to what lies ahead, I press on to reach the end of the race and receive the heavenly prize for which God, through Christ Jesus, is calling us.

PHILIPPIANS 3:12-14

I have fought the good fight, I have finished the race, and I have remained faithful. And now the prize awaits me—the crown of righteousness, which the Lord, the righteous Judge, will give me on the day of his return. And the prize is not just for me but for all who eagerly look forward to his appearing.

2 TIMOTHY 4:7-8

Hebrews 12:1-2 is the key New Testament text on how to run the race of life with focus and endurance—on how to run for your life:

Therefore, since we are surrounded by such a huge crowd of witnesses to the life of faith, let us strip off every weight that slows us down, especially the sin that so easily trips us up. And let us run with endurance the race God has set before us. We do this by keeping our eyes on Jesus, the champion who initiates and perfects our faith. Because of the joy awaiting him, he endured the cross, disregarding its shame. Now he is seated in the place of honor beside God's throne.

William Barclay, the well-known biblical commentator, calls these two verses "a well-nigh perfect summary of the Christian life."[3] These verses picture the Christian race from the starting blocks to the finish line. They fall neatly into six parts.

THE EXHORTATION

The key statement in Hebrews 12:1-2 is "and let us run with endurance the race God has set before us." Everything around this statement in Hebrews 12:1-2 describes how we run our race with endurance. But before we unpack this statement, let's get our bearings within the book of Hebrews. This anonymous epistle was penned in the early AD 60s for believers residing in the city of Rome, likely before the outbreak of Nero's persecution. The litany of Old Testament quotations and allusions point toward Jewish Christians ("Hebrews") as the primary audience. The readers have trusted Jesus as their Messiah and are now suffering mistreatment from both Gentiles and Jews. Hebrews 10:32-36 describes their situation and the author's call to hang in there:

> Think back on those early days when you first learned about
> Christ. Remember how you remained faithful even though
> it meant terrible suffering. Sometimes you were exposed to
> public ridicule and were beaten, and sometimes you helped
> others who were suffering the same things. You suffered
> along with those who were thrown into jail, and when all
> you owned was taken from you, you accepted it with joy.
> You knew there were better things waiting for you that will
> last forever. So do not throw away this confident trust in
> the Lord. Remember the great reward it brings you! Patient
> endurance is what you need now, so that you will continue to
> do God's will. Then you will receive all that he has promised.

The troubles have reached the point where some of the believers are tempted to jettison Jesus and revert to their old way of life. They're in danger of flaming out and fizzling out.

Many believe the book of Hebrews was originally a sermon to stir the audience to keep going. The dominant theme of the letter is the supremacy of Jesus. The first three verses set the tone:

> Long ago God spoke many times and in many ways to our ancestors through the prophets. And now in these final days, he has spoken to us through his Son. God promised everything to the Son as an inheritance, and through the Son he created the universe. The Son radiates God's own glory and expresses the very character of God, and he sustains everything by the mighty power of his command. When he had cleansed us from our sins, he sat down in the place of honor at the right hand of the majestic God in heaven.

After this grand opening, chapters 1 through 10 show that Jesus is greater than angels, greater than Moses, greater than Aaron, and greater than Old Testament sacrifices. The message is to stay focused on Jesus. He is supreme—why on earth would readers want to leave him and go back to their old way of life?

Within this larger context, Hebrews 12:1-2 is like a dose of spiritual smelling salts to help these believers, and us, get a second wind in the race. It's a call for us to run for our lives in the face of increasing opposition and buffeting spiritual headwinds.

The word "race" in Hebrews 12:1 is the Greek word *agona* (from which we get our English word *agony*). Anyone who has ever run any significant distance knows that running a long way involves a degree of agony and exhaustion.

Years ago, while visiting my in-laws in Dallas for Thanksgiving, my wife talked me into running an eight-mile race called the Turkey Trot on Thanksgiving morning. I was running about three miles a day back then and thought a few more miles would be no problem, so off we went. I was right to a point. I felt great for the first three miles. And the next two or three weren't bad either (the first five or six miles were fairly flat). But the last two or three miles were grueling. All the hills were in the final stretch. The finish line in the distance was one of the most welcome sights I've ever seen. I finished the race, but I vowed never to do that again. Since then, I've always wondered why people like to run long distances.

I sympathize with Joe Stowell's attitude toward running:

I have nothing against runners. Some of my best friends are addicted runners. Though I have never seen a runner smiling, apparently there is something fulfilling about it. I even tried it once, waiting for that surge of ecstasy that my friends told me I would experience, only to find that the ecstasy came when I stopped running.[4]

Stowell continues:

Whatever you think about running, it's important to note that the Bible often speaks of living the Christian life as if . . . we were running a race. Following Jesus is clearly more than a leisurely stroll in the park! And the issue is not whether you will run the race. When you became His follower, you were put in the race. The question is not *will* you run, but *how* will you run?[5]

We're called to run the race of life with endurance. And we each have our own race to run. Hebrews 12:1 calls this "the race marked out for us" (NIV). We each have a lane to run in. Our Lord has mapped out a specific race for each of us. Our races vary greatly. No two races are the same. We each face our own set of challenges. As Kent Hughes reminds us,

We each have a specific course mapped out for us, and the course for each runner is unique. Some are relatively straight, some are all turns, some seem all uphill, some are a flat hiking path. All are long, but some are longer. But each of us . . . can finish the race "marked out for us." I may not be able to run your course, and you may find mine impossible, but I can finish my race and you yours. Both of us can finish well if we choose and if we rely on him who is our strength and our guide.[6]

That's the exhortation.

THE ENCOURAGEMENT

The exhortation to run the race is preceded by a wonderful encouragement: "Therefore, since we are surrounded by such a huge crowd of witnesses." We all desperately need encouragement in the race. The word "therefore" that opens Hebrews 12:1 is a transition word that reaches back to the long list of the faithful in Hebrews 11. The "huge crowd of witnesses" pictures a capacity crowd at a stadium. Few things are more electrifying than a stadium full of loyal fans. There's nothing that can match the wave of enthusiasm that sweeps over a packed college football stadium on a Saturday afternoon in the fall.

Many understand this to mean that all the saints who lived before us are spectators in a great stadium in heaven, watching us and cheering us on. But the picture here is not of *them* watching *us* but of *us* watching *them*. In other words, they testify to us and bear witness to us that God can see us through. When we look at the lives of men and women like Enoch, Abraham, Sarah, Jacob, Rahab, David, and Daniel, we are encouraged. They all faced struggles, tests of faith, and temptation, yet they finished the race. They didn't quit. They didn't go back. That's the point the author of Hebrews is driving home. The lives of these Old Testament saints are a motivation and incentive for the original readers and for us not to go back. That's why we need to study the lives of the saints of old. They stayed in the race and finished; so can we.

The *exhortation* is clear: run with endurance.

The *encouragement* is comforting: look to the witnesses.

But there's another thing every runner must do to win: eliminate the encumbrances and the entanglements.

THE ENCUMBRANCES

Here we move from the stands down to the track as the runners are preparing to run, getting ready for the race: "Let us strip off every weight that slows us down." The first thing any runner does is to work to eliminate drag.

The Greek word translated here as "weight" (*ogkos*) is the word from which we get our English word *oncology*, and it refers to a mass, tumor, or weight. Runners do all they can to shed excess body weight. You never see a chubby marathon runner—at least not one who is competitive. They also peel off any shred of excess clothing. You will never see a competitive runner on race day wearing sweatpants or ankle weights.

In the same way, as we run our race, we must throw off everything that holds us back. Anything that slows our progress must go.

These encumbrances in our lives aren't sinful things. They're things that distract and delay us, that sap our energy, that divert our attention, and that dampen our enthusiasm for the things of God. They're anything that dulls our competitive edge. We know they're not sinful things because they're distinguished from sins in the next phrase ("the sin that so easily trips us up"). This tells us that just because something is not a sin doesn't make it right for us. A good thing can become a bad thing if it slows us down or impedes our progress.

What are the encumbrances that can weigh us down? Some examples could be too much recreation and entertainment, our careers, our habits, our hobbies, sports, relationships, lack of discipline, or procrastination. Encumbrances vary from person to person.

We would all do well to search our hearts and ask, *What encumbrances are in my life? What am I doing to rid myself of them?*

THE ENTANGLEMENTS

The author of Hebrews moves seamlessly from "every weight that slows us down" to "the sin that so easily trips us up." These are bad things; they're sin. The use of the definite article, *the*, before the word *sin* could indicate that a specific sin is in view. In the context of the book of Hebrews, the main threat to the believers seems to have been a creeping unbelief (see Hebrews 3:12, 19). Hebrews 11 is all about faith, so in this context *the* sin could be a reference to unbelief (lack of faith) or doubt. After all, the phrase "by faith" occurs twenty-one times in Hebrews 11. The Lord may be warning us to put aside unbelief, which is a faucet for all kinds of other sins.

While that view is certainly possible, I think *the* sin referred to in Hebrews 12:1 is probably broader. We all face entangling, ensnaring sins in our lives. They are often referred to as "besetting" sins because the King James Version refers to this as "the sin which doth so easily beset us." We could call this "the sin which clings so closely." We each have certain sins that cling closely to us, although they're not the same for every person: pride, greed, lust, worry, gossip, laziness, jealousy, impatience, addiction, anger, self-pity, ingratitude, hatred, bitterness, unforgiveness, or a critical spirit. J. C. Ryle exposes our special sins:

But there are particular besetting sins, of which each separate Christian can alone furnish an account; each single one of us has some weak point; each one has got a thin, shaking spot in the wall of defence against the devil, each one has a traitor in his camp ready to open the gates to Satan, and he that is wise will never rest until he has discovered where this weak point is. This is that special sin which you are here exhorted to watch against, to overcome, to cast forth, to spare no means in keeping it under and bringing it into subjection, that it may not entangle you in the race towards Zion. One man is beset with lust, another with a love of drinking, another with an evil temper, another with malice, another with covetousness, another with worldly-mindedness, another with idleness; but each of us has got about him some besetting infirmity, which is able to hinder him far more than others, and with which he must keep an unceasing warfare, or else he will never so run as to obtain the prize.[7]

As the storm clouds gather and the world grows darker, the encumbrances and entanglements are increasing. Sin is nothing new, but its manifestations seem to be proliferating before our eyes. More and more our world mirrors the days of Noah, when "everything they thought or imagined was consistently and totally evil" (Genesis 6:5). Os Guinness laments, "Evil in the advanced modern world flaunts itself under the cover of the cool, the global, the connected and the accessible. . . . This magnification of evil is profound."[8]

Do you know what your entangling sin or sins are? Are you brutally honest and self-aware, or do you hide and make excuses for yourself? Do you seek the Lord about them? Do you pray for his help and strength? Are you serious about guarding your life from them? Do you avail yourself of the means of grace—Scripture, prayer, fellowship, confession, and service? To run effectively and efficiently, we have to get rid of the encumbrances and entanglements.

THE EXAMPLE

Next the author of Hebrews points us to the example: "We do this by keeping our eyes on Jesus, the champion who initiates and perfects our faith." In every ancient Roman arena there was an emperor's box. Every competitor would look to see if the emperor was in attendance on the day of his race and was watching. When we look for our emperor, he's there. And Jesus is not only watching us, he's out ahead of us all the way. He's been through the race himself. He has blazed the trail for us and completed the course. He endured to the point of bearing the cross and its shame.

He's called the "champion who initiates . . . our faith," which means he's our pioneer or leader. He is the embodiment of trust in God—the preeminent example and model of faith. We draw some great encouragement from the lives of the faithful saints in Hebrews 11 who've gone before us, but the consummate example for us to follow is Jesus. We look to him. He is our pursuit and our prize.

Yet far too many believers have their gaze directed on the past—past sins, past sorrows, and past successes. Looking back will paralyze your progress. The apostle Paul had a laser-like forward focus: "I focus on this one thing: Forgetting the past and looking forward to what lies ahead, I press on to reach the end of the race and receive the heavenly prize" (Philippians 3:13-14). "Forgetting" doesn't mean you don't remember the past, but it carries the idea of not being influenced by it. You can't drive a car by looking in the rearview mirror or the back-up camera—at least not very far or very well. You can't run a race if you're looking back over your shoulder.

There's an example of this memorialized in a bronze statue at

Empire Fields in Vancouver. The British Empire and Commonwealth Games were held in the newly constructed Empire Stadium on August 7, 1954. Two competitors—England's Roger Bannister and Australian John Landy—had both run sub-four-minute miles earlier that year, breaking the records of the time. Bannister had accomplished this feat first, and then Landy beat the new record a month later. This was their first meeting, and a crowd of thirty-five thousand was present to watch what was hailed as "The Mile of the Century."

The race was close all the way, and then almost at the end of the race, Landy, who had the lead, looked over his left shoulder to see where Bannister was, which caused Landy momentarily to break stride. At that moment Bannister passed him on his right side and won the race. To this day it stands as one of the most dramatic moments in sports history and has become known as "the Miracle Mile," and the statue at Empire Fields captures Bannister passing Landy while his head was turned.

Looking back will break your stride. Don't be influenced by what's behind. Look ahead. Look to Jesus. He's our Example.

But Jesus isn't just our *Example*. He's our *Enabler*. He's the one who "perfects," finishes, or completes our faith. He's the *Pioneer* who shows the way, but he's also the *Power* that energizes us to make it to the finish line and win. We don't have to persevere in our own strength and willpower. Thank God for that.

THE END

Because of the joy awaiting him, he endured the cross, disregarding its shame. Now he is seated in the place of honor beside God's throne.

HEBREWS 12:2

Endurance requires anticipation and motivation. That's why all races end with reward. The final point of every race is the finish line, followed by the awarding of prizes for those who finished well. No one runs a race without the expectation of reward if they win. This was true of the games in ancient Greece and Rome.

The apostle Paul, near the end of his life, looked toward the goal when he said, "I press on to reach the end of the race and receive the heavenly prize for which God, through Christ Jesus, is calling us" (Philippians 3:14).

Even Jesus endured life here on earth because of the reward at the end of the race. Jesus looked forward to the reward of his exaltation in glory—joy. In the same way, the anticipation of future reward fuels us to keep running.

When rewards are handed out, Max Lucado reminds us, "The small will be great. The forgotten will be remembered. The unnoticed will be crowned, and the faithful will be honored."[9] The Bible doesn't tell us all we would like to know about rewards in heaven, but Lucado boils it down fairly well: "While we're not sure exactly what those rewards are, we do know they include heavenly applause, God's approval, and eternal life. What else would you want?"[10]

KEEP ON

If we're going to survive spiritually in the troubled times that surround us, we'd better hit the ground running every morning. Standing still is a killer. We must run with endurance the particular race God has marked out for us, all the time remembering that—

> *Behind us* are the faithful saints spurring us on.
> *Around us* are encumbrances and entanglements we need to shed.
> *Before us* and *ahead of us* is Jesus, our Example and Enabler.
> *Awaiting us* are rewards.

Maybe you have never entered the race. Many today are trying to win a race they haven't entered. If you've never put your faith in Jesus Christ as Savior and Lord, you aren't even in the race. Hebrews 7:25 says, "Therefore He is able also to save forever those who draw near to God through Him" (NASB). God will save you forever if you come to him through his Son, Jesus. Don't delay. Come now. Get in the race.

Some of us are in the early race. If that's you, get serious. Set the pace early for your own life and for your family. Throw off the encumbrances and entanglements. It never gets easier to get rid of them than now. Disciplines practiced and perfected early in life will be a great benefit as you go farther in the race.

Some of us are in the middle of the race or a little beyond. At this point the race may seem like a slog. You may be hitting the wall. Fix your eyes on Jesus. Look to him to lead the way and give you strength.

Some may be approaching the finish line. Don't give up. Finish strong. Finishing is hard; finishing well is harder. We don't want to end before we finish, with days unredeemed. We want to end and finish at the same time—and finish well. It will be worth it.

Stay focused. Keep running. Don't give up, no matter how hard it gets and no matter how winded you may feel.

Dr. Eric Alexander, a renowned Scottish pastor, relates this story about the importance of persevering as we run the race to win:

> While I was still a theological student, Dr. Martyn Lloyd-Jones came from London to Glasgow to preach at the great St. Andrews Hall. . . . After the meeting finished, I was waiting at the side of the platform for transport home. A long line of people were waiting to speak to Dr. Lloyd-Jones. . . . Interestingly, I noticed that every encounter

ended in the same way: "Keep on!" was the doctor's final exhortation as he shook hands.

As it happened, on the journey home I was in the same car as the doctor, and he engaged me in conversation. After the generalities, I summoned enough courage to ask him a question. "Doctor," I began, "forgive me, but I could not help hearing your last words to every person you spoke with. They were 'Keep on.' It sounded as if that was particularly important to you." He was immediately animated: "My dear man," he said, "there is nothing more important. The Christian life is not a sprint; it is a marathon."[11]

Great words for each of us to live by—*keep on!*
Great words for us to say to one another often—*keep on!*
I believe we're getting near the end. All the signs point in that direction. We need to run like never before.

Keep on!
Run for your life.
The prize awaits you.

CHAPTER 3

MAKE A GOOD CONNECTION

The New Testament does not envisage solitary religion.

C. S. LEWIS

*Don't ever come to church without coming as though it were
the first time, as though it could be the best time and
as though it might be the last time.*

VANCE HAVNER

I like the story of the mother who went to wake her son for church one Sunday morning. When she knocked on his door, he said, "I'm not going!"

"Why not?" asked his mother.

"I'll give you two good reasons," he said. "One, they don't like me. Two, I don't like them."

His mother replied, "I'll give you two good reasons why you *will* go to church. One, you're forty-seven years old. Two, you're the pastor!"

Scenes like this one are becoming common in churches today in America. More and more people seem to be AWOL on Sunday mornings. Increasingly, Sunday has become a day for sleeping in and going out, not turning up for worship.

Statistics bear out the decline in church attendance. One of the most startling aspects of the current trend is the movement of younger evangelicals away from the church. John S. Dickerson writes, "Research indicates that more than half of those born into evangelicalism are leaving the movement during their twenties. And the majority of them never return. This departure figure has never been higher in the United States. The number of those who return has never been lower."[1] Josh McDowell found that "69 percent of evangelical teens leave the church after high school."[2] LifeWay Research discovered that "70 percent of Christian church attendees from the millennial generation quit attending church by age twenty-three."[3] George Barna "estimates that from every five young evangelicals, four will 'disengage' from the church by age twenty-nine."[4]

While the most significant bleeding is coming from the millennial generation, the overall picture of church attendance and participation is not pretty. Thom Rainer puts his finger on what may be the number one reason church attendance is declining:

Most of us have our own ideas why attendance is declining. Many have suggested that our nation is shifting away from its Christian roots, and thus the churches are declining as a smaller proportion of our country are believers in Christ. I certainly will not argue with that premise. Certainly attendance declines are related to massive cultural shifts in our nation. But I would also suggest that one reason for declines has a greater impact than others. Stated simply, the number one reason for the decline in church attendance is that members attend with less frequency than they did just a few years ago. . . . No members left the church. Everyone is still relatively active in the church. But attendance declined over 12 percent because half the members changed their attendance behavior slightly.[5]

Ask most pastors, and they will confirm that members attend church less frequently than they did ten or twenty years ago. I've seen this in the church I pastor. To maintain the same attendance level requires more members because people come less often. The trend is troubling. Many more reasons for this phenomenon could be cited.

Donald Whitney suggests a few of the most common ones:

> Ask why people don't attend church, and you'll get a variety of responses. . . . Some say they don't go to church because they are turned off by what seems an endless asking for money. Others stay away because church services bore them. A percentage of those who have no interest in church say the sermons are irrelevant to their lives. Some refuse to go because when they do attend they leave feeling guilty.
>
> Numbers of people stay home because Sunday is their only day off and they want to spend it doing other things. . . .
>
> A few stay away because they think their lifestyle is too unacceptable to the expectations of churchgoers. A lot of folks are convinced the church simply has nothing to offer them. . . . And one of the most common reasons given why people don't go to church is that there just isn't time.[6]

My main purpose in this chapter is not to diagnose why people don't attend church but to challenge you, in these last days, to find a church that faithfully preaches the gospel of Jesus Christ, loves people, and serves the church and the world, and to consistently show up, support the church financially, and connect with the people there. Why? Because God created us for relationship. We're hardwired for relationship with him and with others. We must have a relationship with God's Son, Jesus Christ, to have true life and salvation. After that, much of our growth as believers comes through the interaction and accountability that fellow believers supply within spiritual community. The Bible calls us to be with God's people regularly because the Lord knows our spiritual survival is at stake. Isolation is not God's will for his children. Isolation in today's environment is dangerous and spiritually deadly.

Filmmaker Alex Gibney directed a documentary titled *Steve Jobs: The Man in the Machine*. Summarizing the thrust of the documentary, one writer says, "What *The Man in the Machine* really wants to present is the contradiction of Jobs's legacy: that he developed a technology that sought to connect while he lived a life of disconnection (alienating colleagues, pushing his girlfriend and daughter away, etc.)."[7] What an irony. The man who connected the world lived an isolated existence.

Jobs's story is far from unique. More and more people, including professing Christians, are settling for detached, disengaged lives and are reaping the consequences.

Challenging the millennial generation, Kevin DeYoung says,

> It's possible we talk a lot about authentic community but we aren't willing to live in it. The church is not an incidental part of God's plan. Jesus didn't invite people to join an anti-religion, anti-doctrine, anti-institutional bandwagon of love, harmony, and re-integration. He showed people how to live, to be sure. But He also called them to repent, called them to faith, called them out of the world, and called them into the church. The Lord "didn't add them to the church without

saving them, and he didn't save them without adding them to the church" [quoting John Stott].[8]

DeYoung concludes with this wise warning: "Don't give up on the church. The New Testament knows nothing of churchless Christianity. The invisible church is for invisible Christians. The visible church is for you and me. Put away the Che Guevara t-shirts, stop the revolution, and join the rest of the plodders. Fifty years from now you'll be glad you did."[9]

There are all kinds of ways to express the need we have as God's people to connect with others. Togetherness. Networking. Fellowship. Doing life together. But whatever you call it, we all need it. Clearly, not every person can be in church. Attendance for some is precluded by health issues or advancing age. But most believers are able to be in church with some degree of regularity, yet a disturbing number simply choose not to come. Why? I'm sure there are many reasons, but one simple one is that it's easier and less demanding to be home alone.

With this backdrop in mind, let's briefly look at five essential reasons why you need to stay connected, especially in treacherous, uncertain times like these.

"AS WE SEE THE DAY APPROACHING"

The first reason we need to stay connected is in Hebrews 10:24-25. This passage addresses the need to live in meaningful community with one another as we wait for the Lord's coming in these last days. It's a clarion call to connect in light of Christ's coming. It's a last-days strategy for spiritual survival:

Let us think of ways to motivate one another to acts of love and good works. And let us not neglect our meeting together, as some people do, but encourage one another, especially now that the day of his return is drawing near.

Anyone who reads the newspaper, watches cable news, or follows world events online realizes our world is on fire. The Middle East remains a global hot spot. Israel is in the crosshairs. North Korea is a nuclear menace. The Russian Bear is roaring out of hibernation. Even those with a superficial knowledge of end-times prophecy realize this world seems to be getting near closing time. Many signs seem to be aligning, giving us every reason to believe the coming of Christ is near. No one on earth knows the time of Christ's coming, but as believers, we're to live looking, with an attitude of expectancy concerning our Lord's coming (see 1 Thessalonians 1:10).

This hope and anticipation should energize every believer with a renewed sense of urgency to be about the Lord's business. Hebrews 10:25 clearly states that a key aspect of that business is to stay connected with one another through the fellowship of the local church. The words "the day of his return is drawing near" or "as you see the Day approaching" (as in NIV) indicate that believers today should be gathering together *more* frequently, not less, as we see the approach of the Lord's coming. With all that's happening in our world today, churches should be packed. As signs of the times proliferate, church attendance should be soaring. Yet, sadly, we see the exact opposite. Malaise and indifference have set in.

Do you remember what it was like in the wake of the terrorist attack on 9/11? Churches were filled to capacity and in many cases overfilled. Faced with the fragility of life, people sought solace in God and reevaluated what's important. However, the spike in attendance waned as life got back to normal. People settled into a pattern that fails to prioritize regular attendance at public worship.

There's a humorous, well-worn, but worthwhile illustration about a church that announced "a special 'No Excuse Sunday'" to "make it possible for everyone to attend church" on a specific Lord's Day. The announcement contained the following incentives:

> Cots will be placed in the foyer for those who say, "Sunday is my only day to sleep."
> We will have steel helmets for those who say, "The roof will cave in if I ever come to church."
> Blankets will be furnished for those who think the church is too cold and fans for those who think the church is too hot.
> We will have hearing aids for those who think the preacher speaks too softly and cotton for those who think he preaches too loudly.
> Scorecards will be available for those who wish to list the hypocrites present.
> Some relatives will be in attendance for those who like to go visiting on Sunday.
> There will be TV dinners for those who can't go to church and cook dinner also.
> One section will be devoted to trees and grass for those who like to see God in nature.
> Finally, the sanctuary will be decorated with both Christmas poinsettias and Easter lilies for those who have never seen the church without them.[10]

Ouch! That hits pretty close to home for a growing number of contemporary churchgoers. The writer of Hebrews leaves no doubt that regular attendance of public worship is not an option for believers; it's a command. When it comes to the church, assembly is required. Regardless of this stern admonition, more and more professing Christians fail to take church attendance seriously. Hebrews

10:25 calls on us to gather for mutual encouragement as we see the day drawing near. In troubled times, we all need encouragement. We need encouragement to read our Bibles, to pray, to love our spouses, to sacrifice for others, to share, to tell others about Jesus, and to turn from sin. For me, as a pastor, just seeing God's people on Sunday morning is an encouragement. Your simple presence is a much greater encouragement to others, especially your pastor, than you will ever know.

The call to assemble is urgent. As Erwin Lutzer says, "Never before in American history has it been so important to become an active part of a network of other believers for worship, encouragement, instruction, and prayer. Bible studies, prayer groups, and discipleship training of believers to be change-agents in their world."[11]

The church is a place of safety and protection as believers come under the supervision and care of pastors who look out for their well-being (see Hebrews 13:17). Failing to have a church home and meet with God's people regularly leaves you isolated, alone, and exposed, and strays from the herd are always the easiest for the lions to pick off. Far too many believers today are voluntarily leaving themselves and their families spiritually exposed outside the church in the devil's domain. I like the story author Anne Lamott tells about a seven-year-old girl who got lost in a big city:

> The girl frantically ran up and down several streets, looking for a familiar landmark. A policeman saw the girl, realized something was wrong, and offered to help. So she got in the car and he slowly drove through nearby neighborhoods. Suddenly the girl pointed to a church and asked the policeman to let her out. She assured him, "This is my church, and I can always find my way home from here."[12]

As the world darkens and Christ's coming draws near, never have so many needed to find their way home, especially in the millennial generation. Encouraging them to regularly be a part of corporate worship and fellowship is a strong beginning point.

WHEN THE CHURCH WAS YOUNG

The second, and perhaps the simplest, reason we need to stay connected with other believers is the pattern in the early church. The emphasis on connection is present in the very first church in Jerusalem a few weeks after the resurrection of Christ:

> They were continually devoting themselves to the apostles' teaching and to fellowship, to the breaking of bread and to prayer.
>
> Everyone kept feeling a sense of awe; and many wonders and signs were taking place through the apostles. And all those who had believed were together and had all things in common; and they began selling their property and possessions and were sharing them with all, as anyone might have need. Day by day continuing with one mind in the temple, and breaking bread from house to house, they were taking their meals together with gladness and sincerity of heart, praising God and having favor with all the people. And the Lord was adding to their number day by day those who were being saved.
>
> ACTS 2:42-47, NASB

The first point mentioned in this snapshot of the early church is the apostles' teaching, which is foundational to everything else. We must gather to hear God's Word or our fellowship is little more than a social gathering. The truth is what ties us together. The faithful preaching of God's Word is the heart muscle of the church, which pumps life into everything else we do. We rally around a common gospel, centered in our great Savior. But these verses in Acts 2 also focus repeatedly on the gathering together of God's people. We're not just *believers*; we're *belongers*.

Notice also that there's a beautiful balance here between the corporate gatherings of the church in the Temple area and smaller, private gatherings for meals in individual homes. We observe this throughout the book of Acts, which establishes a pattern for our gatherings today.

You and I need the corporate church setting to sing and praise God together, to pray, to learn, and to celebrate the Lord's Supper and baptism. There's something about the power of presence. Just being with God's people every week is a strong encouragement. Seeing young families with young children worshiping the Lord; watching people singing, giving, and praying together; and observing the church surrounding those who are dealing with physical ailments or old age are all part of growing deeper in our shared life in Christ.

We also need to connect with other believers in smaller gatherings for meaningful fellowship and discipleship. Hebrews 10:24-25 says we must gather regularly to "spur one another on toward love and good deeds" (NIV). While this can and should happen as we sing and listen to the preaching of God's Word in a corporate setting, in the deepest sense this happens in smaller gatherings.

These smaller gatherings take many forms such as home groups, lunch meetings, women's or men's Bible studies, adult Sunday school classes, and so on. I've even heard about one church that had a group of older men who called themselves ROMEOs (Retired Old Men Eating Out) who met regularly for Christian fellowship.

At the church I pastor, we have ABFs (Adult Bible Fellowship groups) that meet on Sunday mornings at parallel times with our corporate worship services. While it may appear in many forms, small-group ministry is an integral ingredient for healthy spiritual growth.

Of course, in all of this, our goal is not just to get people to church more and keep them busy meeting in more intimate settings. Church attendance and connection is a means, not an end. The end is a growing, thriving, maturing walk with Jesus Christ.

The story is told that a pastor who was new to a small Oklahoma town started his tenure as pastor by stopping by the houses of the church's members and inviting them to come to church the following Sunday. When Sunday rolled around, however, he was disappointed to discover that the members he had invited weren't there and the church was mostly empty. The next week he took out an ad in the local newspaper, inviting people to the funeral of the church.

When the time for the funeral came, the church was packed because people were curious how a funeral for a building might work. A hearse arrived, and pallbearers carried the casket into the sanctuary and placed it in front of the pulpit.

The pastor gave a eulogy for the church, and afterward he opened the casket's lid for the congregation to pay their respects. The people didn't know what to expect—what could possibly be in the casket to represent a dead church?—so they dutifully approached the casket. And once each person looked in, they saw it: their own reflection. The "dead church" was a mirror.

The death of a church is the death of the people because a church is not a building or an organization—a church is its people. And each church is a reflection of the spiritual vitality of those who claim membership there.

How is your church doing? In many ways your church is a mirror image of you. What does the mirror say about you and your family?

Let me add one point here. All pastors, elders, and church

leaders must do all we can in our local churches to provide a setting that encourages God's people to join us. God has commanded all Christians not to forsake assembling together, but we must do all we can to remove as many obstacles as possible and to make it edifying for people to come. God's Word must be preached accurately, clearly, and practically. Our singing must glorify God and flow from passionate hearts. Our fellowship must be enriched by the Lord's presence. The sheep are called to gather, but the shepherds must work hard to make sure the sheep find green pastures that nourish their souls. I love the saying "The world at its worst needs the church at its best." Few would dispute that our world today is at its worst. What we're witnessing is nothing short of tragic. This should provide ample motivation for us to be at our best when we're gathered together on the Lord's Day and then take that with us as we're unleashed into the community throughout the week.

TAKING SIDES

The third reason for us to take our connection to the church seriously as the end draws near is that as church attendance becomes increasingly spotty and intermittent in our culture, one of the ways we give witness to our love for Christ is by going to church. Those who connect frequently with God's people give visible evidence of their commitment to Christ and his Word to their neighbors and friends. Of course, we all know that going to church can be perfunctory and routine and has no saving merit, but what I'm talking about is not duty but delight. Being a real part of a local church with a sense of expectancy and excitement each week testifies to a watching world that we belong to Jesus and love him.

In some ways, attending church is a litmus test of our loyalty to Christ. It's a birthmark and benchmark for believers. Think about it. If we aren't loyal to Christ in something as simple as showing up for church on the Lord's Day, how committed are we in other, more demanding aspects of our faith such as giving sacrificially, serving, praying, reading God's Word, or sharing the gospel with others? Going to church consistently should be the bare minimum—the lowest rung—of our Christian commitment. If we can't carve out time from our schedules to regularly meet for public worship, how likely are we to make deeper sacrifices for our Lord?

Doug McIntosh, in his book *Life's Greatest Journey*, tells the story of an elderly man who lost his hearing late in life. Despite his hearing loss and inability to hear the songs being sung or words being spoken, he attended church every week. When one of his neighbors asked why he continued to go to church when he couldn't hear what was happening, he simply replied, "I want people to know whose side I'm on."[13]

Going to church can never wash away our sins or, by itself, make us more righteous, but increasingly in our culture it does show our friends and neighbors "whose side we're on."

PICTURING THE CHURCH

Fourth, the New Testament employs many metaphors to describe the church of Jesus Christ that stress our closeness to Jesus and to one another and how much we need each other.

Here are a few of the most basic ones:

> - Body (see 1 Corinthians 12): Jesus is the Head; we are the various parts.
> - Flock (see John 10:11-15): Jesus is the Shepherd; we are the sheep.
> - Building (see Ephesians 2:20-21; 1 Peter 2:5): Jesus is the Cornerstone; we are the stones cemented together.
> - Vine (see John 15:1-11): Jesus is the Vine; we are the branches.

Each of these metaphors involves close connection to Jesus and others. We were never intended to live and grow in isolation from other believers. These images also reveal that together we are much more than we could ever be alone. The church is much greater than the sum of its parts.

Nevertheless, going it alone is becoming more common. More and more people claim they're finding all they need online. They stay home and watch a sermon on Sunday and check the worship box for the week. But listening to a sermon online is not enough. Certainly, times have changed since the first century, and we have wonderful, helpful technology that was not available then. Watching sermons online is a great way to keep up with what's going on at your church when you're ill or out of town. That said, sitting at home in front of your computer every Saturday evening or Sunday morning is not what the New Testament envisions for church connection. Spiritual growth and encouragement take place in the context of actual, lived community.

As David Jeremiah says, "Cyber-community seems nice until something bad happens, and then we want face time rather than Facebook."[14] Certainly, in today's world, social media is a great way to stay in touch with others, but the church is a face-to-face community that can never be replaced by Facebook. The pulpit can seem far away during the week. There's no substitute for real community with other believers.

I like the old story about the pastor who visited a member of his church who had stopped attending without giving a reason. The pastor visited the man on a cold evening when the man was home alone, warming himself in front of the fireplace. The man invited the pastor to sit with him and waited for the pastor to lecture him about his church attendance. However, instead of talking, the pastor took the tongs by the fireplace and picked up a burning ember and placed it off to the side, all by itself. The pastor remained silent in all of this, which made the man uncomfortable, so he fixed his attention on the ember whose flame was quietly dimming and then extinguished.

After the ember had been dead for a few minutes, the pastor placed it back in the fire, where it immediately ignited. When the pastor made a move to leave, his host said, "Thank you so much for your visit and especially for the fiery sermon. I'll be back in church next Sunday."[15]

The truth is we cool spiritually and eventually stop glowing without the warmth of our brothers and sisters in Christ. We need each other more than we often realize.

Make sure you stay on fire and spread the heat to others, and do it even more as we see the day approaching. You need the church, and the church needs you. Don't get isolated and exposed.

Your spiritual survival, and that of your family, is at stake in these last days when the world is at its worst.

"ONE ANOTHERING"

A fifth reason to stay connected is found in the many New Testament commands about how we live in connection with one another. The commands in these verses are often referred to as "one anothering."

The New Testament records many "one anothers." Some are repeated several times, so there are about thirty-three unique "one anothers." Here are a few of the main ones. (Note that the New Living Translation usually translates this phrase as "each other.")

> "Love each other" (John 15:12)
> "Wash each other's feet" (John 13:14)
> "Love each other with genuine affection, and take delight in honoring each other" (Romans 12:10)

> "Live in harmony with each other" (Romans 12:16)
> "Build each other up" (Romans 14:19)
> "Accept each other just as Christ has accepted you" (Romans 15:7)
> "Teach each other" (Romans 15:14)
> "Greet each other with a sacred kiss" (Romans 16:16)
> "Wait [to eat the Lord's Supper] for each other" (1 Corinthians 11:33)
> "Care for each other" (1 Corinthians 12:25)
> "Serve one another" (Galatians 5:13)
> "Share each other's burdens" (Galatians 6:2)
> "Be patient with each other" (Ephesians 4:2)
> "We are members of one another" (Ephesians 4:25, NASB)
> "Be kind to each other, tenderhearted, forgiving one another" (Ephesians 4:32)
> "Submit to one another" (Ephesians 5:21)
> "Regard one another as more important than yourselves" (Philippians 2:3, NASB)
> "Encourage each other with these words [about Jesus' return]" (1 Thessalonians 4:18)
> "Encourage each other and build each other up" (1 Thessalonians 5:11)
> "Think of ways to motivate one another to acts of love and good works," "not neglect our meeting together, . . . but encourage one another" (Hebrews 10:24-25)
> "Confess your sins to each other and pray for each other" (James 5:16)
> "Be hospitable to one another" (1 Peter 4:9, NASB)[16]

We sometimes forget that "one anothering" can only be faithfully fulfilled if we are regularly *with* one another. First Thessalonians 5:11

summarizes this idea beautifully. It literally says, "Build up one the one," that is, "one by one." We build up God's people one by one. This is true even in large settings in the church. Ultimately, all ministry is personal and individual. People are built up one by one. We need each other and the community of mutual support to survive and grow spiritually. God and his transformative grace are most evident in the sphere of a loving community. We need each other. Our salvation is personal, but it is not private.

There's an old poem sometimes attributed to William Blake that says this well:

> I sought my soul, and my soul eluded me.
> I sought my God, and my God I could not see.
> I sought my brother, and I found all three.

DEADLY DISCONNECT

Sunandha Kumariratana was the queen of Thailand in the late nineteenth century. Among the laws in that day was one forbidding anyone to touch the queen under threat of death.

While she was journeying to the summer palace with her young daughter on May 31, 1880, the royal boat they were traveling in capsized. There were many witnesses to the capsizing, but they were unwilling to pull her from the watery grave because of the law. A guard on another boat even reiterated the law that the queen was not to be touched. As a result, the queen drowned.[17]

Isolating yourself from others is dangerous and can even be deadly. If you keep others away and never let them touch your life, when you're drowning, they may not be able to come to your aid.

Don't drown needlessly in discouragement, sorrow, grief, loneliness, pain, and trouble. Meet with God's people regularly, joyfully, and often. Allow others to connect with you, and be willing and eager to reach out and touch the lives of others in meaning-ful ways.

And do it all the more as "the day of his return is drawing near."

Your spiritual health and survival hangs in the balance.

CHAPTER 4

PUT ON YOUR ARMOR

*Two things are happening today that I never thought I would
live to see. First, spiritual warfare is getting much more intense as Satan's
attacks become bolder. Second . . . too many Christians
are not taking spiritual warfare seriously or even
believing such a war is going on.*

DAVID JEREMIAH

Gun sales in America today are on the rise. The worse the news gets, the more people seem to buy—many in preparation for what may lie ahead. Television shows like *Doomsday Preppers* and *The Wheel* fuel the fear of some apocalyptic scenario that showcases the need to be armed and ready.

I was talking to a friend of mine a while back when some especially bad news was in the headlines. We were talking about people buying gold to shield themselves from potential market crashes or collapses. He told me, "I'm not buying gold; I'm buying lead." That seems to be a shared sentiment. Increasingly, many are stocking up on food, guns, ammo, and anything else they think can help them survive the uncertain days ahead.

More and more people today are responding to world events out of panic, fear, and an unhealthy obsession about some impending catastrophe. They're focused on being armed and dangerous. But the most important way to arm and protect yourself and your family in these uncertain times is to be armed spiritually. Increasing numbers of people have a small arsenal of physical weaponry but don't have enough spiritual power or protection to match an airsoft gun.

With surging spiritual deception and demonic forces arrayed against us as Christ's coming draws near, every believer needs to be spiritually armed to the teeth. If we fail in this, we are easy prey for the enemy of our souls. The Bible is clear. As the Lord's coming draws near, as the last days run their course, every believer in Jesus Christ needs to be equipped with the full armor of God:

> This is all the more urgent, for you know how late it is;
> time is running out. Wake up, for our salvation is nearer
> now than when we first believed. The night is almost gone;
> the day of salvation will soon be here. So remove your dark
> deeds like dirty clothes, and put on the shining armor of
> right living. Because we belong to the day, we must live
> decent lives for all to see. Don't participate in the darkness
> of wild parties and drunkenness, or in sexual promiscuity
> and immoral living, or in quarreling and jealousy. Instead,
> clothe yourself with the presence of the Lord Jesus Christ.
> And don't let yourself think about ways to indulge your
> evil desires.
>
> ROMANS 13:11-14

These verses are clear that, as the last days draw to a close, we must put on the spiritual armor of light. Without it, we're defenseless. Many passages in the New Testament call believers to "take up arms" spiritually in these last days, but Ephesians 6:10-18 is the central passage on our spiritual warfare as believers. Please read these words slowly and thoughtfully:

> Be strong in the Lord and in his mighty power. Put on the full armor of God, so that you can take your stand against the devil's schemes. For our struggle is not against flesh and blood, but against the rulers, against the authorities, against the powers of this dark world and against the spiritual forces of evil in the heavenly realms. Therefore put on the full armor of God, so that when the day of evil comes, you may be able to stand your ground, and after you have done everything, to stand. Stand firm then, with the belt of truth buckled around your waist, with the breastplate of righteousness in place, and with your feet fitted with the readiness that comes from the gospel of peace. In addition to all this, take up the shield of faith, with which you can extinguish all the flaming arrows of the evil one. Take the helmet of salvation and the sword of the Spirit, which is the word of God.
>
> And pray in the Spirit on all occasions with all kinds of prayers and requests. With this in mind, be alert and always keep on praying for all the Lord's people. (NIV)

THE INVISIBLE WAR

Every believer in Christ senses that he or she faces daily conflict. We all recognize this relentless reality. We have our sin nature on the inside that exerts a strong gravitational pull toward sin and the wicked world around us that draws us to compromise with its values and attitudes.

Nevertheless, many are not aware of the invisible war in the spirit realm that rages around us, or worse yet, they may choose to ignore it.

Our secular world today is increasingly a "world without windows."[1] Secularists believe the unseen is unreal. Yet we deny the unseen world at our own peril. As Lesslie Newbigin warns, "The principalities and powers are realities. We may not be able to visualize them, to locate them, or to say exactly what they are. But we are foolish if we pretend they do not exist."[2]

Just beyond the thin veil of this visible world is a spiritual world every bit as real. Beyond the paper-thin walls of this fading world is a cosmic struggle encircling us. Understanding this invisible war helps us see things as they really are.

You could hardly find a better statement of the Christian life and our spiritual combat than this: "The ideal war is one that no one realizes war is being waged, that is mostly invisible, not because its actions are camouflaged, but because they look like something else. War need never be declared again because we are always at war."[3] It's like modern terrorism. We're always at war, but it's mostly invisible.

Satan is the ultimate terrorist who led the first rebellion, the first insurgency in history as he was lifted up in pride. When he fell into sin, he went on a campaign in heaven to slander God and recruited one-third of the angelic host to join his conspiracy (see Ezekiel 28:15-17; Revelation 12:4). These fallen angels are what the Scriptures refer to as demons. There is only one devil, but there are many demons. They are our enemies in the invisible war.

The intensity of the cosmic conflict is underscored by the word "struggle" in Ephesians 6:12, which in ancient times referred to wrestling in the Greek games. The picture of wrestling emphasizes the closeness of the conflict and the sustained effort and stamina required in this fight. Moreover, the word "against" occurs six times in Ephesians 6:10-12, which underlines the opposition we face in this cosmic clash of forces and the intensity of the struggle. The Lord wants us to know that we're up against a real enemy. The battle lines are clearly drawn. God and his people are on one side; Satan and his demons are on the other. Ray Stedman vividly describes this war:

> Spiritual warfare is not about the struggle of man against man. It is not a political struggle, a social struggle, an economic struggle, or even a religious-theological-doctrinal struggle. It is not a struggle *between* human beings. It is a struggle *within* human beings. . . . The battle is not against people, but against unseen spiritual powers. In fact, the entire human race is under a vicious assault by certain principalities and powers, world rulers of darkness, wicked spirits in high places. . . . Every man, every woman, every child, everywhere is a target of the enemy. The devil has each one of us in his crosshairs. The whole race is opposed by the principalities and powers, the world rulers of this present darkness.[4]

The good news in this war is that, according to the Bible, Satan and his minions are a defeated foe. The Lord Jesus, our Commander in Chief, crushed Satan's head at the Cross. Nevertheless, though Satan is infinitely mismatched and has no chance of winning, he furiously fights the Lord and his people, working to undermine our faith and hinder our progress in the Christian life. Satan's doom is sure. His eternal incarceration in the lake of fire is recorded in Revelation 20:10. However, that defeat is yet to be fully consummated at the second coming of Christ. In the meantime we fight our enemy not *for* victory but *from* victory.

Jesus has won the victory for us already. He has taken the spiritual high ground staked out in Ephesians 1–3. All that's left for us is to hold the spiritual ground he has gained on our behalf. The purpose of our spiritual armor is not to attack Satan or gain new territory.

Notice that the key word "stand" punctuates Ephesians 6:10-13 four times. The same idea of "standing" (holding our ground) and "resisting" is found elsewhere in the New Testament in reference to our warfare against Satan and his host. James 4:7 says, "Resist the devil, and he will flee from you." First Peter 5:9, referring to Satan, concurs: "Resist him, firm in your faith" (NASB).

SUIT UP

To protect us in our battle with the enemy, God has graciously provided us with a spiritual suit of armor because we are defenseless in ourselves and our own strength. We are no match for the forces of evil. As S. Lewis Johnson says, "You notice the Apostle does not say, 'be strong in human plans.' He does not say, 'be strong in human methods.' He does not say, 'be strong in the latest ideas' that sweep over the evangelical church, but 'be strong in the Lord and the power of his might.'"[5] What every believer needs is the Lord. We don't need him and our own strength and ingenuity; we need him and his provision.

Before we identify and describe each individual piece of our "armor," I want to make a few general observations about our equipment. First, we must avail ourselves of the armor God has provided. The spiritual battle we're facing is an epic struggle pitted against Satan and his angels, against the principalities and powers—it is being fought every day right where we live, in our homes, our offices, our marriages, our churches, and in the inner core of our hearts. The Bible is clear that God has provided us with resources to win this war, but we must take advantage of his provision. We have to "take [it] up" and "put [it] on." The armor doesn't cover us automatically. We have to put it on daily.

Second, we must put on *all* the armor. We can't decide which pieces to put on and which to leave off. Every piece is essential. It's the *full* armor—the complete "panoply." The Welsh preacher Martyn Lloyd-Jones notes,

> If you are to be a soldier in this army, if you are to fight victoriously in this crusade, you have to put on the entire equipment given to you. That is a rule in any army. . . . And that is infinitely more true in this spiritual realm and warfare with which we are concerned. . . . You need it all . . . because your understanding is inadequate. It is God alone who knows your enemy, and He knows exactly the provision that is essential to you if you are to continue standing. Every single part and portion of this armour is absolutely essential; and the first thing you have to learn is that you are not in a position to pick and choose.[6]

We need all the armor if we're going to stand firm in these last days.

Third, we need to wear *all* the armor *all* the time. We never know when the enemy will strike, so the only way to be prepared is to always have it on. Around 1171, John de Courcy conquered land in Northern Ireland. John was a courageous warrior who was serious about the worship of God and gave God the glory for his victories. King John in England wanted to capture and kill him but knew it would be very difficult because de Courcy was such a fierce warrior. King John commissioned Sir Hugh de Lacy to find out how to capture de Courcy. To learn about de Courcy's habits and weaknesses, Hugh de Lacy conferred with certain of de Courcy's own men as to how he might be taken, and they said it was not possible since he always wore his armor. The only time each year when he took off his armor in public was Good Friday. His custom on that day was to wear no armor and carry no shield or weapon. He walked around the church five times barefoot and then spent the rest of the day in church, kneeling in prayer. Hugh de Lacy determined that Good Friday was the only opening to capture de Courcy, and so on that day a group of his men descended suddenly upon him. De Courcy found nothing but a cross pole to defend himself and slew thirteen men until it broke. Finally, with no armor and no weapon, the great warrior was captured. In the brief time when he was defenseless, the enemy struck.

Our enemy is no different. His sinister surveillance of our lives is cunning and constant, so we can be sure he knows when we're not wearing our armor. He picks his time when we least expect it and stand unprepared. We have to put the armor on, and we have to put it all on all the time. Without it, we're easy prey.

With these thoughts in mind, let's turn our attention to the individual pieces of our spiritual defense system.

THE BELT OF TRUTH

The pieces of our spiritual armor listed in the New Testament are adapted from the equipment worn in that day by a Roman hoplite, or foot soldier. Paul takes something his audience would have been familiar with and invests it with spiritual meaning. The parallels are striking.

The first piece of the Roman soldier's armor was his belt, which was the first thing he would put on to prepare for battle. No soldier could fight effectively without his belt. It was six inches wide and made of either leather or linen. The belt served two important functions. First, the Roman hoplite would use the belt to gird his loins, which refers to tucking his tunic under his belt so he could move freely and fight effectively without getting his legs and feet tangled in it. Getting tripped up in battle was deadly. Second, the belt supported his weapons. The sword hung from it. Archers used it to attach their quivers of arrows.

With this background, it makes sense that our spiritual armor begins with truth because God's truth is what enables us to move freely and holds everything else together. Truth must come first. Satan is a deceiver—the father of lies. Satan's master campaign of deception is to attack the Word of God. He will do anything he can to undermine it and deceive people. Everything in our lives hangs on our knowledge and application of God's truth.

But how do we put on the belt of truth? Here are a couple of practical thoughts:

> *Listen to good Bible exposition.* Regularly attend a church that teaches biblical truth faithfully and systematically, meditate on what you hear, and apply it to your life. If there's no Bible-teaching church in your town, attend the best church you can find. You can supplement what's lacking by listening to faithful preachers on local Christian radio or downloaded sermons.

> *Read and study the Bible on your own.* Get into a good Bible study where you can encourage others in the truth and be encouraged. One important point to note in Ephesians 6 is that all the verbs and pronouns in this section are in the plural, which of course means that this all applies to every believer. But it also indicates to us that we aren't alone. We're in God's army together. We're a band of brothers and sisters. We are struggling side by side, arm in arm, shoulder to shoulder. We stand for God's truth together. Seeing others standing firm and resisting the devil shores up our own faith and gives us the resolve to hold our ground.

Doing these things will cinch your belt tighter and tighter each day.

THE BREASTPLATE OF RIGHTEOUSNESS

No Roman soldier would ever think of going into battle without his breastplate. This essential armor was a tough, sleeveless garment of leather or heavy linen that protected his full torso, and sewed on it were overlapping slices of animal hooves or horns or pieces of metal for extra reinforcement. Sometimes a breastplate was made of molded metal that conformed to the body. It was like a modern bulletproof vest or body armor. The purpose was obviously to cover lungs and other vital organs, the heart most of all.

Likewise, our hearts are protected against the accusations and condemnation of the enemy by righteousness. The righteousness here is not our own but that of Jesus Christ, which has been credited to us (see 2 Corinthians 5:21). Knowing about this righteousness and appropriating it by faith protects us against the onslaught of the enemy. One of Satan's favorite attacks on our hearts is false accusations. He's "the accuser of our brethren" (Revelation 12:10, NASB). The word "devil" (*diabolos*) means "accuser" or "slanderer." Our protection against the bombardment of accusation and condemnation is the righteousness of Jesus Christ. We rest in his merits—in his righteousness alone (see Romans 8:1, 33). Knowing that we stand accepted before God, not condemned, gives us great fortitude to stand our ground.

THE SHOES OF PEACE

The image of shoes comes from the Roman soldier's *caliga*, or war boot, which was the half-boot worn by Roman legionnaires. It was an open-toed leather boot, tightly fastened to the ankles and shins with leather straps and stuffed with wool or fur in cold weather. These shoes weren't for running (pursuing or fleeing from the enemy); rather, these thick-soled boots were made for long marches and a solid stance. The key in battle was keeping your footing during close combat. The bottoms of the boots were covered with sharp spikes or nails to give traction, enabling the warrior to make quick, sudden moves without slipping and falling.

In warfare, shoes are critical. They're the foundation. They provide stability. Imagine a Roman soldier in armor from head to foot but with no shoes. The ground would quickly tear his feet to shreds, and he would easily lose traction, rendering him helpless.

So, what provides the firm foundation we need for spiritual warfare? What gives us the readiness we need—the preparation that will make us immovable in the battle? Ephesians 6:15 talks about "feet fitted with the readiness that comes from the gospel of peace" (NIV). The peace we have with God through the gospel makes us immovable. Paul refers to this peace earlier in Ephesians 2, and even writes, "Christ himself has brought peace to us" (verse 14).

Scripture tells us that before we were converted, we were enemies of God. We were at war with him, but the death of Christ brought peace (see Romans 5:1, 10). When we trust Christ as our Savior, we are justified by faith. The result is that we have peace with God. This is the gospel of peace. Peace with God is our new position in Christ. And it's on the basis of this new position that we are able to resist the forces of Satan. This is our foundation and footing. When our feet are planted in this peace, we can stand firm against the malicious assaults of the enemy.

THE SHIELD OF FAITH

Ephesians 6:16 says, "In addition to all this, take up the shield of faith, with which you can extinguish all the flaming arrows of the evil one" (NIV). The other pieces of armor up to this point are fastened to the body, but here the shield must be picked up. The word for "shield" used here doesn't refer to the small, round shield we see in movies like *Gladiator* but to a large, oblong one that was four feet tall, two and one-half feet wide, and as thick as a person's hand. When Satan and his forces fire their flaming missiles of doubt, they are extinguished by our faith. Again, 1 Peter 5:9 says, "Resist him, firm in your faith" (NASB).

One other interesting feature of the Roman shield is that it had hooks on each side to join to the shields of others. In the same way, we join our faith with other believers in times of attack to form an impenetrable wall of protection. If we're honest, we all have to admit that sometimes in the fog of spiritual warfare it's easy to feel alone and isolated and give way to discouragement or even depression. The enemy works to magnify this in our lives. Let's never forget to lock shields with our brothers and sisters in Christ—joining our faith with theirs. We must never forget that we're not in the battle alone. We need to stay in close ranks with other believers as the end draws near (see Hebrews 10:25).

THE HELMET OF SALVATION

Every Roman soldier wore a helmet made of bronze or iron, lined inside with felt or sponge to make it tolerable to wear for long periods of time. Nothing is more vital in battle than protecting the brain from battering blows. Applying this to our spiritual lives, guarding our minds is essential in the invisible war. Nothing is more important than keeping our thinking straight and clear. Let's face it—we live in cloudy, chaotic times. The Niagara of negative news—from political polarization to the growing threat of nuclear war—can easily drive us to discouragement and even despair. A sense of gloom seems to hang in the air. Satan and his forces seize this to swamp us with hopelessness.

But the believer in Christ has the helmet of salvation. We have a resource that protects our mind—that keeps us thinking straight in confusing times. That piece of equipment is salvation, more specifically, our future salvation that will be realized when Jesus comes. As Ray Stedman writes,

> [The apostle Paul] is not talking about the salvation of the soul. He is not referring to salvation as regeneration or conversion. In other words, he is not looking backwards, to the moment of conversion. The first three pieces of armor do so, but the next three pieces of armor, including the helmet of salvation, look forward, not back. Paul is talking about a salvation that will be a future event.[7]

The helmet of salvation is final, full salvation or deliverance when the Lord Jesus returns to earth. This understanding is confirmed by 1 Thessalonians 5:8, which refers to the believer's helmet as the "confidence of our salvation" (see also Romans 13:11). Stedman continues,

> [Paul] is talking about the day of the return of Christ, the day when creation will be delivered from bondage by Christ's return to establish His kingdom. This helmet, therefore, is the recognition that . . . the plan of God is moving forward, right on schedule. Jesus Christ is coming back, and He will appear again, and He will establish His own reign in righteousness on the earth. That is the helmet of salvation which will keep your thinking straight in the hour of man's utter confusion and darkness. . . . If you can keep God's eternal plan in view at all times, it will save you from enormous heartache and fear as you read your daily newspaper. When you see the chaos in the world, you will know that even the disorder that Satan seeks to stir up in the world is being used to further God's plan and bring

His kingdom one day nearer. Though we are often shocked whenever we open a newspaper or turn on CNN, God is never surprised. His plan is right on schedule.[8]

God has a plan, and it is on schedule. Every day that passes, its completion is one day nearer. Our hope is not in man but in God. Our knowledge of our future salvation keeps our thinking straight and stable. Keeping God's eternal plan in view will keep you from a great deal of heartache and fear.

That's one of the reasons I believe it's so important to regularly preach and teach on the Lord's coming. We need to be reminded often that Jesus is coming again to bring our salvation to its consummation.

THE SWORD OF THE SPIRIT

The first five items in our spiritual arsenal are defensive in nature. The only offensive weapon listed in Ephesians 6 is the Bible, the Word of God. Picture a Roman warrior with all his armor firmly in place, shoes laced up, and carrying his massive shield on his left arm, yet with no weapon in his right hand. A massacre would ensue. A warrior with no weapon is easily dispatched.

Similarly, every Christian warrior must have a weapon for the war against the spiritual forces of darkness, and that powerful weapon is "the sword of the Spirit, which is the word of God" (see also Hebrews 4:12-13). The Greek word for "sword" refers to the Roman short sword, which was essentially a large knife with a two-edged blade, two inches wide and about sixteen to eighteen inches long. As you can imagine, this was used in hand-to-hand combat. This reinforces the reality of the up-close nature of the spiritual conflict.

Our sword is God's Word. The Word of God cuts, convicts, challenges, and confronts. It's razor sharp. As someone has said, "It's all edge." This helps explain why the Word of God is under sustained attack by the enemy. Satan has relentlessly attacked the Bible down through the ages because it's the one weapon that cuts through his deception and neutralizes his temptations. Satan is at war with the Word of God because he knows its power.

The power of the Word rises from its source. It's called the "sword of the *Spirit.*" The Spirit is the Voice who inspired God's Word (see 2 Timothy 3:16). Human authors wrote the words of Scripture through their own unique personality, vocabulary, and background, but behind the entire process the Spirit worked in such a way that the words inscribed on the page were the very words of God himself (see 2 Peter 1:21). That's why the Bible is so powerful and precious. Every word is inspired or breathed out by the Holy Spirit.

One more point concerning our sword is important. The term used for God's Word (*rhema*) refers to a particular, specific saying of Scripture. For instance, John 3:16 is a *rhema*; Romans 3:23 is a *rhema*. A *rhema* is God's Word applied to a specific situation in your life. Thinking of it this way means the Bible is like an armory in itself, and inside are all kinds of swords you can pull out when you need to go on the offensive against the enemy. When you select the right sword, it slices through everything, right to the heart of the matter.

As James Boice says, "According to Ephesians 6:17, you must know the specific sayings of Scripture—you must have them memorized—if you are to resist and overcome Satan successfully. . . . Satan will not flee from us simply because we tell him to. . . . There is nothing in all life more powerful than the specific words of God."[9]

Jesus perfectly modeled this for us when he was tempted by the devil in the wilderness for forty days (see Matthew 4:1-11). During this duel in the desert, Jesus deftly wielded the Word of God. Each time Satan launched his assault, Jesus responded with "It is written" and quoted a specific verse from the Old Testament book of Deuteronomy. He slashed the temptations to pieces with his sword, totally disarming Satan. Out of ammunition, the defeated devil left Jesus. There's one vital point here we dare not miss—if Jesus used Scripture as his weapon, how much more should we?

Where is your sword all week? Is it safely in the sheath, sitting on the shelf? Or is it in your hand, ready to attack when needed?

Part of the legend of King Arthur is his famous sword known as Excalibur. When the Lady of the Lake brings the sword up from the water, presenting it to Arthur, there's an engraving on opposite sides of the blade—"take me up" and "cast me away." We face these same two options every day with our own Excalibur—the Bible. Our spiritual survival hangs in the balance depending upon which choice we make. Will we take it up and read it, or will we cast it away?

WARFARE PRAYER

I'm no expert on military tactics or strategy, but even I know that in modern warfare, victory or defeat turns on one key factor: who controls the skies. It's all about air power. Whoever wins the air wins the war.

The same is true in the invisible war. Air superiority is decisive. Fittingly, our spiritual armor concludes with a call to control the air with our prayers. Ephesians 6:18 says, "Pray in the Spirit at all times and on every occasion. Stay alert and be persistent in your prayers for all believers everywhere."

Prayer is our secret weapon in the invisible war, and it's something every Christian can do. Prayer requires no special training, no great knowledge, and no special degree of spiritual maturity. All of us can humbly approach the Lord and ask for what we need.

Whatever else you do, pray. There is no victory over the enemy without it.

PUT ON JESUS

We've said quite a bit about our spiritual survival suit in this chapter, but to make it as simple as possible, essentially, the armor is Jesus Christ. Romans 13:12 tells us to "put on the armor of light" (NASB), and then Romans 13:14 says "put on the Lord Jesus Christ" (NASB). In other words, we are to dress up in Jesus.

As David Jeremiah says, "He is the belt of truth, for He is the Way, the Truth and the Life. He is the breastplate, for He is our righteousness. He becomes our shoes of peace, because He is our peace. He is the shield of faith, for He is the author and finisher of our faith. And He is the helmet of salvation, for we are told in the Bible that we have the mind of Christ."[10]

So Christ is the key. Stay close to Jesus. As A. W. Tozer famously said, "The best way to keep the enemy out is to keep Christ in. . . . It is not the praying sheep Satan fears but the presence of the Shepherd."[11]

If we stay Christ-centered and Christ-focused and draw near to him each day, we will stand strong and will survive the spiritual onslaught arrayed against us.

CHAPTER 5

KEEP PUSHING

Prayer is simply the key to everything we need to do and be in life. We must learn to pray. We have to. . . . There is nothing more important, or harder, or richer, or more life-altering. . . . To fail to pray, then, is not to merely break some religious rule—it is a failure to treat God as God. It is a sin against his glory. . . . Prayer is simply a recognition of the greatness of God.

TIM KELLER

Prayer is not overcoming God's reluctance; it is laying hold of his highest willingness.

RICHARD TRENCH

Ray Stedman, who for many years served as pastor of Peninsula Bible Church in Palo Alto, California, tells a story he heard from a retired mariner who navigated his ship through surging, stormy seas over a career of many years. This captain recounted weathering one especially wild storm where survival was by no means assured.

The old mariner said, "The Lord heard the voices of many strangers that night."[1]

I believe the same is true today. Perhaps in the midst of the peril and perplexity in today's world, you're turning to the Lord more often than ever before. In these times I think we all sense a need to take a knee in prayer like never before. As we navigate these last days, few things are more important than our prayer lives. As S. D. Gordon once said, "You can do *more* than pray, *after* you have prayed. But you can *not* do more than pray *until* you have prayed."[2]

Jesus told his followers that their prayer lives must intensify as the days get darker. At the end of his great sermon about the end of days, Jesus said, "Keep alert at all times. And *pray* that you might be strong enough to escape these coming horrors and stand before the Son of Man" (Luke 21:36, emphasis added).

Right after his extensive instruction about the days before his coming in Luke 17, we read in Luke 18:1, "Jesus told his disciples a story to show that they should always pray and never give up." Jesus' follow-up to his teaching about the final days was a story about a desperate widow that highlights the need for persistent prayer. Jesus knew the challenges and cares of the end times must be met with persevering prayer.

Jesus' message is clear: just as the popular slogan said some time ago, we have to *PUSH*—Pray Until Something Happens.

We all sense a need to pray, and to keep praying, but if you're like me, you often feel woefully inadequate. Prayer is *essential*, but prayer is not easy. The great Scottish preacher Alexander Whyte once said, "If you want to humble a man, ask him about his prayer life."[3] That's true, isn't it? If we're honest, prayer is something we all struggle with, even (and perhaps especially) when times are uncertain. We know we need to pray, but sometimes we may secretly wonder if it really works.

Jesus' disciples experienced the same struggle with prayer in their day. The disciples never asked Jesus how to walk on water, how to still a storm, or how to do other miracles, but they did ask Jesus to teach them to pray (see Luke 11:1). We need the same help.

Other than regularly reading and meditating on the Bible, nothing is more essential to your spiritual life—and spiritual survival—than prayer. It's that simple. We need to learn to pray, and there's no better place to look than Luke 11:1-13. These verses provide answers from Jesus to three key questions about prayer:

> *What* are we to pray for? (verses 1-4)
> *How* are we to pray? (verses 5-10)
> *Why* are we to pray? (verses 11-13)

Our focus will be on the last two questions, but let's begin briefly with the most basic question—what should we pray to the Lord about?

WHAT TO PRAY

In response to the disciples' question, Jesus tells them what kinds of things to pray for. The prayer Jesus gives, commonly known as the Lord's Prayer, is shorter in Luke 11 than the version recorded in Matthew 6. They aren't exact, word-for-word copies, which means you don't have to pray these exact words. If the Lord wanted us to pray this prayer verbatim, the version in Luke 11 would be the same as the one in Matthew 6. However, while Jesus didn't give us this prayer to repeat over and over again, there's nothing wrong with using this prayer as long as it's not *routine* or *mechanical*. We should memorize it and cite it as we do other parts of Scripture.

Since the form of the model prayer in Matthew 6:9-13 is longer and more familiar than the one in Luke 11, let's look at that text in its traditional form as our guide.

Our Father who art in heaven,
hallowed be thy name.
Thy kingdom come.
Thy will be done on earth, as it is in heaven.

Give us this day our daily bread,
and forgive us our trespasses,
as we forgive those who trespass against us,
and lead us not into temptation,
but deliver us from evil.

Before we get into the specifics, let's make a few general observations about this prayer.

It's a model prayer. It's a pattern, road map, or skeleton to guide our own praying. It's a sample of the main areas we're to cover in our daily prayers. As I've already stated, it's not a prayer for us to pray in some rote fashion, but a pattern or outline to follow.

It's not the "Lord's" prayer. While it's not wrong to call this the Lord's Prayer, it's more accurate and descriptive to call it the "Disciple's Prayer." The reason is that this was not a prayer prayed by Jesus but a prayer he gave his disciples to guide their own praying. The "Lord's prayer" is in John 17, where Jesus pours out his heart to his Father.

It's a family prayer. We see this in two ways. First, God is called our Father. This prayer is for those born into God's family by faith in Jesus. Second, all the pronouns are plural ("our"). This reminds us that we belong to a great family of faith. We don't pray just for ourselves; we pray for the family. Martin Luther is reported to have said, "Religion is a matter of personal pronouns."[4] That's certainly true in this model prayer. The plural, family nature of this prayer is well-expressed in this poem:

You cannot say the Lord's prayer,
And even once say "I."
You cannot pray the Lord's prayer,
and even once say "my."

Nor can you pray the Lord's prayer
and not pray for another.
For when you ask for daily bread,
you must include your brother!
For others are included in each and every plea.
From the beginning to the end of it,
It never once says "me."

It's a short, simple prayer. The words in the prayer are simple and unadorned. In the original Greek (without the disputed ending in Matthew 6:13), the entire prayer is only fifty-seven words. While there are occasions to pray for lengthy periods of time, and examples of this in the Bible, the model Jesus gave his disciples is strikingly brief.

It's a petitionary prayer. Over the years, I've heard all kinds of definitions and descriptions of prayer. People say prayer is "talking with God," "conversing with God," or "opening our heart to Jesus." The simplest definition of prayer is "asking God for something." All of the Greek words used in the New Testament that are translated "prayer," "petition," "request," or "supplication" have a common basic meaning—to ask for something. Prayer is asking God for something. It's human asking and divine answering. We see this in Matthew 6. The model prayer contains a string of six requests:

> "Hallowed be thy name"
> "Thy kingdom come"
> "Thy will be done"
> "Give us this day our daily bread"
> "Forgive us our trespasses"
> "Lead us not into temptation"

The model prayer is a petitionary prayer.

It's a balanced prayer. While the model prayer contains six requests, there are two main divisions:

> Pray to the Father about the Father (God's glory: *thy* name, *thy* kingdom, *thy* will)
> Pray to the Father about the family (our good: give *us*, forgive *us*, lead *us*)

The prayer moves from God's glory to our good. Notice the change in pronouns from "thy" ("your") to "our" and "us." Our focus and first priority in prayer is on God's glory. Then the model prayer brings us back to earth to pray for our own needs.

God has all the power, the majesty, and the glory; we have all the needs, wants, and poverty. He's got everything; we have nothing. Prayer is the ultimate act of dependence. As E. M. Bounds writes, "Prayer honors God; it dishonors self. It is man's plea of weakness, ignorance, want."[5]

With this overview, let's briefly look at the two divisions of this prayer and the six things we're to pray about.

PRAY TO THE FATHER ABOUT THE FATHER

The three requests in this first half of the prayer cover three areas:

> The Father's person: "hallowed be thy name"
> The Father's program: "thy kingdom come"
> The Father's priorities: "thy will be done"

"OUR FATHER, WHO ART IN HEAVEN"

The prayer begins with the one we seek in prayer—"Our Father." The word "Father" indicates *to whom* we pray, and the word "our" refers to *with whom* we pray. God is referred to as Father fourteen times in the Old Testament, yet always in reference to the nation of Israel, not individuals. Jesus calls God his Father more than sixty times in the Gospels. We have a new relationship with God. He is our Father through faith in Jesus.

When I think about God being my Father, my mind goes to my own dad. He's great at fixing things and working with his hands. He doesn't like talking on the phone, so when I call and my mom answers and I ask for him, my dad knows that I must need something. When he takes the phone, his first words are usually, "What do you need?" I like to think of my heavenly Father in the same way. When I come to him with my troubles and concerns as his child, his response is, "What do you need?"

The phrase "who art in heaven" references whom we're seeking. He resides in the heavens. He's seated on the throne. He is almighty, eternal, and infinite. God is near us—he's intimate. But he's also far beyond us—he's transcendent. First things first: before anything else, remember who it is you're praying to. Stop and think about the Father in the heavens before you go any further.

THE FATHER'S PERSON

The first request is that God's name be honored, revered, and set apart (that's what "hallowed" means). In ancient times, someone's name represented their person or nature—who they are. So this is a request that God be revered, set apart from everything else, and treated as holy. The Puritan Thomas Watson noted that this is the one petition in this prayer that we will make for all eternity:

When some of the other petitions shall be useless and out of date, as we shall not need to pray in heaven, "Give us our daily bread," because there shall be no hunger; nor,

"Forgive us our trespasses," because there shall be no sin; nor, "Lead us not into temptation," because the old serpent is not there to tempt: yet the hallowing of God's name will be of great use and request in heaven; we shall be ever singing hallelujahs, which is nothing else but the hallowing of God's name.[6]

This request is what the angels around the throne in heaven never cease to proclaim in Revelation 4:8—"Holy, holy, holy."

If we pray for God to make his name set apart, then it follows that we must pray and seek that *we* will be holy in our lives. The revering of God's name must begin in my life if I sincerely want to see it hallowed everywhere else. We should honestly ask ourselves, *Is God treated as holy in my life? My marriage? My family?*

THE FATHER'S PROGRAM

Next is "thy kingdom come." This is a longing for God's program to be fulfilled—for the weary, war-torn world we live in to be made right. When you think about it, all prayer is ultimately a cry for the Kingdom to come. When we pray about our fears and uncertainty, the nation and our leaders, temptation, family issues, financial concerns, or health problems, the final answer to every one of these issues of life is the arrival of Christ's Kingdom. The Kingdom is God's answer to all our cries, sighs, and whys. And when we ask for the Kingdom to come, for God's Kingdom to rule on earth, we implicitly pray that our lives will also be subject to him.

Haddon Robinson says, "We must be willing for all of the little kingdoms that matter so much to us now to be pulled down. If we want God's rule over all men and women at some future time, it follows that we will want His control in our lives today. Unless we are sufficiently concerned about making our lives His throne and bringing others into glad submission to Him, we cannot pray with integrity for His kingdom to come."[7]

It's been well said that when we pray "your kingdom *come*," we must pray "my kingdom *go*."

THE FATHER'S PRIORITIES

The final request in this first section of the prayer concerns God's will or priorities—"thy will be done on earth as it is in heaven." How is God's will done in heaven? Completely. Joyfully. Unceasingly. Perfectly. Immediately. This is an appeal for God's sovereignty to be manifested on earth.

Again, what we want for this world must first be true in our lives. We must abandon our will for his will and yield ourselves totally to him. The ultimate issue in our lives is lordship—who's in charge?

PRAY TO THE FATHER ABOUT THE FAMILY

After we pray to the Father about the Father and his glory, we move to praying to the Father about the family and our good. Again, remember that all the pronouns here are plural. We pray for ourselves and others. It's difficult sometimes to avoid self-centered praying. We get so absorbed in our own needs, like the young woman who said, "Lord, I'm not going to pray for myself today; I'm going to pray for others," and after praying for some time, she added, "And give my mother a handsome son-in-law." Our prayers have a tendency to circle back to ourselves.

In the model prayer, Jesus focuses on three requests that we pray for ourselves and other believers.

OUR PROVISION

The first petition is "give us this day our daily bread." This is a humble request for provision. We ask God for what is needed for the day—*daily* bread. Each day brings its share of burdens and needs but also its joys and blessings.

Daily bread includes food but is not limited to that. Everything necessary for our body and our existence is captured in this request. Martin Luther helps us understand the full meaning of "daily bread":

> What does "Daily Bread" mean? Everything that nourishes our body and meets its needs, such as: Food, drink, clothing, shoes, house, yard, fields, cattle, money, possessions, a devout spouse, devout children, devout employees, devout and faithful rulers, good government, good weather, peace, health, discipline, honor, good friends, faithful neighbors and other things like these.[8]

God is our Father. We can trust him to meet our daily needs. As Hudson Taylor reminds us,

> It is not difficult for me to remember that the little ones need breakfast in the morning, dinner at midday, and something before they go to bed at night. Indeed, I could not forget it. And I find it impossible to suppose that our Heavenly Father is less tender or mindful than I. . . . I do not believe that our Heavenly Father will ever forget his children. I am a very poor father, but it is not my habit to forget my children. God is a very, very good Father. It is not his habit to forget his children.[9]

OUR PARDON

The second family request is for pardon from our sins. The model prayer Jesus gives us moves from "give" to "forgive"; from food to forgiveness.

The whole notion of forgiveness raises an important, practical question—if our debt is erased by God when we trust in Jesus and receive his forgiveness, why do we *still* need to ask for God's forgiveness? If all our debts have been paid and we have asked Jesus to forgive our sin once for all, why do we still need to be pardoned? (See Ephesians 1:7; Colossians 2:14.) It's easy to see why we need to ask God to forgive us once. Until we accept Christ's payment for our sins, we're not saved. I have to trust and believe that Jesus died on the cross to cancel my debt. Yet the prayer Jesus taught us in Matthew 6 makes asking for forgiveness part of our *daily* prayers. We ask for *daily pardon* as well as *daily provision*. But why do we need to keep asking for God's forgiveness? The answer is very simple—because we keep on sinning.

At this point, distinguishing two aspects of God's forgiveness is helpful.

1. *Final* forgiveness (relationship): This facet of our forgiveness brings us into an eternal relationship with our Father. Our sins are forever forgiven, blotted out, and removed far away (see Psalm 103:12; Jeremiah 31:34; Micah 7:19; Ephesians 1:7).

2. *Family* forgiveness (fellowship): Our daily sin interferes with our intimacy with our Father. It fractures our fellowship. As believers, we don't lose our relationship when we sin, but we do interrupt our fellowship with the Father. So we have to come daily for a fresh application of his forgiveness to maintain our fellowship with our Father. First John 1:9 says, "If we confess our sins to him, he is faithful and just to forgive us our sins and to cleanse us from all wickedness."

There's an old Dennis the Menace cartoon that pictures Dennis kneeling beside his bed at night, with hands clasped, eyes looking heavenward, saying, "Lord, I'm here to turn myself in." We have to come to God daily to turn ourselves in.

Jesus adds an interesting condition to our forgiveness: "As we forgive those who trespass against us." This is the only petition in this model prayer with a condition attached to it. The reason is because we sin *and* we are sinned against. We aren't the only ones in debt. We have debtors of our own: those who owe us something for what they've done to us. Our call when we are sinned against is to let it go. That's what forgiveness is. Forgiveness is a release, a letting go of destructive feelings like anger, bitterness, and revenge—attitudes that poison our lives. Forgiveness is not tolerating sin, excusing it, forgetting it, or covering it up. Forgiveness is letting it go. It's releasing the other person and also releasing ourselves from the burden of bitterness. Phil Ryken says,

If we must forgive, then how shall we do it? What does it mean to forgive our debtors?

It means to forgive everyone for everything. Forgive the neighbor who backed over your begonias. Forgive the sibling who colored in your books and the parent who never showed you very much affection. Forgive the spouse who doesn't meet your needs and the child who ran away from home. Forgive the coworker who stabbed you in the back and the boss who denied your promotion. Forgive the church member who betrayed a confidence or the pastor who gave you poor spiritual care. Forgive people for whatever they have done to you.

If you are a Christian, you do not have the right to withhold forgiveness from anyone for anything.[10]

Jesus knew this would be the most difficult issue for his disciples and us to understand and apply, so he adds a postscript or appendix in Matthew 6:14-15: "If you forgive those who sin against you, your heavenly Father will forgive you. But if you refuse to forgive others, your Father will not forgive your sins."

This is not saying that our forgiveness merits God's forgiveness. It is saying that a mark of being forgiven is forgiving other people. Our forgiveness of others is evidence of our own forgiving spirit, and God only forgives the truly penitent. Refusing to forgive others is evidence that I myself am unforgiven.

The English poet George Herbert says, "He that cannot forgive others, breaks the bridge over which he himself must pass if he would ever reach heaven; for every one has need to be forgiven."[11] This doesn't mean that Christians never wrestle with forgiveness. But the struggle itself is evidence of God's grace in our hearts. And we may have to forgive over and over again. It can be a process, especially when the wounds are deep. At times, we may have to forgive all over again and continue to forgive as often as necessary. Like the rest of this prayer, forgiveness is part of everyday life for believers.

OUR PROTECTION

The final request in the model prayer ("lead us not into temptation but deliver us from evil") has probably caused more head-scratching than any other. The first thing to recognize is that this is not two separate requests but one petition in two parallel parts. "Lead us not into temptation" and "deliver us from evil" are two sides of the same request.

The main question in this request is why would we ask God not to lead us into temptation? Does God lead us into temptation? According to James 1:13, the answer is no. "When you are being tempted, do not say, 'God is tempting me.' God is never tempted to do wrong, and he never tempts anyone else."

So, what does Jesus mean in Matthew 6:13? The best explanation is that this is a figure of speech to express something positive by stating the opposite. "This is no small matter" means "This is a big matter." When we pray "lead us not into temptation," we're really praying "keep us away from temptation." "Don't let Satan ambush us." "Build a hedge around us." We need to ask the Lord, "If the opportunity to sin presents itself, please remove our desire. If the desire springs up within us, please don't allow us to have the opportunity."

HOW DO WE PRAY?

After telling us *what* to pray, Jesus tells a parable in Luke 11:5-10 that focuses on *how* we pray. His instruction is pointed: we're to pray persistently; we're not to give up. In our prayer life we must PUSH:

> Then, teaching them more about prayer, he used this story: "Suppose you went to a friend's house at midnight, wanting to borrow three loaves of bread. You say to him, 'A friend of mine has just arrived for a visit, and I have nothing for him to eat.' And suppose he calls out from his bedroom, 'Don't bother me. The door is locked for the night, and my family and I are all in bed. I can't help you.' But I tell you this—though he won't do it for friendship's sake, if you keep knocking long enough, he will get up and give you whatever you need because of your shameless persistence."
>
> LUKE 11:5-8

Jesus begins this story by drawing in the listener: "Suppose you went to a friend's house at midnight." The listener or reader is the person in need—that's *us*. We find ourselves in the story.

The parable revolves around a situation that could have arisen in ancient Near Eastern culture. An unexpected visitor arrives at midnight. This was quite common because people often traveled at night when it was cooler. The culture of the day demanded hospitality. It was a social duty and requirement. But the host has a problem: he has visitors and no food.

The cupboards are bare, and there are no 7-Eleven stores or twenty-four-hour Walmarts to shop at. The man is in a real bind. His only choice is to go next door to his neighbor in the dead of night.

To visualize this scene, we have to remember that families in that day lived in one-room houses. The entire family slept on one large mat on the floor. The animals were put to bed in another part of the room at night. The door to the house had a wooden or iron bar through rings in the door panels. Getting up and removing it would be noisy, and lighting a candle to find bread and rummaging through the kitchen would wake up the entire household. The situation presents a *massive* inconvenience, so the man responds, "Don't bother me. . . . I can't help you" (verse 7). Request denied!

The desperate neighbor does the only thing he can do: he knocks again and must have said something like, "Come on, man, you know I need some bread. I can't leave my visitors unfed. You have to help me!" You get the point: this man is not going away.

Jesus says, "If you keep knocking long enough, he will get up and give you whatever you need because of your shameless persistence" (verse 8). The word translated "shameless persistence" can also mean "gall," "nerve," or "bold perseverance."

We must be careful to note that God is not being compared to this tired, reluctant neighbor. Rather, he is being contrasted with him. What we have here is a "how much more" argument. Jesus is saying, "If even this unwilling neighbor will respond to persistence, how much more will our Father answer the persistent prayers of his people?" Our prayers are to be punctuated by commas, not periods.

Persistence in prayer is reinforced by Jesus' call in verses 9-10 to keep asking, keep seeking, and keep knocking. There's increasing intensity and a stacking of the words.

> Ask (prayer is asking for something)
> Seek (a stronger word than ask)
> Knock (relates back to the story of the man persistently knocking on the door)

God is ready to give, so *ask*, *seek*, and *knock*. PUSH—Pray Until Something Happens. As the Scottish theologian P. T. Forsyth writes, "Prayer is never rejected so long as we do not cease to pray. The chief failure of prayer is its cessation."[12]

This raises some important questions: Why does God want us to persist in prayer? Why does he sometimes delay his answers for so long? Why does God so often put us on hold? Why does he leave us waiting on the other end of the phone? What's the point? Do you ever feel like that? If God knows what we ask before we ask, if God hears us immediately, and if God is willing to answer us, why do we need to persist and persevere in prayer? Although much more could be said here about the mystery of prayer, here are five practical benefits of persistent prayer:

1. *Our faith is strengthened.* Our faith grows as we persist in seeking the Lord.
2. *We draw closer to the Lord.* Ben Patterson, in his book *Deepening Your Conversation with God*, says, "Perhaps one reason God delays his answers to our prayers is because he knows we need to be with him far more than we need the

94

things we ask of him."[13] Haddon Robinson says, "Those who are satisfied with the trinkets in the Father's hand miss the best reward of prayer—the reward of communicating and communing with the God of the universe."[14]

3. *Our patience is stretched.* We learn to wait on the Lord.

4. *Our gratitude grows.* That which is easily gained is often lightly appreciated. When we pray and seek the Lord for something over a period of time and the Lord answers our petition, we're filled with joy and thanksgiving.

5. *God may want to do something bigger.* God may delay his answer because he has something bigger in mind. I once heard someone, in reference to the story of the raising of Lazarus, say, "If Jesus had arrived on time he would have healed a sick man, but he waited a few days so He could raise a dead man." We have to persist in prayer and trust the Lord's timing, looking for the benefits his delays bring.

In these last days, as we face greater trials and opposition, we must not give up in our praying. No matter what—keep praying. Keep PUSHing.

WHY DO WE PRAY?

The final facet of Jesus' teaching on prayer in Luke 11 answers the "why" question. Why pray? The answer is simple: because of the nature of God. He is our Father. Our persistent prayer is rooted in the character of God as our Father.

> You fathers—if your children ask for a fish, do you give
> them a snake instead? Or if they ask for an egg, do you give
> them a scorpion? Of course not! So if you sinful people
> know how to give good gifts to your children, how much

more will your heavenly Father give the Holy Spirit to those
who ask him.

LUKE 11:11-13

In verse 11, Jesus again draws in the listener—"You fathers—if
your children ask for a fish . . ." Jesus is telling us we pray because
God is our Father and is predisposed to give us good things, just as
a father wants to bless his children. Jesus' teaching on prayer ends
where it began, with the "Father" (Luke 11:2, 13). The word "Father"
brackets the entire passage.

This gives us confidence and motivation to pray and to persist in
prayer. The realization that our Father loves us and is willing to give
us what is good should motivate us to persist in prayer. I love these
words of Warren Wiersbe: "Prayer isn't bothering God, bargaining
with God, borrowing from God, or burdening God. True prayer is
blessing the Father because we love Him, trust Him, and know that
He will meet our needs, so we come and ask."[15]

Our prayers get sifted through the goodness and wisdom of our
Father. He will always and only give us what is good for us. Pray
persistently, knowing that God is your loving Father who will only
give you good gifts. If what you request is not best for you, God will
not give it.

Dr. Howard Hendricks, a beloved professor for so many years at
Dallas Theological Seminary, told of a time when he was a young
man, before he was married. A certain mother in the church he
attended came up to him one Sunday and said to him, "Howard, I
just want you to know that I'm praying that you'll be my son-in-law."
Dr. Hendricks, when telling this story, stopped at that point and said,
very solemnly, "Have you ever thanked God for unanswered prayer?"
I know I have.

We trust our Father to give us good gifts. But we don't receive just gifts; we receive the *Giver*. God gives us the Holy Spirit (see Luke 11:13). That's the greatest gift of all. He can't give more than himself.

As the world around us grows more chaotic and confusing, turn your panic into prayers. Don't be a stranger to God. Let him hear your voice often. Pray regularly. Pray repeatedly.

No matter what happens, keep PUSHing!

CHAPTER 6

DO THE BEST THINGS IN THE WORST TIMES

Never before in American history has it been more
important for the church to be all that it can be in a society that
is increasingly hostile to Christian values. . . . The darker the night,
the more important every candle becomes.

ERWIN LUTZER

In his book *Shepherding the Church*, Joe Stowell records "an inspiring but little-known inscription hidden away in Harold Church, Staunton, England." The inscription is from 1653, and reflects a dark time for the Anglican Church in Great Britain. At the time, Oliver Cromwell was in power, and his mission was to remove any trace of the monarchy from the country. The Anglican Church thus came within his crosshairs since the head of that church was the king. As Stowell describes it, "Cromwell emptied the monasteries, removed baptismal fonts from the churches, defamed the clergy, and did everything in his power to disengage their place and influence in the culture. If you were an Anglican pastor, those were tough times to be in the religion business."

It is against this backdrop that the inscription from Harold Church was written: "In the year of 1653, when all things sacred were throughout the nation destroyed or profaned, this church was built to the glory of god by sir Robert Shirley, whose singular praise it was to have done the best things in the worst times."[1]

What a praise: doing "the best things in the worst times."

It certainly seems that we're living in the "worst times" for the United States spiritually, morally, and politically. Our nation is rapidly drifting away from God. Christianity is under attack from within and without. Biblical Christianity is in decline and vilified at every turn.

In these worst times, God is calling us to be about doing the best things. But what are the best things we must do? What activities and aspirations should capture our focus as time runs out?

No book in the New Testament answers this question more clearly than 1 Peter. The apostle Peter wrote this letter to believers scattered throughout central and northern Asia Minor (modern Turkey) in the early AD 60s. The audience Peter addressed was suffering persecution. The mistreatment was not empire-wide and did not involve physical suffering or martyrdom but consisted of mocking, slandering, maligning, and reviling (see 2:12; 3:16-17; 4:3-4, 14). The epistle 1 Peter was written to Jewish believers scattered throughout the Roman provinces of Asia Minor to encourage them in the face of localized persecution so that others could witness the true grace of God in their lives (see 5:12). In short, the purpose of 1 Peter is to show how to stand firm in God's grace in a hostile or Christian-unfriendly culture.

Peter develops several themes in his letter, but one thread that runs through the book is the coming of Jesus Christ. The return of Jesus serves as a kind of background music fostering hope and a sense of urgency to do the best things (see 1:7, 13; 2:12; 5:4). In hard times, God's people must stand firm. Peter believed the Lord could come at any moment and he motivates his readers to live in light of that day.

Peter's most detailed presentation of Christ's coming and how we should live in view of that reality is found in 4:7-11. There's no more simple, straightforward passage in the New Testament concerning what we should be doing if we believe Jesus is coming soon:

> The end of the world is coming soon. Therefore, be earnest and disciplined in your prayers. Most important of all, continue to show deep love for each other, for love covers a multitude of sins. Cheerfully share your home with those who need a meal or a place to stay. God has given each of you a gift from his great variety of spiritual gifts. Use them well to serve one another. Do you have the gift of speaking? Then speak as though God himself were speaking through you. Do you have the gift of helping others? Do it with all the strength and energy that God supplies. Then everything you do will bring glory to God through Jesus Christ. All glory and power to him forever and ever! Amen.

Verse 7 opens with the startling words, "The end of the world is coming soon." Many wonder how Peter could say that almost two thousand years ago. How could the end be soon in the early AD 60s? Was Peter mistaken?

The consistent view of the early church was that Christ's coming was near—that is, it could come at any moment (see Romans 13:12; 1 Corinthians 7:29; Philippians 4:5; Hebrews 10:25; James 5:8-9; Revelation 1:3; 22:20). Peter pictures "the end as impending—having drawn near and now in a position to break in at any time. . . . As human history moves alongside the edge of the eschatological future, the line of separation at times seems razor-thin."[2]

Wayne Grudem states, "*The end of all things is at hand* means that all the major events in God's plan of redemption have occurred, and now all things are ready for Christ to return and rule. . . . Thus the curtain could fall at any time."[3]

Daniel Segraves writes,

> Since nothing else must occur before the event that triggers all other eschatological events (the rapture of the church), it is still correct to say, "The end of all things is at hand." This is the doctrine of imminence, which means that, so far as we know, the end can come at any moment. It also means that, as far as the writers of the New Testament knew, the end could have come at any moment.[4]

When thinking about the arrival of the end, there's another aspect to this we should not overlook. None of us knows how near our own end is in the sense of personal, individual mortality.[5] None of us knows how much time we have personally or prophetically. We could encounter some tragedy and depart this world at any time. Prophetically, Jesus could come at any moment to catch his bride to heaven. In that sense, "the end of the world is coming soon." There's an ever-present "soonness" to the end of all things for all of us either way.

After reminding us that Christ could come at any moment, Peter's next word is "therefore." Peter is saying to us that since the Lord could return at any time, triggering the sequence of events that will bring history to a close, here's what we should be doing. Knowing should fuel a sense of urgency and simplicity.

When speaking of the Lord's return, not all believers agree on the details, but we can all agree on the demands of the experience.[6] First Peter 4:7-11 outlines four things we should do if we believe that the Lord is coming soon. We could call these the "Peter Principles" of spiritual survival in the last days, the best things we can do in the worst of times.

KEEP YOUR HEAD CLEAR: PRAY

The end of the world is coming soon. Therefore, be earnest
and disciplined in your prayers.

1 PETER 4:7

Peter's first principle is for believers to stay calm and balanced in
order to have a devoted prayer life. After saying, "The end of the
world is coming soon," Peter follows immediately by calling us to
be "earnest" and "disciplined." He knows that in light of end-times
events, many people are prone to get unbalanced and go to extremes.

We see this today. As things in the world continue to spiral out of
control, some people can't resist the temptation to get caught up in
all kinds of prophetic foolishness and frenzy, which is not conducive
to a rich prayer life. The most egregious form of prophetic hysteria
is date-setting for the coming of Christ or the end of the world. A
charismatic leader will claim to know when Jesus is returning to
earth, and in extreme examples, followers may even liquidate their
possessions to prepare. The last two centuries are littered with failed
predictions, disgraced "prophets," and disappointed followers.

What's amazing is that Jesus claimed during his earthly ministry that even he did not know the day of his coming (see Matthew
24:36). Anyone who claims to know the specific time of Christ's
coming is claiming to know something the Father didn't tell even the
Son while he was on earth. This is the height of arrogance and folly.

A biblical approach to the end times will never promote panic or
frantic activity. The New Testament knows nothing of apocalyptic
hysteria. Rather, in view of the end of all things, believers are to be
"earnest" and "disciplined." Being earnest means being sensible, pru-
dent, balanced, and proportionate in our reactions and possessing a
clear mind.

The word *disciplined* means literally "sober" or "not drunk." In other words, we are to be sober-minded, clearheaded, and mentally alert for the purpose of prayer. We are to be earnest and disciplined so that we are disposed to pray. Believing that the end of all things is at hand should spur us on to a disciplined prayer life. When we're sane and sober, we can pray more effectively and appropriately, and as the troubles of the last days increase, prayer is more important than ever. As we await the end of all things, we're to pray, not panic.

In our present day, prayer is needed on every front—individually and corporately in our families, churches, and society. Perilous times must be faced with prayer. Nothing else will do.

As Charles Swindoll notes, "When something alarms you, pray. When current events confuse you, pray. If the world looks like it's spinning out of control, pray. In fact, prayer is what sharpens our awareness so that we are able to be more discerning. It gives us genuine hope and confidence in Christ in the midst of confusion. When you're panicking, you're not praying."[7]

To survive spiritually, don't get caught up in end-times hysteria. Don't panic; pray.

KEEP YOUR HEART WARM: LOVE

> Most important of all, continue to show deep love for each other, for love covers a multitude of sins.
>
> I PETER 4:8

According to Jesus, one of the signs of the Second Coming is that "the love of many will grow cold" (Matthew 24:12). Paul reminded Timothy that in the last days, "people will love only themselves" (2 Timothy 3:2). The final days will be marked by lack of love, and more and more our world is descending into the cold, hateful place predicted in Scripture.

In contrast, the badge of Christianity is love (see John 13:34-35). As we see the end approaching, Peter reminds us that believers are to be marked by a "deep love" for one another. The word translated "deep" was used in ancient times of a horse at full gallop when its muscles were stretched to the limit. Peter is saying that our love for one another is to be stretched out to the limits but never reaching its breaking point. Our love for our fellow believers is to keep "stretching, in both depth and endurance."[8]

First Peter 4:8 focuses on our love for one another as believers, but I believe it's valid to extend this command outward to the world around us. As our world becomes colder and more callous, believers should be a haven of warmth and winsomeness. Yet sadly, many believers are responding to the world's hostility in kind. Erwin Lutzer challenges this attitude: "We are not a majority, but God keep us from becoming an angry, vindictive minority! Self-pity loses sight of the promises of God and leads to a mindset of withdrawal, an attitude that says, 'Since they hate us, let them rot.' How unlike our Master!"[9]

A reason for or result of loving others is included: "For love covers a multitude of sins." Love doesn't *condone* sin, but it does *cover* it. When we love others, we will be gentle with their weaknesses and failures and won't broadcast their sin to humiliate or injure them. We should derive no delight from finding and exposing the faults and sins of others.

KEEP YOUR HOME OPEN: SHARE

Cheerfully share your home with those who need a meal or a place to stay.

I PETER 4:9

As love is in short supply in these last days, the love of believers must increase and intensify. One concrete expression of love is reaching out in hospitality to strangers. Hospitality is a specific aspect or subset of love.

The beautiful Christian virtue of hospitality is mentioned repeatedly in the New Testament (see Romans 12:13; 1 Timothy 3:2; 5:9-10; Titus 1:8; Hebrews 13:1-3; 3 John 1:5-8). As this world becomes a colder and more isolating place, we are to keep our homes open and show the warmth of Christ to strangers.

With the influx of immigrants and refugees into the United States and other nations, it's common to hear people speak of those who oppose unrestrained immigration as *xenophobic*, which means a fear of strangers. This slur is the opposite of what Peter references by his use of the word *philoxenos*, which means to love or befriend strangers. Believers are to have an affectionate concern for strangers always but even more in light of the any-moment coming of Christ. Max Lucado underscores the simplicity and impact of hospitality:

> Something holy happens around a dinner table that will never happen in a sanctuary. In a church auditorium you see the backs of heads. Around the table you see the expressions on faces. In the auditorium one person speaks; around the table everyone has a voice. Church services are on the clock. Around the table there is time to talk.
>
> Hospitality opens the door to uncommon community. . . . When you open your door to someone, you are sending this message: "You matter to me and to God." You may think you are saying, "Come over for a visit." But what your guest hears is, "I'm worth the effort."[10]

Hospitality is simple yet sublime. It's something almost every believer can do, yet as our society becomes more disconnected and distracted, it's becoming more and more rare.

THE END TIMES SURVIVAL GUIDE

There's an important condition added to our hospitality. It must be expressed "cheerfully," not with grumbling or complaining. We all know that showing hospitality can be costly in both money and time. It can be messy, inconvenient, and occasionally frustrating. When extending hospitality, God's people need to display a positive, cheerful attitude.

I like the story of a poor, tired, hungry traveler, walking a country road in England, who came to an inn bearing the name "George and the Dragon." The man knocked on the door.

"Is there any food I can have?" the man asked when he saw a woman's head pop out of a window to see who was at the door.

The woman saw his shabby clothes and knew he probably wouldn't be able to pay. "No!" she practically yelled.

"Can you spare some ale?"

"No!" she said again.

"That's all right. But is there any room in your stable for me to rest?"

"No!"

The traveler thought a moment before speaking again. "Is George around? Could I have a word with him instead?"[11]

In these times, as our world becomes a colder, less inviting place, we each need to take stock and honestly ask ourselves, *When it comes to showing hospitality to strangers, am I George . . . or the dragon? Am I willing to move outside my comfort zone to befriend and bless strangers the Lord brings across my path?*

KEEP YOUR HANDS BUSY: SERVE

God has given each of you a gift from his great variety of spiritual gifts. Use them well to serve one another. Do you have the gift of speaking? Then speak as though God himself were speaking through you. Do you have the gift of helping

> others? Do it with all the strength and energy that God supplies. Then everything you do will bring glory to God through Jesus Christ. All glory and power to him forever and ever! Amen.
>
> 1 PETER 4:10-11

Jesus gave his disciples specific, final instructions about how they were to use their gifts, talents, and possessions in his absence in the form of a parable found in Matthew 25:14-30. Jesus told a similar parable in Luke 19. There a nobleman entrusts his possessions to his servants before he embarks on a long trip and leaves them with these final instructions: "Invest this for me while I am gone" (Luke 19:13). The King James Version translates this, "Occupy till I come." Jesus is saying we must maximize the abilities, gifts, and opportunities he gives us while we wait for him to return. Our instructions are clear: keep your hands busy.

Every believer in Jesus Christ has at least one spiritual gift given to us by the Master to use in his service. No believer has all the gifts, and a believer can have more than one gift, but there is no such thing as an ungifted believer.

A spiritual gift is a skill or ability given by God for regular use to perform a function in the body of Christ with ease and effectiveness. More simply, a spiritual gift is a God-given ability for Christian service. (For a list of spiritual gifts, see Romans 12:6-8; 1 Corinthians 12:8-11, 28-31; Ephesians 4:11.)

Many wonder what the difference is between a natural talent or ability and a spiritual gift. One distinction is that natural talent comes by natural birth, whereas spiritual gifts come by new birth. Having said that, the two are not always easy to distinguish in their expression because natural talents and skills are also from God. They are clearly different, but they often complement each other. God in

9 KEY TRUTHS ABOUT SPIRITUAL GIFTS

1. Every believer has a spiritual gift or gifts.

2. A gift is received at the moment of salvation.

3. A gift is a divine enablement that manifests God's grace.

4. It's to be used to serve others.

5. It's a stewardship.

6. There is great variety in spiritual gifts.

7. There are two basic categories of gifts: speaking gifts and serving gifts.

8. We must depend on God in the use of gifts.

9. The ultimate purpose of these gifts is to glorify God.

his providence knew he was going to save us and gave us natural talents at birth that can be enhanced by our spiritual gifts at our new birth.

One benefit of knowing your spiritual gift is that it helps you to know where to focus your time and effort for the greatest impact in God's service. So, how can you discover your spiritual gift? Let me suggest five simple steps.

First, there are two broad categories of gifts: speaking gifts and serving gifts. Begin by determining which broad category your gifting falls in; then read the New Testament gift lists to get more specific.

Second, pray for the Lord's guidance. He wants you to discover your gift and use it more than you do.

Third, don't make this overly complicated. Begin to do something and trust God to lead you into your sweet spot of spiritual service. We discover by doing. That's the same way we discover our natural talents for things such as sports or music. As the old saying goes, "It's hard to steer a parked car."

Fourth, as you begin to serve or speak, listen to the input and evaluation of others. They serve as a valuable, objective resource and sounding board.

I like the story of a young farmer who was out plowing in his field one day. He stopped for a rest, wiped the perspiration from his brow, and looked up into the sky. The clouds had formed two letters—PC. "That's it!" he exclaimed. "Preach Christ! The Lord is telling me to preach Christ!"

He went to several churches in the area and tried to speak, but his messages weren't well delivered and didn't inspire or encourage the congregation. Finally, an old deacon called him aside and said, "Son, what makes you think you've been called to preach?"

The man said, "I saw it written in the clouds. PC—Preach Christ."

The deacon said, "Son, I think you missed it. I believe the Lord was telling you to *plant corn*."[12]

Others can help you in discerning God's calling and gifting. When you're functioning in the area of your gift, others will take note of it and ask you to do it and enjoy watching you do it.

Fifth, think about what you enjoy and what you do with ease and effectiveness. When you use your gift, you will enjoy it, which means you're probably on the right track. When you use your gift, you will be fulfilled, and you won't be totally fulfilled unless and until you use it.

Ray Stedman summarizes:

Now we close with this question: Who are you, anyway? Every morning you ought to ask yourself that. Who am I? And your answer should come from the Scriptures: I am a son of God among the sons of men. I am equipped with the power of God to labor today. At the very work that is given to me today God will be with me, doing it through me. I am gifted with special abilities to help people in various areas, and I don't have to wait until Sunday to start to utilize these gifts: I can do it at my work, I can do it anywhere. I can exercise the gift that God has given me to do. As soon as I begin to find out what it is, by taking note of my desires, and by asking others what they see in me, and by trying out various things, I am going to set myself to the lifelong task of keeping that gift busy.[13]

God supplies the strength we need to exercise our gifts whether they involve speaking or serving. His supply is limitless to enable and energize us.

My friend Pastor Philip De Courcy lives in California but was born and raised in Belfast, Northern Ireland. When he and his wife and three daughters were on their way to the ceremony to become US citizens, Philip was feeling patriotic and asked them what they liked best about America. Philip went first and waxed eloquent about the freedom Americans enjoy. As others were thinking about their answer, from the back seat one of his daughters said, "My favorite thing about America is free refills."

If you've ever been to Europe, that answer makes sense. Over there, when you order a soft drink, it's expensive, and you have to pay for every refill. For a young person, what could be better than free refills? And for a believer, what could be better than a God who gives free refills of his grace and strength? His power can never be diminished or exhausted. He is always available, and his help is unlimited.

A doxology closes the passage above—"All glory and power to him forever and ever! Amen." (1 Peter 4:11)—reminding us that in all our service, we get no glory. All the glory goes to the Lord.

Corrie ten Boom was a wonderful model of this idea of God receiving all the glory. Although she received notoriety during her lifetime, she said of her own position, "When Jesus rode into

Jerusalem on Palm Sunday on the back of a donkey, and everyone was waving palm branches and throwing garments on the road, and singing praises, do you think that for one moment it ever entered the head of that donkey that any of that was for him? If I can be the donkey on which Jesus Christ rides in His glory, I give him all the praise and all the honor."[14]

THE END

In light of the end of all things, God doesn't call us to acts of fanaticism or hysteria, and he doesn't necessarily call us to heroic feats of bravery or courage. The actions in 1 Peter 4:7-11 are simple things we can all do every day.

"The end of the world is coming soon," Peter writes. "Therefore..."

> Keep your head clear.
> Keep your heart warm.
> Keep your home open.
> Keep your hands busy.

These are the best things we can do in the worst times. These are things we can all do every day.

And never forget to give God all the glory.

CHAPTER 7

FIND YOUR FRAIDY HOLE

We cannot talk about standing on the Rock of Ages
and then act as if we are clinging to our last piece of driftwood.

ANONYMOUS

Do you remember the movie *Twister*? It's one of my all-time favorite movies—not because I enjoy disasters but because I live in Oklahoma, where, unfortunately, tornadoes are a part of life. I've lived here for all but three years of my life, so I've seen hundreds of tornado watches and warnings, heard the haunting blare of warning sirens, and seen my share of funnels in person and from storm chasers' videos. Central and northern Oklahoma are part of a region that has been dubbed "Tornado Alley." Oklahoma is known for three things: football, oil, and tornadoes.

Tornadoes are such a part of Oklahoma life and culture that most homes have what has come to be known as a "fraidy hole" or an underground storm shelter. "Fraidy hole" is an appropriate name because few things are more frightening than a tornado—the dark, ominous skies; the wall cloud; the spinning funnel; the debris cloud.

When new families move to Oklahoma, it's not unusual for them to experience serious anxiety and even panic when the first tornado watches and warnings are issued.

None of the houses my wife and I had lived in since we'd been married had a storm shelter, so when we built our current home, one nonnegotiable feature was a fraidy hole. A home without a shelter was not an option.

Meteorologists in Oklahoma urge everyone to have a safe place to hide in the event a twister comes calling. Every spring, when tornado season ramps up and twisters spin across the landscape, local meteorologists track tornadoes, calling on those in the storm path to go to their designated safe places. Our new safe place is the fraidy hole underneath the floor in our garage. It's very snug, but it's safe. We've already used it once. And my wife loves it.

As the storm clouds gather and our world spins out of control, we all sense the need to have a spiritual fraidy hole or shelter where we can retreat to ride out the storms. Jesus highlighted the sweeping fear that will mark the end times:

> You will hear of wars and threats of wars, but don't panic.
> MATTHEW 24:6

> People will be terrified at what they see coming upon the earth.
> LUKE 21:26

In these distressing days, we need a safe place away from the panic. We need a refuge. I can't think of a better spiritual fraidy hole than another famous "46 defense," Psalm 46:

> God is our refuge and strength,
> A very present help in trouble.

Therefore we will not fear, though the earth should change
And though the mountains slip into the heart of the sea;
Though its waters roar and foam,
Though the mountains quake at its swelling pride.

Selah.

There is a river whose streams make glad the city of God,
The holy dwelling places of the Most High.
God is in the midst of her, she will not be moved;
God will help her when morning dawns.
The nations made an uproar, the kingdoms tottered;
He raised His voice, the earth melted.
The LORD of hosts is with us;
The God of Jacob is our stronghold.

Selah.

Come, behold the works of the LORD,
Who has wrought desolations in the earth.
He makes wars to cease to the end of the earth;
He breaks the bow and cuts the spear in two;
He burns the chariots with fire.
"Cease striving and know that I am God;
I will be exalted among the nations, I will be exalted in the
     earth."
The LORD of hosts is with us;
The God of Jacob is our stronghold.

Selah. (NASB)

THE 9/11 PSALM

The terrorist attack on September 11, 2001, was an American tragedy. The surprise attack against America shook us to the core individually and nationally. We were left reeling. The stunning images of that day still arouse deep feelings in all our hearts. The day after 9/11 I was at Dallas Theological Seminary, and the sorrow was palpable. An unusually sober, solemn atmosphere hung over the campus. As we were going into chapel, I overheard someone ask the venerable professor Dr. J. Dwight Pentecost what he was thinking about in light of all the recent events. I'll never forget his reply. All he said was "Psalm 46, Psalm 46." His response has stayed with me all these years.

Then, at the National Prayer Service on Friday, September 14, Billy Graham offered words of comfort to the families of the fallen, the survivors, and the entire nation. During his comments, he read Psalm 46. Those words struck a chord.

I remember turning to Psalm 46 several times that week in 2001, and I found peace, security, and calm.

The great reformer Martin Luther faced numerous dangers and threats on his life from the pope and his forces in the sixteenth century. At one point he spent eleven months in hiding at Wartburg Castle. In the face of opposition, excommunication, and pressure from every side to back down, he stood firmly for the truth of salvation by God's grace through faith alone. Luther's favorite Bible passage was Psalm 46. The words of that psalm inspired him to write his triumphant hymn "A Mighty Fortress Is Our God." When Luther became fearful, discouraged, or insecure, he would say to his friend and coworker Philipp Melanchthon, "Come, Philipp, let us sing the Forty-Sixth Psalm," and they would lift their voices to God in praise.[1]

When I feel insecure or afraid, I often find myself turning to Psalm 46 as well. It's the divine fraidy hole when the twisters of life are spinning out of control. With all that's going on in our world today as the end of the age closes in, my time in Psalm 46 has become more frequent. As we move deeper into the last days, perilous times will increase in frequency and intensity.

Added to the mounting international, global concerns are our fears about our own lives that can make cowards even of the best of us. Ann Landers was a popular syndicated advice columnist. At one time she was receiving ten thousand letters a month from people with all kinds of problems. "Someone asked her if there was one common denominator among all her correspondents. She said that the great overriding theme of all the letters she read was *fear*—fear of nearly everything imaginable until the problem became, for countless readers, a fear of life itself."[2]

I've been there; so have you. How can we feel secure in a world filled with insecurity?

The answer today to our fears and insecurity is the same as it was in Martin Luther's day and the same as it was on 9/11—Psalm 46. We all need a huge dose of Psalm 46. It can be our fraidy hole in these stormy times.

I like the story about the little boy who was afraid of the dark. One night his mother told him to fetch the broom that was out on the back porch. "Mama, it's dark out there," the little boy said. "You know I'm afraid of the dark."

His mother responded, "Jesus is out there, so you don't have to be afraid. He'll protect you."

The little boy asked, "Are you sure he's out there?"

"Yes, I'm sure," the mother said. "He is everywhere."

The little boy thought about that and then cracked the door open. He called out, "Jesus? If you're out there, would you please hand me the broom?"

Just like that little boy, our security in the darkness comes from knowing God is with us. Security is found in God's presence. That's the simple, strong message of Psalm 46—the answer to panic and peril is the presence of God.

God's presence as the source of our security is highlighted

repeatedly in Psalm 46 (see verses 1, 5, 7, 11). The only safe, secure place in these last days is in knowing God is with us. God's presence is our fraidy hole.

GETTING OUR BEARINGS

Before we begin to unpack Psalm 46, we need to think for a few moments about the background of this psalm. We can't be sure about its historical setting, but many believe it's from the days of Hezekiah, one of the kings of Judah. In 701 BC, the Assyrian king Sennacherib was leading his army on a ruthless march through the Mediterranean world. Twenty years earlier Sennacherib's predecessor had stormed the northern kingdom of Israel's capital, Samaria, and deported the ten northern tribes, depopulating the nation. Once again, like a swarm of locusts, they descended on the tiny nation of Judah, conquering and consuming everything in their path. Sennacherib marched through Judah in 701 BC with a massive army of almost two hundred thousand.

By the time he got to Jerusalem, more than two hundred thousand Jews had been taken captive, along with much spoil. Forty-six cities had fallen. Sennacherib besieged Jerusalem, and it was only a matter of time before the city would fall. The Assyrians engaged in psychological warfare, sending messengers outside the walls of the city to taunt the people and their God in an effort to persuade them to surrender. As you can imagine, the city was gripped with crippling fear. This was a 9/11 scenario for Judah.

The Assyrian king sent a letter to King Hezekiah mocking God and urging him to surrender. I love the words of 2 Kings 19:14: "After Hezekiah received the letter from the messengers and read it, he went up to the Lord's Temple and spread it out before the Lord." Hezekiah spread the letter out before the Lord as if to say, "Read this, Lord. Look at what I'm facing. Help me." Hezekiah did what we must do in times of trouble. He turned panic into prayer. He laid it all out before the Lord and left it all in God's hands.

In 2 Kings 19:35, we read, "Then it happened that night that the angel of the LORD went out and struck 185,000 in the camp of the Assyrians; and when men rose early in the morning, behold, all of them were dead" (NASB). Did you catch the words "that night"? The very night when Hezekiah prayed, the Lord intervened dramatically. A lone angelic warrior dispatched from heaven destroyed the Assyrian juggernaut. The citizens of Jerusalem woke up the next morning to a killing field littered with almost two hundred thousand corpses. Proud King Sennacherib retreated to Nineveh in total humiliation. He was sent packing. Back in Nineveh he was later assassinated by his own sons.

One interesting historical footnote confirms that something dramatic happened to the Assyrian army in Judah. The Taylor Prism, a hexagonal clay document in the British Museum, contains Sennacherib's account of the siege of Jerusalem in 701 BC. In his chronicle, Sennacherib never explains why he failed to conquer Jerusalem, capture its king, and annex Judah as part of his kingdom. The Assyrian military machine that steamrolled everything in its path inexplicably failed to subdue the tiny nation of Judah and its capital city, Jerusalem.

The reason for Sennacherib's epic failure? The destroying angel.

It is thought that Psalm 46 commemorates this deliverance. It's a psalm of trust or confidence. The divine deliverance of Judah in Hezekiah's day serves as a foretaste or preview of what God will do when he finally defeats all his enemies and ushers in his kingdom of peace (verse 9). That's the day we anticipate.

There are three movements, stanzas, or natural breaks in the Psalm, each ending with the word *Selah* (probably a musical notation denoting a pause). Each stanza addresses a different situation with a corresponding reaction rising from faith:

Situation 1: Nature, in upheaval.
Reaction: I will not fear. (vv. 2–3)
Selah!

Situation 2: Jerusalem, under attack.
Reaction: I will not be moved. (vv. 4–7)
Selah!

Situation 3: Battlefield, after war.
Reaction: I will not strive. (vv. 8–11)
Selah![3]

The threefold outline we will use is simple:
> Our Refuge (verses 1-3)
> Our River (verses 4-7)
> Our Ruler (verses 8-11)

OUR REFUGE

The Lord is "our refuge and strength" in times of trouble. He is our hiding place. He is our fraidy hole.

The word "trouble" in Psalm 46:1 refers to a tight place or tight spot. It's when you feel like you're painted into a corner. King Hezekiah and Judah were certainly in a jam in the events that are believed to have given rise to this psalm. From the Taylor Prism, we know Sennacherib boasted that he had Hezekiah "shut up like a bird in a cage" in the city of Jerusalem. Hezekiah was trapped. The siege encircling the city was airtight. Yet God was with Hezekiah, and he's with us, too, if we know him. God is our refuge, our security, our hiding place. He's our strength who helps us. The Lord hides us and helps us when we find ourselves in the tight places and traps of life—when we face our own Sennacheribs.

But we must remember that God doesn't hide us and help us to take us out of the fray but only to protect and strengthen us for a time until we can get back into action. Warren Wiersbe says it well: "He hides us that He might help us, and then He thrusts us back into the battle that we might accomplish His will in this world. God does not hide us to pamper us, but to prepare us, He strengthens us that He might use us."[4] That's an important reminder.

The truths in Psalm 46 are real no matter how bad it gets. The word "though" occurs four times in the psalm in the New American Standard Bible, each time highlighting in poetic language some devastating national peril or cataclysm:

> - "*though* the earth should change": nothing is more stable and predictable than the earth's landscape; only extreme conditions can alter it.
> - "*though* the mountains slip into the heart of the sea": nothing is more immovable than a mountain.
> - "*though* its waters roar and foam," "*though* the mountains quake at its swelling pride": the oceans threaten to overwhelm the mountains.

These four phrases symbolize an unimaginable, threatening doomsday scenario. Using highly charged, symbolic language, the psalmist is saying, "No matter how bad it gets, we have a refuge," even if a spiritual F-5 tornado is bearing down on us.

How can the psalmist say that in the face of such peril and upheaval? How can we? Because we have one who hides us and helps us.

There's a great story from the life of Frederick Nolan, who served as a missionary in North Africa. Nolan was trying to get away from his enemies during a time of persecution, and hiding places were scarce. Eventually, he was so weary that he had to give up running and take refuge in a small cave, fully expecting that his enemies would find him. While he waited for his enemies to arrive, he watched with fascination as a spider began to spin a web over the entrance of the cave. It started small, but in just a few minutes, the web covered the entire entrance of the cave. Nolan's enemies came just as he had expected, but after some deliberation, they passed on. There's no way that Nolan could be in the cave, they reasoned, because he would have had to break the spider's web to get in. Nolan escaped and later wrote about this incident, "Where God is, a spider's web is like a wall. Where God is not, a wall is like a spider's web."[5]

As Proverbs 18:10 reminds us, "The name of the LORD is a strong fortress; the godly run to him and are safe." When all else is moving, we go to the one who is immovable. When everything is shifting, we go to the one who is secure. As Erwin Lutzer says, "We must cling to what is unmovable in an age when everything that has been nailed down is being torn up."[6]

Vance Havner told a story about an elderly woman who was greatly disturbed by her many troubles, both real and imaginary, and visited every doctor in town. Finally, someone in her family tactfully told her, "Grandma, we've done all we can for you. You'll just have to trust God for the rest." A look of absolute despair spread over her face as she replied, "Oh dear, has it come to that?" Havner wisely commented, "It always comes to that, so we might as well begin with that!" It *does* always come to that for all of us. We must trust God as our refuge and strength.

There's a comforting truth here about God and his help. Psalm 46:1 says God is "a very present help" (NASB). The New Living Translation says that God is "always ready to help in times of trouble." He's not just a help; he's *always* present to help us.

This means:

> God is always available.
> God is instantly present in any situation.
> God is easy to find.
> God is accessible.

Psalm 46:5 alludes to the destruction of the Assyrian army: "God will help her when morning dawns" (NASB). The King James Version translates it, "God shall help her, and that right early." Or as we would say, "in the nick of time."

Remember, when Hezekiah prayed while the Assyrian army was camped outside Jerusalem, 2 Kings 19:35 says "that night" God sent his angel to wipe out the Assyrian army. God's help was in the nick of time. It was available. Of course, not every cry to God is met with an immediate response, but the point is that God's help is timely. He is always right on time, even if his timetable is not our timetable.

The people of Judah woke up in the morning, and God had miraculously delivered them from the Assyrians. I'm sure you've gone to bed sometime, burdened and distressed about some difficulty you were facing, only to awake in the morning to discover that God had sorted it all out while you slept. His help is timely.

Several years ago I had the privilege to speak at Harvest Christian Fellowship in Riverside, California, where Greg Laurie pastors. We were sitting in his office chatting when his granddaughter came into his office, and Pastor Laurie handed her a small toy. I could tell he couldn't wait to give it to her. She was so happy, but it quickly became clear that the toy wasn't working. She asked him if he could fix it, and he immediately took it from her and began working on it. He worked and worked on it to no avail. He was undeterred. We continued to talk, but his focus was on that little, inexpensive toy. I was pleased and even amused to see this well-known pastor spending thirty minutes tediously working on a flimsy toy that wouldn't last but a few days. Yet his granddaughter had a need, so he was immediately available for her. He was instantly accessible to help with the problem. And finally, he got it to work. I think he was happier about it than his granddaughter was.

God is like that for his children. He's accessible when we need help. He *wants* to help us.

Far too many believers see God as far off, inaccessible, and maybe even uninterested in what's happening to them. The psalmist tells us God is a refuge that's approachable and easy to find.

When peril raises its head, go to your fraidy hole, your safe place, your refuge—find your Father. As Isaiah 41:10 says, "Don't be afraid, for I am with you."

OUR RIVER

The middle stanza of Psalm 46 references a river: "There is a river whose streams make glad the city of God" (verse 4, NASB). This center stanza presents a striking contrast between the raging waters and foaming oceans that rattle us (verses 1-3) and the calm, flowing river that refreshes us (verses 4-7).

Most great cities of the world are situated on or near a river. Paris has the Seine. London, the Thames. Washington, DC, the Potomac. New York City, the Hudson. Tokyo, the Sumida. Vienna, the Danube. The reference to the city of God in Psalm 46 is clearly Jerusalem, which is interesting, because Jerusalem has no natural water source. It's one of the few major ancient cities not built on a river, which left it in a precarious position. Without a water supply within or alongside the city, if it was besieged, the people were finished.

Anticipating the Assyrian invasion and siege, Hezekiah wisely cut an underground tunnel to bring water from the Gihon Spring outside the city into the Pool of Siloam and then from there underneath the city through a tunnel into a repository. This left no water on the outside for the Assyrians while providing Jerusalem with its own underground river inside the walls of the city.

The tunnel Hezekiah dug, which is still around today, is over 1,700 feet long, hewn out of solid rock. Known today as Hezekiah's Tunnel, this marvelous feat of engineering was dug from each end, meeting in the middle. The water or river it channeled into the city was the water supply that provided for the inhabitants of Jerusalem during the siege.

That water source is used by the psalmist as a picture of the greater spiritual resource of the Lord himself for his people. What the tunnel and water supply were physically to the people, God is spiritually. Everything that a river is to a city, God is to his people. He's the fountain of life, the source of refreshment and joy. As Robert J. Morgan says,

> Think of it. On the surface, there was no water. No river. No refreshment. No life-giving currents. Outside the city, an amassed army. But deep below the level of the streets and homes, beneath the ground level of ancient Jerusalem, there was a hidden river coursing through the rocks. There was a secret spring, a reliable source of water to refresh the trapped inhabitants who, though besieged, were assured of victory. . . .
>
> There's spiritual meaning here. Far beneath the ground level of life, below our homes and streets and everyday activities, there is a secret spring for Christians—a reliable source of refreshment the enemy cannot figure out, and whose flow cannot be interrupted.[7]

God is our Refuge, so we need not fear.
God is also our River, so we need not faint.

OUR RULER

The final stanza of Psalm 46 underscores the sovereignty of God. In these verses two main points surface.

BEHOLD HIS WORKS

Psalm 46:8-9 brings us to the end of history, long after the Assyrian army has been wiped out. In these verses the Prince of Peace has been enthroned on earth. This looks ahead to the future, messianic kingdom of Jesus on earth:

> Come, behold the works of the LORD,
> Who has wrought desolations in the earth.
> He makes wars to cease to the end of the earth;
> He breaks the bow and cuts the spear in two;
> He burns the chariots with fire.
>
> PSALM 46:8-9, NASB

This passage has never been fulfilled at any time in the past and will only be fulfilled when Jesus comes back to earth someday to crush his foes, bring an end to human warfare, and establish his kingdom on earth (see Revelation 19:11–20:6). As Charles Swindoll says,

> The songwriter now surveys a battlefield. He invites us to view the mute reminders of war, a terrain littered with bodies and debris. Chariots lie on their sides, burned, and now rusty. Dust and debris cover broken bows and splintered spears. War itself has been decimated. The song describes a scene not unlike the aftermath of World War II. The beaches of Normandy; the cities of Berlin and Hiroshima; sections of London; the islands of Iwo Jima, Guadalcanal, and Okinawa. Rusty tanks. Sunken

boats covered with barnacles. Concrete bunkers. A silence pervades. It is as though our God has said, "That is enough!" When the Lord acts, He's thorough.[8]

At this point, all the tumult and cataclysm will cease. Man's day will end. The sovereign Messiah will reign over all the earth.

BOW TO HIS WAYS

Psalm 46:10 gives the proper response to the destruction the Lord brings to the earth at the end of the age. "Cease striving and know that I am God," or as it's sometimes translated, "Be still, and know that I am God!" (as in NLT). This verse is one of the most misinterpreted verses in the Bible.

Most often we hear this verse quoted as a call to contemplation and quiet reflection before God—of ceasing our frantic activity and busyness and resting before God. However, in the context of Psalm 46, where the final victory of the Messiah has just been described, this is not a call to contemplation or reflection but a redemptive call to surrender and know God personally before his judgment is unleashed.[9] It's a call to the nations to surrender. The Lord is calling humans to abandon their rebellion against him and to surrender to him.

God is saying, "You can never win your war against me, so quit while you can. Throw down your weapons and surrender."

In his book *God's Trombones*, James Weldon Johnson begins one poem about the Prodigal Son with these words: "Young man— / Young man— / Your arm's too short to box with God."[10] That's what the psalmist is saying here: "Give up the fight. Jesus is coming. His Kingdom is coming. Your arm is too short to box with God." The psalmist urges all people to surrender to him now.

According to Scripture, every knee will bow one day before

Jesus (see Philippians 2:10). He will be exalted among the nations. Ultimate security will come for all who bow to the Lord. In the meantime, we find our security in bowing to him now and recognizing his presence with us in every circumstance of life.

Psalm 46:11 says, "The LORD of hosts is with us" (NASB). The words "with us" in the original Hebrew are one word, *immanu*, from which we get the word "Immanuel"—God with us. This is the name that Jesus would bear (see Matthew 1:23). The ultimate expression of God's presence with us is the coming of his Son Jesus Christ into the world to become one of us and to die in our place on the cross.

SAFE AND SOUND

As the last days march on and the signs of the times proliferate, we will all undoubtedly face more and more challenges to our personal and national security in an age of terror. We will all face daily challenges to our security in the arenas of health, finances, marriage, and family. But in all of this, remember—the answer to our problems, perils, and panic is the presence of God. We find our refuge and security in our great God. He's our fraidy hole as the storm clouds gather on the horizon.

There's a true story about a family from Canada that was consumed with fear about a coming war. They were terrified, so they decided to run away to the safest place on earth. After much research they found the perfect place, and in the spring of 1982 they relocated to this quiet little spot known as the Falkland Islands, an obscure piece of British real estate. The family relaxed and enjoyed five days of tranquility before the Argentineans invaded their backyard and began the famous Falklands War.

We sometimes wish we could run away from our fears and the things that make us feel insecure. But there's nowhere to run. Fear follows us. We can't outrun our fears. The only way to successfully overcome fear is to confront it and avail ourselves of God's resources. The Lord is our refuge and strength. He is our stronghold. When God is great, our fears are not. As our view of God expands, the fears of life diminish. As J. I. Packer reminds us, "The world dwarfs us all, but God dwarfs the world."[11] Allow Psalm 46 to expand your view of Christ and your fear of God.

Depend on him as your *Refuge*.

Draw upon him as your *River*.

Defer to him as your *Ruler*.

God is our *Refuge*; we need not fear.

God is also our *River*; we need not faint.

God is our *Ruler*; we need not fret.

A series of earthquakes rattled London in 1750, sending shock waves throughout the city. The first tremor struck on February 8. Early in the morning one month later, on March 8, Charles Wesley was preaching when a second earthquake hit. It was much stronger than the first one. As you can imagine, pandemonium ensued. Yet Wesley quoted Psalm 46 to the panicking parishioners. He later recounted how God had given him the words he needed to reassure the congregation.

Another earthquake rocked England's south coast just ten days later, prompting a man to predict a coming earthquake of even greater magnitude. The people believed his prophecy, fearing that the end of the world was near.

That prophecy never came to pass, but Charles Wesley published a collection of hymns that was written to calm the masses and came to be known as the "Earthquake Hymns." The collection includes a hymn based on Psalm 46.[12]

Our world is shaking today and feels like it's becoming less safe all the time. But even in tectonic times, remember: God is our Refuge, he is our River, and he is our Ruler.

THE BEST OF ALL, GOD IS WITH US

John Wesley, the great founder of Methodism (and brother of Charles) preached his final sermon on February 17, 1791, at age 87. The next day, feeling very ill and weak, he was put to bed in his home. During the days of his illness, he often repeated the words from one of his brother's hymns: "I the chief of sinners am, but Jesus died for me!" Wesley died on March 2, and as he lay dying, his friends gathered around him. He lovingly grasped their hands, saying, "Farewell, farewell." At the end, Wesley cried out, "The best of all is, God is with us." Lifting his arms, he raised his feeble voice one last time again, repeating the words, "The best of all is, God is with us."

If you know Jesus, you can say the same thing no matter what may come your way—"The best of all is, God is with us."

The presence of God is your ever-present, always-accessible fraidy hole as the end draws near.

CHAPTER 8

REMAIN UNDER THE INFLUENCE

All Christians are committed to be filled with the Spirit.
Anything short of a Spirit-filled life is less than
God's plan for each believer.

BILLY GRAHAM

On the night before he died, Jesus gave a long message to his closest followers sharing his heart with them about his coming departure and how they should live in his absence. The sermon known as the Upper Room Discourse is found in John 13–17. Jesus told his disciples many things, but he repeatedly mentioned the Holy Spirit, whom he would send to be with them in his physical absence (see John 14:15-17, 25; 15:26; 16:7-15).

Then, after his resurrection, just before he ascended to heaven, Jesus' final words to his followers were about the Spirit:

"Do not leave Jerusalem until the Father sends you the gift he promised, as I told you before. John baptized with water, but in just a few days you will be baptized with the Holy Spirit. . . . But you will receive power when the Holy Spirit comes upon you. And you will be my witnesses, telling

people about me everywhere—in Jerusalem, throughout
Judea, in Samaria, and to the ends of the earth." After saying
this, he was taken up into a cloud while they were watching,
and they could no longer see him.

ACTS 1:4-5, 8-9

Of all the things Jesus could have shared in his farewell address,
he underscored the disciples' need for the presence and power of the
Holy Spirit. If Jesus believed the Holy Spirit was important enough
to mention over and over in his final instructions to his disciples, we
need to take notice and learn about the Spirit's ministry in our lives
in these end times. Nothing is more vital to your spiritual survival
and success as you await Christ's coming than the Spirit.

Many believers today mouth the words about believing in the
Spirit, but when it comes to their daily lives, he is out there somewhere on the periphery. Many today in the church are guilty of *loving*
the Father, *adoring* the Son, and *ignoring* the Spirit.

In his classic book *Knowing God*, J. I. Packer calls the study of
the Holy Spirit "the Cinderella of Christian doctrines" and adds,
"Comparatively few seem to be interested in it."[1] Sadly, the Holy
Spirit can be just a footnote in our theology—the minor key in our
worship. Many Christians are settling for "two-thirds" of God. I once
heard someone say, "The sin of the world is rejecting the Son; the sin
of the church is neglecting the Spirit." We must make sure this isn't
true of us. We need the Spirit's power to survive.

FOCUSING ON THE FILLING

There are many ministries of the Holy Spirit in the New Testament
that we need to understand, but none is more central to the believer's
daily life than the filling of the Spirit. Evangelist D. L. Moody once
gathered a group of pastors together to discuss Christian holiness and

productivity in daily living. At the end of their time together, Moody offered this summary: "I can tell you in five words how Christians can become more holy, useful, and fruitful—*be filled with the Spirit!*" Moody was right. These five words hold the key to our spiritual survival and service in these final days. There's no substitute.

In the troubled, temptation-filled times we all face, we're prone to believe that everything we do depends on us, that we simply have to try harder or be smarter, but we must not fall into the trap of thinking that we have the power to live the Christian life in our own strength. We can't live the Christian life without the filling of the Holy Spirit. We must have power beyond ourselves to flourish, especially in times like these. Simply stated, we can't survive spiritually without the work of the Spirit in our lives. Spiritual survival without the Spirit is a deadly oxymoron.

Spirit power is necessary for spiritual prosperity. Spirit saturation is necessary for spiritual survival. Spirit filling is necessary for spiritual flourishing.

But what does it mean to be filled with the Spirit?

The biblical entry point for understanding the Spirit-filled life is found in the book of Ephesians. Ephesians is a book that's rich in teaching about the Holy Spirit. Several key truths about the Spirit are highlighted:

> sealing of the Spirit (1:13; 4:30)
> accessing the Father through the Spirit (2:18)
> indwelling of the Spirit (2:19-22)
> unifying of the Spirit (4:1-3)
> grieving the Spirit (4:30)

Ephesians 5:16-21 is a key New Testament passage that tells us about the filling of the Spirit:

Make the most of every opportunity in these evil days. Don't act thoughtlessly, but understand what the Lord wants you to do. Don't be drunk with wine, because that will ruin your life. Instead, be filled with the Holy Spirit, singing psalms and hymns and spiritual songs among yourselves, and making music to the Lord in your hearts. And give thanks for everything to God the Father in the name of our Lord Jesus Christ. And further, submit to one another out of reverence for Christ.

This passage begins by telling us that we need to "make the most of every opportunity in these evil days." I don't have to tell you that the end times are evil days—not just bad days or tough days but downright evil days. We see it all around us. We've fallen so far that evil is now cool.

If we're to survive spiritually and "make the most of every opportunity" in evil days, the apostle Paul tells us that we must have a power and strength beyond ourselves. To put it bluntly, you will fail on your own. I will fail on my own. We are wholly inadequate on our own to meet the demands and challenges of life. We must stay under the influence of the Holy Spirit.

Since this is true, we need to look together at what it means to be filled with the Spirit, how we can be filled, and what it will look like if we're filled. Along with Bible study and prayer, nothing is more important to your spiritual survival than being Spirit-filled.

Learning about the Spirit-filled life was one of the major turning points in my own spiritual life. Knowing about the Spirit's power and influence available to me was life-changing. We need the Spirit's filling all the time, but in these evil days at the end of the age, our need is magnified even further.

THE MEANING

The best definition of being filled with the Spirit is being controlled or influenced by God the Holy Spirit—being under the influence of the Spirit. Where do we get this definition?

VOCABULARY

The first key to understanding the filling of the Spirit comes from the vocabulary or terminology used. There are three Greek words used for the filling of the Spirit, and they all carry the idea of being controlled, influenced, or gripped by something. We observe the meaning of these words as they are used in other contexts, for example, the people in the synagogue being "filled with rage" when Jesus taught (Luke 4:28, NASB), sorrow having "filled" the hearts of the disciples when Jesus announced he was leaving them (John 16:6, NASB), Ananias allowing Satan to "fill [his] heart" in lying about the gift he brought to the apostles (Acts 5:3), and the false prophet Bar-Jesus being "full of every sort of deceit and fraud" (Acts 13:10). In the same way that these people were gripped or controlled by an emotion or outside force, believers are to be filled with the Holy Spirit.

CONTRAST

The second key is the contrast between drunkenness and the filling of the Spirit. Three times in the New Testament the filling of the Spirit is contrasted or at least mentioned in conjunction with getting drunk:

> He will be great in the eyes of the Lord. He must never
> touch wine or other alcoholic drinks. He will be filled with
> the Holy Spirit, even before his birth.
>
> LUKE 1:15

Others in the crowd ridiculed them, saying, "They're just drunk, that's all!"

Then Peter stepped forward with the eleven other apostles and shouted to the crowd, "Listen carefully, all of you, fellow Jews and residents of Jerusalem! Make no mistake about this. These people are not drunk, as some of you are assuming. Nine o'clock in the morning is much too early for that. No, what you see was predicted long ago by the prophet Joel:

'In the last days,' God says,
  'I will pour out my Spirit upon all people.
Your sons and daughters will prophesy.
  Your young men will see visions,
    and your old men will dream dreams.'"

ACTS 2:13-17

Don't be drunk with wine, because that will ruin your life. Instead, be filled with the Holy Spirit.

EPHESIANS 5:18

Everyone knows that a person who is drunk is under the control of alcohol. Drunkenness puts a person under the influence of alcohol, and according to Ephesians 5:18, this leads to a ruined life, or as the New American Standard Bible has it, "dissipation." Notice in Ephesians 5:18 that being drunk is contrasted with being filled with the Spirit. Just as being drunk leads to being under the control of a foreign influence, being filled with the Spirit leads to *his* control— being under *his* influence.[2]

Both parts of this verse are equally true and operative—"don't be drunk with wine" and "be filled with the Holy Spirit." Both are commands (imperatives in Greek). Christians often settle for half of this verse. We may not get drunk, but we also aren't filled with the Spirit. It's not enough not to be drunk with wine. Getting drunk is a sin of commission, while not being filled with the Spirit is a sin of omission.

I like the story of the children's Sunday school class where the teacher asked, "What is a sin of omission?" One little boy, after weighing the question, raised his hand and said, "Those are the sins we wanted to do but never got around to." Actually, sins of omission are *good* things we never got around to doing. Not being filled with the Spirit is a sin of omission.

Leighton Ford tells of a visit his brother-in-law, Billy Graham, made to a very large and influential church. His host told him of an unfortunate experience. One of the officers in that church had repeatedly gotten drunk, and so they had to discipline him and put him out of the church fellowship. Mr. Graham asked, "How long has it been since you put somebody out of the church for not being filled with the Holy Spirit?" His host looked startled. So Mr. Graham continued, "The Bible says, 'Don't get drunk with wine,' but the very same verse says, 'Be filled with the Spirit.'"

Billy Graham was making a valid point. The positive command to be filled with the Spirit is just as binding as the negative command not to be drunk with wine.

THE COMMAND

After the contrast between getting drunk with wine and being filled with the Spirit, we observe three important things about the command to be filled. First, the command is in the present tense. This indicates that it's an ongoing, repeated experience, not something that happens once for all. We could translate this as "Keep on being filled." Stanley Toussaint writes, "You can't go on last week's experience, last year's experience, or yesterday's experience. It is something that you must experience in the eternal *now*. Be filled with the Spirit constantly."[3]

There's an important distinction I need to point out between the *filling of the Spirit* and the *indwelling of the Spirit*. These are two distinct ministries of the Spirit. Believers in the New Testament are never commanded to be indwelled by the Spirit. Every believer in Christ has the Spirit from the moment of salvation (see Romans 8:9). The indwelling of the Spirit occurs once for all at the moment of salvation; the filling of the Spirit occurs again and again throughout our Christian life.

There's also a distinction between the *filling* of the Spirit and the *baptism* of the Holy Spirit. These two ministries of the Spirit are sometimes confused with one another. Every believer in Christ is baptized by Jesus into his body by the agency of the Spirit at the moment of conversion (see 1 Corinthians 12:13). The baptizing work of the Spirit is a universal, unrepeated work in the life of every believer.

The baptism and indwelling of the Spirit are part of the "standard" package that comes with salvation—they aren't optional equipment.[4] The fullness of the Spirit is received by every believer at the moment of conversion, but we must be filled (influenced and controlled) again and again. There is one indwelling and one baptism of the Spirit but many fillings.

As believers in Christ today, we are no longer waiting for the Holy Spirit; rather, *he* is waiting for *us*—waiting for us to surrender to him and yield our lives to him completely.

The filling of the Spirit must be repeated in our lives again and again.

There's an old story I heard years ago about a man who came forward to the altar every week at his church when the preacher asked who needed to dedicate their life to the Lord and get filled with the Spirit. After many weeks of the same routine, one man in the congregation turned to the man next to him and said, "Why does that man go down front every week to get filled with the Spirit? What's his problem?" The other man whispered back, "He leaks."

That's the problem for all of us. We leak. We must all be filled again and again.

Second, the command to be filled with the Spirit is *passive*. We could translate it "keep being continuously filled." It's something that's done to us. We allow it or yield to it. We allow the Spirit to take control of our lives. This makes all the difference.

I love the story about the medical doctor and evangelist Walter Lewis Wilson. Wilson was a believer who struggled with the futility and spiritual barrenness of his life. In 1913, a French missionary asked him, "Who is the Holy Spirit to you?" Wilson replied, "One of the Persons of the Godhead . . . Teacher, Guide, Third Person of the Trinity." The missionary said, "You haven't answered my question." Wilson responded, "He is nothing to me. I have no contact with Him and could get along quite well without Him."

The next year, on January 14, 1914, Dr. Wilson heard James M. Gray preach a sermon on Romans 12:1: "I beseech you therefore, brethren, by the mercies of God, that ye present your bodies a living sacrifice, holy, acceptable unto God, which is your reasonable service" (KJV). Gray said, "Have you noticed that this verse does not tell us to whom we should give our bodies? It is not the Lord Jesus. He has His own body. It is not the Father. He remains on His throne. Another has come to earth without a body. God gives you the indescribable honor of presenting your bodies to the Holy Spirit, to be His dwelling place on earth."

The message hit home. Wilson went home, fell on the floor before the Lord, and prayed, "My Lord, I have treated You like a servant.

When I wanted You, I called for You. Now I give You this body from my head to my feet. I give you my hands, my limbs, my eyes and lips, my brain. You may send this body to Africa, or lay it on a bed with cancer. It is your body from this moment on."

The following day two people came to his medical office selling advertising, and they both left believing in the Lord. From that point on, he was an effective, fruitful witness for the Lord—a Spirit-filled believer.[5] His life was changed. Surrendering to the Spirit made all the difference. Wilson was a dynamic personal evangelist and founded Central Bible Church in Kansas City, Flagstaff Mission to the Navajos, and the institute later to become Calvary Bible College. Wilson later wrote, "With regard to my own experience with the Holy Spirit, the transformation in my life on January 14, 1914 was much greater than the change that took place when I was saved."[6]

Surrendering to the Spirit makes all the difference.

The third key to the command is that it's *plural*, which means it's for every believer. The command to be filled with the Spirit is not just for pastors, elders, missionaries, mature believers, or some elite group. The Spirit-filled life is for every Christian. None of us are to get drunk. All of us are to be filled with the Spirit. Being Spirit-filled should be the normative experience of every Christian. Stanley Toussaint writes, "We *can* be filled with the Holy Spirit. All of us are to be filled with the Holy Spirit; it is a command. The filling of the Holy Spirit is the chassis—the drive train—of our Christian experience."[7]

In sum, being filled with the Spirit means we are to continuously allow our life to be controlled by the Spirit. The filling of the Spirit is not about me getting more of the Spirit but about the Spirit getting more of me. As I once heard someone say, the Spirit must not only be *resident* in our lives; he must be *president*.

There's another story I like about the famous preacher D. L. Moody and the filling of the Holy Spirit. Moody was scheduled to speak several places in England. In advance of his arrival, a meeting was held by several church leaders. A pastor protested, "Why do we need this 'Mr. Moody'? He's uneducated, inexperienced, etc. Who does he think he is anyway? Does he think he has a monopoly on the Holy Spirit?"

Another pastor responded, "No, but the Holy Spirit has a monopoly on Mr. Moody."[8] That's what every believer should desire for his or her life.

Now that raises a second key issue—how can you and I be Spirit-filled and remain under the influence?

THE MEANS

Not every believer in Jesus Christ is Spirit-filled. Every believer is Spirit-indwelled and Spirit-baptized but not necessarily Spirit-filled. There are certain spiritual conditions that must be met to experience the controlling of the Spirit. I've always found it interesting that there are no specific steps laid out in Ephesians 5:18 for being filled. No conditions are expressly given. There's no ritual or formula. The verb "be filled" is passive, so we know that this is something we allow to happen, not something we do ourselves. But how does it happen?

There's a sense in which we could say that "anybody who really loves the Lord Jesus and wants to please Him is *going to be filled* with the Holy Spirit."[9] We don't want to make the Spirit-filled life more complicated than necessary. A. W. Tozer says, "Throw your heart open to the Holy Spirit and invite Him to fill you. . . . Every man is as full of the Spirit as he wants to be. Make your heart a vacuum and the Spirit will rush in to fill it."[10]

Keeping this in mind, I do believe there are two main clues or hints in other places in the New Testament about the means to being Spirit-filled. These two passages give us keys to how this filling takes place. The first is John 7:37-39, which calls on us to trust in the Lord:

On the last day, the climax of the festival, Jesus stood and shouted to the crowds, "Anyone who is thirsty may come to me! Anyone who believes in me may come and drink! For the Scriptures declare, 'Rivers of living water will flow from his heart.'" (When he said "living water," he was speaking of the Spirit, who would be given to everyone believing in him. But the Spirit had not yet been given, because Jesus had not yet entered into his glory.)

The first attitude that puts us under the Spirit's influence is trust in the Lord ("everyone believing in him"). It's coming to the Lord and saying, "I need you. I trust in you. I can't live today in my own strength. I put myself under your control."

The second passage is Colossians 3:16-17, which calls us to open our lives to God's Word and obey it. Note the striking parallels between Ephesians 5:18-21 and Colossians 3:16, which reads, "Let the message about Christ, in all its richness, fill your lives. Teach and counsel each other with all the wisdom he gives. Sing psalms and hymns and spiritual songs to God with thankful hearts."

Ephesians and Colossians are often considered tandem epistles by the apostle Paul, written about the same time during his first Roman imprisonment and delivered by the same courier. There's a clear correlation between what Paul says in Ephesians 5:18-21 about being filled with the Spirit and what he says in Colossians 3:16-17 about letting Christ's word dwell within you. The results of each are the same, so they appear to be parallel. This shouldn't surprise us, since the Spirit is the Author of the Word. The two are always in sync.

This means that allowing the Word to richly dwell within, to be at home in our lives, is a key means for the Spirit to take over. We must give our minds to the truth of God's Word, our hearts to its teaching, and our wills to its commands. To be open to the Word and under its influence is to place ourselves under the control of the Spirit. I once heard a preacher say, "When the Word dwells within us, the Spirit swells within us."

The means of being filled is to trust in the Lord and open our hearts and lives to his Word. Any heart that is open toward God and in submission to the Scriptures will be filled with the Spirit. When we do these things, the Spirit takes over and goes to work.

So what happens when a believer is filled with the Spirit? What does it look like? How do you know if you're Spirit-filled?

THE MANIFESTATIONS

I don't know if you've noticed, but anytime the New Testament speaks of someone being filled with the Spirit, it's always followed by the word "and." There's always an "and" to the work of the Spirit. There are always results of being filled with the Spirit. What are those results we should be looking for? What will a life look like when the Spirit takes over?

First, notice what's not in Ephesians 5:19-21. Not flashy, spectacular, sensational experiences—speaking in tongues, being slain in the Spirit, being translated into some ecstatic state, or miraculous signs and wonders. The focus is rather on three main manifestations, which are all in the present tense, indicating that these results are continual and ongoing in the life of the Spirit-filled believer.

MUSIC (GLADNESS)

The first result of the Spirit's control is a glad heart full of joy manifested in music.

Ephesians 5:18-19 says, "Be filled with the Holy Spirit, singing psalms and hymns and spiritual songs among yourselves, and making music to the Lord in your hearts." We're to sing from our hearts, not just move our lips, and "to the Lord"—our songs are directed to the one who delivered us from wrath and gives us the power to live a life that pleases him. God wants to hear you sing to him with all your heart. God wants to hear you sing praises to him.

A Spirit-filled Christian is a joyful, singing Christian who loves to praise the Lord for his greatness, grace, mercy, goodness, and majesty. Do you love to sing? Do you go around every day with a song in your heart? A Spirit-filled Christian is a singing Christian and lives a life filled with joy and music. It's a dead giveaway. The same is true of churches. Dead churches and dead Christians don't sing; "they just kind of stand there and mumble."[11]

THANKFULNESS (GRATEFULNESS)

The second manifestation or result of being filled with the Spirit is a thankful heart. This means a Spirit-filled believer is not bitter, grumbling, complaining, negative, sour, or grumpy but thankful and grateful. There are four key aspects to our thankfulness to God.

When are we to give thanks? "Always" (NASB).

What are we to give thanks for? "Everything."

Whom are we to give thanks to? "God the Father."

How are we to give thanks? "In the name of our Lord Jesus Christ."

We understand giving thanks for the good things, and we can even understand giving thanks "*in* everything" (1 Thessalonians 5:18, NASB). But "*for* everything" is a different matter. How do we give thanks "always . . . for all things" (NASB)? Does this include even sin? John Stott clarifies the meaning:

> God abominates evil, and we cannot praise or thank him for what he abominates.
>
> So then the "everything" for which we are to give thanks to God must be qualified by its context, namely *in the name of our Lord Jesus Christ to God the Father*. Our thanksgiving

is to be for everything which is consistent with the loving Fatherhood of God and the self-revelation he has given us in Jesus Christ.[12]

Spirit-filled believers are thankful.

SUBMISSION (GRACIOUSNESS)

A third manifestation of the Spirit's control is submission. This refers to repenting of self-centeredness and putting others ahead of ourselves. Submissive people are concerned about others, are concerned about what others think, and think of others, not just themselves.[13] Spirit-filled submission is humble and gracious.

So, *what is the Spirit-filled life?* A life under the influence and control of the Spirit.

How can we be filled? By trusting in the Lord and obeying God's Word.

What are the results of being filled? Gladness, gratefulness, and graciousness.

Today, as evil abounds, there are all kinds of opportunities around us. We need to be filled with the Spirit to meet the demands of life. We can't do it in our own strength. What follows Ephesians 5:18-21 is a discussion of marriage, family, and work (5:22–6:9). We all know how broken and hurting the family is today. The Spirit-filled life spills over into every area of our relationships. We have to be Spirit-filled to have marriages and families that please the Lord and witness to the world around us.

HOLD ON

A. J. Gordon, one of the founders of Gordon-Conwell Theological Seminary, told of seeing a house across a field when he was out walking, with a man vigorously using a hand pump next to the house. The man was pumping rapidly without ever slowing down or resting. Amazed at this sight, Gordon walked toward it until he saw it was not a man after all, but a painted wooden figure. Wire held the hand to the pump, and the water pouring out came from an artesian well. Rather than the man pumping the water, the water was pumping the man.

When you see a person whose work for the Lord is effective and produces results—someone who is filled with gladness, gratefulness, and graciousness—that is a person who is filled with the Holy Spirit. When we keep our hands on the pump, the Spirit will fill us and use us.[14]

When this happens, you won't just survive spiritually; you will thrive, and others will be blessed by and through you.

Your spouse needs a Spirit-filled husband or wife.

Your family needs a Spirit-filled mother or father.

Your church needs a Spirit-filled member.

Your friends need a Spirit-filled companion.

Your neighbors need a Spirit-filled neighbor.

Your community needs a Spirit-filled citizen.

The days are evil. Depravity and darkness are spreading. Redeem the time. Take full advantage of every opportunity. But don't try to go it alone.

Whatever else you do in life, make sure you remain under the influence of the Holy Spirit.

Your spiritual survival depends on it.

CHAPTER 9

TUNE IN TO HEAVEN'S FREQUENCY

The world hopes for the best,
but Jesus Christ offers the best hope.
JOHN WESLEY WHITE

When the Wisconsin Badgers were playing the Michigan State Spartans in October 1982, Badger Stadium was packed with expectant fans. It began to seem, however, that Michigan State might have the better team.

Despite the uncertainty of the game, and at seemingly inappropriate times, the Wisconsin fans erupted in cheers and applause. How could devoted fans be so excited when there wasn't any cause for celebration on the field?

On the same day as the Wisconsin Badgers game, the Milwaukee Brewers were playing the St. Louis Cardinals in game four of the 1982 World Series. Many of the Badgers fans that day were watching their team struggle on the field but listening to the Brewers win.

While what they could see on the field at times looked grim, they were cheering a victory they could not see.[1]

This story resonates with me because it reminds me of our present situation on earth as God's people. Let's face it—here on earth things don't seem to be looking too good for God's team. As believers, it can sometimes feel like our team is losing . . . and losing badly. We see it around the world on many fronts. The church is suffering persecution in many places, where believers are severely mistreated and even martyred for their faith. Closer to home, believers are frequently the object of mocking and maligning. In courts, workplaces, schools, and the halls of government, people have become increasingly unwelcoming and even antagonistic toward those who follow Jesus. Watching the "game" as it unfolds in front of us can be difficult at times and can even diminish our hope and drive us to despair.

But like those beleaguered Badgers fans, while we're watching the game in front of us, at the same time, we can tune in to another "game" and cheer on a victory that's invisible to us now but no less real—a total victory in heaven that's coming soon to planet Earth.[2]

This world needs hope. You and I need hope. And our only hope as the score gets more and more lopsided down here is to stay tuned in to heaven's frequency, listening and looking every day for the final victory that's coming through Jesus Christ.

IS THERE ANY HOPE?

On December 17, 1927, a US submarine off the coast of Massachusetts was attempting to surface when it was struck by a US Coast Guard destroyer and sank immediately. The crew scrambled to secure themselves behind watertight doors. The entire crew was entombed in a prison house of death. Every effort was made to rescue the crew, but nothing worked. Near the end of the ordeal, a diver put his ear to the side of the vessel and heard a faint tapping from inside. Recognizing it as Morse code, he heard the same question formed slowly over and over—"Is . . . there . . . any . . . hope?"[3]

That's the key question people everywhere are asking today: "Is there any hope?" There's a growing hopelessness out there today—even among some believers.

I like the story about the wife who said to her husband, "Should we watch the six o'clock news and get indigestion or wait for the eleven o'clock news and have insomnia?" That's about how bad it's gotten. Key questions on the minds of many people are "Where is everything headed?" "What's the world coming to?" and "Is there any hope?"

One of the most quoted Old Testament passages in the New Testament answers this question as clearly and succinctly as possible. Let's look now at Psalm 2.

LIFE'S TWO GREAT QUESTIONS

The first two psalms are the driveway into the Psalms. Their positioning in the book of Psalms is deliberate. They answer the two great questions of life. Psalm 1 answers the question, *Where am I going?* This is the most urgent individual matter. The psalm, in more traditional translations, opens with the word "blessed" and ends with the word "perish." This psalm sets forth two paths for humanity—the way of the righteous (those who receive the Lord and are blessed) and the way of the wicked (those who reject the Lord and perish). Every person falls into one of these two groups. Every person needs to make sure he or she belongs to the community of the righteous through faith.

Psalm 2 answers the second great question: *Where is the world going? Where is history headed?*

That's why these psalms are Psalms 1 and 2. We meet the two great issues of life at the front door of the Psalms. I need to know where I'm going, and I need to know where history is going.[4] I need to see the whole show. You and I need to have a biblical worldview in these last days to buoy our lives and fill us with hope. We need to know the end game.

Psalm 2 is God's decisive declaration of the outcome of world events. There's no greater comfort in the chaotic, uncertain times in which we live than to know where it's all headed. Psalm 2 is all about hope for planet Earth. More specifically, it's about hope for planet Earth in Jesus Christ. It tells us that the world has been promised to the Messiah. His triumph is certain. Here is Psalm 2 in its entirety:

Why are the nations so angry?
    Why do they waste their time with futile plans?
The kings of the earth prepare for battle;
    the rulers plot together
against the Lord
    and against his anointed one.
"Let us break their chains," they cry,
    "and free ourselves from slavery to God."

But the one who rules in heaven laughs.
    The Lord scoffs at them.
Then in anger he rebukes them,
    terrifying them with his fierce fury.
For the Lord declares, "I have placed my chosen king on the
        throne
    in Jerusalem, on my holy mountain."

The king proclaims the Lord's decree:
"The Lord said to me, 'You are my son.
    Today I have become your Father.

Only ask, and I will give you the nations as your inheritance,
  the whole earth as your possession.
You will break them with an iron rod
  and smash them like clay pots.'"

Now then, you kings, act wisely!
  Be warned, you rulers of the earth!
Serve the LORD with reverent fear,
  and rejoice with trembling.
Submit to God's royal son, or he will become angry,
  and you will be destroyed in the midst of all your
      activities—
for his anger flares up in an instant.
  But what joy for all who take refuge in him!

Before we probe deeper into Psalm 2, let's get a brief understanding of its background. Psalm 2 is one of the most frequently quoted psalms in the New Testament. According to Acts 4:25, David is the author of this psalm. It's a messianic psalm. We know this because it's quoted in the New Testament as referring to Jesus. It's been called the Drama of the Ages. Psalm 2 outlines the agelong rebellion of mankind against God and his Son and how it all ends in God's victory. At its core, it's a psalm of hope.

Psalm 2 is divided into four parts or stanzas, each with a different speaker, but I want to look at it under two headings derived from our image of the Badgers' football game: "The Chaos We See" and "The Conquest We Can't See."

Watching the game in front of us here on earth can push us to despair. Of course, we have to live here on this earth and watch the game on the field. But if we have no farther horizon, no outside perspective beyond this world, we will lose hope quickly. Our spiritual survival will be in jeopardy. We can't survive long without hope. Tuning in to heaven's frequency is our only hope. Listening and learning about the invisible victory going on far away is our ultimate encouragement. But before we consider what's happening on heaven's frequency, let's begin by surveying the scene that's unfolding before our eyes.

THE CHAOS WE SEE

The first stanza of Psalm 2 unveils a shocking, agelong, global insurrection and conspiracy against God. In this stanza the speaker or voice is that of the nations or lost humanity.

The first word of Psalm 2 is "Why?" or we could translate it "How could they?" The psalmist can hardly believe what he sees and hears. He sees "the rulers plot together against the LORD and against his anointed one," which is a reference to the Messiah.

Here we witness the nations rising up in cosmic treason against God and his Messiah in rebellion against God's sovereignty. The Bible says that lost humanity is against God and Jesus. I know that may sound strong, but that's what the Bible says. In fact, that's what Jesus says too (see John 15:18). The rage of humanity against God may not show up with the same fury at all times in all places, but its strong undercurrent is always present. The world hates God, detests his Messiah, and despises Messiah's people.

Lost humanity may love the Jesus they've created but not the Jesus who is God in human flesh and the only way to God. The world is against the real Jesus.

What could possibly possess people to have such rage against the true God and his Son?

The defiant voice of sinners, banded together in their rebellion, speak with one collective voice in Psalm 2:3: "Let us break their chains and free ourselves from slavery to God."

What lost humanity wants more than anything is freedom from God. This is the heart of sin, a rejection of God's rule in favor of our own. The lost don't want God to reign over them. People want what they want with no restraints.

The world wants sexual freedom. The sexual revolution began in the 1960s and was followed by changing attitudes toward homosexual behavior that continues today. The result is pervasive immorality, the pollution of pornography, and the peril of widespread gender confusion. Carl F. H. Henry once described the modern generation as "intellectually uncapped, morally unzipped and volitionally uncurbed."[5] That's what we see today.

The world also wants intellectual freedom. Against all reason, they hold doggedly to the notion that all the beauty, order, and constancy of creation came about by the collision of time and chance. And because the created order is the result of random chance, marriage can be redefined by judicial fiat.

Lost humanity wants spiritual freedom. They want to decide whether there is a God, and if there is a God, they want to decide who he is and how they come to him. I love the words of the Scottish theologian P. T. Forsyth: "The first duty of every soul is to find not its freedom but its Master."[6] But lost humanity wants it the other way around. Yet sadly, the search for freedom results in deeper enslavement. It results in chaos. Because of unrestrained freedom, our world is a mess and reeling out of control. We live in a world gone wild. It's tragic to see the resulting chaos and confusion in homes, schools, lives, and marriages.

When people lose God, they lose themselves. That's what we see in Romans 1:18-32—the tragic consequences of defying the Lord and his Christ. Paul says of lost humanity, "Claiming to be wise, they instead became utter fools. . . . Since they thought it foolish to acknowledge God, he abandoned them to their foolish thinking and let them do things that should never be done. Their lives became full of every kind of wickedness" (verses 22, 28-29).

As Frederick Buechner says, "The power of sin is centrifugal. When at work in a human life, it tends to push everything out toward the periphery. Bits and pieces go flying off until only the core is left. Eventually bits and pieces of the core itself go flying off until in the end nothing at all is left."[7]

This ongoing, agelong rebellion of lost humanity against God and his Son began in the Garden of Eden, continues today, and will stretch all the way to the second coming of Christ.

According to Acts 4:23-31, the premier historical example of this rebellion occurred in the crucifixion of Jesus. The apostles quote Psalm 2 and fill in the blanks with Herod and Pilate.

Comparing the rebellion of modern man with what happened at the tower of Babel, Os Guinness observes, "In their vaunting pride, advanced modern humanists are competing with their ancient rivals in rebellion. They are straining every nerve and brain cell to make a name for their projects and themselves. But they too are driven by an insatiable need to succeed, for only success after success can allow them to avert their eyes from the strains and stresses on humanity and on the earth behind them."[8]

We have front-row seats to this game as human rebellion is on full display. God has placed us here to live and witness for him. We must represent heaven here on earth. We're not just spectators; we're in the game. We're ambassadors for Christ to this lost world (see 2 Corinthians 5:20). We're to do all we can while we can. Individuals must be rescued from the uprising against God.

Nevertheless, Scripture tells us that the rebellion of this world won't improve. It's going to get worse as the end nears. But praise God! There's a frequency we can listen to every day that inspires us with an invisible victory that is going on now in heaven and is coming to earth someday, maybe very soon.

THE CONQUEST WE CAN'T SEE

Tuning in to heaven's frequency—the invisible victory—we hear about final victory on planet Earth from three sovereign voices: the voice of the Father, the voice of the Son, and the voice of the Spirit. What we have here is powerful inter-Trinitarian communication.

THE VOICE OF THE FATHER—MOCKERY

Heaven's response to earth's upheaval begins with the voice of God the Father. The response of the Father to humanity's rebellion is laughter. Yes, God laughs: "The one who rules in heaven laughs. The Lord scoffs at them" (Psalm 2:4). This is the only time recorded in the Bible when God laughs. This is not the laughter of humor or hilarity but divine derision, mockery, and contempt.

God openly mocks humanity's puny rebellion. God is not fazed in the slightest. He's unimpressed. As the prophet Isaiah reminds us, "All the nations of the world are but a drop in the bucket. They are nothing more than dust on the scales. He picks up the whole earth as though it were a grain of sand" (Isaiah 40:15).

But if God is sovereign over this world, we might look around at the mess we see and wonder, *Why doesn't God do something? Why doesn't God fix it all right now?* As I heard someone say, "I know God is in control, but sometimes I wish he would make it more obvious." We all probably share that sentiment sometimes.

Psalm 2 assures us that someday God *will* make his control obvious. He will do this by installing his Son on a throne on earth: "I have placed my chosen king on the throne in Jerusalem, on my holy mountain" (Psalm 2:6).

Most scholars believe Psalm 2 is a "Royal Psalm," that it relates to the coronation of the kings of Judah. Many see it as going beyond Solomon and his successors, ultimately pointing to the Messiah. While some reference to human kings is possible, I prefer to view this psalm as about Jesus only. Several things said here cannot be said of any king other than Jesus. For instance, only to Jesus will the whole earth be given as his possession. Christ is presently enthroned in heaven, but Psalm 2 looks ultimately to the return of Christ to earth and his glorious enthronement on David's throne and his thousand-year rule of peace and prosperity over the earth (see Revelation 20:1-6).

Notice in Psalm 2:6 that the placing of Jesus on David's throne to rule the world is stated in the past tense ("I *have placed* my chosen king on the throne"). It's as good as done. Nothing can stand in the Son's way.

THE VOICE OF THE SON—VICTORY

That brings us to the third stanza, where the speaker shifts from the Father to the Son of God—the Messiah. All that the Father has planned and purposed in eternity will be performed by the Son in history. The decree of Yahweh controls history. The Son says,

> The LORD said to me, "You are my son.
>   Today I have become your Father.
> Only ask, and I will give you the nations as your inheritance,
>   the whole earth as your possession.
> You will break them with an iron rod
>   and smash them like clay pots."
> PSALM 2:7-9

When Jesus comes back to this earth, he will come as King of kings and Lord of lords to inherit a global kingdom, putting a sudden, sweeping end to the agelong rebellion of man (see Daniel 7:14,

27; Revelation 20:1-6).[9] Jesus will destroy rebellious humanity. He will do it with ease, effortlessly, like someone smashing fragile clay pots with an iron rod.

Josiah Wedgwood was an English potter, the founder of the Wedgwood company, and he is known as the one responsible for the industrialization of pottery. He would often walk through his factory in England and smash inferior pieces of pottery with his walking stick, saying, "This will not do for Josiah Wedgwood."

There's a day coming when Jesus will smash to pieces everything that is contrary to his will. He will, in essence, say, "This won't do for the Son of God." He will take the planet back and restore paradise.

Jesus is saying to us, "Don't tolerate now what I won't tolerate then. If it won't do for Christ in the future, put it out of your life now. Don't be ruled by the world that will someday be ruled by Christ."

THE VOICE OF THE SPIRIT—OPPORTUNITY

The final stanza in this psalm records the message of the Holy Spirit speaking through the psalmist. The Spirit's invitation goes out to all who will receive the Son. Instead of resisting God, sinners must turn from sin and self and serve the Lord with fear. The choice is clear. Those who fail to bow in submission to the Son have a rendezvous with judgment. As Old Testament scholar Derek Kidner says, "There is no *refuge* from him: only *in him*."[10] One day, "those who worshipped him on earth will confess him gladly. Those who didn't will confess him regretfully."[11]

C. S. Lewis poignantly describes the coming of Christ's victory to earth:

God will invade. . . . When that happens, it is the end of the world. When the author walks on to the stage the play is over. . . . For this time it will be God without disguise; something so overwhelming that it will strike either irresistible love or irresistible horror into every creature. It will be too late then to choose your side. . . . That will not be the time for choosing: it will be the time when we discover which side we really have chosen, whether we realised it before or not. Now, today, this moment, is our chance to choose the right side. God is holding back to give us that chance. It will not last for ever. We must take it or leave it.[12]

Jesus came the first time in mercy, to save. The second time he will come in wrath, to judge. The end-times events predicted in the Bible are all lining up. The stage is being set. We see the buildup all around us. The signs of the times point to the soon coming of the Lord Jesus Christ.

He may be coming soon. Our decision to submit to him is urgent.

Jesus is earth's only hope. He is *your* only hope. He is *my* only hope.

Let me close this chapter with four simple applications or meditations to give us hope in a world gone wild and to ensure our spiritual survival.

1. YOU CAN'T UNDERSTAND HISTORY APART FROM JESUS CHRIST

Jesus alone holds the key to the meaning of history. The world has been promised to the Messiah. All of history is wrapped up in him. History culminates in his second coming to earth to rule and reign over the earth (see Revelation 19:11–20:6). George Eldon Ladd states, "Here is a simple but profound biblical truth which cannot be overemphasized: apart from the person and redeeming work of

Jesus Christ, history is an enigma. . . . Christ, and Christ alone, has the key to the meaning of human history."[13] James Hamilton adds,

> We need Jesus.
>
> We need Jesus not only for our own personal salvation. We need Jesus so there is hope for the world. By his death and resurrection Jesus has taken control of history. Jesus has seized destiny—not just his destiny—all destiny. Jesus is the one who ensures that the universe will have meaning. Jesus is the one who will judge the wicked and vindicate those who have trusted in him. Jesus is the one who will right the wrongs and heal the hurts and wipe away the tears.
>
> We need Jesus. Without Jesus there is no hope.[14]

I like the story of a father who was intently watching the final minutes of a close football game on television, when his little boy came running in, asking him to play. The father sent him away with promises that he would play soon, but the son kept coming back at intervals and asking if it was time yet.

Searching for anything that would allow him to watch the game in peace, the father saw a picture of the world on a newspaper in front of him and tore it into pieces, like a jigsaw puzzle. The father gave the pieces to his son and said, "When you've put the picture back together, then it will be time to play."

Thinking this task would take his son a while, the father settled in to watch the remainder of the game. But no sooner had he settled in than his son returned with the picture of the world reassembled. "I did it, Daddy," he said. "Is it time now?"

The father couldn't believe that his son had finished the puzzle so quickly, but there it was: the world was taped back together. "How did you do this so quickly?" the father asked.

"It was easy," the boy said. "I saw there was a picture of Jesus on the other side, and when I put that picture together, the world came together too."[15]

When Jesus is put together in his rightful place, the world comes together. Jesus is the only one who puts the world together. He is the Alpha and Omega.

2. HISTORY IS HEADED TO THE FEET OF JESUS

Have you ever wondered what the world is coming to? If Psalm 2 tells us anything, it tells us that the world is coming to Jesus. In spite of how things look on earth, Psalm 2 assures us that Jesus rules. His Kingdom is coming to earth, and all must bow to him. This is the ultimate worldview.

The sculptor Bertel Thorvaldsen created a marble statue of Christ that was placed in the National (Lutheran) Cathedral in Copenhagen, Denmark. The figure's arms are extended, welcoming all who will come. Yet the statue has an unusual feature. To look directly into the face of the statue, it's necessary to kneel. It's impossible to get a clear view from any other position.

A famous story recounted from English literature concerns the essayist Charles Lamb and a group of literary men who began to surmise what they would do if the noble and gifted men of the past were to enter into the room. They began to call out the names of various greats and what they would do if that person appeared in their midst. Lamb said, "If Shakespeare were to enter, we would rise to our feet in admiration for his accomplishments. But if Jesus Christ were to enter, we would fall down at His feet and worship Him in adoration."[16]

Bertel Thorvaldsen and Charles Lamb were dead right. The only proper response to the person and presence of Jesus Christ—who is eternal God—is to fall on our knees or on our faces in wonder and adoration. We don't rise in *admiration* to shake his hand; we fall in *adoration* to kiss his feet.

All of history is ultimately headed to the feet of Jesus Christ. If all history is headed there, that's where we should live our lives now in humble worship as we await his coming.

The words of P. T. Forsyth capture the essence of our humble worship: "The world thus finds its consummation not in finding itself, but in finding its Master; not in coming to its true self but in meeting its true Lord and Saviour; not in overcoming but in being overcome."[17]

We overcome, not by overcoming, but by being overcome in awestruck worship of our Savior.

3. JESUS IS IN TOTAL CONTROL OF THE PRESENT AND THE FUTURE

Although it looks today like evil is unchecked and humanity's rebellion is triumphing, the invisible victory in heaven today is real and will be manifest soon on earth.

There's a great story about Ray Stedman when he was in England years ago preaching in some London churches. On one occasion he spoke in a Methodist chapel, and the congregation was singing "Our God Reigns," which was a new song at that time. However, when Stedman looked at the song sheet the congregation was using, he noticed that the typist had made an error. Instead of "Our God Reigns," the song was titled "Our God Resigns."

That's a funny story, but many Christians live that way today, as if God has resigned. All they can see is the game on the field in front of them. But God has not resigned. Rather, as the song says, our God *reigns*! Stedman writes, "This is what we must declare. We must show it on our faces, and let it be heard in our voices."[18] Jesus is coming someday as King.

Every day should find us "Singing in the Reign" as we anticipate and celebrate the coming of Jesus to take his inheritance.

On April 15, 1865, President Abraham Lincoln died at 7:22 a.m. At that moment, the doctor whispered, "He is gone." As others in the room knelt by Lincoln's bedside, a minister prayed that God would receive his servant Abraham Lincoln into heaven. The room then fell silent until Secretary of War Edwin Stanton poignantly declared, "Now he belongs to the ages."[19]

Some humans, like Abraham Lincoln, are so great in their impact that they belong to the ages, but only of Jesus can we truthfully say that the ages belong to *him*. Jesus controls the destiny of the ages. He will triumph over the world.

4. WE CAN REST TODAY IN OUR KNOWLEDGE OF WHAT'S COMING AND WHO'S COMING IN THE FUTURE

Kent Crockett tells this story: "A mother asked her son why he always read the end of the book first. The boy replied, 'Mom, it's better that way. No matter how much trouble the hero gets into, I don't have to worry, because I know how it's going to end.'"[20]

I like that. God has announced to us how the story will end. Jesus wins, Satan loses, and all who trust in Jesus will live happily ever after.

In the meantime, as we await the final victory, we live in a turbulent world. The chaos and rebellion in the world are real. There's no way to mitigate the current condition of planet Earth. But we must not let the "game" we see dampen our spirits and plant seeds of hopelessness in our hearts. Don't give in to despair and cynicism. As Corrie ten Boom reminds us, "Look at yourself, you'll get depressed, look at the world, you'll get distressed, look at Jesus, you'll find rest."

As the score down here gets more lopsided, tune in every day to heaven's frequency and check the score up there. It's all under control. The victory is sure, and all who submit to Jesus will share his triumph.

Today's *invisible* victory will soon become his *invincible* victory.

Don't give up. Don't give in. Don't give out.

The best is yet to come!

CHAPTER 10

WAKE UP

Let us be alert to the season in which we are living. It is the
season of the Blessed Hope. . . . It is imperative that we stay fully alert to
the times in which we live. . . . All signs today point to this being the season
of the Blessed Hope. . . . All around us, we have the evidence of Jesus' soon
return. Each day our focus should be on the Coming One. Our focus on the
Blessed Hope is the most important discipline of our Christian life.

A. W. TOZER

Polling reveals that most American evangelicals have a sense that
the end times are upon us. The Religion News Service reported that
according to a 2013 poll, "41% of all U.S. adults, 54% of Protestants
and 77% of Evangelicals believe the world is now living in the biblical end times."[1]

Polls have also found that

> 58 percent of Americans think that another world war is
  "definite or probabl[e]."
> 41 percent "believe Jesus Christ will return" by the year 2050.
> 59 percent "believe the prophecies in the Book of Revelation
  will come to pass."[2]

Further, "research conducted by the Brookings Institute's Center for Middle East Policy on Americans' attitudes toward the Middle East and Israel found that 79 percent of Evangelicals say they believe 'that the unfolding violence across the Middle East is a sign that the end times are nearer.'"[3] These statistics reveal that people everywhere, and especially evangelicals, believe history is winding down—that the world is getting near closing time.

As a result, some Christians are overly focused on Christ's return. It's all they think about. They're preoccupied with prophecy. This leads to all kinds of unhealthy speculation such as recklessly setting dates for Christ's return, spending countless hours "prepping" for the apocalypse, trying to figure out the identity of the Antichrist and the meaning of 666, and seeing every flood, earthquake, eclipse, or hurricane as a significant sign of the times.

The majority of believers, however, seem to lean toward the other extreme with at best a tepid interest in Jesus' coming. These sluggish, slumbering saints are hitting the snooze button rather than waking up and watching for Jesus' coming.

In his teaching about the end of days, Jesus presents a balance between these two extremes we see today—between the alarmists and the apathetic. Jesus calls on his followers to be awake and alert.

LAST-DAYS LIVING

Jesus talked often about the future. He may have talked about the future more than any person who ever lived. In the New Testament, "Jesus refers to His second coming 21 times, and over 50 times we are told to be ready for His return."[4] Jesus wasn't preoccupied with the end times in an unbalanced way. He always talked about the future to change the way people live in the present.

The call to readiness dominated the teaching of Jesus, especially in the final days of his life on earth. Time and again, he emphasized that his followers must keep watching and stay alert. In his great prophetic sermon in Mark 13, delivered just days before he died on the cross, Jesus gives the basic blueprint or outline of the events that will immediately precede his coming. This sermon, often called the Olivet Discourse since it was given by Jesus on the Mount of Olives just to the east of Jerusalem, is also recorded in Matthew 24–25 and Luke 21.

In this sermon, Jesus provides a litany of signs that will portend his return to earth. Jesus clearly teaches about signs of the times. He says that the generation that sees these signs will witness his second coming to earth (see Mark 13:30). However, this sermon is much more than a list of signs of the times. Jesus highlights how his followers are to live in light of his coming.

He says, "You, too, must *keep watch*! For you don't know what day your Lord is coming. Understand this: If a homeowner knew exactly when a burglar was coming, he would *keep watch* and not permit his house to be broken into. You also must *be ready* all the time, for the Son of Man will come when least expected" (Matthew 24:42-44, emphasis added).

The parable of the ten bridesmaids should reverberate in our hearts with a call to readiness:

> The Kingdom of Heaven will be like ten bridesmaids who took their lamps and went to meet the bridegroom. Five of them were foolish, and five were wise. The five who were foolish didn't take enough olive oil for their lamps, but the other five were wise enough to take along extra oil. When the bridegroom was delayed, they all became drowsy and fell asleep.
>
> At midnight they were roused by the shout, "Look, the bridegroom is coming! Come out and meet him!"

All the bridesmaids got up and prepared their lamps. Then the five foolish ones asked the others, "Please give us some of your oil because our lamps are going out."

But the others replied, "We don't have enough for all of us. Go to a shop and buy some for yourselves."

But while they were gone to buy oil, the bridegroom came. Then those who were ready went in with him to the marriage feast, and the door was locked. Later, when the other five bridesmaids returned, they stood outside, calling, "Lord! Lord! Open the door for us!"

But he called back, "Believe me, I don't know you!"

So you, too, must keep watch! For you do not know the day or hour of my return.

MATTHEW 25:1-13

Notice all the bridesmaids fall asleep, but five are ready and five are not. Jesus' point is simple: only those who are ready and prepared will enter his Kingdom.

In Mark's account of Jesus' sermon, he closes with a clear call to spiritual alertness. As you read these words, notice the repeated use of "watch" and "stay alert."

Now learn a lesson from the fig tree. When its branches bud and its leaves begin to sprout, you know that summer is near. In the same way, when you see all these things taking place, you can know that his return is very near, right at the door. I tell you the truth, this generation will not pass from the scene before all these things take place. Heaven and earth will disappear, but my words will never disappear.

However, no one knows the day or hour when these things will happen, not even the angels in heaven or the Son himself. Only the Father knows. And since you don't know when that time will come, *be on guard! Stay alert!*

The coming of the Son of Man can be illustrated by the story of a man going on a long trip. When he left home, he gave each of his slaves instructions about the work they were to do, and he told the gatekeeper to *watch* for his return. You, too, must *keep watch!* For you don't know when the master of the household will return—in the evening, at midnight, before dawn, or at daybreak. *Don't let him find you sleeping* when he arrives without warning. I say to you what I say to everyone: *Watch* for him!

MARK 13:28-37, EMPHASIS ADDED

Jesus refers to the four watches of the night according to Roman reckoning: evening, midnight, before dawn ("cockcrow"), and daybreak. He emphasizes that he can come at any time.[5] Vigilance is required.

The apostles followed Jesus' lead and issued the call to readiness to their generation. Their words are a much-needed wake-up call:

This is all the more urgent, for you know how late it is; time is running out. Wake up, for our salvation is nearer now than when we first believed. The night is almost gone; the day of salvation will soon be here.

ROMANS 13:11-12

They speak of how you are looking forward to the coming of God's Son from heaven—Jesus, whom God raised from the dead. He is the one who has rescued us from the terrors of the coming judgment.

I THESSALONIANS 1:10

Be on your guard, not asleep like the others. Stay alert and be clearheaded.

1 THESSALONIANS 5:6

Look, I will come as unexpectedly as a thief! Blessed are all who are watching for me, who keep their clothing ready so they will not have to walk around naked and ashamed.

REVELATION 16:15

The reference in that final verse to having clothes stripped off and walking around naked may be an allusion to what happened to guards in that day who fell asleep. Their punishment was having their clothes stripped off and burned and being sent home naked and in disgrace.[6]

The message is clear: those waiting for Christ to come must fight spiritual drowsiness.

I like the story of the college professor who would walk into the lecture hall each morning and place a tennis ball on the corner of his podium. The tennis ball didn't seem to have any purpose—at the end of the lecture, the professor would put it back in his jacket pocket and leave. The students wondered why he did this but were never quite sure—until a student fell asleep in class. The professor walked over to the podium and, without any change in his intonation or notes, picked up the tennis ball and fired it at the sleeping student, scoring a direct hit on his head.

At class the following day, the professor placed a baseball on the podium. The entire class was wide awake from then on.[7]

The words of Jesus should serve as a tennis ball to the head for those of us who are drowsy and dozing in these last days. With all that's going on in our world today, we have every reason to be awake and alert. In these last days, Jesus should have our rapt attention.

er1 GE

AWAKE AND ALERT

I hope you're convinced that Jesus is coming, that he could come at any time, and that you need to be watchful and alert. John MacArthur tells a great story that underscores this truth:

> Jesus is telling you, "I'm coming, I'm coming." I remember a preacher was preaching on the second coming. And he was one of those guys who believed that you shouldn't have any notes, you ought to preach strictly off your head. And he forgot his point. All he could remember was, "Behold, I come quickly; behold, I come quickly." And it should have jogged his mind, so he said it about five times and nothing happened. The final time he thought, "If I hit the pulpit real hard and say, 'Behold, I come quickly,' maybe something will jar loose and I'll remember." Instead he knocked the pulpit over and fell in the lap of a lady in the first row. And he apologized. She said, "Why are you apologizing? You warned me eight times you were coming." She got the point.[8]

I hope *we* get the point. Jesus places high value on his followers being awake and alert. The Rapture is possible any day, impossible no day. In light of the imminence of Christ's coming, the key issue that should grab our hearts is being alert and awake. That's what Jesus repeated over and over.

So, what does it look like for a believer today to be watchful and alert?

WHAT IT DOESN'T MEAN

One thing we know "watching" doesn't mean is setting dates for Christ's coming.

Jesus clearly says, "No one knows the day or hour when these things will happen, not even the angels in heaven or the Son himself. Only the Father knows. And since you don't know when that time will come, be on guard! Stay alert!" (Mark 13:32-33). The two parables Jesus employs, the fig tree and the gatekeeper, further demonstrate that no one can know the exact time of the Master's return (see Mark 13:28-29, 34).

Speculating about the precise moment of Jesus' return is not part of faithful preparation. For any person to claim to know what even Jesus did not know during his sojourn on earth is the height of arrogance and folly. The litany of signs in Mark 13 demonstrates that followers of Jesus can know the general season of Christ's return— otherwise they wouldn't be signs. Nevertheless, Jesus says no one on earth can know the time of his coming. The issue for faithful disciples is not calendars and clocks but commitment. Never listen to anyone who claims to know the time of Jesus' coming. Whenever someone sets a date for Christ's coming, you can be sure that's not the date.

Second, waiting for Christ is not passive, like waiting at a bus stop for the bus to show up. Waiting and watching for Jesus is active. Mark 13 contains nineteen specific imperatives or commands from Jesus. This should let us know that being awake and alert for his coming requires action.

Moreover, the parable Jesus gives in Mark 13:34 depicts a man going away on a journey and assigning various tasks for his servants while he's away. This parable instructs us that watching for Jesus is not just sitting around passively waiting; rather, it involves keeping the house ready for his arrival. The beds must be made, the floors must be swept, and the garden must be tended. Watching is more than just waiting, looking up into the heavens every day.

There's a story I've told before about a bunch of sailors returning from a long voyage at sea. As the boat approached shore the men were all looking for their wives and girlfriends on the shore, eager to see them. As the men searched the crowd of women lined up, the air of excitement and expectancy grew. One sailor, however, was left all alone as all the other men found their wives and girlfriends. His wife wasn't there.

Worried, he rushed home and found a light on. He was relieved to see his wife when he went inside. She said, "Honey, I'm so glad to see you. I've been waiting for you!" His response displayed his disappointment. "The other men's wives and girlfriends were *watching* for them!"

Likewise, Jesus doesn't call us to be passive waiters but to be active, engaged watchers.

WHAT IT DOES MEAN

Jesus emphasizes at least three main actions that fill in for us what it looks like to be alert and awake in the last days. The first is *protection*. We must stand strong in the truth and guard our lives from spiritual deception. The sermon in Mark 13 begins with these words from Jesus: "See to it that no one misleads you" (NASB). He later adds the warnings "Be on your guard" and "Take heed" (verses 9, 23, NASB). The repeated warnings are clear that we must be on guard against false teaching that will proliferate as Christ's coming draws near.

Referring to the parable of the gatekeeper in Mark 13:34, Ray Stedman says:

Now, what is he to watch for? Is he to watch for the master's return? That is the way this is usually interpreted. But that is not it, for he is to start watching as soon as the master leaves. They know he will not be back right away. What then is he to watch for? He is to watch lest somebody deceive them and gain entrance into the house, and wreck and ruin and rob all they have. . . . Don't let anything derail you from being what God wants you to be in this day and age. This is the way you watch. We are not to be looking up into the sky all the time, waiting for his coming. That will happen when he is ready. We are to watch that we are not deceived.[9]

Alertness involves protection. And what is the best defense against the false teaching and deception that will proliferate in the end times? Knowing the truth of God contained in the Bible. Staying awake and alert means we must read, study, and apply the Bible for ourselves and also regularly listen to gospel-centered, biblical preaching at a local church. Charles Swindoll says, "In this age of darkness, we can't afford to doze off spiritually. We need to stay awake. We need to keep our eyes open and our Bibles open, avoiding dangerous deception."[10]

Second, spiritual alertness includes *preparation*. We can't be ready and alert if we're unprepared. Mark's Gospel gives us an important clue about what it means to be prepared for Christ's coming. Mark uses a literary device known as an inclusio to make his point. An inclusio consists of similar material placed before and after a specific text that serves to bracket, bookend, or frame the text, emphasizing what is most important in the section in between the bookends.

Mark 13 is strategically bracketed by two accounts of "unnamed women who are the epitomes of faithfulness, demonstrating incredible loyalty and devotion to God."[11] The preceding bookend is the poor widow in Mark 12:42-44, who gives everything she has to the Lord. She's the gold-medal giver in the Bible. The following bookend is an unnamed woman who anoints Jesus' feet with expensive perfume (see Mark 14:1-9). Her sacrifice is "profuse, pure, and precious."[12] By bookending chapter 13 with these two stories, Mark gives clear examples of the lavish sacrifice and devotion that characterize preparedness. Being prepared for the Lord's return includes liberally sacrificing our time, money, talents, and energy to serve the Lord's interests and to help others.

How prepared is your life for the coming of Christ? Are you awake, alert, active, and attentive, using what you've been given in the Lord's service? Or are you dull and drowsy?

Steven Cole relates this personal story about always being prepared:

> I once worked at the swanky Drake Hotel in Chicago. Years before I was there, in July of 1959, Queen Elizabeth was scheduled to visit Chicago. Elaborate preparations were made for her visit. The waterfront was readied for docking her ship. Litter baskets were painted and a red carpet was ready to be rolled out for her to walk on. Many hotels were alerted to be ready. But when they contacted the Drake, the manager said, "We are making no plans for the Queen. Our rooms are always ready for royalty."[13]

Make sure your life is always ready for royalty. Live each day alert and prepared by laboring and living sacrificially for our coming King as we await his arrival.

I like a story I've heard about preacher Warren Wiersbe. As the story goes, when he was a young preacher, his account of end-times prophecy was meticulously crafted and left little margin for guesswork. After one service where he laid out his account, a member of the congregation approached him and said, "I used to have the Lord's return planned out to the last detail, but years ago I moved from the planning committee to the welcoming committee."[14]

Wiersbe explains, "This does not mean that we should stop studying prophecy, or that every opposing viewpoint is correct, which is an impossibility. But it does mean that, whatever views we hold, they ought to make a difference in our lives."[15] The focus of end-times prophecy is not to build a calendar but to change our lives in preparation for our Lord's coming.

The third aspect of our alertness for last-days living is *proclamation*. In Mark 13:10, Jesus says, "The Good News must first be preached to all nations." Jesus is saying that before he comes again, all the world must hear the gospel. This doesn't have to be fulfilled before Jesus comes for his bride at the Rapture, but it must happen before Jesus can return to earth at the end of the future time of tribulation.

Part of our marching orders for last-days living is faithfully proclaiming the gospel (see Matthew 28:18-20). How can we legitimately claim to be awake and alert and at the same time be oblivious to the perishing world around us? Watching and witnessing go together. We can't get so caught up in our own ambitions and pursuits that we turn a blind eye and a deaf ear to those around us who don't know Jesus. Neither can we get so caught up in the details of the end times that we lose sight of the spiritual needs that surround us. As my friend Randall Price says,

> What good is it to be able to understand the seven heads described in Revelation 13:1 if we don't use our own head? Or what profit is it to discern the ten toes of Daniel 2 . . . if we don't move our own two feet? And what value is it to know about the great mouth that speaks lies (Daniel 7:8; Revelation 13:5), unless we open our own mouth and speak the truth? In every generation where prophecy has been properly proclaimed, the results have been a harvest of souls to the glory of God.[16]

We need to ask the Lord every day to give us opportunities to be witnesses for him. He wants to use us more than we want to be used.

The famed evangelist D. L. Moody had many positive practices in his life, but one is especially worth attempting to emulate. Moody committed to share the gospel with someone every day. He didn't want a day to go by without telling someone about Jesus. R. A. Torrey, a close friend of Moody, tells this story:

> Mr. Moody got home and had gone to bed before it occurred to him that he had not spoken to a soul that day about accepting Christ. "Well," he said to himself, "it is no good getting up now; there will be nobody on the street at this hour of the night." But he got up, dressed and went to the front door. It was pouring rain. "Oh," he said, "there will be no one out in this pouring rain." Just then he heard the patter of a man's feet as he came down the street, holding an umbrella over his head. Then Mr. Moody darted out and rushed up to the man and said: "May I share the shelter of your umbrella?" "Certainly," the man replied. Then Mr. Moody said: "Have you any shelter in the time of storm?" and preached Jesus to him.[17]

May God help us to have at least something of Moody's heart for the lost as this age draws to a close. Alertness includes being on the lookout every day for those around us who haven't found spiritual refuge in Jesus from the coming storm.

Let's not fall asleep on the job.

I CAN SEE CLEARLY NOW

I had to get glasses in sixth grade to correct my bad nearsightedness. A couple of years later I was able to get contact lenses and lose the obnoxious glasses (this was back before glasses were fashionable). Hard contact lenses have been an integral part of my life since then.

Everything was fine until my early forties, when my close-up vision started to get fuzzy. Reading almost anything became a chore.

I refused to surrender to the problem because I thought my only option was to get reading glasses or bifocals. But the frustration finally drove me to get help. To my surprise, my optometrist told me about another option called monovision. With monovision the dominant eye is corrected to 20/20 for distance while the other eye is corrected for near vision. It took about a week for my brain to adjust to the new situation, but since then it has been fantastic. I can see 20/20 far away and clearly up close—with no glasses.

Watching for the coming of Jesus is like spiritual monovision. We're to always be watching the horizon for his coming with one eye, anticipating his return, yet at the same time seeing plainly what's up close that needs our attention as we live our daily lives. Jesus knows we need both lenses to live a balanced life.

Spiritually, if all we have is distance vision we miss the up-close obligations and opportunities of everyday life, but if all we have is near vision, we lose perspective and life gets fuzzy and out of focus. We need both. Jesus wants us watching and working—awake and active.

ULTIMATE SURVIVOR

The bestselling book *Unbroken* captured the world's attention as it chronicled the survival of Louis Zamperini for forty-seven days stranded in a rubber raft after his B-24 malfunctioned and was ditched in the Pacific during World War II. One man didn't survive the ordeal, but Zamperini and the pilot were finally retrieved by Japanese sailors and endured more than two harrowing years in a Japanese POW camp, where he was the object of vicious brutality by a guard nicknamed "The Bird."

After the war ended in 1945, Zamperini returned home but found no peace. Rage, shame, violent flashbacks, and constant nightmares consumed him. Zamperini had survived physically but was dead spiritually.

With his drinking out of control, both Zamperini and his new marriage were falling apart. In October 1949, Zamperini was desperate, so he went to hear Billy Graham preach in Los Angeles and received Christ as his Savior. He found peace for the first time in his life. In his book *Devil at My Heels*, he tells about the beginning of his spiritual survival:

[I] asked Jesus to come into my life. I waited. And then, true to His promise, He came into my heart and my life. The moment was more than remarkable; it was the most *realistic* experience I'd ever had. I'm not sure what I expected; perhaps my life or my sins or a great white light would flash before my eyes; perhaps I'd feel a shock like being hit by a bolt of lightning. Instead, I felt no tremendous sensation, just a weightlessness and an enveloping calm that let me know that Christ had come into my heart.[18]

What a description—"a weightlessness," "an enveloping calm." That's what Jesus gives to all who turn to him in simple faith and trust. The Bible describes it like this: "We praise God for the glorious grace he has poured out on us who belong to his dear Son. He is so rich in kindness and grace that he purchased our freedom with the blood of his Son and forgave our sins" (Ephesians 1:6-7).

As you finish this book, make sure you're alive and awake spiritually. Make sure you've found the ultimate secret to spiritual survival. Do what Louis Zamperini did: trust Jesus. Receive him and his forgiveness. Let him lift your burden. Experience the wonderful weightlessness of grace.

Remember, Jesus is coming for those who have come to him.

Come to him now.

Be an ultimate survivor.

NOTES

INTRODUCTION: ULTIMATE SURVIVOR

1. Ed Hindson, *Final Signs: Amazing Prophecies of the End Times* (Eugene, OR: Harvest House, 1996), 191.
2. Erwin W. Lutzer, *Where Do We Go from Here? Hope and Direction for Our Present Crisis* (Chicago: Moody, 2013), 39.
3. Sean Sullivan, "5 Moments That Show Why Margaret Thatcher Mattered in American Politics," *Washington Post,* April 8, 2013, https://www.washingtonpost .com/news/the-fix/wp/2013/04/08/5-moments-that-show-why-margaret-thatcher -mattered-in-american-politics/.
4. Howard LaFranchi, "Margaret Thatcher: 'This Is No Time to Go Wobbly' and Other Memorable Quotes," *Christian Science Monitor,* April 8, 2013, https://www .csmonitor.com/USA/Foreign-Policy/2013/0408/Margaret-Thatcher-This-is -no-time-to-go-wobbly-and-other-memorable-quotes.
5. Os Guinness, *Impossible People: Christian Courage and the Struggle for the Soul of Civilization* (Downers Grove, IL: IVP Books, 2016), 195.
6. Megan G. Oprea, "Why America Is Obsessed with Survivalism," *Federalist,* March 28, 2016, http://thefederalist.com/2016/03/28/why-america-is-obsessed-with -survivalism/.
7. Lutzer, *Where Do We Go from Here?,* 44.
8. I believe the Rapture will occur before the Tribulation, so I don't think believers will be on earth for the final period of Great Tribulation before the second coming of Jesus to earth. This is commonly called the pre-Tribulational view of the timing of the Rapture. If you want to know more about the various views of the timing of the Rapture and why I believe the pre-Tribulational view is most consistent with Scripture, see my book *The End: A Complete Overview of Bible Prophecy and the End of Days* (Carol Stream, IL: Tyndale, 2012), 121–88.

CHAPTER 1: USE THE 46 DEFENSE

1. Doug Farrar, "How Ryan's 46 Defense Ruled Football," *Sports on Earth*, June 28, 2016, http://www.sportsonearth.com/article/186694084/buddy-ryan-46-defense-bears-eagles-nfl.
2. Robinson Meyer, "The Most Popular Passages in Books, according to Kindle Data," *Atlantic*, November 2, 2014, https://www.theatlantic.com/technology/archive/2014/11/the-passages-that-readers-love/381373/.
3. Robert J. Morgan, *Worry Less, Live More: God's Prescription for a Better Life* (Nashville: W Publishing Group, 2017), xv.
4. Jim Folk and Marilyn Folk, "Anxiety Disorder Statistics," AnxietyCentre.com, April 25, 2017, http://www.anxietycentre.com/anxiety-statistics-information.shtml.
5. Don Joseph Goewey, "85 Percent of What We Worry about Never Happens," *HuffPost* (blog), August 25, 2015, https://www.huffingtonpost.com/don-joseph-goewey-/85-of-what-we-worry-about_b_8028368.html.
6. Morgan, *Worry Less, Live More*, 55.
7. Horace Greeley, *The Autobiography of Horace Greeley: Or, Recollections of a Busy Life* (New York: E. B. Treat, 1872), 405.
8. Morgan, *Worry Less, Live More*, 53.
9. "From Spurgeon's 'Faith's Check Book,'" Gospel Web, September 24, 2014, http://www.gospelweb.net/SpurgeonDevotions/Spurgeon0330.htm.
10. Morgan, *Worry Less, Live More*, 120.
11. "Spurgeon's 'Faith's Check Book.'"
12. Steven J. Lawson, *Philippians for You* (Purcellville, VA: The Good Book Company, 2017), 197.
13. James Montgomery Boice, *The Sermon on the Mount: Matthew 5–7* (Grand Rapids, MI: Baker Books, 2006), 223.

CHAPTER 2: RUN FOR YOUR LIFE

1. Philip De Courcy, "Run for Your Life," Know the Truth, June 30, 2015, https://www.ktt.org/resources/truth-matters/run-your-life.
2. Ibid.
3. William Barclay, *The Letter to the Hebrews*, rev. ed. (Louisville, KY: Westminster John Knox Press, 1976), 171.
4. Joe Stowell, "The Great Race," Strength for the Journey, http://getmorestrength.org/daily/the-great-race/.
5. Ibid.
6. R. Kent Hughes, *Hebrews: An Anchor for the Soul*, vol. 2 (Wheaton, IL: Crossway, 1993), 160.
7. J. C. Ryle, *Heading for Heaven* (Reprint, Carlisle, PA: EP Books, 2009), 33–34.
8. Os Guinness, *Impossible People: Christian Courage and the Struggle for the Soul of Civilization* (Downers Grove, IL: IVP Books, 2016), 55.
9. Max Lucado, *Max on Life: Answers and Insights to Your Most Important Questions* (Nashville: Thomas Nelson, 2010), 207.
10. Ibid.

11. Eric Alexander, "Keep On," Ligonier Ministries, September 1, 2012, http://www.ligonier.org/learn/articles/keep-on/.

CHAPTER 3: MAKE A GOOD CONNECTION

1. John S. Dickerson, *The Great Evangelical Recession: 6 Factors That Will Crash the American Church . . . and How to Prepare* (Grand Rapids, MI: Baker Books, 2013), 98.
2. Ibid., 99.
3. Ibid.
4. Ibid.
5. Thom S. Rainer, "The Number One Reason for the Decline in Church Attendance and Five Ways to Address It," *Christian Post*, August 23, 2013, http://www.christianpost.com/news/the-number-one-reason-for-the-decline-in-church-attendance-and-five-ways-to-address-it-102882/.
6. Donald S. Whitney, *Spiritual Disciplines within the Church: Participating Fully in the Body of Christ* (Chicago: Moody, 1996), 16.
7. Alex Almario, "The Myth of Steve Jobs and the Truth about Us," Philstar Global, September 18, 2015, http://www.philstar.com/supreme/2015/09/19/1501293/myth-steve-jobs-and-truth-about-us.
8. Kevin DeYoung, "Stop the Revolution. Join the Plodders," Ligonier Ministries, September 9, 2016, http://www.ligonier.org/blog/stop-the-revolution-join-the-plodders/.
9. Ibid.
10. "No Excuse Sunday," BibleBelievers.com, https://www.biblebelievers.com/NoExcuseSunday.html.
11. Erwin W. Lutzer, *Where Do We Go from Here? Hope and Direction for Our Present Crisis* (Chicago: Moody, 2013), 39.
12. Anne Lamott, "Finding Our Way Home," *Our Daily Bread* (Grand Rapids, MI: RBC Ministries), quoted at "Philippians Illustrations 2," Precept Austin, February 21, 2015, http://www.preceptaustin.org/philippians_illustrations_2.
13. Doug McIntosh, *Life's Greatest Journey: How to Be Heavenly Minded and of Earthly Good* (Chicago: Moody, 2000), 30.
14. David Jeremiah, *Living with Confidence in a Chaotic World: What on Earth Should We Do Now?* (Nashville: Thomas Nelson, 2009), 93.
15. "The Lonely Ember," StoriesforPreaching.com, https://storiesforpreaching.com/category/sermonillustrations/church/.
16. This list is adapted from Mike Hubbard, "The 'One Anothers' of the New Testament," Genesis Church, September 6, 2009, https://blog.genesiseureka.com/2009/09/06/the-one-anothers-of-the-new-testament/.
17. Moniek, "On Pain of Death, Do Not Touch Queen Sunandha!" History of Royal Women, June 5, 2015, https://www.historyofroyalwomen.com/sunandha-kumaritana/on-pain-of-death-do-not-touch-queen-sunandha/.

CHAPTER 4: PUT ON YOUR ARMOR

1. Peter Berger, quoted in Os Guinness, *Impossible People: Christian Courage and the Struggle for the Soul of Civilization* (Downers Grove, IL: InterVarsity Press, 2016), 77–78.
2. Lesslie Newbigin, *Lesslie Newbigin: Missionary Theologian: A Reader*, comp. Paul Weston (Grand Rapids, MI: William B. Eerdmans, 2006), 47.
3. Quoted by Ray Pritchard, *Stealth Attack: Protecting Yourself against Satan's Plan to Destroy Your Life* (Chicago: Moody, 2007), 18.
4. Ray C. Stedman, *Spiritual Warfare: How to Stand Firm in the Faith* (Grand Rapids, MI: Discovery House, 1999), 20–21.
5. S. Lewis Johnson, "The Christian's Conflict" (sermon, Believer's Chapel, Dallas, TX, 2006), https://s3-us-west-2.amazonaws.com/sljinstitute-production/new_testament/Ephesians/18_SLJ_Ephesians.pdf.
6. D. Martyn Lloyd-Jones, *The Christian Soldier: An Exposition of Ephesians 6:10-20* (Grand Rapids, MI: Baker Books, 1977), 179.
7. Stedman, *Spiritual Warfare*, 133.
8. Ibid., 134, 136, 137.
9. James Montgomery Boice, *Ephesians: An Expositional Commentary* (Grand Rapids, MI: Baker Books, 1997), 253.
10. David Jeremiah, *Spiritual Warfare* (San Diego, CA: Turning Point, 2002), 80.
11. A. W. Tozer, *Born after Midnight* (Chicago: Moody, 2015), 52.

CHAPTER 5: KEEP PUSHING

1. Charles R. Swindoll, *Finding God When the World's on Fire: Strength & Faith for Dangerous Times* (Franklin, TN: Worthy Inspired, 2016), 8–9.
2. S. D. Gordon, *Quiet Talks on Prayer: When Praying People Engage a Giving God, Amazing Things Are Bound to Happen*, rev. ed. (Uhrichsville, OH: Barbour, 2013), 17–18.
3. Quoted at Danny E. Olinger, "Prayer and the Ministry," Orthodox Presbyterian Church, reprinted from *New Horizons* (February 2006), https://www.opc.org/nh.html?article_id=62.
4. Quoted in J. I. Packer & Carolyn Nystrom, *Praying: Finding Our Way through Duty to Delight* (Downers Grove, IL: IVP Books, 2006), 213.
5. E. M. Bounds, *E. M. Bounds on Prayer* (Peabody, MA: Hendrickson, 2006), 198.
6. Thomas Watson, *The Lord's Prayer*.
7. Haddon W. Robinson, *What Jesus Said about Successful Living: Principles from the Sermon on the Mount for Today* (Grand Rapids, MI: Discovery House, 1991), 200.
8. Martin Luther, "Small Catechism" quoted at Ray Pritchard, "Daily Bread Living" (sermon, Keep Believing Ministries, October 8, 2009), http://www.keepbelieving.com/sermon/daily-bread-living/.
9. Hudson Taylor, quoted at John Stott, "Four Things John Stott Learned from Hudson Taylor," OMF, November 30, 2016, https://omf.org/uk/2016/11/30/four-things-john-stott-learned-from-hudson-taylor/.
10. Philip Graham Ryken, *The Prayer of Our Lord*, rev. ed. (Wheaton, IL: Crossway, 2002), 76.

11. George Herbert, quoted in Ryken, *The Prayer of Our Lord*, 76.
12. P. T. Forsyth, *The Soul of Prayer* (Vancouver, BC: Regent College, 2002), 16.
13. Ben Patterson, *Deepening Your Conversation with God: Learning to Love to Pray* (Minneapolis: Bethany House, 2001), 28.
14. Robinson, *What Jesus Said about Successful Living*, 192.
15. Warren W. Wiersbe, *Prayer 101: Experiencing the Heart of God* (Colorado Springs: David C Cook, 2016), 84.

CHAPTER 6: DO THE BEST THINGS IN THE WORST TIMES
1. Joseph M. Stowell, *Shepherding the Church: Effective Spiritual Leadership in a Changing Culture* (Chicago: Moody, 1997), 15.
2. D. Edmond Hiebert, *1 Peter* (Chicago: Moody, 1992), 268–69.
3. Wayne Grudem, *1 Peter*, Tyndale New Testament Commentaries, ed. Leon Morris (1988; repr., Grand Rapids, MI: Eerdmans, 1997), 172–73.
4. Daniel L. Segraves, *First Peter: Standing Fast in the Grace of God* (Hazelwood, MO: World Aflame Press, 1999), 239.
5. Stuart Briscoe, *1 Peter: Holy Living in a Hostile World*, Understanding the Book series, rev. ed. (Wheaton, IL: Harold Shaw, 1993), 167.
6. Warren W. Wiersbe, *The Bible Exposition Commentary*, New Testament, vol. 2 (Wheaton, IL: Victor Books, 1989), 422.
7. Charles R. Swindoll, *Insights on James, 1 & 2 Peter*, Swindoll's New Testament Insights (Grand Rapids, MI: Zondervan, 2010), 218.
8. Edmund Clowney, *The Message of 1 Peter*, The Bible Speaks Today, ed. John R. W. Stott (Downers Grove, IL: IVP, 1988), 179.
9. Erwin W. Lutzer, *Where Do We Go from Here? Hope and Direction for Our Present Crisis* (Chicago: Moody, 2013), 38.
10. Max Lucado, "Open Your Door, Open Your Heart," UpWords, October 8–14, *Christianity.com*, https://www.christianity.com/devotionals/upwords-max-lucado/open-your-door-open-your-heart-upwords-week-of-october-8-14-11639250.html.
11. "Hospitality," *Preaching.com*, https://www.preaching.com/sermon-illustrations/hospitality/.
12. Denis Lyle, "Failures in Our Relationship to the Holy Spirit," SermonIndex.net, http://www.sermonindex.net/modules/articles/index.php?view=article&aid=22498.
13. Ray C. Stedman, *From Guilt to Glory*, vol. 2 (Palo Alto, CA: Discovery, 1978), 118–19.
14. "Humility," Chinese Christian Bible Study Data Website, http://ccbiblestudy.net/Topics/89Character/89GE20.htm.

CHAPTER 7: FIND YOUR FRAIDY HOLE
1. Steven Lawson, "Luther and the Psalms: His Solace and Strength," October 15, 2012, Ligonier Ministries, https://www.ligonier.org/blog/luther-and-psalms-his-solace-and-strength/.
2. David Jeremiah, *Slaying the Giants in Your Life* (Nashville: Thomas Nelson, 2001), 3.

3. Charles R. Swindoll, *Living the Psalms: Encouragement for the Daily Grind* (Brentwood, TN: Worthy, 2012), 134.

4. Warren W. Wiersbe, *The Bumps Are What You Climb On* (Grand Rapids, MI: Baker Books, 2002), 141.

5. Bob Abramson, "The Power of a Spider Web," Mentoring Ministry, March 26, 2013, https://www.mentoringministry.com/2013/03/the-power-of-a-spider-web/.

6. Erwin W. Lutzer, *Where Do We Go from Here? Hope and Direction for Our Present Crisis* (Chicago: Moody, 2013), 25.

7. Robert J. Morgan, *The Strength You Need: The Twelve Great Strength Passages of the Bible* (Nashville: W Publishing Group, 2016), 63–64.

8. Swindoll, *Living the Psalms*, 138–39.

9. Steven J. Lawson, *Psalms 1–75*, Holman Old Testament Commentary, gen. ed. Max Anders (Nashville: Holman Reference, 2003), 246.

10. James Weldon Johnson, *God's Trombones* (New York: Penguin Books, 2008), 21.

11. J. I. Packer, *Knowing God* (Downers Grove, IL: InterVarsity Press, 1973), 8.

12. Morgan, *The Strength You Need*, 67.

CHAPTER 8: REMAIN UNDER THE INFLUENCE

1. J. I. Packer, *Knowing God* (Downers Grove, IL: InterVarsity Press, 1973), 68.

2. Stanley D. Toussaint, "Living in the Power of the Holy Spirit," *Veritas* (July 2004), Dallas Theological Seminary, http://www.dts.edu/download/publications/veritas /veritas-2004-july.pdf. Much of the information in this chapter is adapted from this brief article and time in classes with Dr. Toussaint at Dallas Theological Seminary when I was a student.

3. Toussaint, "Living in the Power of the Holy Spirit," 6.

4. David Jeremiah, *God in You: Releasing the Power of the Holy Spirit in Your Life* (Sisters, OR: Multnomah, 1998), 89.

5. Robert J. Morgan, *On This Day: 365 Amazing and Inspiring Stories about Saints, Martyrs & Heroes* (Nashville: Thomas Nelson, 1997), January 14.

6. Ibid.

7. Toussaint, "Living in the Power of the Holy Spirit," 6.

8. "D. L. Moody," Bible.org, https://bible.org/node/10435.

9. Toussaint, "Living in the Power of the Holy Spirit," 3.

10. A. W. Tozer, *Man: The Dwelling Place of God* (Camp Hill, PA: WingSpread, 2008), 39.

11. Toussaint, "Living in the Power of the Holy Spirit," 5.

12. John R. W. Stott, *The Message of Ephesians*, The Bible Speaks Today, ed. John R. W. Stott (Leicester, England: Inter-Varsity Press, 1979), 207.

13. Toussaint, "Living in the Power of the Holy Spirit," 6.

14. Max Anders, *What You Need to Know about the Holy Spirit in 12 Lessons* (Nashville: Thomas Nelson, 1995), 140.

CHAPTER 9: TUNE IN TO HEAVEN'S FREQUENCY

1. "Cheering the Invisible Victory," *Preaching Today*, http://www.preachingtoday .com/illustrations/1998/july/4466.html.

2. We can see this victory in some ways today. Despite the persecution of Christians, Christianity is actually growing across the non-Western world.

3. Ben Patterson, *Serving God: The Grand Essentials of Work & Worship*, rev. ed. (Downers Grove, IL: InterVarsity Press, 1994), 39.

4. Dale Ralph Davis, *The Way of the Righteous in the Muck of Life: Psalms 1–12* (Scotland: Christian Focus Publications, 2010), 27–28.

5. Quoted at Steve Kumar, "The Battle for Truth," *Think Why?*, November 20, 2008, https://thinkwhy.wordpress.com/2008/11/20/the-battle-for-truth/.

6. Richard Lischer, ed., *The Company of Preachers: Wisdom on Preaching, Augustine to the Present* (Grand Rapids, MI: Eerdmans, 2002), 100.

7. Frederick Buechner, *Beyond Words: Daily Readings in the ABC's of Faith* (New York: HarperCollins, 2004), 368–69.

8. Os Guinness, *Impossible People: Christian Courage and the Struggle for the Soul of Civilization* (Downers Grove, IL: IVP Books, 2016), 139.

9. The kingdom spoken of in Psalm 2 is not a present, spiritual kingdom. It's the future, literal, earthly, Davidic kingdom promised in 2 Samuel 7:12-16. Two points in Psalm 2 support this view. First, "Jerusalem" is mentioned as the place where Messiah's throne will be established. There's no reason in Psalm 2 to take this in any way other than literally. Second, Messiah's kingdom will be established not by *salvation* but by *subjugation*. This supports a future, literal kingdom and argues against any notion of a present spiritual kingdom that is being slowly expanded by the preaching of the gospel.

10. Derek Kidner, *Psalms 1–72*, Kidner Classic Commentaries (Downers Grove, IL: InterVarsity Press, 2008), 70.

11. Max Lucado, *Because of Bethlehem* (Nashville: Thomas Nelson, 2016), 115.

12. C. S. Lewis, *Mere Christianity* (New York: HarperCollins, 2001), 65.

13. George Eldon Ladd, *A Commentary on the Revelation of John* (Grand Rapids, MI: Eerdmans, 1972), 82.

14. James M. Hamilton Jr., *Revelation: The Spirit Speaks to the Churches*, Preaching the Word, ed. R. Kent Hughes (Wheaton, IL: Crossway, 2012), 151.

15. "The World Is a Puzzle," StoriesforPreaching.com, https://storiesforpreaching.com /the-world-is-a-puzzle/.

16. Sinclair B. Ferguson, *Child in the Manger: The True Meaning of Christmas* (Carlisle, PA: Banner of Truth Trust, 2016), 177.

17. P. T. Forsyth, *The Justification of God: Lectures for War-Time on a Christian Theodicy* (Eugene, OR: Wipf and Stock, 1999), 227.

18. Ray Stedman, "Our God Reigns," Daily Devotions, News and Information, February 24, 2016, https://808bo.com/2016/02/24/ray-stedman-our-god-reigns/.

19. "Now He Belongs to the Ages," April 15, 2008, *Lincoln Studies: Abraham Lincoln and the American Civil War*, http://lincolnstudies.blogspot.com/2008/04/now-he-belongs -to-ages.html/.

20. Kent Crockett, *Making Today Count for Eternity* (Sisters, OR: Multnomah, 2001), 17.

CHAPTER 10: WAKE UP

1. "Shock Poll: Startling Numbers of Americans Believe World Now in the 'End Times,'" Religion News Service, September 11, 2013, http://religionnews.com/2013 /09/11/shock-poll-startling-numbers-of-americans-believe-world-now-in-the-end -times/.

2. Jeff Brumley, "Global Events, Prophecy Stir Talk of 'End Times' Beliefs," *Florida Times-Union*, July 16, 2010, http://www.jacksonville.com/article/20100716 /NEWS/801248442.

3. Walter Einenkel, "New Survey Shows That about 80% of Evangelicals Believe the 'End Times' Are Near," *Daily Kos*, December 8, 2015, http://www.dailykos.com/story /2015/12/7/1457887/-New-survey-shows-that-about-80-of-Evangelicals-believe-the -end-times-are-near.

4. "The Certainty of the Second Coming," Grace to You, November 24, 1991, https://www.gty.org/library/sermons-library/66-3/the-certainty-of-the-second -coming.

5. I believe Jesus' Olivet Discourse concerns his Second Advent, not the Rapture. I believe the Rapture and the return are two phases of Christ's future coming. The Olivet Discourse addresses the signs of the Second Coming that the final generation living on earth will witness, but we can apply the same principles of alertness to our lives as we await the Rapture. For a more detailed discussion of the Rapture, see my book *The End: A Complete Overview of Bible Prophecy and the End of Days* (Carol Stream, IL: Tyndale, 2012), 121–76.

6. Grant R. Osborne, *Revelation*, Baker Exegetical Commentary on the New Testament (Grand Rapids, MI: Baker Academic, 2002), 594.

7. "Illustration: Staying Alert," *Preaching.com*, https://www.preaching.com/sermon -illustrations/illustration-staying-alert/.

8. John MacArthur, "Ready or Not—Here I Come!, Part 2," Grace to You, July 22, 1984, https://www.gty.org/library/sermons-library/2374/ready-or-nothere-i-come -part-2.

9. Ray C. Stedman, *The Ruler Who Serves: Mark 8–16* (Waco, TX: Word Books, 1976), 145–46.

10. Charles R. Swindoll, *Mark*, Swindoll's Living Insights (Carol Stream, IL: Tyndale House, 2016), 334.

11. Abraham Kuruvilla, *Mark: A Theological Commentary for Preachers* (Eugene, OR: Cascade Books, 2012), 284.

12. Ibid., 298.

13. Steven J. Cole, "Lesson 15: Are You Ready for That Day? (1 Thessalonians 5:1-8)," Bible.org, November 6, 2016, https://bible.org/seriespage/lesson-15-are-you-ready -day-1-thessalonians-51-8.

14. "Wiersbe—Story of Young Man Preaching on Last Days," Family Times, http://www.family-times.net/illustration/Last-Days/201555/.

15. Warren W. Wiersbe, *Wiersbe Bible Study Series: 2 Peter, 2 & 3 John, Jude* (Colorado Springs: David C. Cook, 2013), 69.

16. Randall Price, *Jerusalem in Prophecy* (Eugene, OR: Harvest House, 1998), 50.

THE END TIMES SURVIVAL GUIDE

17. R. A. Torrey, "Why God Used D. L. Moody," first published 1923, Wholesome Words, https://www.wholesomewords.org/biography/biomoody6.html.
18. Louis Zamperini and David Rensin, *Devil at My Heels: A Heroic Olympian's Astonishing Story of Survival as a Japanese POW in World War II* (New York: HarperCollins, 2011), 243.

THE COMING APOSTASY

MARK HITCHCOCK
JEFF KINLEY

INTRODUCTION

In nineteenth-century France, disgruntled workers developed a subversive tactic that involved throwing a shoe into factory machinery, causing it to grind to a halt, ruining all productivity. This act of aggression became known as *sabotage* (from *sabot*, the French word for shoe).[1] A single shoe thrown into the gears could wreak untold havoc on a well-oiled machine.

Today, we are witnessing the relentless sabotage of Christianity and the church from within. Subtle saboteurs are tossing one theological shoe after another into the machine, causing spiritual bewilderment and breakdowns.

Satan has always worked to sabotage the work of God through human false teachers. And although Satan has many shoes and strategies, his two main areas of sabotage are against the *written* Word of God (the Scriptures) and the *living* Word of God (the Savior, Jesus).[2] The devil's first recorded words in the Bible are spoken to Eve in the Garden of Eden, and they drip with doubt and denial: "Indeed, has God said . . . ?"[3] Since that time, the hiss of the serpent has echoed down through the ages, from generation to generation, as he questions, undermines, and sabotages the Bible. As David Jeremiah says,

[Satan] isn't just given to one approach. If he can't take the Word of God away from us by undermining its authority, he will take us away from the Word of God by giving us another basis of authority. Satan has developed just such a substitute, and it seems to have a great attraction for many people.

It's called *experience*.

People become so wrapped up in their spiritual experience that they no longer look to the Word of God for their authority. Their experience becomes the determining force in their lives.[4]

Dr. Jeremiah closes with this powerful observation:

Two groups, then, are vying for our minds—but with the same end in view. [Liberal scholars] would take the Bible away from us, and those who hold to the experiential view would take us away from the Bible.[5]

We could not agree more. Sound doctrine is under siege. The Bible is being either reduced, outright rejected, or replaced by how people feel about whatever moral or theological topic is under consideration.

However, nothing we see should surprise us. The Bible predicted that this day would come. Scripture tells us that the tide of apostasy will crest as the end draws near. This portent of the end is referred to in 2 Thessalonians 2:3 as the falling away or the final great apostasy. That season may be arriving very soon. In light of this sobering reality, our main goal in this book is to unmask the current sabotage aimed at the authority and sufficiency of the Bible and targeting the exclusivity of Jesus as the only way to God. We also want to arm you with the truth, heighten your discernment, and recalibrate your thinking and living in accordance with the plumb line of God's truth. These are serious issues for the church and for every believer. A great deal is at stake.

May the Lord be pleased to use this book in the life of every reader as He has graciously used it already in the lives of its authors.

CHAPTER 1

GOD AND GHOST SHIPS

Some have . . . suffered shipwreck in regard to their faith.

1 TIMOTHY 1:19

Captain David Morehouse was accustomed to the choppy waters of the North Atlantic, but he wasn't prepared for what caught his eye this winter's day. Sailing some four hundred miles east of the Azores Islands, Morehouse encountered a disturbing sight. It was a ship, which in itself is not unusual to spot on the open sea. What was odd was that this particular two-masted brig seemed to be in great distress. Its canvas sails tattered by a relentless wind, the ship drifted aimlessly in open water. From his vantage point aboard the *Dei Gratia*, Captain Morehouse was unable to see anyone on deck of the wayward vessel. And so, after calling out and receiving no reply, the British captain gave orders to come alongside the mystery ship. He sent a boarding party to inspect the ship, but his first mate and two crew members failed to find a single soul aboard.

Instead, what they discovered was a full cargo containing 1,701 barrels of crude alcohol, along with a six-month supply of food and water. What was missing was the ship's only lifeboat. Gone, too, were its captain, Benjamin S. Briggs, his wife, Sarah, and their two-year-old daughter, Sophia, along with eight crew members. However, they found closets of clothes left behind, suggesting a sudden departure. During the one-hour inspection, the *Dei Gratia*'s boarding crew also observed a disassembled pump and three and a half feet of water sloshing around in the hull. But aside from these curiosities, the 108-foot-long vessel appeared to be seaworthy.

The creaking ship discovered by Captain Morehouse on December 5, 1872, turned out to be the *Mary Celeste*. Records later showed the ship had set sail on November 7 from New York headed for Genoa, Italy. But something happened along the way, and the *Mary Celeste* was now long overdue. And those now aboard the *Dei Gratia*, whose Latin name means "by the Grace of God," could only hope and pray that same grace would watch over the lost ship's passengers and crew.

The tragic tale of the *Mary Celeste* has become one of the most puzzling mysteries in maritime history. Many theories have been offered to make sense of this perplexing story and what happened—everything from pirates to storms and high seas, even sea monsters. Experts still scratch their heads as to why Captain Briggs would give orders to abandon a ship that showed no signs of imminent danger.

But nearly 150 years past that cold December day, and after speculation in articles, books, poems, and even movies, we are today no closer to knowing what led to the *Mary Celeste*'s fate than Morehouse was. In the absence of captain or crew, the ship had drifted off course in the open sea for some two weeks before being discovered. Instead of reaching its intended destination, the *Mary Celeste* has gained the enduring infamy of being history's quintessential ghost ship.

OUR CURRENT CONDITION

Unless you've spent the past few years cast away on a deserted island, you've no doubt come to the conclusion that ours is a planet in peril. We are a culture in chaos, a human race caught in the epicenter of a global storm. Like the *Mary Celeste*, we are adrift as a planet, lost in a turbulent sea of confusion and uncertainty. And it's no longer just the experts who recognize the imminent crises threatening our world. According to a nationwide poll, 41 percent of adults believe we are living in the "end times."[1] An acute awareness of our world's troubles has finally filtered down to the average person. And the reigning consensus is that planet Earth is showing all the signs of rapidly approaching disaster on multiple levels.

In other words, we're in deep, choppy waters here.

This moment in time is a markedly different one than our parents' or grandparents' generation knew. Though previous generations may have witnessed world war, economic recession, and political upheavals, this present dark hour carries a distinctly apocalyptic cargo. Upon first glance, the happenings in recent history may more closely resemble a bad dream or a sci-fi movie scenario. Despite some who naively imagine things getting better, an honest, open-eyed appraisal of humanity's situation reveals much more dystopia than utopia. This is reality, not some hopeful, future fantasy. Further, it's *your* reality. The world in which you live is becoming increasingly volatile, rising and falling like a ship's bow in a furious tempest, wildly tossed about. Instability, unrest, and uncertainty are constants in this contemporary global drama. The world is changing—and not for the better.

Of course, it's human to question and to wonder whether history's hurricane is about to make landfall. Having saturated ourselves in sin, we have to wonder, *Is Revelation finally setting sail toward our shores?*

Scan culture's horizon, and what do we see? Rage-filled citizens rioting in the streets, looting local businesses due to perceived injustice in their community. Immigrants and refugees embroiled in an unprecedented international crisis, the consequences of which are as yet unknown. Mass shootings, combined with an ongoing epidemic of violence and homicide, have almost anesthetized us to murder.[2] And the body count among the unborn continues to rise, nearing 1.5 billion butchered worldwide in the name of "reproductive rights."[3]

The ancient Canaanites got nothing on us.

But that's not all. Keep looking around, and you'll see state and federal authorities, along with Supreme Court justices, passing laws and declaring edicts sanctioning, legalizing, endorsing, promoting, and even wholeheartedly celebrating homosexual activity and same-sex marriage. Men who self-identify as women are allowed to use women's restrooms, exposing young girls to potential trauma, abuse, and attack. Our society's moral conscience has dulled to the point where we now proudly call evil "good" and good "evil." This sad commentary on our nation tragically parallels an earlier time in Israel's history when "everyone did what was right in his own eyes."[4] Today, there's even a proposal within some psychiatric circles to destigmatize sexual offenses such as pedophilia, instead referring to people who commit these offenses as "minor-attracted persons."[5] In our contemporary moral climate, just about anything goes—except, of course, biblical morality. Our culture's collective decadence is eclipsed only by the individual depravity of those who define it. It's a critical breach in humanity's hull, letting in a flood of lunacy disguised as "enlightenment" and "progressive thought." And the water keeps pouring in.

Political correctness has become one of our new idols, and one that demands we pay regular veneration and worship. It dare not be ignored or angered lest we feel its wrath. To merely disagree, for example, with trendy, "richer" views of morality is to be charged with hate speech or bigotry. Historical Judeo-Christian values are systematically being sandblasted from the walls of conscience with pagan, Mardi Gras morals chiseled in their place. To suggest there is still an absolute, objective morality regarding issues such as sexuality or marriage is to be instantly judged, cast into the public court of shame and ridicule, and summarily stoned to death by popular opinion and social media. As a result of this and other glaring evidences of moral decay, many believe we are witnessing in real time the systematic collapse of Western civilization. It's almost as if it were all part of a larger, sinister plan and strategy.

Yes, something is very wrong with *humanity*, something as a race we collectively refuse to acknowledge. In truth, the root causes of our evil obsessions go much deeper than social, psychological, or even moral causes. What lies under the surface of our universal insanity is a spiritual problem, a deadly virus, birthed in our first parents and passed down from generation to generation.

But keep looking, now internationally, and we see that global economic stability has never been so volatile, with multiple nations teetering toward default and financial collapse. According to the World Economic Forum, earth's economy is currently vulnerable on a number of fronts and more than ever at risk to suffer "global shocks." These economic tremors do not respect national borders and can potentially shake whole financial systems and societies to their foundations.[6] Like at no other time in recorded history, the international community has become linked together. What happens financially in one nation often dramatically impacts another, with one country's economic crisis sending concentric ripple effects to ten others, or more. This has led to an unprecedented interdependence in an ever-emerging one-world financial market.

In its Global Risks 2014 Report, the World Economic Forum states, "A fiscal crisis in any major economy could easily have cascading global impacts."[7] Put simply, this worldwide economic house of cards could collapse at any time, an unfolding scenario which seamlessly syncs with Revelation's portrayal of future economic disaster.[8]

Look around, and you'll see that our world is also facing a number of humanitarian crises, one of which is the more than 780 million hungry people in the world today.[9] Though the vast majority of these are from developing countries, they nevertheless represent one out of every eight people on the planet. Imagine the scale of impact when global famine eventually hits the world, as forecast in Revelation. Chances of thriving, both in third-world and developed countries, will rapidly go from unlikely to virtually impossible. Additionally, human trafficking, sex trafficking, and sex slavery together globally form a $32 billion industry involving some 21 million victims worldwide.[10]

What on earth have we become?

From a geopolitical perspective, the Middle East remains a delicate minefield, easily set off by a single misstep. Add to this ticking time bomb Iran's stealthy efforts to develop nuclear weapons capabilities. Iran's stated desire is to remove the Jewish nation as the cancerous "tumor" in the body of the Islamic world, wiping Israel from the face of the earth.[11] Meanwhile, Israel has its own problems as ongoing conflict with Syrian-based Hamas threatens to erupt like a powder keg at any given moment. Recurring missile strikes from both sides are now a regular part of life in the Middle East.

According to Bible prophecy, Russia is poised to be an end-times player and continues to reinforce its reputation as a world bully, having previously established its presence on Israel's border. Drunk on its own power, Russia's next move remains unknown, but this nation could very well be positioning itself for the apocalyptic war Ezekiel predicted.[12]

But there's more.

The Islamic State in Iraq and Syria (ISIS) is the latest unwelcome arrival on the world terrorist scene. Even so, it has managed to have a massive, devastating impact in a relatively short span of time. Begun as a splinter group from al-Qaeda, this barbaric death cult has become well known for military campaigns, invasions, brutal torture, and public executions, including crucifixion. It is apocalyptic Islam on steroids, a brand of jihadist ideology that believes the coming of their Mahdi (messiah) can be hastened as the world is engulfed in chaos and carnage.[13] Ironically, their favorite method of execution is beheading. Reviving an ancient form of bloody barbarism, ISIS has branded itself as a group of modern-day human butchers. Beheadings have now happened right here in the United States, even in rural communities.[14] And these wicked warriors do not discriminate, as they brutally slaughter hundreds of women and small children. The masked monsters of ISIS also produce their own "snuff videos," featuring selected beheadings and executions, posting them online in an attempt to bolster their cause and terrorize peace-loving people worldwide.

This growing terrorist body is well financed and organized. Its short-term goal is to create a "caliphate" (Islamic State) in Syria and Iraq. Forcing over a million Iraqis from their homes, many of them Christians, ISIS has also taken control of oil fields and seized cities in that region. But their gruesome aspirations are not confined to the Middle East. A US Army Intelligence bulletin has warned of potential attacks in America by ISIS supporters and sympathizers targeting US military personnel and their families, threatening to "show up [at their homes] and slaughter them."[15]

Of course, the terrorist roots of this radicalism can be traced back to a several-thousand-year-old hatred of Jews. Now, like a deadly virus, this evil enmity has mutated, branching out with the goal of destroying other equally despised infidels (Christians, friends of Israel, or anyone unwilling to submit to the oppressive religious demands of these sadistic serial murderers).

As if this weren't enough, on American soil, lone-wolf terrorist attacks (sometimes erroneously labeled "workplace violence") have burst the bubble of our assumed protective insulation from this threat. A new tentacle of terrorism has developed as individuals now self-radicalize with bloody vendettas targeting non-Muslims. Unfortunately, there is no guaranteed and effective preventative measure against such rampages.

Negotiation has proved impossible with an ideology whose adherents believe they've been given a "holy mandate" to subjugate or kill outsiders. They do not debate, argue, barter, or waver in fulfilling their mission but are wholly committed to their unholy cause. And there is every indication this brand of terrorism will continue gaining momentum as sleeper cells infiltrate free societies in order to conquer and destroy them. Who would have ever dreamed words like *jihad* and *terrorism* would earn permanent places in our national vocabulary? The imminent threat of another terrorist attack, whether on a local or large scale, is not a matter of *if* but rather *when*, as our military and intelligence leaders believe these jihadists are already on American soil.[16] We do know there are currently some thirty-five Islamic terrorist training camps scattered all across America.[17] These Muslim extremists have also pledged to one day "raise the flag of Allah in the White House."[18]

We have officially passed through the looking glass and into another reality altogether. And there is every indication our world is drifting toward destruction.

But this is what happens when mutiny ensues and humanity defiantly casts God overboard. These are the consequences to resisting and rejecting Him, ripple effects from refusing to acknowledge the Creator's existence and regal right to rule His own creation. God turns us over to ourselves. Billions of people, bound by an enslaving depravity.

However, if our eyes are fixed only on humanity and world events, we could easily be overcome with fear and uncertainty, and often this fear leads to unhealthy isolation and reclusiveness as we withdraw from engaging culture and being Christ's witnesses in the world. Weathering this current sin-storm, Christ's disciples can also default to self-reliance instead of dependence on our Lord, as what's wrong with our world can have a debilitating effect on our faith in God. Looking at the chaos surrounding us, we may even wonder if He is still at the helm. Is God really guiding history? Is He still in charge? Or has He abandoned us altogether?

Were it not for the reality of a sovereign God who superintends both history and humanity, we would surely despair. Thankfully, Scripture assures us the God of heaven is still in control. The real question is, Do we believe that? Daniel 4:35 proclaims, "All the inhabitants of the earth are accounted as nothing, but He does according to His will in the host of heaven and among the inhabitants of earth; and no one can ward off His hand or say to Him, 'What have You done?'"

In light of the darkness around us, the prophet Isaiah delivers much-needed perspective in Isaiah 40:6-31. Open your Bible and read it for yourself, allowing his words to marinate in your mind.

MEANWHILE, AT HOME . . .

All across the world, abandoned ships rust on shores and beaches. Some are half sunken while others lie fully submerged under oceans and lakes. These are vessels that suffered shipwreck due to neglect, abandonment, or mutiny. Some were left to drift, sailing aimlessly at the unpredictable whim of the wind and the waves. Many met their fate at the hands of pirates. Forcibly boarding unsuspecting ships, these sea terrorists seized cargo, killing passengers and crew before either scuttling the vessel or leaving it to the ocean's mercy. Still other ships found themselves wandering upon the waters or resting on the ocean floor because of war, storms, fire, disease, a damaged rudder, or running out of fuel or food. Bad winds or no winds easily contribute to the demise of once-worthy ships. Even so, the common denominator for these ghost ships is that they are all *lost*, adrift in the ocean's vast expanse, without help or hope, and with no helmsman to guide them toward safe harbor.

Sadly, what is true of ships can also be true of people. The same perilous danger that threatens seagoing vessels also endangers those who call themselves Christians. It's why the apostle Paul admonished the Corinthians, "Test yourselves to see if you are in the faith; examine yourselves! Or do you not recognize this about yourselves, that Jesus Christ is in you—unless indeed you fail the test?"[19]

Peter, writing to the scattered believers living in a decadent society under the rule of a pagan government, urged, "Therefore, brethren, be all the more diligent to make certain about His calling and choosing you; for as long as you practice these things, you will never stumble; for in this way the entrance into the eternal kingdom of our Lord and Savior Jesus Christ will be abundantly supplied to you."[20]

In a world racing toward Revelation, Jesus' church today finds herself sailing through turbulent waters of her own. She's perilously taking on water while some of her more naive passengers seem perfectly content, satisfying themselves at the weekly Sunday buffet. Mirroring the churches Christ chastised in Revelation 2–3, the collective state of Christendom today faces an internal threat far more deadly than a terrorist attack. As we will discover, the bride of Christ is not exactly "shipshape." In places, she has suffered a hull breach, lost her rudder, failed to catch wind, and gone adrift from the course God has charted for her.

What lies dead ahead is the hidden reef of apostasy, and no one understood this more than Paul, as the much-traveled apostle suffered literal shipwreck himself three times![21] Using this as a powerful metaphor, he puts on display examples of *spiritual* shipwreck, even calling out individuals by name:

> This command I entrust to you, Timothy, my son, in accordance with the prophecies previously made concerning you, that by them you fight the good fight, keeping faith and a good conscience, which some have rejected and *suffered shipwreck* in regard to their faith. Among these are Hymenaeus and Alexander, whom I have handed over to Satan, so that they will be taught not to blaspheme.[22]

There are several important observations and principles we can draw from Paul's words:

1. Losing or abandoning faith is equivalent to apostasy, or suffering "shipwreck."
2. The two men Paul mentions weren't the only ones to abandon the faith.
3. There are tangible, painful consequences to deserting the faith.

Granted, all Christ-followers encounter storms and suffer through occasional seasons of sin. This is a normal part of the challenge and messiness of temptation and sanctification. But there is a vast difference between getting water in your boat and your boat actually sinking, and there is a big distinction between temporarily sailing off course and suffering a fatal shipwreck. The good news is that God has promised to faithfully discipline His children when they, by either active or passive choices, veer off course and straight into sin.[23] At times we may wander, sailing too close to the rocky shore and becoming stuck on those hidden reefs, yet without actually capsizing and permanently going under.

However, for others, there is no rescue from the angry sea or salvage from below. These once-professing believers may have set out on their Christian pilgrimage with good intentions and noble motives. They may have even had a correct course heading, been under great teaching, or participated in a healthy faith community. But as important as those things are, by themselves they are not enough. Thus these self-proclaimed God-followers eventually become spiritual "ghost ships" themselves. It's not an issue of losing their salvation but rather of demonstrating their true identity. They flirted with the idea of being disciples of Jesus at some point in their lives, but their eventual falling away revealed them to be counterfeit Christians. As Jesus bluntly warned, *professing* Him, no matter how confidently, doesn't necessarily mean *possessing* Him.[24] This is why the Holy Spirit inspired John to write, "The one who says, 'I have come to know Him,' and does not keep His commandments, is a liar, and the truth is not in him."[25]

Bottom line: people drift, falter, and sink. So do churches and even whole denominations. Having merely parroted faith in Jesus, they can, and often do, deviate off course. Some succumb to doctrinal error or, like the church at Ephesus, lose the wind in their sails, manifested in the absence of a passionate love for Jesus Christ.[26]

This "falling away from the faith" (known as *apostasy*) can be a nebulous concept, perhaps because it's seldom studied, preached, or understood by a generation of churchgoers who measure their spiritual temperature by how much they "enjoyed" the church service and evaluate their spiritual progress by conformity to rules and religiosity. But our Christian faith goes much deeper than this. Part of maturing as believers means addressing some of the weightier issues of God's Word. As we grow, we discover that, along with all the benefits God offers (His presence; peace; provision; and steadfast, unconditional love), there are also some major concerns He has for His church, specifically, her tendency to drift, both doctrinally and personally. These dangers exist because of the world in which we live, the enemy bent on destroying us, and our own hearts that are so prone to wander.[27] But the closer we get to God's heart, the more our hearts become sensitive and open to the deeper issues God's Word addresses. We begin to want what He wants. That's part of what it means to "seek first [God's] kingdom and His righteousness."[28] At times we may think the really important truths and issues concerning the church are meant only for pastors and leaders. But individual Christians also have a responsibility to preserve the unity and purity of the church.[29] We are *all* meant to understand and "handle the truth." If not, much of Paul's epistles would be irrelevant to the average believer, something we know is not true, as "*all* Scripture is inspired by God and profitable" for us.[30]

As this book will explain, the coming apostasy is a serious sign of the end times and one of Scripture's weightier truths. Understanding it is essential if we are to navigate the waters of today's confusing culture.

THE CAPTAIN OF OUR SALVATION

Apostasy represents an abandonment of faith, and it can happen over time without a person realizing it. In fact, just the opposite may occur, as pride mixed with false doctrine leads to an attitude of superiority, complacency, and self-righteousness. Nevertheless, it's there. Lying just beneath the surface, it is poised to penetrate the very thing keeping us afloat—our faith. Perhaps you've known those who set out seeking safe harbor in Christ only to end up splintered on the jagged rocks of unbelief. Without being moored by the biblical anchor of authentic faith, they drift in an age of unprecedented pseudo-Christian thought. At times they are driven by the winds of progressive theology, postmodern thought, or godless philosophies and values. Perhaps they are emotionally driven by political correctness and even a reimagining of God Himself. In an era of endless information, where self-appointed truth-proclaimers peddle phony faith formulas to innocent, untrained church members, it's no surprise that many become lost in the disorienting fog. This is why every professing believer in Jesus desperately needs a magnetic compass, a map, an anchor, a lighthouse with a clear beacon—an unfailing GPS guiding them every step of the way.

It's also why we need a Captain.

Jesus promised *He* would build His church, "and the gates of Hades will not overpower it."[31] And He has made, and will make, good on that promise. Even so, it's not enough to merely quote verses, claiming immunity from the enemy's attacks. Obviously, because of Christ's efficacious payment for sin, every believer will make it safely to heaven. But that doesn't guarantee a life exempt from sporadic episodes of apathy, self-absorption, moral failure, doctrinal deviance, or even being temporarily misled by false teachers. There is no automatic guarantee of continuous safe spiritual passage. But even in the midst of our messiness and meandering, God is still committed to us—much more committed to us than we are to Him.[32] Yes, Christ will build His church. He has established her and preserved her through both history *and* heresy. And death will not defeat or permanently derail her. But that doesn't mean she isn't vulnerable to rough seas in these last days in which we live. There are clear and present dangers threatening her—threatening *you*, too. There are issues some may consider minor or nonessential but that still cause us to deviate from faith's map. And the longer we continue traveling off course, even if only by a few degrees, the farther from our intended destination we drift.

Pilots who miscalculate flight plans by even one degree could miss their target destinations by hundreds of miles, or worse, run straight into a mountain. Pharmacists who make just one error combining chemicals while filling a prescription could potentially poison their patients.

The same is true for us, which is why we must always strive to stay on target with God and His Word. While Christians may disagree about certain peripheral areas of doctrine, that does not in any way diminish the importance of doctrine itself. And we cannot flippantly dismiss any part of God's Word, because what we believe really does matter.

THE *LORD'S* PRAYER

On Jesus' final night with His disciples, they had dinner together, after which he took them on a walk to a place that was very familiar to them.[33] Located just outside Jerusalem's walls, this garden of olive trees proved to be a favorite gathering spot for Jesus and the Twelve. The word *Gethsemane* comes from two Hebrew words that when combined mean "a place for pressing oil." In ancient culture, heavy slabs of stone were used to crush olives until all the oil had been extracted. The oil was then poured into clay jars for household use. Jesus was well aware of this common practice. He also knew what that word prefigured for Him. Arriving in the garden that night, Christ experienced a sense of dread as He contemplated being crushed by the Father's fierce wrath due to our sin. And so, securing a solitary spot, Jesus fell on His face, pouring out His heart to the Father in prayer.

In that most intimate and passionate prayer, the Son of God explicitly asks the Father *not* to take His followers out of the world but rather to "keep them from the evil one." The reason for this, He says, is that His disciples do not belong to the domain of this world—or of its god.[34] But exactly how would Christ's current and future disciples remain well insulated from Satan's deceptive and destructive influence? The answer is found in the very next verse. They need only for the Father to "sanctify them in the truth," Jesus prays. He then affirms, "Your word is truth."[35]

The life-changing, lasting influence of God's Word in our lives is a primary countermeasure to Satan's attacks. As Jesus' followers, we must keep this in mind when confronting the godless world in which we live. But we also must realize there are other threats too, some coming from within the church itself.

The unfortunate reality today is that the world and the church are often indistinguishable. As worldly philosophies and values infiltrate the body of Christ, moral values adjust and new theologies emerge. This creates a fatal breach, allowing other compromising half-truths and deceptive false teachings into the body. And why would this be such a major concern? Why is it such a big deal? Few things made Paul's blood boil more than false teachers deceiving and misleading God's people.[36] More about this later.

The principle we draw from Jesus' prayer is that we are purified and protected by engaging, believing, and living out God's truth. Put simply, when we think *biblically*, we are less likely to drift aimlessly. But failing to seal our minds from unbiblical thinking, beliefs, and doctrine causes us to sail perilously close to catastrophe. By adjusting Scripture to fit our own thinking (instead of vice versa), we stray from God's heart and mind. And we miss His best for us.

We've written this book for several important reasons: (1) to help you understand what apostasy is; (2) to help you understand that it's surging all around us and is a serious sign of the end times; (3) to guard you from spiritual shipwreck and the danger of sinking; and

(4) to help you understand the truth so that you stay on course as you await Christ's return.

Many people today pray for a great revival, and though it may happen, no such revival is prophesied. On the contrary, according to Scripture, a great apostasy is coming.

But how close are we?

CHAPTER 2

THE FIFTH COLUMN

In 1939, the Spanish Civil War was coming to an end, and General Mola prepared his attack on Madrid. He had four columns of troops ready to take the city, and someone asked Mola which of these would be the first to attack. "The fifth," was his world-famous answer.

General Mola's most important line of attack was not the military outside the city; it was rebel sympathizers inside the city. They went about unnoticed but were already preparing for his advance. The term *fifth column* has come to mean those who sympathize with an attacker and aid the attacker from the inside.[1]

The fifth column within Christianity is apostasy. Let's face it: the word *apostasy* is ugly and harsh—and misunderstood. Yet the subject is hardly foreign to the Bible. We would all love to talk about positive things and leave the negative to others, but apostasy is an important issue in the New Testament. From its earliest days, the church has faced the advance of apostasy. Many of the New Testament letters were written to confront various forms of false teaching within the churches. Although apostasy is nothing new for the church, in recent times the surge is palpable. As A.W. Tozer wrote, "Christians now chatter learnedly about things simple believers have always taken for granted. They are on the defensive, trying to prove things that a previous generation never doubted."[2] Think of how much more true that statement is today.

TWO WARS

The world today is witnessing two great wars in progress—two wars waged on two fronts. One front is in the East, where radical Islamists are prosecuting a brutal, bloody, barbaric war to establish a caliphate. They want to raise up one religion to dominate the world. The specter of radical Islam casts its ominous shadow across the globe. The other front is in the West. The war in the West is a philosophical war—an attempt to remove one religion, Christianity, from any influence. The war in the East is to establish a religion. The war in the West is to eradicate a religion.

These two wars are closely related. The diminishing role of Christianity in the public square has left the West unable or at least unwilling to stand up against pure evil in the form of ISIS and other militant jihadists. Paralysis and powerlessness are increasingly the response of the West to unmitigated evil. Secularism and humanism have dulled the ability to discern evil, even its most blatant manifestations, and to act against it aggressively.

Christianity is being eviscerated from within and without. From the outside, atheists, secularists, and humanists unload a relentless barrage against the faith. And on the inside, theological liberals and all sorts of false teachers diminish and even deny essential Christian doctrine and morality. This is apostasy, and it's eating away like a cancer at the heart of biblical Christianity.

THE GREAT FALLING AWAY

Before we go any further, let's remind ourselves of the meaning of *apostasy*. Apostasy in general is defection or departure from the tenets of some religious community. The Greek word *apostasia* means "rebellion" or "abandonment." Christian apostasy in its broadest terms is defection or departure from the truth of Scripture. Andy Woods describes it this way:

> The English word apostasy is derived from two Greek words. The first word is the preposition *apo*, which means "away from." The second word is the verb *histēmi*, which means, "to stand." Thus, apostasy means, "to stand away from." Apostasy refers to a departure from known or previously embraced truth. The subject of apostasy has little to do with the condition of the unsaved world, which has always rejected divine truth and therefore has nothing from which to depart. Rather, apostasy pertains to the spiritual temperature within God's church.[3]

Apostates are those who profess faith but rebel or fall away from it. They never possessed Christ and eternal life but simply professed faith.[4] Apostates are consistently characterized by two things in the New Testament: false doctrine and ungodly living. Apostates believe wrong and behave wrong. "They profess to know God, but by their deeds they deny Him."[5] Apostates are the fifth column within the visible church.

Some apostates deny the faith and leave the church. Others deny the faith and stay within the church. While both are harmful, those who remain and persist in eroding the foundation of the church of Jesus Christ are worse. We live in days of rampant, surging, encroaching apostasy. The fifth column is firmly entrenched in almost all the major denominations in America today and has overrun most theological seminaries in what is nothing short of a landslide. Every aspect of Christianity is under sustained attack. Doctrinal underpinnings are being challenged and jettisoned at an accelerated pace. We are witnessing a startling departure from the truth on the part of individuals, churches, and even entire denominations. Sound doctrine is under siege.

The rise of modern technology, which has aided the spread of the gospel and the reach of sound biblical teaching, has also given voice to an endless barrage of teaching from those who regularly undercut the truth of Scripture. The blogosphere is fertile ground for shallow, shady, and even satanic teaching that clouds and confuses many believers and provides ammunition for apostates. Gaining a following is easier than ever.

Of course, the church has always been plagued by apostasy but nothing like what we see today. Recently, for example, a professor at a respected Christian college said that Islam and Christianity worship the same God. Of course, this statement is incorrect on its face because the God of Christianity is a triune God (one God in three persons—Father, Son, and Holy Spirit) while Islam denies the deity of Christ. Christianity teaches that Jesus is the only way to God, so if you deny Him, you cannot come to God. The college moved to fire the professor who said God and Allah are the same, which we applaud, but her statement (and the conversation it generated) unveils a growing sentiment that clear biblical doctrine is cloudy, confused, and even contradicted.

Apostasy has been around since the beginning of the church. But could the surge of apostasy over the last few decades be another sign that the coming of the Lord is near? Is the rise of apostasy a harbinger of the end times? Could the church today be on the threshold of that terrible dark period predicted at the end of the age?

TIMES OF THE SIGNS

The key to putting together a puzzle is the picture on top of the box. All the pieces, when fitted together, will look like this picture. The Bible lays out a detailed picture of the end-times template or scenario, which serves as the picture on top of the box. Our world today is looking more and more all the time like that picture. Here are a few of the key puzzle pieces we see fitting into place.

REGATHERING OF THE JEWISH PEOPLE

Many of the end-times prophecies of Scripture hinge in one way or another on the presence of the Jewish people in their ancient homeland. Against all odds, the Jewish people, after almost two thousand years of dispersion, are coming back to their land. Almost 40 percent of the Jewish people have returned, and as Scripture predicts, they are under constant attack or the imminent threat of attack. The modern state of Israel has been rightly called the super-sign of the end times.

RISE OF GLOBALISM

Globalism is another discernible sign of the times. Scripture predicts in many places that the world in the end times will be under the rule of one man.[6] The world will come full circle in the end times. Just as Nimrod ruled the world in the days after the Flood, before people were scattered across the face of the earth, Satan will bring the world back together again under the rule of one man he controls.[7] Globalism, accelerated by technology and an international economy, strikingly foreshadows what Scripture presents.

RATIFICATION OF A PEACE TREATY

According to Scripture, the end times will begin with a peace treaty between the final world ruler (the Antichrist) and the nation of Israel.[8] Other biblical references point toward a brief time of global peace as the end times begin.[9] The global cry today for peace in troubled times points toward where things are headed. The world is anxious to find someone who can bring security and peace to our ravaged planet.

RUMORS OF WARS IN THE MIDDLE EAST

World focus on the Middle East is another sign of the times. The staging ground for many of the events of the end of the age is in this region. The spotlight of the world is on the ravaged Middle East today, just as we should expect if the coming of the Lord is near.

The nations listed in Ezekiel 38:1-7 (including Russia, Iran, and Libya) are all existing nations with the will and desire to attack Israel, just as Ezekiel prophesied over 2,500 years ago.

REBELLION OF APOSTASY

Many other significant signs could be mentioned. Yet one sign of the end times that is often ignored or overlooked is the rise of apostasy, or the final great falling away. Andy Woods writes, "Apostasy is another sign, often taking place right under our noses, which we fail to recognize as a sign of the end. Apostasy is the specific scriptural sign given indicating that the church is nearing the completion of her earthly mission."[10] The New Testament says that the final great apostasy is coming. To understand this future event, we have to turn to 2 Thessalonians 2.

APOSTASY AND THE APOCALYPSE

The apostle Paul's letters to the Thessalonians were written during his second missionary journey during his stay in Corinth.[11] While these epistles address many important topics, their outstanding feature is a focus on the future. They are often called the "eschatological epistles" since the coming of the Lord is mentioned in every chapter.

Second Thessalonians 2 is one of the great prophetic chapters of Scripture. No other chapter in the entire Bible covers the same prophetic ground. To understand this chapter and its content, we have to know a little background. Sometime not long after Paul wrote his first letter to the Thessalonians, teachers arose in the church who were espousing false doctrine. The nature of this particular false teaching was that the Day of the Lord had come and the church was already in the Great Tribulation. The Tribulation or Day of the Lord is the final time of global judgment that precedes the second coming of Christ. Apparently, this false teaching erupted in several forms, one of which was a forged, spurious letter that claimed to be from the apostle Paul. Before straightening this problem out, Paul frames the issue:

> Now concerning the coming of our Lord Jesus Christ and
> our being gathered together to him, we ask you, brothers,
> not to be quickly shaken in mind or alarmed, either by a
> spirit or a spoken word, or a letter seeming to be from us,
> to the effect that the day of the Lord has come.[12]

While it may seem strange to us that the new believers at Thessalonica would entertain the teaching that the end-times Day of the Lord had arrived, we have to remember that they were enduring serious persecution (as reflected in 2 Thessalonians 1). Their current persecution made them susceptible to the notion that the Day of

the Lord had already arrived. It all made sense in light of their circumstances. Nevertheless, the reality of being in the Day of the Lord
raised a major issue. Paul, in his first letter to them (1 Thessalonians),
promised them deliverance from the future time of tribulation by
means of their catching away or Rapture to heaven.[13] If what they
were now being told was true, it would mean either that Paul's previous teaching about their deliverance was wrong or that Paul had been
correct, and they had been left behind.[14] Neither of these prospects
was appealing, and they were seriously shaken "with the impact of a
major earthquake, and they were continuing to feel the disturbing
aftershocks of that report."[15]

The question facing the Thessalonians is whether their present sufferings indicate they had already entered the tribulation
period. Paul's answer to this question is an emphatic no. He tells
the Thessalonians they are not in the Day of the Lord. In order to
drive his answer home, he points to two things that must transpire
before that day can come, which hadn't happened yet: "Let no one
deceive you in any way. For that day will not come, unless the rebellion comes first, and the man of lawlessness is revealed, the son of
destruction."[16] Two things must happen before the end times can
begin: an event must occur (the rebellion) and a person must appear
(the rebel).

Paul's point is clear: because neither of these events had taken
place, the Day of the Lord could not have come. But it will come
someday.

THE APPROACHING APOSTASY
The first event that must come before the final Day of the Lord is
the apostasy, or the rebellion. Paul is saying that the final Day of the
Lord cannot come until there is a widespread departure from the true
faith. Some take the departure here to be a physical departure, or the

Rapture of the church to heaven. While that view has some merit, most expositors believe that this refers to a theological departure or rebellion.[17]

The definite article appears before the word "apostasy" signaling that this is not just any departure from the faith but one that is unique and that the readers apparently knew about. It is *the* apostasy. This final apostasy will entail a large-scale, widespread falling away on the part of those who profess to know God. Some scholars see the apostasy in 2 Thessalonians 2:3 in broader terms, referring to a "world-wide rebellion against authority at the end of the age"—that is, a general uprising against God.[18] While that will certainly occur, in the context of 2 Thessalonians 2:1-3, the apostasy seems to describe a departure on the part of those who profess to know God. John Calvin notes,

> Paul therefore uses the term rebellion or 'apostasy' to mean a treacherous departure from God, not on the part of one person or a few individuals, but such as would spread far among a wide circle of people. Now, nobody can be called an apostate but he who had previously professed to follow Christ and the Gospel. Paul, therefore, is predicting a general rebellion in the visible church.[19]

Referring to 2 Thessalonians 2:3, G. K. Beale says, "The apostasy will not occur primarily in the non-Christian world but rather within the covenant community."[20] Christendom is headed for a great falling away. At the time 2 Thessalonians was written, there were, no doubt, some errors in the church, but there was no widespread apostasy within Christianity in the ordinary sense of the term. The churches were still true to the Lord. Paul is declaring that the Day of the Lord cannot come until there is first a pervasive, global departure from the faith. The Scriptures speak often of this coming apostasy (see the next section, "From Bad to Worse").

In the twenty-first century the situation is entirely different than it was for the Thessalonian church. Today there is certainly widespread apostasy. The sad fact is that there are many who are not preaching the true gospel and moreover are denying the central doctrines of our Christian faith. Many are teaching that Christ is only a man, that He was not born of a virgin, that He was not sinless, that He did not rise from the dead, that salvation is not through His atoning sacrifice, that people can get to heaven other than through Jesus, and that He is not coming again. They deny that the Scriptures are the inerrant, infallible Word of God and decide what parts of the Bible are important and which parts are optional or even outdated. They reject the biblical standards for holy living and accept practices such as homosexual activity, even among church leaders. To a certain degree, apostasy is already here and swelling in strength and intensity.

The second event that must occur before the final Tribulation can begin is the revelation or unveiling of the "man of sin." This man of sin is none other than the final Antichrist. "Man of sin" is one of his many aliases recorded in Scripture. The verses that follow describe the outrageous nature of his sin: "[He] opposes and exalts himself against every so-called god or object of worship, so that he takes his seat in the temple of God, proclaiming himself to be God."[21] The Antichrist's outrageous self-deification will be the final step downward in man's rebellion against the true God.

The relationship between the apostasy and the Antichrist is clear. The final great falling away will prepare the world for the reception of the final Antichrist. John Stott summarizes this well:

What he does is to clarify the order of future events. *The day of the Lord* (2b) cannot be here already, he says, because *that day will not come* until two other things have happened. A certain event must take place, and a certain person must appear. The event he calls *the rebellion* (*apotasia*, "the Great Revolt" JB; "the final rebellion against God" REB) and the person *the man of lawlessness*, the rebel. Although Paul does not call him the "Antichrist," this is evidently who he is. John writes of the expectation of his coming.[22]

Charles Ryrie adds, "It is as though the infidelity of those who profess to be religious will prepare the way and perhaps even furnish the occasion for the final display of revolting against God in the person of the Man of Sin. But the Day of the Lord will not be present until this great apostasy sweeps the earth."[23] As those who profess to know the truth turn wholesale from it, they will embrace the ultimate lie—worshiping a man as God.

FROM BAD TO WORSE

A handful of New Testament passages tell us that apostasy will be one of the defining characteristics of the last days. Each of the following passages provides important insight into the nature of apostasy in the last days.

I TIMOTHY 4:1-3

First Timothy 4:1 states, "The Spirit explicitly says that in later times some will fall away from the faith, paying attention to deceitful spirits and doctrines of demons."

The time frame of when this apostasy will occur is defined as "later times." The word "later" or "latter" indicates that these times were still future when Paul wrote this epistle. The word used here for "times" is the Greek word *kairois*. It refers to seasons or shorter segments of time. It is plural to indicate that there will be more than one of them—that is, these times of apostasy will recur intermittently throughout the church age.[24]

2 TIMOTHY 3:1-13

This extended passage contains some of the final words of the apostle Paul—words of warning. In these verses, Paul catalogs nineteen characteristics that will prevail during various seasons throughout the last days of the church. These conditions will worsen as the church age progresses. We will look at this passage in more detail in chapter 6.

2 PETER 2:1-22; 3:3-6

In 2 Peter 2:1-22, the apostle writes a lengthy diatribe against apostates that he predicts will come into the church to deceive God's people and deny and disobey the truth. Second Peter 2:1-2 says, "False prophets also arose among the people, just as there will also be false teachers among you, who will secretly introduce destructive heresies, even denying the Master who bought them, bringing swift destruction upon themselves. Many will follow their sensuality, and because of them the way of the truth will be maligned."

In 2 Peter 3:3-4, Peter continues, "Know this first of all, that in the last days mockers will come with their mocking, following after their own lusts, and saying, 'Where is the promise of His coming?'" Peter says apostates will even deny the second coming of Christ.

JUDE 1:1-25

Jude, a half-brother of Jesus, writes his entire brief epistle as a warning that the apostates Peter had warned about a few years earlier have already arrived, worming their way into the church. I (Mark) have always found it interesting that the little epistle of Jude, which is the only book in the Bible devoted exclusively to apostasy, is right before the book of Revelation. In many ways, Jude serves as the vestibule or foyer for the book of Revelation by revealing what the visible, professing church will be like in the days before the events of Revelation unfold.

SIGN OF THE TIMES?

In Scripture, apostasy possesses a "specific eschatological orientation."[25] The apostasy we see swelling today is all headed toward the final, full-blown falling away predicted in 2 Thessalonians 2:3, which Scripture says will break out as the end times begin to unfold. Many today are expecting a great global revival as the end nears. Of course, that's possible, and we hope and pray it will come, but John Phillips gives some helpful biblical perspective:

> The river of apostasy is rising today. The "perilous times" of which Paul wrote are upon us. Soon the river will overflow its banks as all the tributaries of delusion and deception join the mainstream. When it reaches flood level, that river will inundate the earth in the final apostasy, which is the enthronement of the Devil's messiah as this world's god and king. . . . Some think we can look for a worldwide spiritual awakening before the Rapture of the church, but this passage in 2 Thessalonians indicates the opposite; a worldwide departure from the faith can be expected. God might indeed send a revival before He calls home the church, but the Scriptures do not prophesy one.[26]

Deepening apostasy is a sign of the times. Apostasy to some degree has always been within the church, but a future, distinct period of moral darkness and spiritual deception is coming. There is no doubt today that deepening deception and surging apostasy are upon us. What we see in the visible church today is nothing short of shocking.

We are witnessing the increase and intensification of apostasy we should expect if the coming of Christ is near. While things could always get worse, we find it difficult to believe that they could get much worse than the theological and moral malaise we have witnessed in the last fifty years, and especially the last decade. We seem to be on the leading edge of the final apostasy, and as the end nears, the battle will intensify.

In case you think we're overreacting or are alone in our assessment of apostasy as a sign of the end times, here are some quotes from well-known, respected pastors and prophecy teachers who share this viewpoint.

John Walvoord, former president of Dallas Theological Seminary, in his book *The Church in Prophecy*, believes what we see today is a sign of the times:

> The increment of evil, the growth of hypocrisy, selfishness, and unbelief within the bounds of professing Christendom are according to Scripture signs of the approaching end of the age. Though there are thousands of faithful congregations and many pious souls still bearing a faithful testimony to Christ in our modern day, it is hardly true that the majority of Christendom is bearing a true testimony. It is the exception rather than the rule for the great fundamentals of the church to ring from the pulpit and for the pew to manifest the transforming grace of God in life and sacrificial devotion. In a word, the last days of the church on earth are days of apostasy, theologically and morally, days of unbelief, and days that will culminate in divine judgment.[27]

Walvoord concludes, "The Scriptures predict that there will be a growing apostasy or departure from the Lord as the church age progresses, and its increase can be understood as a general indication that the Rapture itself is near."[28]

J. Dwight Pentecost, a noted authority on Bible prophecy, states,

> Abundant evidence on every hand shows that men are departing from the faith. Not only do they doubt the Word; they openly reject it. This phenomenon has never been as prevalent as today. In the period of church history known as the Dark Ages, men were ignorant of the truth; but never was there an age when men openly denied and repudiated the truth. This open, deliberate, willful repudiation of the truth of the Bible is described in Scripture as one of the major characteristics of the last days of the church on earth.[29]

John Harold Ockenga was a leading figure of American evangelicalism in the mid-twentieth century. He pastored Park Street Church in Boston and helped found Fuller Seminary and Gordon-Conwell Theological Seminary. Commenting on apostasy as a sign of the times, he said, "In this present great apostasy from New Testament Christianity we could see a sign which will warrant us in believing that Christ's coming may not be far away. There has always been some measure of apostasy and at times that apostasy has been great, but not as it has been in the last fifty years."[30]

Donald Grey Barnhouse, the great Presbyterian pastor, said, "Watch for such an apostasy, says Paul; that will be the sign of the day of the Lord. Well, it is possible that we may be seeing the first stages of such apostasy in our day. If ever there was a turning away from the truth, it is in our day. . . . But we're seeing the tip of the iceberg."[31]

John Horsch, writing back in the early part of the twentieth century, said,

The apostasy that is evident on every hand is an unmistakable sign of the times. It should arouse believing Christendom from its lethargy and listlessness to a realization of conditions as they are. In consequence of the apostasy the church finds itself today face to face with a crisis such as it has never passed through in its history.[32]

These are the last days of apostasy for the church. We are not yet in the final, great falling away that will immediately presage the arrival of the end times, but we are on the vanguard.

In the pages to come we want to get more specific about some of the areas where apostasy is accelerating and give practical, hopeful encouragement that will help us wake up and stand up and run our leg of the race faithfully, passing the baton intact to the next generation if our Lord doesn't come first.

CHAPTER 3

FAITH OF OUR FATHERS

As for you, speak the things which are fitting for sound doctrine.

TITUS 2:1

We live in a world where feelings trump rational thought, where a statement may be considered "true" not because it actually is but simply because it feels right or because someone wants it to be true. Take any biblical truth—whether concerning God's sovereignty, the reality of eternal punishment, or marriage between a man and a woman only—and if it clashes with someone's personal belief or desire for what reality should be, it is simply redefined or dismissed altogether. The prevailing spirit of the age is one where individuals can now craft their own truth-world, one that fits them and their perception of reality.

It is in this sense that humans have essentially crowned themselves little gods. And as fantastical as that may sound, it's how most people practically function. We take truth, doctrine, and moral decisions into our own hands and fall for the deception our first parents embraced in the Garden. Questioning the clearly revealed will and Word of God, Adam and Eve believed that personal fulfillment and happiness lay somewhere outside their loving Father's provision. And so, drifting from His truth and plan, they bit the bait and bought the lie, becoming "like God."[1]

And here we are.

Thousands of years later, we still think we can deviate from God's Word and somehow not die. The intoxicating lure of being in charge of our own lives and of scriptwriting our own reality is often a temptation too pleasurable to resist. But it is only when we acknowledge that there is a God and we're not Him that our minds can clear and we can begin enjoying a satisfying relationship with our Creator. Ours is not a blind faith, and when we believe without reason, we are easily persuaded away from God's truth by a more promising or persuasive argument.

So it brings us to the question: Why do you believe what you believe? The question is not as much about evidence as it is about *impetus*. In other words, what factors motivate you toward acceptance and ownership of a particular belief? When you say you believe a biblical truth, where does that belief come from? Some might say:

> My parents taught it to me.
> It's what my pastor believes.
> I read it in a Christian book.
> A famous Christian said it.
> It just feels right.
> It's what I've always believed.
> It gives me comfort to believe it.
> It makes me happy.
> It seems more inclusive.

> I can't imagine God behaving otherwise.
> I seriously studied it.
> It's in the Bible.

When you look at the sources of our faith and why we choose to embrace a certain doctrine or truth as our own, it becomes clear that only one source is 100 percent reliable. The bottom line of any belief is that if it can't be backed up by Scripture, it's nothing more than wishful thinking, speculation, or theory. So then, how exactly is belief formed? What is it? Does having a conviction really matter anymore? And if so, why?

According to the Bible, biblical belief is more than intellectual agreement. It's more than just a spiritual nodding of the head. Rather, it occurs when both the mind and the will engage God's truth. Volition is involved, as faith is a conscious choice. Belief connects with the spirit. And that belief then informs and influences a person's thinking, focusing the lens through which he or she sees God, life, others, the world, and reality itself. That kind of faith, stemming from Scripture, gives us a discernment that helps us navigate the confusing, contradictory world in which we live.

Some today argue, "What difference does it make what you believe as long as you love God and others? Aren't those the greatest commandments?" Yes, those are the greatest commandments, but if that were the sum total of all God wanted us to know, believe, and do, the sixty-six books of the Bible would be reduced to two verses. There is a greatest commandment, but it in no way diminishes our responsibility to all the others. Besides, who is this God we are commanded to love with all our heart? What do we know about Him? What has He done? What is He like?

It is not possible to effectively love or worship a God about whom we know nothing. Further, the more we know about this great God, the more we are drawn into deeper love for and worship of Him. Therefore, we must encounter truth about Him, otherwise our love has no real object, and we end up once again with a god manufactured in our own minds.

If we truly believe all of the Bible is divinely inspired, then *every word* of it is, as Paul wrote, "useful to teach us what is true and to make us realize what is wrong in our lives. It corrects us when we are wrong and teaches us to do what is right. God uses it to prepare and equip his people to do every good work."[2]

The beauty of this is that it means God intends for us to go beyond merely "savoring the Psalms." He also invites us to dive into Deuteronomy, study 2 Timothy, and read Revelation. It means we care about 2 Chronicles as well as Colossians. How tragic that Christians often treat books of the Bible like outdated clothes in the closet: "I don't like that one anymore. This one doesn't fit me. It's old, out of season, or no longer in fashion. No one is wearing that style anymore."

But although truth may indeed go "out of style" in society, God and His Word never change. Therefore, those who believe His truth recognize that they will, at times, become unpopular or even hated as their beliefs race toward a head-on collision with culture. According to Jesus, this is part of discipleship and to be expected.[3]

WHY TRUTH MATTERS

Have you noticed how people today are selective about which parts of the Bible they accept as historical, true, relevant, and necessary for life in the twenty-first century? Even in some mainline denominations, many are choosing to go with the "basics of the faith," ignoring, dismissing, or outright denying the rest of God's Word as optional or even, as popular author Rob Bell has suggested, "irrelevant" to today's culture.[4] Sort of like passing over the pickled okra at the salad bar, there is a growing movement among Christianized millennials toward a *figurative* rather than literal understanding of the Bible. Among their discussions is a reimagining of gender, the Genesis creation account, marriage and divorce, the role of women in the church, and homosexuality.[5]

This is definitely not your father's faith. Nor is it Paul's.

But it's a fair question to ask: How much does the *content* of our faith really matter? Is there really only one faith to which we should all subscribe? Or are there just a few core truths, with the rest of it being whatever we want to believe?

One way to address this issue is to remember that truth doesn't exist in a vacuum. We live in a world where there is both good and evil, virtue and vice. There is a God and an actual devil, and there is a sinful nature inside each of us that resists God and rebels against Him. Satan, self, and a planet saturated with sin together create an environment where lies and evil are as plentiful as the air we breathe:

> Lies about God, humanity, happiness, and the afterlife
> Theories of origins birthed in darkened minds and intellects devoid of truth or the willingness to entertain it
> Lies about what and who we are as humans
> Purposeful deceptions about gender, strategically planted in our collective consciousness by the great deceiver himself

Breathing this atmosphere sometimes makes it difficult to distinguish between the truth, half-truths, and full-blown lies. Every day, we walk through a minefield of falsehood. This is why the author of Hebrews wrote that mature believers are those "who because of practice have their senses trained to discern good and evil."[6] Growing in the grace and knowledge of our Lord and Savior is part of what safely maneuvers us through that minefield.[7] Simply put, understanding and believing God's truth enables us to discern the distinction between the truth and Satan's subtle lies.[8]

But that's not all. Sound doctrine does much more for you:

> It nourishes you in the faith.[9]
> It keeps you true to God when, in the last days, people downplay the importance of biblical teaching, even dismissing and denying it.[10]
> It helps you to encourage other believers in the truth and to refute those who blatantly contradict Scripture.[11]

For example, in His encounter with the Samaritan woman, Jesus not only exposes and corrects her flawed theology but He also enlightens her understanding regarding the nature of true worship:

You Samaritans know very little about the one you worship, while we Jews know all about him, for salvation comes through the Jews. But the time is coming—indeed it's here now—when true worshipers will worship the Father in spirit and in truth. The Father is looking for those who will worship him that way. For God is Spirit, so those who worship him must worship in spirit and in truth.[12]

Jesus isn't afraid of offending this woman or hurting her feelings, because He knows that's not what love is or how it operates. Instead, He genuinely cares for her and wants her very best; therefore, He communicates the truth in a way that makes sense to her, even though it may be a bit uncomfortable in spots.

Think about it. God conceived of and created not only the human body but also the mind and the spirit.[13] So it stands to reason that He would know how they best operate, how they connect with Him, and how they bring Him maximum glory. Jesus is teaching here that worshiping in spirit cannot be divorced from the knowledge of the truth. Logically and chronologically, true worship must begin with the revelation of God's truth to our minds. Mindless worship, therefore, is an oxymoron. Being spiritually or emotionally caught up in worship requires some previous knowledge of the One you are worshiping. Otherwise it is nothing more than an imaginative exercise, a fantasy of faith. Authentic worship begins with *knowing* something about God. So knowledge of God (sound teaching) naturally leads to worshiping God, and we should never experience one without the other.

God made us to *know*. He designed our minds to reason, wonder, inquire, explore, and comprehend. As a result, the Christian faith is more than just wishing, hoping, or believing. It involves a level of intellectual confidence in the truth God has revealed, from general revelation (creation and conscience) to special revelation (Christ and Scripture).[14] Therefore, belief based on knowledge about God and His revealed truth is what actually *enables* us to enter into worship and become what Jesus calls a "true worshiper."[15] Otherwise we may worship a false image of God, which is what the Bible calls idolatry. It cheats us out of the full experience of enjoying who He really is![16]

Paul writes,

Though we walk in the flesh, we do not war according to the flesh, for the weapons of our warfare are not of the flesh, but divinely powerful for the destruction of fortresses. We are destroying speculations and every lofty thing raised up against the knowledge of God, and we are taking every thought captive to the obedience of Christ.[17]

What are these "fortresses" Paul speaks about here? A fortress is a stronghold, a place of strength. Paul identifies them here as "speculations," which are human (or demonically inspired) thoughts, ideas, beliefs, theories, opinions, philosophies, doctrines, and so on—anything that contrasts with the true knowledge of God as found in Scripture. Paul includes "every lofty thing," meaning those ideas or philosophies that are proposed or presented as wise, learned, established, scientific, or superior to the Word.

Paul calls them "fortresses" because they are mental and spiritual strongholds that capture our thinking concerning God, truth, and life. They take our thoughts captive, enslaving them into false patterns of thinking. But the Christian influenced by the Word can rescue those thoughts by exposing the lies for what they really are. Thus we turn the tables on Satan's strategies, taking those thoughts captive to the obedience of Christ.

A few years ago, I (Jeff) wrote a book about the doctrine of the sin nature—what it is, how it operates, and how we can overcome it. Using the metaphor of zombies, I portrayed the sin nature as the "living dead" within that longs to consume us. As a result, I was invited to speak and exhibit my book at an international zombie convention in Seattle. Out of the over seven thousand zombie and horror movie enthusiasts in attendance, several hundred came to hear me speak. Perhaps they were curious what a Christian author could possibly say at a zombie convention.

The moderator of the session (John) was an avowed atheist. And just to mock me and ridicule my faith, he wore a priest's collar during the entire interview. As we both took the stage, he introduced me this way: "Author Jeff Kinley will now tell us more about his zombie book, and also I'm sure a little bit about his imaginary friend . . . *God.*"

Following that introduction, he began firing question after

question, attacking both the church and Christianity with an air of superiority and self-righteousness (and with some well-chosen expletives thrown in). Some of what he said about the state of the church I agreed with. But with every "lofty thing" and "speculation" he shot my way, I countered with reasonable truth from Scripture. Finally, frustrated that his antagonistic arguments were getting him nowhere (*and* steadily losing his credibility with the audience), he threw up his hands and asked, "Okay, so enough about the book. Just answer me this. Why would a guy like you ever get into this 'Jesus thing' in the first place?"

I looked at him, amazed, thinking, *Did I hear him correctly? Did he really just ask me to share my Christian testimony with all these people?*

I thanked God for His sovereignty and ability to overrule the futile plans of men. I told my story of coming to faith in Christ and how He still helps me overcome my personal zombie within (sin nature). Afterward many people stayed around to ask questions and purchase books, so I didn't get to say good-bye to John. However, later that afternoon, I paid him a visit at his booth (he was a newspaper journalist turned comic book writer). I offered him a signed copy of my book, and he gratefully accepted. As I turned to leave, he offered an unexpected apology.

"Hey, I'm sorry if I was a little too hard on you up there today."

I smiled and gave him a firm handshake.

We parted as friends.

Fortunately that day my knowledge of Scripture helped me destroy human speculations and philosophies. Had I not been "nourished on the words of faith and of sound doctrine," John and his arguments could have eaten me for lunch . . . like a *zombie!*

Most of the spiritual battles we face don't happen on a stage in front of hundreds of people but out there in the real world—in the classroom, at work, or with neighbors, friends, or even family. Much of the time our battleground is more hidden, taking place in the privacy of our own minds. And I don't always win those skirmishes. Sometimes I know the truth but fail to follow it. Other times I rationalize it for my own selfish benefit.

So knowing Scripture is only half the battle. Like Jesus, when tempted by Satan's deceptions, we have to go beyond merely quoting the truth to *obeying* it.[18]

But with all this talk about knowledge and sound doctrine, you might think, *Wait a minute. Didn't Paul say "knowledge puffs up, but love is really what edifies"?*[19] That's absolutely true. Knowledge, when not accompanied by humility, obedience, love, and worship, can easily birth pride in us. Often when people know something others don't, they feel superior and use that knowledge to put others down while at the same time exalting themselves. This is true of those who reject God's revelation about creation, replacing it with their own theories. Paul says these people became "futile in their speculations, and their *foolish* [literally 'unintelligent' or 'without understanding'] heart was darkened." The result is that "professing to be wise, they became fools."[20]

But Christians can also fall prey to this type of arrogance. When we pursue knowledge for knowledge's sake or when we fail to apply what God's Word reveals to us, we are setting ourselves up to become proud and bloated. That's why we must always receive God's truth with humility, responding with love and worship toward Him. Real knowledge of God is far more than fact gathering. Doctrine isn't simply a systematic collection of truths or storing up "Bible ammunition." No, the *Word* of God always leads us to the *person* of God. It is never an end unto itself. Truth comes *from* God *to* us in order that we may respond accordingly and live that truth back to God. "For from Him and through Him and to Him are all things. To Him be the glory forever. Amen."[21]

This is the purpose of all knowledge and sound doctrine. It's why Paul writes to the Philippians,

This is my prayer: that your love may abound more and more in *knowledge* and depth of insight, *so that* you may be able to discern what is best and may be pure and blameless for the day of Christ, filled with the fruit of righteousness that comes through Jesus Christ—to the glory and praise of God.[22]

For the Colossians, he prays,

For this reason also, since the day we heard of it, we have not ceased to pray for you and to ask that you may be filled [influenced] with the *knowledge* of His will in all spiritual wisdom and understanding, *so that* you will walk in a manner worthy of the Lord, to please Him in all respects, bearing fruit in every good work and *increasing in the knowledge of God.*[23]

Jesus even defined "eternal life" itself as *knowing* the Father: "This is eternal life, that they may know You, the only true God, and Jesus Christ whom You have sent."[24]

Biblical knowledge is meant to be both intellectual *and* experiential.[25] It's a package deal—two sides to the same coin and meant to be enjoyed together. Knowledge without response is like an incomplete sentence or a song without a chorus. Information about God must always lead to an intimacy with Him. It's as much true now as it will one day be in heaven, when our intimacy with God will be exponentially enhanced by a more complete knowledge of Him.[26]

Can you see how growing in your knowledge of God and His Word is essential to becoming mature and complete in your faith?[27]

CHRISTIAN CONTENDERS

So how do we apply this knowledge as it relates to the coming apostasy and the false doctrine currently swirling around us? It's important to note that though the purity of the Christian faith has been preserved and passed down for two thousand years, as history records, it hasn't always been a smooth handoff. There have been seasons and even centuries where the truth taught in the church was altered, modified, and even denied, all in the name of God. It took courageous men of faith like Martin Luther, John Calvin, and Ulrich Zwingli calling the church *out* and *back* to her scriptural roots. And in doing so, they also called her *up*, toward godliness and maturity in Christ. This is the faith we are commanded to defend. In Jude's letter we read, "Beloved, while I was making every effort to write you about our common salvation, I felt the necessity to write to you appealing that you *contend earnestly for the faith* which was once for all handed down to the saints."[28]

"The faith" Jude refers to is the body of truth found in Scripture. This truth is not a fluid, ongoing revelation but rather one that was "once for all" delivered to God's people. This is one reason why we reject so-called visions and supposed visits to heaven claiming new revelation not found in Scripture. The Christian faith has been entrusted to *us*, deposited into our hearts and minds. God is counting on us to "guard what has been entrusted" to us and to "hold on to the pattern of wholesome teaching" we have learned.[29] Paul exhorted Timothy, "Through the power of the Holy Spirit who lives within us, *carefully guard* the precious truth that has been *entrusted* to you."[30]

But exactly why would Jude call us to vigorously contend for the faith? And why would Paul strongly exhort us to guard that faith?

Why does Scripture urge us to fight for the truth? Simple: "Certain persons have crept in unnoticed, those who were long beforehand marked out for this condemnation, ungodly persons who turn the grace of our God into licentiousness and deny our only Master and Lord, Jesus Christ."[31]

Plainly put—false teachers. Wolves disguised as sheep. Counterfeits. *Apostates.*

It's not a topic you hear much about in the church today, even though the Bible addresses the subject repeatedly and prophetically. But why not? Why does theology seem so important to Jude and Paul? Why does God take the truth so seriously? Shouldn't we stick to everyday issues, problems, and "practical applications" for our lives?

This is where we need a paradigm shift in the church. According to Jesus and the New Testament writers, theology and doctrine *are* practical matters. And they are definitely not just for preachers, theologians, and "Bible nerds." The Word of God was written for the common person. God wants every one of His children to read and comprehend His Word.

Besides, even the youngest believer knows some theology and doctrine. When you say, "I believe Jesus died on the cross for me to take away my sin," *that's* doctrine and theology.[32] Theology is the study of God, and doctrine simply refers to a system of teaching or a body of belief. Our faith is not primarily a feeling. It is *belief* based on fact. It's more about grounded assurance than personal philosophy. Like other disciplines such as math or science, we can't simply make up facts or imagine things about God and then base our lives on those thoughts. To do so is to make a radical departure from Scripture and the historical beliefs of the early church. Instead, we always must calibrate our thoughts about God to biblical truth, regardless of contemporary or popular thinking, faith fads, or theological trends. That's because *true* knowledge begins with God.[33]

You wouldn't adamantly assert that 2 + 2 = 73 or that the sun revolves around the earth, even if you "believed it with all your heart." That's because you obviously know those things aren't true. And because you're a thinking person, you also know that merely saying something doesn't somehow make it true or real. Even *believing* something doesn't make it true. It's either true or not, independent of our belief in it.

Another reason truth is so critical to our faith is that it reflects the character and nature of God. God is true, and His Word is truth.[34] All truth is His. So when we pursue, discover, believe, and live out His truth, we honor Him and exalt His character.

Sound doctrine is also important to us because believing something that is *un*true about God is idolatry. We typically step into this trap when we believe or entertain a subtle or blatant lie about God. This is essentially substituting biblical truth about Him with our own. Therefore, what we believe about God, Christ, heaven, and the Christian life is not elective but essential. To be apathetic about belief confines us to a state of immaturity and destines us for spiritual impotence. And no disciple of Christ wants that.

We must also allow Scripture to inform and influence our beliefs, because our thinking is inherently limited and flawed. God understands this, so the Holy Spirit in us partners with the Word of God, illuminating His truth and moving us toward maturity in our thinking, character, and behavior.[35]

Lastly, sound doctrine shields us against Satan's deceptive lies and half-truths. The more truth we know and personally engage, the more protected we will be in the midst of spiritual warfare. This prevents us from being deceived by the devil's many schemes.[36] If we are to effectively contend for the faith in this world, we must be men and women who know *what* and *why* we believe. This is God's call on every Christian.[37]

DETECTING COUNTERFEITS

Doctrinal discernment is a spiritual life skill you learn over time, not in a single sermon or book. It acts like perpetual faith radar, sounding an internal alarm whenever Scripture is being misrepresented or compromised.

Imagine for a moment you were training to become a pilot. You would expect to log hundreds of hours in classes and receive personal instruction from an experienced pilot, right? Then there would be many hours of in-flight training and multiple test runs long before you ever took a solo flight. You wouldn't assume you could fly a fighter jet just because you watched *Top Gun* a few times! You wouldn't buy a sweatshirt that says, "Harvard Law School" and then expect to argue a case before a judge and jury, would you?

However, that's pretty close to what happened in the case of a teenager named Frank Abagnale. Devastated by his parents' divorce in 1963, Frank channeled his disappointment and frustration by birthing an elaborate con scheme, successfully posing as an airline pilot. He also masqueraded as a lawyer and even a doctor. All along the way, Abagnale funded his ruse by forging checks, which soon totaled millions of dollars. Eventually caught, he spent years in French, Swiss, and American prisons before being offered a chance to work for the FBI's Bank Fraud Division. His story was so incredible it was adapted into a movie called *Catch Me If You Can*, starring Tom Hanks and Leonardo DiCaprio. But even though people called Frank Abagnale "Captain" and "Doctor," he was neither. He was in reality an imposter. A deceiver. A fake. And he knew all along what he was doing.

Unfortunately, many today misrepresent God and Scripture, all the while believing they're speaking the truth. There are, to be sure, those who intentionally deceive others for power and profit. Other false teachers are sincere and confident, even though what they spout is pure heresy. But sincerity is no substitute for biblical integrity. From online webcasts, blogs, and television appearances to church pulpits and Barnes & Noble bookshelves, apostasy by any other name smells just as rotten.

That may sound a bit harsh and restrictive, maybe even confining or narrow-minded. If it sounds this way, it's because it is.

Read Jesus' words in Matthew 7:13-14: "You can enter God's Kingdom only through the narrow gate. The highway to hell is broad, and its gate is wide for the many who choose that way. But the gateway to life is very narrow and the road is difficult, and only a few ever find it" (NLT).

Interestingly enough, the Lord's very next words warn about false teachers: "Beware of false prophets who come disguised as harmless sheep but are really vicious wolves. You can identify them by their fruit, that is, by the way they act."[38]

Without a clear understanding of Scripture and a constant calibration of our hearts and minds to God's Word, the truth in us can fade and even morph to accommodate our feelings or the changing times. So how can the average Christian tell the difference between counterfeit truth and the real thing? How can you know if a pastor, teacher, speaker, blogger, or author is speaking the truth about God and the Bible? How can you detect false doctrine?

The good news is that we can know whose message is false and whose isn't, even when the teachers are all dressed like us sheep. We do this by examining their teachings and the fruit of their ministries. Does what they say square up with the Word? Does it harmonize with a historical understanding of Bible doctrine? What do their ministries generally produce—disciples of Jesus or spiritual "groupies"? Even someone's personal testimony must be authenticated by Scripture.

This isn't to say any of us fully understands all that happened at the moment of salvation or that we're able to eloquently articulate it. But as we grow, we begin to grasp the deep well of truth behind something as simple as trusting Christ for salvation. Otherwise, someone can claim almost anything about God or a personal experience with Him, and unless you've trained your mind, you can easily be misled or mistaught by persuasive words, emotion, and a compelling presentation. But when you are a student of the Bible, God's thoughts over time become embedded in your thinking. Scripture then acts like a "truth filtering system," sifting out Satan's clever lies. This kind of discernment is further developed and sharpened by walking the narrow road in the companionship of the One who personifies Truth.[39]

For five years, I (Jeff) lived in Mobile, Alabama, where I served as student pastor at a local church. During that time, we held youth events on the USS *Alabama*, a World War II battleship. Permanently docked in Mobile Bay, the *Alabama* is one of that state's top tourist attractions. We rented out the entire ship, and our students had fun exploring its many features, as well as enjoying some healthy competition, after which I would speak on spiritual warfare. However, during one of our visits, a girl began complaining of being seasick.

"It's all the rocking back and forth of the ship," she said. "I don't know how much more I can take."

In my attempt to calm her down, I carefully explained that the *Alabama* wasn't really rocking back and forth as she had thought. The 42,000-ton ship's hull was securely resting on the bottom of Mobile Bay, permanently anchored in concrete. The ship wasn't actually rocking at all. It was all in her mind.

Believer, your Bible is an immovable bedrock of truth, anchored in God Himself. And though your senses may make you feel like its truth is rocking back and forth, it nevertheless remains solid and eternal.

Martin Luther purportedly wrote,

Feelings come and feelings go,
And feelings are deceiving;
My warrant is the Word of God—
Naught else is worth believing.
Though all my heart should feel condemned
For want of some sweet token,
There is One greater than my heart
Whose Word cannot be broken.
I'll trust in God's unchanging Word
Till soul and body sever,
For, though all things shall pass away,
His Word shall stand forever!

Rest assured. Despite what culture or popular Christian thought may propose, God's truth does not change, progress, or emerge. And though it's not your job to correct the entire world regarding false teaching or to become the "doctrine police," you are still called to stand for and proclaim what is true, and even when necessary to expose false teaching and heresy.[40] Always ask, "What does the Bible say?" not "Does it make me feel good, happy, or accepted by others?" Evaluate others' truth claims, and trace your own beliefs back to Scripture.[41] This is your "true north," your compass in a confusing culture, your immovable bedrock in an ever-raging storm.[42]

CHAPTER 4

CULTURE OF COMPROMISE

One of the best-known tabletop games is Jenga. In this game of skill, wooden rectangles are stacked together to construct a tower. Players take turns removing one of the rectangles without causing the tower to fall. As blocks are removed, they are placed on top of the tower, so the structure gets progressively taller and less stable. Finally, someone pulls out a block, and the whole structure collapses and falls apart all over the table.

Many in the church today are playing theological Jenga. They're pulling out one doctrinal or moral truth after another, leaving gaping holes as the citadel of the faith grows less and less stable. But like a game of Jenga, eventually one key block is removed, and the structure can no longer stand. The whole thing collapses in a jumbled pile. Of course, no human opposition or distortion of the truth can ever bring down God's tower of truth, but in human terms, the visible church of Jesus Christ is weakening before our eyes.

The compromises we see today in the professing church are both doctrinal and moral. The doctrinal foundations of the faith—such as the inspiration and sufficiency of the Scriptures, the virgin birth of Jesus, the deity of Christ, forgiveness by grace alone through faith alone in Christ alone, and the literal, visible return of Jesus to earth— are no longer considered essential and in many cases are viewed as detrimental to progress. I'm reminded of a story from the ministry of Billy Graham. At the close of his early Los Angeles Crusade, his ministry and preaching was described in *Time* magazine by an Episcopalian rector, who was quoted as saying, "I believe he's putting the church back 50 years." At the ministers' breakfast during the closing week of the crusade, Graham, who rarely responded to his critics, said, "I'm afraid I've failed. I had hoped to put the church back 2,000 years."[1]

Along with the doctrinal departure from the truth, moral standards are being pulled out one after another like Jenga blocks. Francis Schaeffer pointed out this danger years ago: "If our reflex action is always accommodation regardless of the centrality of the truth involved, there is something wrong."[2]

William Booth (1829–1912), who founded the Salvation Army, was a passionate follower of Jesus Christ. On the eve of the twentieth century, Booth predicted that the gospel would not fare well in the new century. He predicted that by the end of the twentieth century, many in the church would be preaching

> Christianity without Christ,
> Forgiveness without repentance,
> Salvation without regeneration, and
> Heaven without hell.

Booth's words seem prophetic. That's exactly where we find ourselves today. As the saying goes, "The living faith of the dead has become the dead faith of the living." We see this all around us. Compromise has sucked the life out of the living faith. Many church-goers yawn today over the truths for which their forefathers shed blood and even died.

Recent polls disclose that 70 percent of Americans with a religious affiliation say that many religions—not just their own—can lead to salvation and eternal life, while 57 percent of evangelical regular church attenders believe that many religions can bring salvation.[3] These statistics represent an unprecedented sea change in opinion. They show that the greatest danger to the church today is not humanism, paganism, atheism, or agnosticism. The greatest danger is not increasing hostility against our faith from the culture. Our greatest danger is apostasy on the inside, arising from false teachers—theological liberals who deny and distort biblical doctrine and lead others down the same path.

Christians often fear what's happening in our culture. We fear what the government may do to our churches, and that concern is certainly not without justification. Yet we need to remember that in Revelation 2:5, it wasn't Caesar who would come close the doors of the church; it was Jesus Christ. Jesus would close the doors and vacate the premises. Jesus told the church at Ephesus that He would remove the lampstand of the church. He would pull the plug and turn out the lights. We mourn a decaying culture, and rightly so, but the greatest danger to our churches and to each of us individually is falling away from the truth of God's Word. As Vance Havner once said, "The biggest danger to the church is not woodpeckers on the outside, but termites on the inside." The termites of compromise gradually gnaw away at the insides of the church and individual lives, leaving empty shells behind.

Many today are openly, even militantly, against the truth, but others' stances are much more murky. Trying to discern their positions on key theological or moral issues is like nailing Jell-O to the wall. Their approach is akin to a theological smorgasbord. As I heard someone say recently, "Vague is now vogue." Yet either way, the church is now caving to pressure from the world.[4] How did we get here? Why is this happening? How do we regain our footing in a culture of downward-sliding values?

TWO KINDS OF COMPROMISE

For many today, compromise is easy. They have no problem compromising on many things, even essential Christian beliefs and morals. For others, *compromise* is a dirty word. In their view, nothing worthwhile should ever be compromised. The truth, it appears, lies in the middle of these extremes. Not all compromise is bad. Broadly speaking, there are two kinds of compromise—wise and worldly. Wise compromise is an attempt to find a way between two extremes. It gives up personal preferences and selfish desires for the sake of unity and peace. Wise compromise is good. We compromise all the time in marriage, family, business, and even politics. No one can have everything their way all the time. Many things in life can be compromised without violating any essential principle. Biblical submission—a willingness to yield to others, a lack of self-centeredness, and a concern with what others think—is a form of wise compromise.

Worldly compromise, on the other hand, is bad. It backs away from essential moral principles. It surrenders truth to error, morality to immorality, and good to evil. That's what's happening in many churches and entire denominations today. A.W. Tozer observes, "The blessing of God is promised to the peacemaker, but the religious negotiator had better watch his step. . . . Darkness and light can never be brought together by talk. Some things are not negotiable."[5]

The Old Testament prophet Daniel is an apt illustration for the balance between wise and worldly compromise. He and some of the other youth from the Jewish nobility were deported from Jerusalem to Babylon by King Nebuchadnezzar. Through his assistants, Nebuchadnezzar instituted a program to fully assimilate these young Israelites into Babylonian life and culture. The plan was to change their language, education, names, and diet. Daniel and his friends wisely agreed to many of the changes. They agreed to learn a new language. (After all, they needed to know the language of Babylon to get along.) They agreed to the three years of advanced education that probably involved mathematics, astrology, astronomy, and agriculture. They even agreed to change their names. Nothing in the law prevented them from taking Babylonian names. But when it came to the matter of diet, they refused to change.[6] Why? Because God had given clear dietary restrictions in the law. The food Nebuchadnezzar presented to them had been offered to idols as a sacrifice and violated the proscriptions in the law. That's where Daniel and his friends drew the line. Daniel would not change, compromise, or concede—even in the face of death. He had convictions based on God's Word. There's an old saying: "Great doors swing on small hinges." Daniel's refusal to compromise God's truth was the small hinge on which the great door of his life would swing.

Years ago, G. K. Chesterton made this powerful statement: "The object of opening the mind, as of opening the mouth, is to shut it again on something solid." Those who have trusted in the gospel—the Good News of Jesus Christ—have closed their minds on the solid truth that He is God in human flesh who provides the only way to God the Father and that life must be ordered according to God's

Word, the Bible. These convictions can never be compromised. We can compromise on many things in life, and we are wise to do so, but we are not to be open minded when it comes to the gospel and its implications for daily life.

In the musical *Fiddler on the Roof*, Tevye is a loving father who is confronted, one at a time, with things his children want to do that displease him. He at first denies them, but when he is alone, he begins to weigh both sides of the issue. He says to himself, "On the one hand . . ." as he considers the aspects of one side of the issue. Then he says to himself, "But on the other hand . . ." as he lists other factors involved. He then grants the child's request, even though it goes against his wishes. But when one of his daughters wants to marry a young Russian communist, he forbids her. As he begins to reason with himself in his common pattern of "On the one hand . . ." and "On the other hand . . . ," he cannot allow it. In this instance, he says, "There is no 'other hand.'"

That is true when we come to the faith. There are some nonnegotiables in the Christian life. When it comes to the gospel of Jesus Christ and the moral implications that flow from it, there is no "on the other hand."

WHY SO MUCH COMPROMISE AND APOSTASY?

One thoughtful question to ask at this point is, Why is there so much compromise today and an epidemic of apostasy? Why are so many falling away, apparently so quickly and easily? Why are biblical essentials being jettisoned so casually? What leads people within the church to depart from the truth of God's Word? Of course, many reasons and rationales could be given, but these five seem to stand out in Scripture.

The first three are fairly straightforward and simple. We will spend more time examining the final two. First, many compromise out of love for the world—plain and simple. They love their sin and don't want to follow God's Word.[7] They substitute God's wisdom with their own. They put themselves above the Bible rather than under it. Second, others compromise because of superficial attention to God's Word. They don't know the Bible and don't take it seriously. They drift away from the truth.[8] Third, compromise can sometimes result from all-out, blatant rebellion and defiance.[9]

Fourth, many compromise because the Bible and the words of Jesus can be hard and narrow. Jesus often lost followers because His teachings were too hard.[10] His words rub against the grain of our sinful nature. For this reason, compromising beliefs or behavior makes it much easier to live self-centered lives and avoid any clash with the world around us. In his early life, Mark Twain moved to a mining town in Nevada. It was a wide-open town with brothels and bars on every corner. Twain said, "I immediately recognized it was no place for a Presbyterian, so I decided not to be one." He compromised. Many have followed his example. Finding it hard to be a Christian, they either quit trying or compromise their convictions.

Fifth, many want to please people. They can't stand to be mocked, maligned, and mistreated. The allure of acceptance is strong. Taking the broad road and fitting in is less stressful. Swimming upstream is difficult and tiring. Compromise always lowers the standard. It's seldom offensive. It tells people what they want to hear, which is why it's so appealing. Telling people they can believe whatever they want and live however they want is much more comfortable than telling people the truth, even though only the truth can really set them free.

We in the church today are under constant pressure to weaken our theology and our morality to make people feel good. We hear things like "You don't have to believe the gospel of Jesus Christ to go to heaven. There are many roads to heaven." Or "Nobody will go to hell. Hell is not a literal place." Or "God's will is for you to be rich and healthy all the time." Or "You can love who you want to love. God will never judge you. He's all about love." Or "Why believe in a book written so long ago?"

The rising tide of progressivism is applauded by many like John Shore:

> It is inevitable that liberal/progressive Christians will be the majority of Christians in America. We feel the waters of that sea change already swelling everywhere around us. Today's conservative evangelical Christians who are rallying against "postmodern relativism," "revisionist secular theology," "a naturalistic doctrine of God," or however else they might label the theology of the left, are like yesteryear's horse-and-buggy owners rallying against them dangnabit newfangled automobiles.[11]

Unbeknownst to him, Shore's sentiments are actually prophesied in Scripture. His attitude fulfills what the Bible says will prevail in the last days. The apostle Paul's final charge to his protégé Timothy prophesies what we see today:

> I solemnly charge you in the presence of God and of Christ Jesus, who is to judge the living and the dead, and by His appearing and His kingdom: preach the word; be ready in season and out of season; reprove, rebuke, exhort, with great patience and instruction. For the time will come when they will not endure sound doctrine; but wanting to have their ears tickled, they will accumulate for themselves teachers in accordance to their own desires, and will turn away their ears from the truth and will turn aside to myths.[12]

Ear-tickling sermons are rampant today. As Tim LaHaye and Jerry Jenkins write,

> False teachers rarely exist in a spiritual vacuum. They start
> appearing because people want to hear and act on their
> flesh-stroking doctrines. In many ways, spirituality is as
> much a commodity as is electronics or beef and is subject
> to similar laws of supply and demand. . . . In other words,
> the people demand to hear ungodly fables, and soon false
> teachers start appearing to supply the demand—like flies to
> a garbage dump.[13]

A consistent mantra of contemporary apostates is their concern that Christians today will be hated or doomed to irrelevance if we stand for the truth. If we want to win the world, we have to tell them what they want to hear, caving to their cravings, compromising our convictions so that others will be more enticed to join us. The most important virtue is not offending anyone. But if that's our goal, we have to raise the question—what are we converting people to?

Ironically, those calling for compromise and no offense in areas of sexual morality won't hesitate to berate Christians for their greed, selfishness, and lack of care for the poor. When it comes to pressing social justice issues on Christians, they quote the Bible literally and assume a no-holds-barred approach. They pull no punches when it comes to certain kinds of sinful behavior. Yet when it comes to homosexuality and other culturally accepted sins, we have to put on pillow-sized boxing gloves and pull all our punches lest anyone take the slightest degree of offense. As Doc Holliday says to his friend Wyatt Earp near the end of the movie *Tombstone*, "My hypocrisy knows no bounds."

Theological liberals and progressives also employ the tactics of shame and humiliation. They claim the moral high ground and look down on conservative, Bible-believing Christians as unloving, negative, and nasty. Yet when we disagree with them and their take on Scripture, we are immediately labeled as bigots and haters and accused of suffering from one phobia or another. We can't be allowed to have an honest disagreement with their view. We have to be branded, vilified, and castigated for our position. But no matter how loudly they denounce our stand on God's Word, we cannot allow fear of shame or humiliation to cause us to cower and compromise.

DO WE HAVE A STANDARD?

While many modern theological progressives have a low view of Scripture, they do appeal to it at times to support their views while at the same time discounting the parts they don't like. One of their favorite passages is John 8—the story about the woman caught in adultery, who was brought to Jesus by His enemies. This beautiful story is twisted to support all kinds of unbiblical notions of moral compromise. Rachel Held Evans, for example, believes Jesus broke the law of God to help the woman in this story. She writes,

> Jesus once said that his mission was not to abolish the law, but to fulfill it. And in this instance, fulfilling the law meant letting it go. It may serve as little comfort to those who have suffered abuse at the hand of Bible-wielding literalists, but the disturbing laws of Leviticus and Deuteronomy lose just a bit of their potency when God himself breaks them.[14]

This is a not-so-subtle discounting of the validity and authority of the Bible and a blasphemous charge that Jesus sinned. However, Evans misses the point. J. Carl Laney provides helpful insight into the meaning of this text:

Yet, the law that required death for the adulteress also demanded that qualified witnesses be the first to begin the stoning (Deut. 17:7). Were these witnesses qualified according to the requirements of the Mosaic Law?

Jesus' words "If any of you is without sin" refer to the key qualification in the Mosaic law, namely that the witnesses be nonmalicious (Deut. 19:16-19, 21; cf. Ex. 23:1-8). A malicious witness promotes violence, perverts justice, and misuses the law for selfish purposes, precisely what the religious leaders were doing in this case. Jesus knew that those testifying against the women were not doing so out of pure hearts and a concern for right. Their conspiracy, inequity, and selfish purposes disqualified them from participation in the execution called for by Mosaic law. . . . Jesus was not applying "situation ethics." He called adultery sin and commanded the woman to cease sinning. Jesus was not relaxing the moral standards of God. Rather He was carefully applying the law. The law called for stoning, but it also required that the witnesses be qualified.[15]

Another way to view this incident is that "Jesus is not breaking the law or shrugging off the Old Testament law. Rather, Jesus is calling these men out on their double-standard, thinking the law applied more to adulterous [women] than to adulterous men."[16] In either case, there is no need to view Jesus as a law-breaking compromiser as Held Evans suggests. The grace and forgiveness Jesus extended to the woman in John 8 should not be used to soften Jesus' stance against sin. We have to remember that after saving her life, Jesus famously said to her, "Go and sin no more," which in the context refers to the sin of adultery.[17]

Notice Jesus didn't whitewash her sin. He called it what it was.

Additionally, the same Jesus who rescued the woman in John 8 from the murderous mob told his followers one chapter earlier that the world "hate[s] me because I accuse it of doing evil."[18] Later in John's Gospel Jesus says,

> If the world hates you, remember that it hated me first. The world would love you as one of its own if you belonged to it, but you are no longer part of the world. I chose you to come out of the world, so it hates you. Do you remember what I told you? "A slave is not greater than the master." Since they persecuted me, naturally they will persecute you. And if they had listened to me, they would listen to you. They will do all this to you because of me, for they have rejected the one who sent me. They would not be guilty if I had not come and spoken to them. But now they have no excuse for their sin. Anyone who hates me also hates my Father.[19]

We must not take Jesus or any of Scripture in bits and pieces, divorced from the overall context. Yes, sexual sins are not the only sins in the Bible. Injustice and greed are sins, and we must never shy away from naming them. But none of us can choose our favorite sins to condemn and let others slide out of fear that we will become unpopular with the world.

I have to admit that we all use Jesus sometimes to support our pet views while at the same time ignoring what He says about our own sinful habits and attitudes. None of us are without blame in using Jesus or other parts of Scripture for our own agendas. But let's at least be honest about how prone we are to misuse Scripture and do the best we can to interpret the words of Jesus and all of the words of Scripture fairly, accurately, and completely in their original context. Anything less is unacceptable.

LET ME ILLUSTRATE

To help you see the depth of the doctrinal confusion and compromise today, here's one example of thousands that could be cited from the blogosphere. The author of this blog is a *New York Times* bestselling author, and her online community is visited by hundreds of thousands of readers every day:

> The better way, the underneath perfection of things that
> I feel deep in my bones looks like this: There is no war.
> All hungry people are fed. All lonely people are loved. . . .
> People of all races, religions, genders, sexualities, cultures,
> and abilities are valued equally in our one human family.
> There is Justice. Peace. Love. Equality.
>
> This sort of unseen order of things—in my view—is
> heaven on Earth. Christians might call it the Kingdom of
> God. My Jewish friends call it Shalom while my atheist
> friends call it Love or Peace. Lovingkindness. Our Buddhist
> brothers and sisters might call it. [sic] ALL PEOPLE who
> are working to bring the above unseen order of things to
> Earth now—whether they are atheist, Jewish, Buddhist,
> Hindu, Muslim, or Christian—THESE people are my faith
> partners. I don't really care what label you give yourself, I
> care about the unseen order of things you believe in and are
> working towards. . . .
>
> But if we want a little scripture to support the idea of
> disregarding labels—we could look at Matthew 7:21. "Not
> everyone who calls out to me, 'Lord! Lord!' will enter the
> Kingdom of Heaven. Only those who actually do the will of
> my Father in heaven will enter."
>
> Do I think this scripture is a threat of hell? Hell no. I
> don't think any scripture is a threat—I think scripture is an

invitation into an unseen order of things that is truer than anything we can actually see.[20]

Notice the repeated language of "feeling" and "what I think." Feeling and human opinion is the modern Bible. The author does appeal to Matthew 7:21 and believes it does not refer to people being judged, yet ironically the entire context of Matthew 7:15-23 concerns false shepherds who lead unsuspecting sheep away from the narrow path that leads to salvation and down the broad road that leads to destruction. What the author is doing in her blog tragically fulfills the stern warning of Jesus in the very passage she quotes. This blogger joins the chorus of voices who deny and disregard the inerrancy and sufficiency of Scripture and the exclusivity of Jesus as the way to God.

Many would claim that compromise on these issues is harmless and benign. They wonder why all the fuss over a few theological points. For them the words *doctrine* or *doctrinal* are pejoratives. They view doctrinal, theological truths as irrelevant, impractical, divisive, unloving, and even unknowable. The problem is that they have no love for these truths or appreciation for the dire, eternal consequences that hang in the balance. Jesus spoke often of the eternal destruction of those who reject Him and His teaching.[21]

I like the story about the New York family that bought a ranch out West where they intended to raise cattle. Friends visited and asked if the ranch had a name. "Well," said the would-be cattleman, "I wanted to name it the Bar-J. My wife favored Suzy-Q, one son liked the Flying-W, and the other wanted the Lazy-Y. So we're calling it the Bar-J-Suzy-Q-Flying-W-Lazy-Y Ranch."

"But where are all your cattle?" the friends asked.

The reply: "None survived the branding." Make no mistake: compromise can be deadly!

FAITHFUL PEOPLE

When confronted by apostasy, I find solace in tracing the lives of great saints from the past who stood in their day against a similar tide and refused to compromise even in the face of withering opposition. One of these faithful people was Athanasius of Alexandria. The life of Athanasius is an epic saga. He served as bishop of Alexandria for forty-five years. He knew five popes and five emperors. He survived five exiles—nearly twenty years—as well as persecution under Emperor Diocletian.

Athanasius is best known for his lengthy battle against the heresy of Arianism. Arius, a church leader from Alexandria, Egypt, believed that Jesus was not coequal and coeternal with God the Father and claimed that Jesus was a created being. He taught that Christ the Son was simply a creature—the greatest of all created beings. Athanasius didn't shrug off the issue as unimportant or inconsequential. He understood that the entire Christian faith was at stake. The controversy with Arias raged on for several years. At one point, when it looked like the entire Roman Empire was moving away from orthodoxy into Arianism, a concerned, exasperated colleague of Athanasius exclaimed, "The whole world is against you!" Unfazed, Athanasius made this famous response, "Then it is Athanasius against the world."

Another early giant of the faith was Tertullian, a lawyer from Carthage (in North Africa) who served the church in the third century. He authored a book titled *On Idolatry*. The book deals with the issue of Christians who made a living by making idols. When believers in his day were told that because they were Christians they should not be involved in the business of making idols, they said, "We have to live. There's no other way by which we can live."

Tertullian's response was "Do you have to live?"

What a probing question. It cuts to the heart of compromise. We always have some excuse for our compromise. The ultimate justification would be "I have to live." Yet the truth is, you and I do not. We *think* we have to live. Many today believe that they have to live and even have to live a comfortable life without any clash with our culture. The truth is, however, you and I *don't* have to live. The ultimate claim upon our lives is loyalty to Christ. Our ultimate loyalty is not to our physical life—it's to Christ. We don't have to live, but we do have to be loyal to Him. That's what life is all about.

As leaders, churches, and denominations swerve from the truth and increasingly fall away, we need to stand like Daniel, like Athanasius, and like Tertullian for the truth of God's Word. No matter how strong and sustained the opposition may grow, we must joyfully, graciously stand for the truth, lovingly share it with others, and strive to live it out in our lives every day by the power of the Holy Spirit.

CHAPTER 5

WHEN TOLERANCE IS INTOLERABLE

I have this against you, that you tolerate the woman Jezebel.

REVELATION 2:20

American Airlines Flight 11 pushed back from gate 26 in what was expected to be a routine flight from Boston to Los Angeles. Captain John Ogonowski and his Boeing 767-200ER taxied down the runway with nine flight attendants and eighty-one passengers on board and took off at 7:59 a.m. No one could have dreamed that forty-seven minutes later, they would all be dead. When the airliner rocketed into the World Trade Center's North Tower at 440 mph, 9,717 gallons of jet fuel exploded, catapulting everyone aboard into eternity.

The whole world changed in an instant.

What precipitated the events of that disastrous September day was a mere handful of men. Consumed by a jihadist ideology, they had committed themselves to the destruction of human life.

And so, storming their way into the cockpit, they took control of Flight 11 while simultaneously attacking and killing passengers and crew.

The ringleader of this unholy war from the sky that day was Egyptian terrorist Mohamed Atta. He was accompanied by four fellow terrorists (all from Saudi Arabia). When the body count was totaled, 1,466 additional persons perished in the North Tower, with another 624 in the South Tower. American passenger jets transformed into explosive missiles manned by maniacal Muslims. It was the worst hijacking in history. And though sudden and unexpected, it had actually been years in the making.

In these last days, it's not just planes that are being hijacked. The Bible claims, "The human heart is the most deceitful of all things, and desperately wicked. Who really knows how bad it is?"[1]

Because humanity is inherently depraved, we initiate and participate in other types of hijackings: kidnapping truth, moral values, and even common sense. Through crafty deception over time, our sin nature, partnering with the spirit of the age, takes hostage the good things of God in an attempt to redefine, reimagine, and in some cases wipe them completely from humanity's hard drive.

We're seeing this pirating of morals and standards occur today as it relates to the concept of *love*. Seeking to justify homosexual activity and same-sex marriage, LGBT activists coined the catchphrase "Love Is Love." The argument behind this slogan is that if any person feels romantic affection or attraction toward any other person (regardless of their gender or age), then of course it *must* be love, right? Hence "Love Is Love." Admittedly, if you redefine what *love* is, as well as from where it originates, then virtually any definition or expression of this love immediately becomes legitimate and justifiable. *Morally* right. Even a "human right." Redefined and viewed this way, love itself is no longer a definitive standard by which all mankind should operate but rather an ever-evolving whim birthed out of individual preference. Marital and sexual love then become affections and emotions one can feel for anyone—other men or women, even multiple persons involving multiple genders or no "gender" at all. *Each person* (that is to say, each deceitful, wicked heart) decides what love is, not some ancient book or supposed deity.

Of course, if there is truly no God or authoritative Scripture, then logically there is no ultimate standard for morality—or for reality, in that case. What is "good" or "right" for you is just as valid as anyone else's choices. For with no God to create, reveal, guide, judge, or reward, then everyone's life decisions are equally credible . . . and meaningless.

By the same token, with no God, there can also be no authoritative or conclusive way to know whether what you feel for someone else is a genuine spiritual connection, an emotional feeling, or a social compulsion. There's no way to determine if "love" is merely a physical urge brought on by chemicals. If we are just "molecules in motion," we are incapable of knowing *anything* for certain. As C. S. Lewis wisely observed,

> Supposing there was no intelligence behind the universe, no creative mind. In that case, nobody designed my brain for the purpose of thinking. It is merely that when the atoms inside my skull happen, for physical or chemical reasons, to arrange themselves in a certain way, this gives me, as a byproduct, the sensation I call thought. But, if so, how can I trust my own thinking to be true? It's like upsetting a milk jug and hoping that the way it splashes itself will give you a map of London. But if I can't trust my own thinking, of course I can't trust the arguments leading to Atheism, and therefore have no reason to be an Atheist, or anything else.

Unless I believe in God, I cannot believe in thought: so I can never use thought to disbelieve in God.[2]

So then, there cannot even be such a thing as "real love" without God. Moreover, Scripture tells us the following:

> "We know what real love is because Jesus gave up his life for us."[3]
> "This is how God loved the world: He gave his one and only Son, so that everyone who believes in him will not perish but have eternal life."[4]
> "God showed his great love for us by sending Christ to die for us while we were still sinners."[5]

The Bible also unquestionably asserts that love *comes from* God. So then, love is not love; *God* is.[6] Further, the only way we can truly know love in any kind of meaningful relationship is by first experiencing His love for us.[7] And this is nowhere more true than in the marriage relationship. As a husband and wife experience God's love, they are able to experience a deeper love for each other.[8]

Of course, non-Christians can experience some aspects of love. They can perform unselfish acts of service on behalf of others. They can know the emotional bliss and satisfaction of having another person in their lives. They can appreciate how that person fills a void where loneliness once dwelled. They can enjoy the wonderful companionship of human relational love. However, they can never fully experience all that love is and has to offer until they receive it from the God who is love.

Finally, a person cannot give away what they do not personally possess. Encountering God's unconditional love and salvation gives believers a capacity for emotional fulfillment, selfless service, perseverance, and forgiveness that is exponentially enhanced beyond what the average person can know. Sadly, many professing Christians do not "grow in the grace and knowledge of our Lord and Savior Jesus Christ"[9] so as to deepen their exposure to His love and participation in it.

But what we are seeing happen today is more than just people missing out on God's love. Instead, there has been a deliberate, conscious movement to reject the biblical definition of love and marriage, replacing it with one that better harmonizes with culture's crumbling moral standards.

Following the US Supreme Court's 2014 ruling in favor of same-sex marriage, Starbucks flew a 38-foot-wide by 19-foot-tall "pride flag" over its corporate headquarters in Seattle. Anthony Hesseltine, a senior operations buyer for Starbucks, remarked at the time, "The whole message is about diversity and accepting people for their differences. If you think about a rainbow, no one color is dominant. It's a harmonization of different colors, each color contributing to the whole."[10]

Diversity and harmony. And two more hijackings.

Our society is bowing at the altar of tolerance and worshiping at the shrine of open-mindedness. Values that have historically been championed by the Christian faith are systematically being replaced, treated like burned-out lightbulbs by a culture that's in a romantic relationship with darkness.[11] Think of how our world is redefining the following Christian concepts:

> Acceptance (Romans 15:7)
> Unity and diversity (Galatians 3:27-29; 1 Corinthians 12:12-13)
> Compassion (Colossians 3:12-13)
> Justice (Proverbs 28:5; 29:7; Micah 6:8; Romans 12:19)

> Spirituality (Matthew 5:21-28; Galatians 5:16; Ephesians 5:18)
> Bigotry and prejudice (Acts 10:28; Romans 10:12-13; Colossians 3:11; James 2:9)
> Hatred (Proverbs 6:16-19; Romans 12:9)
> Forgiveness (Ephesians 4:32; Colossians 3:13; 1 Thessalonians 5:15)
> Truth (John 4:24; 8:32; 14:6; 17:17)
> Martyrdom (Matthew 10:28; Luke 11:50-51; Hebrews 11:37-40; Revelation 2:10; 6:11)

When comparing the way each of these concepts is defined in culture with Scripture's description of them, you can see how they have been twisted and fashioned into weapons against those who follow Jesus. It's a turning of the tables, a changing of the price tags. And it's a modern-day example of the prophet Isaiah's words:

> Woe to those who call evil good, and good evil.
> Who substitute darkness for light and light for darkness;
> Who substitute bitter for sweet, and sweet for bitter! [12]

Paul echoed Isaiah, writing that those who deliberately reject the Creator and His right to rule in their lives "exchange the truth of God for a lie." The consequence of this spiritual rebellion is that God "gives them over" to judgment.[13] And humanity continues devolving deeper into the depths of depravity, to the point where they

> became full of every kind of wickedness, sin, greed, hate, envy, murder, quarreling, deception, malicious behavior, and gossip. They are backstabbers, haters of God, insolent, proud, and boastful. They invent new ways of sinning, and

they disobey their parents. They refuse to understand, break their promises, are heartless, and have no mercy. They know God's justice requires that those who do these things deserve to die, yet they do them anyway. Worse yet, they encourage others to do them, too.[14]

TELLING THE TRUTH

So we can see from Scripture that many of today's promoted values and "truths" are nothing more than lies, reimagined imitations of the real thing. *Hate* has been redefined to mean "your biblical values clash with mine; therefore, you are a *hater*." Ironically, what the world now calls "hate" is met with *actual* hate in return. But this is nothing new. The same thing happened in Jesus' day. Our Lord demonstrated more love toward sinners than anyone ever could. And yet motivated by this same (real) love, He also told the truth to those who were unrepentant regarding their sin. And they, in turn, vehemently hated Him for it.[15] It's also part of what got Him killed.

Some Christians will use the popular "Jesus hung out with sinners" argument to justify friendships or to tolerate sin in the body of Christ. And though believers should always seek to build bridges and friendships with the lost, what sometimes escapes our notice is that many of those sinners Christ spent time with were keenly aware that their sinful condition and their condemnable lifestyles posed a problem. Yes, Jesus accepted them into His presence, but He did not accept them into His *Kingdom* until they acknowledged their need for Him and trusted Him to forgive their sins. It is these He promises to "never reject."[16]

So in these last days, Scripture's values and virtues have been hijacked by a post-Christian civilization birthed and fed by Satanic delusion and darkened hearts and minds. In fact, nothing appears to be sacred anymore in a world ramping up to Revelation. Morals, values, virtues, origins, sexuality—all are up for grabs, recycled and resold to those whose consciences are not cleansed by Scripture. Even the rainbow we see in the sky has been taken hostage and redefined to symbolize the various gender, sex, and relationship choices currently promoted and celebrated in our age.

Nevertheless, God made the rainbow, and it has absolutely nothing to do with sexuality. It does, however, have symbolic meaning, a sign of a promise God made to Noah and to successive generations that He would never destroy humanity with water again.[17] Ironically, this promise came after He had brought devastating global judgment on mankind because of the godlessness, violence, and moral corruption that now fills our planet![18]

THE "UNPARDONABLE SIN"

But perhaps the biggest hijacking of all is what our culture has done to "tolerance." The way some people talk, you'd think tolerance is the most important virtue. In the spirit of tolerance, some colleges and universities have now created "safe spaces" on their campuses to "protect" students from divergent opinions. So, for example, if you claim to be transgender, lesbian, or "otherkin" (those who identify as partially or totally nonhuman—like a dragon or a fox), then the school will provide a space where you can be protected from shame, ridicule, oppression, or persecution.[19] Yes, *persecution*. Clearly, humanity has taken a Romans 1 turn for the bizarre. What is marketed and sold as tolerance today hardly resembles its corresponding Christian virtue.

In contemporary society, tolerance means being open to divergent ideas and being completely accepting of those who aren't like you. Sounds good, right? Even *Christian*-like. I mean, who wouldn't want to be known as open and accepting?

Those who are faithful Christ-followers already are. Christian tolerance means we demonstrate patience with non-Christian coworkers, classmates, friends, and family. It means we listen and care. We exercise tolerance because we love people and know God can change people. We pray for them and are patient toward them because we remember a time when God and others treated us with the same kind of tolerance.[20] It means they can come to God just as they are. After all, *we* did.

But along with compassion, understanding, and empathy, there is also a time to call sin what it is. As believers, we serve in a dual role of both priest and prophet, being both compassionate and confrontational. And though balancing that role can be challenging, the two responsibilities can exist together at the same time. We can be tolerant yet simultaneously unwavering toward God's Word. One may sound more "loving" than the other. But is it?

When my (Jeff's) son Stuart was two years old, his older brother accidentally fell on top of him, breaking his collarbone. The incident also broke my heart as we were all playing together when it happened. Psalm 103:13 says, "As a father has compassion on his children, so the LORD has compassion on those who fear Him." I felt that while driving Stuart to the hospital. And during his recovery, nobody exhibited more compassion for Stuart than I did. Every time I saw him wincing in pain, my heart ached. I wished so badly that I could have taken his suffering and discomfort away. But my compassion could not overrule the fact that he still needed to go to the doctor, to be examined and X-rayed, to have his arm placed in an uncomfortable sling, and to constantly be told to remain immobile for weeks to come. The cold, hard truth was that he would have to endure some tough days ahead. And as his father, I didn't just cuddle him and help him get dressed, but I also had to deny his requests to go outside and play.

That's because truth and compassion are not enemies. They're partners. And one without the other often leads to a misrepresentation of both. As Christians, we have a tendency to pendulum swing when it comes to dealing with the outside world. In our attempt to reach the lost, we can try so hard to be relevant that we compromise the truth. Conversely, in "standing for what we believe," we can also commit the error of the Pharisees, neglecting "the weightier matters of the law: justice and mercy and faithfulness."[21] But none of God's attributes—from His amazing grace to His terrifying wrath—are ever mutually exclusive. They never conflict with or contradict themselves. It is only our limited understanding of those attributes that creates confusion. However, in God's economy, there is perfect harmony and divine balance among them all.

In practice, both the world and the church tend to upset that balance by overemphasizing one to the exclusion of the rest. What we need is a proper understanding of Scripture's values and virtues and skill in applying them to real-life people and circumstances.

Yes, because of truth, there is a time for unwavering intolerance. Parents have to display intolerance toward certain behaviors and attitudes in their children. Pastors must be intolerant of false doctrine and anyone who might threaten the well-being of their sheep. Husbands are intolerant of things that may harm their wives or marriages. Governments ought to be intolerant of evildoers, administering just punishment. And as Christians, we must show intolerance toward any thought, philosophy, or value that raises itself up against the knowledge of God.[22] In all these cases, intolerance isn't hatred or bigotry but genuine love, care, fairness, and justice.

Paul was intolerant of blatant sin in the church, pronouncing swift and thorough condemnation of those who participated in it in 1 Corinthians 5:1-7. However, just three verses later, he reminds the Corinthians to continue their friendships with unbelievers who are immoral, covetous, swindlers, and even idolaters. In this sense, we should never allow the world to outlove us. At the same time,

Paul urged the Corinthians to limit fellowship with so-called "believers" who practice such sins. That's an example of how truth and love coexist in harmony with one another. Sadly, however, many in the Christian community are embracing this redefined tolerance, even reading and reinterpreting the Bible in light of it. And perhaps nowhere is this more blatant than when it comes to the sin of homosexuality. While Mark covers this issue more comprehensibly in chapter 7, it is worth noting that influential bloggers and authors like Matthew Vines have openly accepted and promoted homosexuality as not only tolerable but as coming from God Himself! The idea is that since homosexuals are all "born that way," Christians should accept, and even endorse, homosexual practice.

How ironic is it that our world (and some who claim to know Jesus) allows tolerance for everything *except* the Christian worldview? Where does this indiscriminate tolerance mind-set come from? And more important, where is it taking us? How does a believer make sense of a culture that equates unbridled tolerance with love, even calling it *God's* love? This is where hijacked spiritual values especially pervert and twist biblical truths. They are reckless inclusion, careless love, and morals devoid of wisdom. These are the open gates through which apostasy enters. And we cannot and should not ever rely on human government to acknowledge God and support His standards.

Christian tolerance means making room in our hearts for those who are different from us. It also means accepting those who are weak in the faith or who have yet to mature in their relationship with God.[23] But as with any other virtue, it is tempered with wisdom. There are boundaries to how much tolerance we exhibit and for how long. We might tolerate our neighbor's barking dog for a few hours but not for an entire evening. We can tolerate a coworker's dissenting opinion but not when it begins to hinder productivity or company morale. We can tolerate a relative's negative opinion of us but not when that relative begins infecting others with lies and unfounded rumors. And we can tolerate people who are enslaved by sin yet never tolerate the sin itself.

However, unless we're careful, we can be guilty of the same sin as the church at Thyatira, one of five Revelation congregations to receive a blistering rebuke from Jesus. This community of faith over-flowed with tolerance—the *bad* kind.

While Jesus praised the church at Ephesus because they did *not* "tolerate evil people," He then condemned the church at Thyatira *because* of their tolerance.[24] The Thyatiran believers happily coexisted with a woman in their church (nicknamed "Jezebel"), who referred to herself as a prophetess. Her teaching led the congregation away from holy living and into immorality and the "deep things of Satan."[25] And Christ was not pleased.

So we dare not have this attitude toward God's grace, abusing it for our own selfish pleasures.[26] But on the flip side of being libertine is what legalists do to God's commands, twisting, redefining, and reassigning more meaning to them than Scripture does, "teaching as doctrines the precepts of men."[27] Jesus sternly warned the Pharisees of His day, "Isaiah was right when he prophesied about you hypo-crites; as it is written: 'These people honor me with their lips, but their hearts are far from me.'"[28] And again, "Woe to you, scribes and Pharisees, hypocrites! For you are like whitewashed tombs which on the outside appear beautiful, but inside they are full of dead men's bones and all uncleanness. So you, too, outwardly appear righteous to men, but inwardly you are full of hypocrisy and lawlessness."[29]

Legalists hijack the Christian concept of obedience, terrorizing God's people with it. This is actually a form of worldliness and car-nality, because it feeds and enables the sin nature in its relentless pursuit to justify itself.

But Jesus said, "If you love Me, you will keep My commandments."[30]

Notice it's love for Christ that motivates obedience to Him, not vice versa. And our love for Christ is directly proportionate to our understanding of His truth and the gratitude and affection that knowledge properly produces. We must therefore avoid this doctrinal and spiritual error at all costs lest we fall into the same trap as those in the world.

TOLERANCE AND THE TAIL END OF HISTORY

So how does this phenomenon of tolerance play into last-days apostasy? From what we've seen, today's tolerance is not simply a weakening of truth or values but rather a deliberate denial of them. The effects of this spiritual delusion are a part of the ear-tickling, end-times "myths" about which Paul solemnly warned Timothy. And Satan, who is both the god of this world and the prince of the power of the air, is he who fuels the grand illusion. Consistent with his nature, he lives up to his reputation as a liar, and the father of lies.[31]

Thankfully for us, though God does not tolerate sin, He does have patience with sinners. This truth prompted Habakkuk to argue,

Your eyes are too pure to look on evil;
You cannot tolerate wrongdoing.
Why then do you tolerate the treacherous?
Why are you silent while the wicked swallow up those more
    righteous than themselves?[32]

No doubt you've had the same sentiment as you observe the world around you. While you know God is intolerant of sin, it appears He still allows an awful lot of it to continue.[33] But that's another reason why knowing Scripture is so important. The Bible also says there is coming a time when God's patience will come to an end. Peter reminds us, "The Lord is not slow in keeping his promise, as some understand slowness. Instead he is patient with you, not wanting anyone to perish, but everyone to come to repentance."[34]

Paul echoes this in Romans 2:4-5, warning unbelievers not to take for granted God's "forbearance" (tolerance):

> Or do you show contempt for the riches of his kindness,
> forbearance and patience, not realizing that God's kindness
> is intended to lead you to repentance?
> But because of your stubbornness and your unrepentant
> heart, you are storing up wrath against yourself for the
> day of God's wrath, when his righteous judgment will be
> revealed (NIV).

Clearly God's patience and tolerance are like sisters with similar DNA. Out of His grace and mercy, He withheld judgment on sins previously committed.[35] Even today, not all sin is punished immediately, but that does not mean God will wait forever. His present patience and tolerance is not *for* but rather *with* sinners. As long as there is breath (that breath itself being a gracious gift from God), there is still time for repentance.[36]

But His tolerance and patience will one day give way to global wrath. This begins in the seven years of Tribulation, where the "wrath of the Lamb" and of His Father are poured out upon earth and its inhabitants. Interestingly enough, even those who suffer this wrath know where it comes from, as Revelation 6:15-17 prophesies:

> Then the kings of the earth, the princes, the generals, the
> rich, the mighty, and everyone else, both slave and free,
> hid in caves and among the rocks of the mountains. They
> called to the mountains and the rocks, "Fall on us and hide
> us from the face of him who sits on the throne and from

the wrath of the Lamb! For the great day of their wrath has come, and who can withstand it?" (NIV)

The Day of the Lord will be a day of ferocious intolerance. How much better to turn to God's grace while it is still freely offered?

By every indication, these and other "hijackings" will occur up to, and beyond, Christ's return for His church at the Rapture. Immoral values and behavior will continue to be not only tolerated but promoted and celebrated, while at the same time biblical standards and those who adhere to them will be demonized. This will create growing tension for believers who desire to reach others for Christ but find themselves hindered by the fact that they are viewed as narrow minded, bigoted, unscientific, or homophobic. This will likely contribute to an even greater marginalization of the church in society. As Nero famously made the church a convenient scapegoat for the burning of Rome, so our world will increasingly vilify believers in the years to come. Do not be surprised when Christians are treated with contempt and seen as "holding back progress" or "keeping us in the dark ages." We are slowly becoming society's outcasts.

But if it's any consolation, so was the first-century church.

So in one sense, the world will become more tolerant while at the same time turning more rigid and biased toward Christians and their Christ. And this is yet another reason to eagerly anticipate the imminent return of Jesus Christ, like those early believers did.

Because we are living in the last days, time is not our friend. That's one reason Paul urged the Ephesian Christians to "[make] the most of your time, because the days are evil."[37] This reality ignites our hearts and lives not with panic but with purposeful urgency. It keeps us on track, laser focused on the faith that has been faithfully passed on to us.[38] In the church, what unites people from diverse backgrounds, races, and experiences is not that we are simply *tolerant* of one another but that we are bound together by a common faith in Jesus Christ. This is the essence of fellowship.[39] The apostles laid the foundation of the church, with Jesus Christ as the chief cornerstone. We are His "living stones." And we have to keep building the body, especially as we "see the day drawing near."[40]

This therefore, is *your* time in God's story. You want a strong ending, not a whimpering finish. So will you be a discerning Christian, one who sees through the deceptive fog of our day? Will you be a last-days revolutionary who takes up the banner of Christ, no matter what it costs? Will you champion His truth, refusing to tolerate mediocrity in your own heart? Will you fight the good fight and finish your course?

Will you keep the faith?

CHAPTER 6

MORAL FREEFALL

An Avianca Airlines jet crashed in Spain in 1984. The investigation into the crash uncovered an alarming conversation on the black box cockpit recorder. A few minutes before the plane plowed into the side of a mountain, a commanding voice from the plane's automatic warning system repeatedly cautioned in English, "Pull up! Pull up!" Believing the device was malfunctioning, the irritated pilot said, "Shut up, Gringo!" and shut the system off. Within minutes, the plane slammed into the side of a mountain, killing everyone on board.[1]

Similar to the airplane's warning system, the Bible, God's instruction manual and warning system, is quoted and obeyed as long as it fits an agenda, tells people what they want to hear, and agrees with their decisions and direction in life. Yet when the Bible warns them to "Pull up!"—to stop some sinful behavior or belief—they don't want to hear it and want to shut it up. Tragically, the result is a spiritual death spiral—a moral freefall without a parachute. This is true of an individual, a family, a church, and a nation.

BEHAVIOR FOLLOWS BELIEF

I like the story of the two hunters who came upon a huge hole in the ground. One hunter said to the other, "I can't even see the bottom of that hole! How deep do you think it is?" The other replied, "I don't know. Let's throw something down and listen for how long it takes to hit bottom."

"I saw an old automobile transmission nearby," the first hunter said. "Let's throw that in and see." So they found the transmission, hauled it over, and tossed it down the hole. While they listened for the transmission to hit bottom, they heard a rustling behind them. Then they saw a goat crash through the brush, run up to the hole, and jump in headfirst.

They were puzzled by this, and while they tried to sort it all out, an old farmer walked up. "You didn't happen to see my goat, did you?" he asked.

The first hunter said, "Funny you should ask. We were just standing here a minute ago when a goat ran out of the bushes and jumped headfirst into the hole!"

The farmer replied, "That can't possibly be my goat. I had him chained to a transmission!"[2]

In the same way that the goat followed the transmission, behavior follows belief. What we believe inevitably pulls our behavior with it. A. W. Tozer says, "It would be impossible to overemphasize the importance of sound doctrine in the life of the Christian. Right thinking about all spiritual matters is imperative if we would have right living. As men do not gather grapes of thorns nor figs of thistles, so sound character does not grow out of unsound teaching."[3]

Doctrinal departure from the truth eventually makes its way into the lives of people. A person becomes what he or she believes. Wandering away from the truth of the gospel leads inevitably to moral apostasy as night follows day. From the other side, what we believe is displayed in how we behave. In the Bible, apostasy involves both wrong belief (doctrine) and wrong behavior (doing). One's creed determines one's conduct and ultimately one's character.[4]

LAST DAYS DEPARTURE

The key New Testament text on the moral freefall in the visible church of the last days is 2 Timothy 3:1-13. The beginning of this passage highlights nineteen terrible characteristics of apostasy in the last days:

> Realize this, that in the last days difficult times will come.
> For men will be lovers of self, lovers of money, boastful,
> arrogant, revilers, disobedient to parents, ungrateful,
> unholy, unloving, irreconcilable, malicious gossips, without
> self-control, brutal, haters of good, treacherous, reckless,
> conceited, lovers of pleasure rather than lovers of God,
> holding to a form of godliness, although they have denied its
> power; Avoid such men as these.[5]

The Message paraphrase of 2 Timothy 3:1-13 is helpful here with its graphic description of the attributes of the last days' apostasy:

> Don't be naive. There are difficult times ahead. As the end
> approaches, people are going to be self-absorbed, money-
> hungry, self-promoting, stuck-up, profane, contemptuous
> of parents, crude, coarse, dog-eat-dog, unbending,
> slanderers, impulsively wild, savage, cynical, treacherous,

ruthless, bloated windbags, addicted to lust, and allergic to God. They'll make a show of religion, but behind the scenes they're animals. Stay clear of these people.

These are the kind of people who smooth-talk themselves into the homes of unstable and needy women and take advantage of them; women who, depressed by their sinfulness, take up with every new religious fad that calls itself "truth." They get exploited every time and never really learn. These men are like those old Egyptian frauds Jannes and Jambres, who challenged Moses. They were rejects from the faith, twisted in their thinking, defying truth itself. But nothing will come of these latest impostors. Everyone will see through them, just as people saw through that Egyptian hoax. . . .

Unscrupulous con men will continue to exploit the faith. They're as deceived as the people they lead astray. As long as they are out there, things can only get worse.

There are five important keys to understanding this passage. First, Paul tells Timothy and us to "realize this." To put it in our language, Paul is saying, "Mark this, underline it, highlight it, don't miss it." In other words, this message about apostasy in the last days is something we need to pay full attention to and lay hold of. These verses are like a divine warning label about the last days. When Paul wrote 2 Timothy, he was languishing in a Roman dungeon. His earthly demise was near. His time on earth was winding down. His final inspired words drip with a sense of urgency.

Second, in the New Testament, the phrase "last days" relates to the entire time period between the ascension of Christ and His return.[6] We often call this period of time the inter-advent age or the church age.

The word "times" in 2 Timothy 3:1 means "seasons." We could translate verse 1, "In the last days wild seasons will come." What Paul is saying in the context of 2 Timothy 3:1 is that during the last days—a period of now almost two thousand years—there will be shorter seasons, periods, or intervals that will be especially difficult, terrible times of apostasy or falling away.[7]

The word "difficult" (*chelepoi*) in 2 Timothy 3:1 connotes the idea of "grievous" or "terrible." The only other place this Greek word is found in the New Testament is Matthew 8:28, where the two demoniacs were so *chelepoi* ("violent" or "wild") that no one could pass by. Plutarch used this word to describe "an ugly, infected, and dangerous wound."[8]

Putting all this together, Paul is telling us that the last days won't be uniformly evil but will be punctuated by repetitive cycles of ugly, dangerous, wild times. We're living in those uncontrollable times now.

Third, this passage says that while there will be seasons or times of apostasy that are especially terrible within the last days, the overall progression will be for things to worsen. We are told in verse 13 to expect apostasy to get worse as the church age progresses: "Evil men and imposters will proceed from bad to worse, deceiving and being deceived." In other words, as this extended period of time known as the last days unfolds, these perilous, uncontrollable times of apostasy will become more frequent and more intense as the return of Christ nears.

Fourth, we need to recognize that the conditions or symptoms described in 2 Timothy 3:1-13 are conditions *within* the visible church. Obviously, the kinds of sins listed here have always been prevalent in society at large. That's nothing new. The shocking thing here is that the sins of the culture become the sins of the church. Professing Christians are pictured living on the lowest level. The entire context of 2 Timothy 3 is describing people who profess to know God and hold to a form of godliness yet deny its power. Paul says clearly that there will be no lack of religion but that people will deny its power to transform the lives of people and society. As Ray Stedman says, "Paul tells us that the primary cause of these repetitive cycles of stress and danger is the hypocritical lives of people who profess to be Christians. They outwardly seem pious and religious but inwardly do not have the power of God in their lives. . . . When our light dims, the whole world sinks deeper into darkness."[9]

Don Carson states, "This appearance of godliness can have many different shapes. It may be fine liturgy or it may be a lot of exuberant noise. It may bubble over in a lot of fluent God-talk. What is missing, however, is the transforming power of the gospel that actually changes the lives of people."[10]

Fifth, the chief sin of the last days' apostasy, the one that heads the list, is that "men will be lovers of self." That's the real focus this list points to. Self-love is the polluted fountain from which the other eighteen characteristics flow. It is followed by "lovers of money" and then later comes "lovers of pleasure rather than lovers of God." (Notice it's not "lovers of pleasure *more* than God" but "*instead of God*." Love of God is replaced by love of pleasure.)

The present moral insanity and apostasy we're witnessing signals a radical shift from reverence for God to love of self. In the last days, a kind of reverse Copernican revolution is occurring. The center of all existence is self instead of God, creating a black hole of depravity, where all kinds of sins and rebellion brew:

The real problem with this vortex of ungodliness is that those who profess to be the people of God will be the ones displaying these characteristics. . . . They will give lip-service but not life-service. . . . They will have a form, but will deny the power that form would indicate they have. . . . In the last days religion will prosper, but so will wickedness, because what will pass for religion won't have any dynamite in it. Holding to a form of religion but denying its dynamite.[11]

Therefore, what we learn from this passage is that during the last days there will be times of especially serious, terrible, ugly moral apostasy in the visible church and that the overall trend and trajectory will be for the decadence and departure within the professing church to grow progressively worse.

LEANING LIVES

On a children's news TV show several years back, one of the segments reported that Italy's Leaning Tower of Pisa could possibly collapse, and to foster interaction with the audience, the reporters asked children to submit their solutions to the problem.

Several of the audience's fixes were featured, including a cable to haul the tower back, refrigeration coils to freeze the tower in place, and building adjacent to the tower to support the structure unobtrusively. But the most perceptive idea was a young boy's suggestion to "just build the buildings around it the same way and nobody will notice."

Many professing Christians today are adopting the same solution when it comes to the leaning world we live in. Rather than living godly lives as a witness to the crooked world, they build their lives on a slant so as not to attract any negative attention.[12]

The lowered standards within many churches and denominations are barely distinguishable from the world's. This reminds me of a story Philip DeCourcy shares about country music legend Willie

Nelson, who bought a golf course. Someone once asked Willie what par was on the course. He answered, "Anything I want it to be. See that hole over there? It is a par 47." He added wryly, "And yesterday, I birdied it."[13] This is a funny story, but what isn't funny is that many within the church today regard morality the same way, lowering the behavioral bar so they can easily reach it. DeCourcy goes on to say,

> It seems that an increasing number of people don't believe in fixed or universal axioms of moral behavior. Right and wrong is determined by whatever the situation requires or whatever they believe is in their best interest. Ours is a day not unlike the time of the Judges when, because there was no king in Israel every man did what was right in his own eyes (Judges 21:25). Ours is also a day not unlike that of the prophet Isaiah when men call evil good, and good evil (Isa. 5:20). Our increasingly secular society is rewriting the rules on morality (Judges 2:10). In a postmodern world there is no king or kingdom that rules over all, "all the ways of man are pure in his own eyes" (Prov. 16:2, 25; 21:2; 30:12). Each man is a law unto himself, and each social group its own kingdom. Man is autonomous, and free to indulge his sexual desires, decide his gender, live his life, and even end his life as he sees fit. This is the brave new world of ethics![14]

And this brave new world has invaded the church. We see it in the divorce rates within evangelical churches that are no different, and in some cases are even higher, than those of non-Christians. Lowered standards are also apparent in the prevalence of premarital sex and cohabitation among young adults who profess to be Christians, as well as pornography viewing among believers. In many vital areas, the church is not much different from the world.

THE ONLY OPINION THAT COUNTS

Moral apostasy, metastasizing out of the cancer of doctrinal apostasy, will escalate as the church age progresses, reaching its zenith just before Christ returns to catch to heaven all who have humbly accepted His Son as their Savior from sin.[15] The escalation of apostasy during this age is setting the stage for the final, ultimate apostasy that will occur under the Antichrist just before Christ returns to earth.[16]

In the meantime, as we await our Lord's return, our calling is to study and obey God's Word.

Umpire Babe Pinelli once called Babe Ruth out on strikes. When the crowd booed, Ruth challenged the umpire. "There's 40,000 people here who know that last pitch was a ball." The witnessing coaches and players prepared for Ruth to be ejected from the game. But Pinelli had a cool head and simply replied, "Maybe so, Babe, but mine is the only opinion that counts."

The church today needs to remember that when it comes to doctrine and morality, the only opinion that counts is God's. Second Timothy 3:14-17 makes this clear. Scripture is made up of the very words of God Himself. A chapter that opens under the ominous cloud of apostasy closes under the pure sunlight of the God-breathed Scriptures. God's Word is set forth as the answer to apostasy:

> But as for you, continue in what you have learned and have
> firmly believed, knowing from whom you learned it and
> how from childhood you have been acquainted with the
> sacred writings, which are able to make you wise for salvation
> through faith in Christ Jesus. All Scripture is breathed out by
> God and profitable for teaching, for reproof, for correction,
> and for training in righteousness, that the man of God may
> be complete, equipped for every good work.[17]

Second Timothy 3:14 begins with the two little words—"but . . . you" (*su de* in Greek). In some ways, these are the key words in 2 Timothy. Four times Timothy is called to stand apart from what's happening around him.[18] He was the opposite of many contemporary Christians who have decided to *fit in* rather than *stand out*. He was faithful to learn and live out God's Word in his life.

God's Word is our source for detecting and rejecting apostasy.[19] Philip Ryken, the president of Wheaton College, writes that "according to tradition, coal miners would take a canary with them underground for safety. Canaries are fragile birds, and thus they are the first to suffer the harmful effects of unhealthy air. In the event of a lack of oxygen or a sudden influx of noxious gas, the canary would pass out and the miners would know that they needed to return to the surface."[20] Today, in the same way, God's Word is alerting us to the toxicity of the surrounding moral atmosphere. The Bible is like the canary down the mine shaft warning us of the deadly fumes seeping into the church. But the Bible is also the clear air that's the answer to the church's polluted environment.

Hearing and humbly obeying its call in our own lives to "pull up" is the only answer to our moral freefall.

CHAPTER 7

THE WATERSHED MOMENT FOR THE CHURCH

June 26, 2015, was a watershed moment in American history. The United States Supreme Court, in a case known as *Obergefell v. Hodges,* held that "the right to marry is a fundamental right inherent in the liberty of the person, and under the Due Process and Equal Protection Clauses of the Fourteenth Amendment couples of the same-sex may not be deprived of that right and that liberty."[1] The ruling further prohibits any state from hindering the marriage of same-sex couples and abrogates all statutes and state constitutional provisions that define marriage as the union of a man and a woman.

This ruling dealt a devastating blow to those who believe the Bible and its definition of marriage as a monogamous, heterosexual union and to all who hold the traditional view of marriage that has been recognized from time immemorial. With one stroke, natural marriage was no longer the exclusive definition of marriage in America. As saddening as the ruling is, it is not surprising to anyone who has followed the cultural trajectory of this issue. It was just a matter of time since the onset of the sexual revolution of the 1960s.

Nevertheless, what has been even worse than the US Supreme Court decision, if that's possible, is the response of many professing Christians, even Christian leaders, to this issue. In many quarters of professing Christianity the decision was met with acceptance, approval, and even applause, so much so that many mainline denominations and progressive "Christians" beat the Supreme Court to the punch.

A year before the *Obergefell* decision, the Presbyterian Church (USA) approved homosexual marriage. "The top legislative body of the Presbyterian Church (U.S.A.) voted by large margins . . . to recognize same-sex marriage as Christian in the church constitution, adding language that marriage can be the union of 'two people,' not just 'a man and a woman.'"[2]

About two weeks before the Supreme Court's decision, Tony Campolo, a well-known, outspoken Christian leader, came out in favor of gay marriage. Campolo's rationale was explained in CBN News:

It was [Campolo's] own relationship with his wife and the many same-sex couples they know and spend time with that persuaded him that the primary purpose of marriage is about spiritual growth. He also wrote that homosexuality is "almost never a choice" and the church should offer love and acceptance to those who have same-sex attraction. "It has taken countless hours of prayer, study, conversation and emotional turmoil to bring me to the place where I am finally ready to call for the full acceptance of Christian gay couples into the Church."[3]

Rob Bell, former pastor of Mars Hill Church, and his wife, Kristen, appeared with Oprah Winfrey on her *Super Soul Sunday* program. When asked about the church embracing same-sex marriage, Rob Bell said, "We're moments away. I think the culture is already there. And the church will continue to be even more irrelevant when it quotes letters from 2,000 years ago as their best defense."[4] His total discounting of Scripture is stunning.

Influential author and blogger Rachel Held Evans, who no longer considers herself an evangelical, offers full support for same-sex marriage, basing her position almost exclusively on feelings and a desire to affirm others rather than Scripture. She says, "As I've made it clear in the past, I support marriage equality and affirm my gay and lesbian friends who want to commit themselves to another person for life."[5] Many more similar, equally shocking quotes could be added to these. The blogosphere is filled with sympathetic endorsements by professing Christians who support homosexual relationships in the name of love and acceptance.[6]

Simply stated, the tide on this issue has turned in our culture, especially with those under age fifty and overwhelmingly with those under age thirty. For believers who have lived in America over the last few decades, our heads are still spinning. What on earth has just happened? How did we get here? While many factors contribute to a shift like this, three stand out.

First, behind this shift is a well-organized satanic strategy. The home is the foundation of society—the first human institution created by God. The main New Testament passage on spiritual warfare is Ephesians 6:10-18, which follows on the heels of a passage about marriage and the family. Satan is the avowed enemy of traditional, natural marriage and the home. There's no doubt that changing views on homosexual behavior—one of the defining issues of our time—is Satan's overt strategy to pervert, repurpose, and reinvent human identity. The devil's end game is to deceive and destroy every trace of conscience found in humanity, God's crown of creation. Satan is working to pry people away from the truth in every form—doctrinal and moral.

As the coming of Christ draws near, we should expect the enemy to step up his assault on the truth to prepare the world for the final great falling away predicted in 2 Thessalonians 2:2-3. The stunning pace with which homosexual behavior has gained approval can only be explained in supernatural terms. Something beyond human forces is energizing this issue and galvanizing the marginalization and mocking of those who disagree.

Second, the Bible and sound biblical teaching are fast becoming relics. The Bible today is not faithfully taught in a growing number of churches. Confidence in God's Word as inspired and inerrant is eroding dramatically. People don't know what the Bible says, or don't care, or selectively believe what they want. Everything has become squishy and uncertain. With no final authority, the demise of a Christian worldview is upon us, and morality is a moving target subject only to the currents of culture. Christian Smith laments this trend from objective truth to subjective feelings: "While the vast majority of US teenagers identified themselves as Christians, the 'language,' and therefore experience, of Trinity, holiness, sin, grace, justification, sanctification, church, Eucharist, and heaven and hell appear, among most Christian teenagers in the United States at the very least, to be supplanted by the language of happiness, niceness and earned heavenly reward."[7] Smith and his colleagues call this new faith "Moralistic Therapeutic Deism," a belief system that embraces the existence of a god who demands little more than to be nice, "with the central goal of life to be happy and feel good about oneself."[8] In the prevailing climate of moralism and relativism, even within churches, we should not be surprised at what's happening.

Third, many professing believers are gripped by compromise and cowardice. In a society that increasingly delights in same-sex relationships and demonizes those who disagree, many are not willing to stand and face the fire. It's easier to cave and cower. Expect more and more professing Christians to take the path of least resistance and to just stay quiet or surrender to the waves of compromise and tolerance.

Nevertheless, the calling on God's people is to hold fast to Scripture and to love others, even in the face of being mocked and maligned for our convictions regarding this important issue.[9] True love for others involves graciously telling them the truth.

MORAL APOSTASY

Some might ask why we are highlighting homosexual behavior as a watershed for apostasy among the other sins in our culture. There are all kinds of sins out there, so why are we dedicating a chapter to this one? Are we just picking on this sin because it's an easy target? While we can't speak for all Christians, we believe there are three main reasons why homosexual behavior is a watershed issue related to apostasy.

First, in a unique way, this sin is contrary to nature and rubs against the grain of God's created order. Three times in Romans 1 Paul emphasizes that homosexual sin is contrary to nature or unnatural.[10] With this sin, a line is crossed that is different from other sins. A divinely appointed barrier is breached. Romans 1:27 seems to make that clear: "In the same way also the men abandoned the natural function of the woman and burned in their desire toward one another, men with men committing indecent acts and receiving in their own persons the due penalty of their error." In this one verse homosexuality is called unnatural, indecent, error, and bringing a due penalty.

In an attempt to blunt this point, many today argue that all sins are the same. Homosexuality is no different from telling a lie, gossiping, or getting drunk, they argue, so why make such a big deal of it? Those who oppose the rapid acceptance of homosexual behavior are accused of overreacting on this issue and failing to maintain a sense of proportion. To be fair, this point is also often cited by those who are against homosexual behavior in an effort to be evenhanded. After all, all of us are sinners—and we say "amen" to that. But is that the end of the matter? Are all sins really the same?

The answer to this question is yes and no. Yes, all sins are the same in that they break God's law. They make the offender a lawbreaker.[11] They put the transgressor at odds with the law. In that sense all sins are the same. But no, all sins aren't the same in their effect and consequences. Any reading of the Old Testament law codes reveals a vast difference in punishment for various offenses. Differing punishment reveals that some sins are more serious than others.

The same thing is true in legal statutes today. Few would argue that traffic offenses are no different from rape, bank robbery, or kidnapping. Yes, all offenses break the law. All violations make you a lawbreaker. But no, not all have anywhere near the same consequences or call forth the same punishment. In Scripture, homosexuality is not treated like other sins.[12]

If someone shoots at a large plate-glass window with a BB gun, the BB breaks the glass. A small hole is made. The BB-shooting perpetrator is a glass breaker. If another person shoots a large plate-glass window with a bazooka, the bazooka shell shatters the glass. The bazooka-wielding perpetrator is also a glass breaker. But in this latter case, the glass is obliterated. It is not a tiny hole that is left behind but a colossal cavity. The window and all the structure around it are blown away. Both parties are glass breakers, and in this sense their acts are the same, yet who would argue that these acts are equal?

Certainly not the owner of the window. The nature of these acts is vastly different. Consequences matter. Punishments are tailored to meet the extent of the damage inflicted. So when someone says all sins are the same to God, we need to make sure we accurately frame the issue.

The second reason homosexual behavior is a watershed issue for culture and the church—a bright red line—is that until very recently, belief that homosexual behavior is wrong was pervasive. Growing up in the '60s and '70s, people of all ages and walks of life considered same-sex physical intimacy wrong. Almost no one, including even the most hardened unbelievers, considered homosexual behavior acceptable. The avalanche in the last twenty years that has culminated in the nationwide legality of same-sex marriage has been nothing short of breathtaking. The radical redefining of marriage goes to the heart of humanity and society. The first human institution God created was marriage. Changing its definition means that nothing is sacred—nothing is off limits. Everything is up for grabs.

Third, more and more professing Christians are capitulating to the culture and accepting same-sex relationships. According to research conducted by the Pew Research Center, "the divide between evangelicals and mainline Protestants over gay marriage is getting wider. The survey found that 70 percent of white evangelicals and 57 percent of black Protestants don't support making same-sex marriage legal [that means one-third of white evangelicals and nearly one-half of black Protestants support it]. However, 62 percent of white mainline Protestants and 56 percent of Catholics are in favor of same-sex marriage."[13] The surrender of so many on this issue sounds the alarm for a reasoned response, a call to biblical discernment, and an answer to the question, How do we hold fast to Scripture and love all people, all the while being hated and demonized by the world for simply believing the Bible?

BACK TO THE BIBLE

For two thousand years the church of Jesus Christ has believed that homosexual behavior is sinful. Having a same-sex orientation is not sinful in itself, but acting on that orientation is contrary to Scripture. The distinction between having a same-sex orientation and acting on that desire is important, and we need to keep this point clearly before us.

Belief that homosexual activity is wrong was almost universally accepted even two or three decades ago among Christians and non-Christians alike. Stating the matter as simply as possible, Christians have believed, "God intended humans to express their sexuality within the confines of a marriage between a man and a woman only, not with someone of the same gender."[14]

Then, suddenly, when activists began to turn the tide of public opinion, progressives in the church had an epiphany that homosexual behavior is acceptable to God. In a lemminglike rush, many could hardly give their blessing fast enough. But could it be that the change in position was borne not of *epiphany* but rather *expediency*—a desire to be embraced and accepted by the secular culture? Is the retreat rising from a desire to avoid the label of homophobia and to appear more loving and tolerant than believers who hold to the millennia-long interpretation of God's Word?

Turning to God's Word, there are four main biblical passages (or groupings) that refer negatively to the issue of homosexual activity:

1. The story of Sodom (Genesis 19:1-13)
2. The Levitical texts (Leviticus 18:22; 20:13)
3. Paul's description of fallen society away from God (Romans 1:26-32)
4. Two lists by Paul, each containing a reference to homosexual

practice of some kind (1 Corinthians 6:9-10 and 1 Timothy 1:8-11)[15]

Let's look very briefly at each of these. (The Leviticus passages will be discussed in connection with 1 Corinthians 6.)

GENESIS 19:1-13

The famous passage in Genesis 19 refers to the homosexual desires of the men of Sodom toward the two male visitors to their city—who were angelic beings in human form—and God's cataclysmic judgment of the city. Since that time, Sodom has become equated with divine judgment. John Stott writes, "To be sure, homosexual behavior was not Sodom's only sin; but according to Scripture it was certainly one of its sins, which brought down upon it the fearful judgment of God."[16] The Epistle of Jude confirms the link between Sodom's sexual sin and its destruction.[17]

ROMANS 1:26-32

Romans 1:26-27 says, "God gave them over to degrading passions; for their women exchanged the natural function for that which is unnatural, and in the same way also the men abandoned the natural function of the woman and burned in their desire toward one another, men with men committing indecent acts and receiving in their own persons the due penalty of their error."

While much could be—and has been—said about these verses, there's no doubt that the other activities listed in Romans 1:28-31 are sinful, and Romans 1:28-31 immediately follows the verses dealing with homosexuality. In this context, which catalogs serious sins, arguing that Paul didn't consider homosexual behavior to be a sin is quite a stretch. Kevin DeYoung says it well:

Homosexual practice is sinful because it violates the divine design in creation. According to Paul's logic, men and women who engage in same-sex sexual behavior—even if they are being true to their own feelings and desires—have suppressed God's truth in unrighteousness. They have exchanged the fittedness of male-female relations for those that are contrary to nature.[18]

I CORINTHIANS 6:9-10

First Corinthians 6:9-10 is an ugly list of sins that are incompatible and irreconcilable with the Kingdom of God and the gospel: "Or do you not know that the unrighteous will not inherit the kingdom of God? Do not be deceived; neither fornicators, nor idolaters, nor adulterers, nor *effeminate*, nor *homosexuals*, nor thieves, nor the covetous, nor drunkards, nor revilers, nor swindlers, will inherit the kingdom of God" (emphasis added).

Don't overlook the serious words of warning: "Do not be deceived." Many today, in failing to take these words seriously, *are* being deceived.

Two of the words used in these verses refer to homosexual behavior:

> *Malakos*, sometimes translated "effeminate," means "soft to the touch." Among the Greeks it referred to males who assumed the passive role in homosexual intercourse.
> *Arsenokoitai*, found in 1 Corinthians 6:9, is a compound of *arsen* (man) and *koite* (bed). An accurate translation is "bedder of man," or someone who takes men to bed. The clear meaning of the word is men engaged in homosexual behavior. Paul probably referred back to Leviticus 18:22 and 20:13 in coining this word.[19] The Levitical passages call for

the death penalty for homosexual intercourse and call it an "abomination." The related words in Romans 1:27, *arsenes en arsesin* ("men in men"), are a vivid, graphic reference to male homosexuals' intimacy.

Kevin DeYoung highlights the seriousness of these verses:

If 1 Corinthians 6 is right, it's not an overstatement to say that solemnizing same-sex sexual behavior—like supporting any form of sexual immorality—runs the risk of leading people to hell. . . . When we tolerate the doctrine which affirms homosexual behavior, we are tolerating a doctrine which leads people further from God. This is not the mission Jesus gave his disciples when he told them to teach the nations everything he commanded.[20]

1 TIMOTHY 1:8-10
Another vice list that condemns homosexual behavior is found in 1 Timothy 1:8-10:

We know that the Law is good, if one uses it lawfully, realizing the fact that law is not made for a righteous person, but for those who are lawless and rebellious, for the ungodly and sinners, for the unholy and profane, for those who kill their fathers or mothers, for murderers and immoral men and homosexuals and kidnappers and liars and perjurers, and whatever else is contrary to sound teaching.

Paul uses the word *arsenokoitai* in 1:10 (the same word used in 1 Corinthians 6:9) and clearly links this behavior with other sinful activities that are contrary to God's law.

TO BELIEVE OR NOT TO BELIEVE

Added to these texts, the biblical view of marriage set forth in Genesis 1–2 excludes homosexual acts by implication even if it never specifically prohibits them.[21] The positive principles in Genesis 1–2 and the consistent prohibitions of sexual immorality in the Old and New Testaments confirm monogamous, heterosexual marriage as the only one-flesh relationship God accepts and blesses. Scripture is very clear on this issue in spite of all the noise we hear today. Those who claim there is no unanimity on this issue among scholars must remember that until very recently there was. Just because people in recent days, influenced by cultural trends, have begun to question the long-standing interpretation of key passages does not mean the issue is foggy.

The question is, Do we believe the Bible is God's inspired Word, and are we willing to take what it says at face value, using accepted principles of interpretation? That the Bible prohibits homosexual behavior is clear cut to any objective interpreter. Those trying to twist Scripture to support homosexual behavior, or at least to muddy the waters, have utterly failed to make their case from Scripture.

Summarizing the New Testament prohibitions, Peter Coleman notes, "St. Paul's writings repudiate homosexual behavior as a vice of the Gentiles in Romans, as a bar to the Kingdom of God in Corinthians, and as an offense to be repudiated by the moral law in 1 Timothy."[22] Rod Dreher encourages young people and progressive Christians to hit the pause button on this issue:

> Homosexuality is a clear, bright line. The Rachel Held Evanses need to ask themselves if they would be willing to follow Jesus Christ if in doing so, they would have to take a countercultural position on the issue. To embrace same-sex marriage from a Christian viewpoint is a radical shift,

one that repudiates two millenia of Christian thought and teaching.

Are we really so sure that we 21st century Americans have this right, and everyone that came before us, including St. Paul, was wrong?[23]

These are sage words for us all to take to heart.

ARGUMENTS IN SUPPORT OF HOMOSEXUAL RELATIONS

Entire books have been written dealing with the arguments pro and con for homosexual behavior, so the purpose here is not to plumb the depths of this issue. In this section, however, we want to briefly state and answer a few of the most common contentions offered by proponents of homosexuality to support their view.

WHAT'S LOVE GOT TO DO WITH IT?

One prevalent argument in favor of homosexual relationships is that love trumps all. If people love each other, what they do or who they do it with cannot be wrong. While this sounds appealing in our contemporary, tolerant culture, it is shortsighted. Love, which is an essential part of any intimate relationship, is not the sole criterion that authenticates it.[24] After all, what if a person loves several people? What if a person loves an animal? What if an adult loves a child and the child says he or she loves the adult? What if someone loves someone who is married to another person?

Love is found in obedience to the law and the purpose of our Creator, not in rebellion against it. As John Stott says, "No man is justified in breaking his marriage covenant with his wife on the ground that the quality of his love for another woman is richer. Quality of love is not the only yardstick by which to measure what is good and right. . . . There seems to be no limits to what some people will seek to justify in the name of love."[25] Love cannot be the sole criterion for sexual relationships. Love and law are not incompatible.[26]

JUSTICE FOR ALL?

For many, the full acceptance of homosexual activity is a simple matter of justice and nondiscrimination. We often hear about "gay rights," which implies homosexuals are suffering an injustice that needs to be righted. Desmond Tutu, former archbishop of Cape Town, among many others, pushes this point. But is this reasoning sound?

God is a God of justice and righteousness. He is infinitely just, and He wants His creatures to love and respect all people without distinction. However, it does not follow that homosexual behavior should be condoned as a matter of justice. Speaking about homosexuality and justice, John Stott says, "Talk of 'justice' is inappropriate, since human beings may not claim as a 'right' what God has not given them."[27] Since the Creator has not given human beings the right to express their sexuality with members of the same sex, any talk of justice or rights on this topic is misplaced. People may believe homosexual relationships are acceptable, but appealing to justice or rights to substantiate this position is contrary to Scripture. "Sexual intimacy is legitimate, according to Scripture, only within the confines of heterosexual marriage. For this reason, homosexual practice cannot be regarded as a permissible equivalent, let alone a divine right."[28]

JESUS WAS SILENT ABOUT HOMOSEXUALITY

Some point to the fact that Jesus never condemned homosexuality as evidence of His implicit approval. There are two problems with this notion. First, Jesus did not address *many* sins. He never condemned child abuse, bank robbery, or drug abuse, but certainly all of those activities are sinful. Jesus never had to condemn homosexual behavior because everyone in the Jewish culture of His day understood that it was contrary to the Mosaic law.[29]

Second, Jesus frequently referenced Sodom (and a few times Gomorrah) to warn His listeners of impending doom.[30] The word *sodomy* comes from the homosexual sin of Sodom. Any argument that Jesus supported homosexuality is an argument from silence that disregards His numerous negative references to Sodom.

APPROVAL AND APPLAUSE

As we've seen, no fair-minded case can be made that Scripture supports homosexual acts or fails to condemn them. Homosexuals who fulfill their sexual desires are violating the will of their Creator. But the issue doesn't end there. The Bible not only prohibits same-sex relations but it also forbids approving or applauding this activity. In the same context in Romans 1 where Paul prohibits same-sex relations, he concludes, "Although they know the ordinance of God, that those who practice such things are worthy of death, they not only do the same, but also give hearty approval to those who practice them."[31]

Today, the cheering section for same-sex relationships and even homosexual marriage is mushrooming in our culture and within the church. Acceptance has given way to approval, which has in turn led to applause. This viewpoint has grown to such an extent that those who voice any objection are increasingly ostracized, maligned, and muzzled. Scores of pastors, church leaders, and denominations across the country lend hearty approval to what's happening in our culture and heap disdain on any who disagree. Evil is called good while good is called evil.

Romans 1:32 is a sobering warning against this attitude. Approving and applauding the sins listed in the preceding context (including same-sex relations) is harshly condemned by God. Romans 1:32

actually says that commending these sins is *worse* than committing them. How can that possibly be? Thomas Schreiner explains: "The person who commits evil, even though his or her actions are inexcusable, can at least plead the mitigating circumstances of the passion of the moment. Those who encourage others to practice evil do so from a settled and impassioned conviction."[32]

C. E. B. Cranfield, the eminent New Testament scholar, says, "There is also the fact that those who condone and applaud the vicious actions of others are actually making a deliberate contribution to the setting up of a public opinion favourable to vice, and so to the corruption of an indefinite number of other people."[33] When people "[take] delight in the sinfulness of others . . . wickedness has sunk to its lowest level."[34]

What we're witnessing today is the graphic fulfillment of this principle. The applause is drowning out the voice of disagreement. According to Romans 1:32, those who are applauding the Supreme Court decision legalizing same-sex marriage are practicing an evil graver than those who are guilty of homosexual sin. That's sobering. It's the bottom rung on the ladder. When this point is reached to the extent we see today, the final falling away predicted in Scripture could certainly be just around the corner.

FINAL APOSTASY

The homosexual revolution has hit like a flood in the last twenty years. A red line has been crossed that few believed possible. In the wake of this departure, culture has already absorbed and accepted this behavior and moved past it to every form of gender confusion one can imagine. Nothing seems off limits or taboo. Every person does what is right in their own eyes. Issues of gender and identity are the new hot topic. In a recent article, ABC News identified fifty-eight genders for Facebook users to choose from.[35] Some have identified more than eighty different gender identifications. The question is being raised, Have we reached the end of gender? Many websites have eliminated any request for gender because they can't list them all or aren't sure how many to list. We even have gender-neutral translations of the Bible. Homosexuality was only the beginning—the opening volley. Having lost God, man has now lost himself. Where's it all headed?

Jesus said the world in the days before His second coming will be like the days of Lot in the city of Sodom:

> It was the same as happened in the days of Lot: they were eating, they were drinking, they were buying, they were selling, they were planting, they were building; but on the day that Lot went out from Sodom it rained fire and brimstone from heaven and destroyed them all. It will be just the same on the day that the Son of Man is revealed.[36]

What is happening today is no coincidence or happenstance. Satan is spearheading a global onslaught against God and man to pave the way for the final apostasy predicted in 2 Thessalonians 2:2-3. We are living on its leading edge. This may be the beginning of the end.

Christ's coming may be very soon!

HIS WORD, THE LAST WORD

Same-sex issues—one single controversial reality—is having a profound effect on the church and individual Christians who don't know either what to believe or how they should respond biblically. We've seen in this chapter that we cannot approve what God disapproves. The church of Jesus Christ is a place for all of us to learn to say no to sin and to find spiritual help to live a life that pleases God. Every believer must take up the cross, dying to self and following Jesus regardless of our specific entangling sins. Our choice today on this issue is not between lazily condoning sinful behavior or lashing out in anger and condemnation. "There's another way. It's possible to show love and also speak of transformative truth. It just isn't easy."[37]

As Satan mounts his final, furious assault against the truth and seeks to erase every vestige of morality, we can rest humbly in the knowledge that God honors those who rely upon Him, submit to His will, and seek to lovingly encourage others to do the same.

Dawson Trotman, founder of the Navigators, used four code letters to refer to his nightly study of God's Word: HWLW. Whenever he was home with his wife or with a group of people at night and the conversation was waning, he would end with "HWLW"—"His Word the Last Word." One of them would recite a portion of Scripture, and they would head to bed. Trotman developed this practice as a way to keep the last thoughts of his day fixed on the Lord.

That's a great practice for ending the day, but it's an equally effective way to face the issues of our day. In every issue of life, our attitude should be HWLW—"His Word the Last Word."

May the Word of God have the Last Word in our lives, our families, our nation, and in His church as we await His coming.

CHAPTER 8

WILL THE REAL JESUS STAND UP?

[Jesus] said to them, "But who do you say that I am?"

MATTHEW 16:15

Jesus Christ is the most pivotal, revolutionary, and controversial figure in human history. Concerning this, there is no debate. This one man accomplished more in His short life than kings and empires have done over centuries. And though the world's libraries are filled with volumes written about Him and His impact on humanity, one familiar work has become a classic. In his memorable poem "One Solitary Life," Dr. James Allan Francis describes Jesus' humble beginnings and ignominious death. But he goes on to describe Jesus' matchless influence:

> *Nineteen centuries have come and gone*
> *And today Jesus is the central figure of the human race*
> *And the leader of mankind's progress*

All the armies that have ever marched
All the navies that have ever sailed
All the parliaments that have ever sat
All the kings that ever reigned put together
Have not affected the life of mankind on earth
As powerfully as that one solitary life.[1]

But despite Jesus' colossal impact on history and humanity, there exists today widespread confusion as to who He actually was . . . and is. There are, in fact, some who claim He never was at all.[2] And then there are those, like author Bart Ehrman, who assert that Jesus Himself never actually claimed to be deity; rather, His recorded claims were nothing more than a legend created by His followers after His death.[3]

But even among those who believe Jesus was God in the flesh, there are divergent views concerning His identity, mission, and accomplishments. Within Christendom exists a multiplicity of images floating around in the heads of those who profess to know Him. Therefore, history's refrain has become a recurring question confronting each new generation: Who *is* Jesus Christ? Or perhaps a more appropriate postmodern, theologically emerging question would be "Who is Jesus *to you?*"

Popular perception of Jesus is changing in culture and even in the church. Scripture's Jesus is getting a makeover, and in some cases undergoing an *extreme* makeover. Take a survey of Main Street or a typical college campus, and you will likely find a surprising percentage of people haven't the slightest clue as to His real identity. I (Jeff) have done this in England, where young people's answers ranged from "I've no idea" to "Isn't he that bloke who did magic?"

Thanks to the overwhelming secularization in society, we're

beginning to see a dramatic drop in the most basic biblical knowledge about Jesus. A recent Barna Group study revealed that fewer than 50 percent of millennials believe Jesus was God, and 56 percent of millennials either believe He was sinful like other humans or have confusion on the issue.[4]

But among those in America with a rudimentary knowledge of Christ, many have rejected long-held beliefs about the Son of God, favoring instead a reimagined version of Him. To them, He's due for an upgrade—Jesus 2.0, a new and improved Christ for a new generation. In an age of evolving spirituality, Jesus has come to mean anything you want Him to mean, really—a *customized* Savior for all peoples and preferences. A morphing Messiah.

JESUS VS. "JESUS"

Every new generation is responsible to engage and respond to God's revelation of Himself and His Son. However, in the absence of an understanding firmly anchored in Scripture, people's perceptions of Christ become skewed, blurred, and distorted. As a result, counterfeit Christs have appeared on the scene. And the values promoted in these various subdivisions of the Christian community give us insight into the "Christ idea" they follow. Here are a few you may recognize.

HIPSTER JESUS

Hipster Jesus is cool and very *chill*. After all, He has to be if we're going to reach a demographic of skinny-jeans-wearing, beard-growing, Pabst Blue Ribbon–drinking twentysomethings, right? Hipster Jesus is a handsome, handy, do-it-yourselfer. He's really into storytelling. In fact, *everything* is about story. He feeds the poor and gives handouts to the homeless. He stands up for human rights. In some circles, He may even have socialist leanings, since that's the way many in the younger generations view the early church. But though Hipster Jesus is big on diversity, His following is to a large degree white. And for some reason, Hipster Jesus doesn't go over that well in poor communities. This Jesus is very concerned about the environment and climate change. He wants His followers to be responsible stewards of the planet. He recycles and buys His clothes secondhand. He likes coffee shops and indie music. He prefers "worship arts pastors" to "ministers of music." He might be gluten free. He doesn't get too bent out of shape with specific doctrines or stress about whether pastors preach expository or topical sermons. He's more into *general* theology, if any at all. He sees value in returning to traditional liturgy.

EQUALITY JESUS

This Jesus is much more liberal than Hipster Jesus, though in places there is some overlap. He isn't concerned about the "antiquated morality" fundamentalist Christians claim that Scripture teaches. So if certain Bible verses don't exactly square with our society's evolving beliefs or practices involving gender, sexuality, or marriage, this Jesus isn't going to get upset if you reinterpret or ignore them. Equality Jesus can't be accused of being on the wrong side of history. Those who subscribe to Equality Jesus say He is all about love and inclusion . . . as *they* define it, of course. His favorite word is *all*, and to His followers, phrases like "whosoever will come" and "just as I am" don't simply mean Jesus accepts you as you are; they mean He is perfectly okay with whoever you *want* to be. Those who believe in Equality Jesus not only redefine words like *love* and *hate* for a new age, but they also reclassify various sins, designating attitudes like bigotry and discrimination as among the most heinous, evil transgressions one could ever commit. Equality Jesus is a superhero social-justice warrior and will probably let everyone into heaven eventually. On the other hand, He may decide to keep out those pharisaical, bigoted, Bible-thumping conservatives.

PATRIOTIC JESUS

This Jesus is the older counterpart to the one portrayed by the hipster crowd. Patriotic Jesus is ultraconservative, especially when it comes to moral issues. He leans far to the right in His politics, and His followers are expected to be heavily involved in the political process. There is no short supply of politically laced sermons in the Patriotic Jesus church culture. In fact, pastors routinely surrender their pulpits to like-minded politicians who happen to stop by. As a result, these politicians gain the "evangelical vote" when they campaign for "Judeo-Christian values" or moral issues that gain this particular religious or socioeconomic demographic's sympathy. Sometimes these voters ignore a personal lack of character in their chosen candidates because they're strong on the "right" issues.

Patriotic Jesus loves America and thinks it is the best nation He ever founded. It makes Him happy when His people fly the American flag in church and celebrate all the really important patriotic holidays. In that sense, this Jesus is very American. His followers talk about America being a "city on a hill" and a "light for all the nations." The United States is seen as sort of a new Israel or some kind of collective covenant people. There's talk about America being a "Christian nation," although Patriotic Jesus' followers sometimes struggle to articulate what that means. Patriotic Jesus supports the US military.

In many ways, Patriotic Jesus looks a lot more like a product of America than of heaven, much more earthly than eternal. He seems more concerned with temporal, national issues than He is with the destiny of people's souls. This Jesus is blatantly white and popular with middle- to upper-middle-class households.

CHRIST CARICATURES

There are many other Christ caricatures in our culture that we could discuss, but they also fall far short of the Savior we see described in Scripture.

What makes these Christ caricatures compelling is that there are some elements of truth sprinkled into these interpretations of the incarnate Christ—truth easily ascertained from reading the Gospels. The Jesus of the Bible does care about social justice and those who are oppressed. On morality, He would be deeply offended and angered by sex trafficking, violence, and today's barbaric slaughter of innocent babies. And He does receive anyone who calls on His name for salvation. And when His people find themselves fortunate enough to be in a democracy, they can and should participate in the political process, especially when government promotes godless values and threatens religious liberty. The real Jesus suffered God's wrath to remove the penalty and power of sin for all sinners who trust in Him.

But despite what these aforementioned caricatures of Christ get right, they fail to provide the clarity and *totality* of who Jesus is as portrayed in Scripture. A *partial* Jesus is no Jesus at all. We cannot choose those parts of Him that appeal to us while ignoring the rest of who Scripture says He is. Christianity is not a biblical-truth buffet, where we hold our noses and pass over the items that fail our personal taste test. We do not set the menu of truth; God does.

Beyond trying desperately to relate Jesus to the next generation, what we've witnessed in some church movements is a redefinition of the very essence of Jesus Himself. Is this a case of the church trying too hard? Loosely based on the Bible's Jesus, these caricatures of Him are like suffering through a bad movie that's "inspired by true events" or "based on the book." In such films, the depictions of characters often bear little or no resemblance to the actual persons they represent. Though some who promote these incomplete Christ caricatures may have honorable motives, by force fitting our Christ into our culture, we end up creating a "hybrid Jesus," one who may be more suited to today's changing world but is far away from the real Jesus known in Scripture. These images of Jesus may have some strengths, but their attempt to make Him more relevant than He already is proves to be a failed experiment. The portrait of Jesus that Scripture paints cannot be improved upon.

God needs no help with His theology, and He doesn't stutter when He speaks. Like Moses, we may protest His proclamations, but we cannot argue their veracity.

Altering or arguing the biblical concept of the Christ, even in the most minute way, blurs our vision of Him, quickly turning our incomplete, self-manufactured image of Him into an idol.

COMING INTO FOCUS

By detaching ourselves from Scripture's Jesus, we not only end up with the wrong Jesus, but we also short-circuit the very power of the gospel. Like the Father and the Spirit, remove any attributes of Jesus, and He suddenly becomes another Jesus altogether. Therefore, we do not need a "fresh vision" of Christ; we need a much more biblical one.

In His address to the seven churches in Revelation, Jesus reviews and repairs His distorted image by unmistakably presenting Himself with clarity and authority. There He describes Himself as a redeeming, loving, glorified, all-encompassing, sovereign, death-conquering, sword-wielding, judgment-bringing, Second Coming Lord and King![5] Is that how you see Him? Or is He still walking around in sandals, passing out fish and healing sick people? The vision of the resurrected, glorified Christ in Revelation is both terrific and traumatic, unbelievable and unforgettable. And it is only *after* imparting this vision that Jesus begins His extremely "tough love" rebuke of the churches. Hence, we can never become the Christians we were meant to be or properly understand our mission apart from a clear concept and understanding of who Jesus Christ is.

What would Jesus say to those churches today who are known not for proclaiming this Revelation Christ but rather for their happy messages, large crowds, and elaborate stage presentations? What would He say to congregations where there is much talk about *relationship* but little talk about *repentance*? There's celebration without sacrifice. A high value placed on friendship but not much emphasis on lordship. This is where the threat of apostasy is most subtle. Like a hairline fissure in a foundation, it's only the beginning of an eventual catastrophic collapse. Unless a contextually complete portrait of Jesus is taught, sung, believed, and celebrated, we end up missing the mark and getting the short stick of spirituality. God wants us to know and embrace *all* of His Son, not just the parts we prefer. We must see the big picture of Him, not conveniently chosen snapshots of His life, character, and ministry.

The good news is that it's not left up to us to define who God's Son is. God has already done the heavy lifting for us, providing us all we need to know through the revelation of Scripture. And that is to our advantage because our judgment can't be trusted anyway. Due to sin's effects on our minds and on our ability to comprehend spiritual truth, God did for us what we could never do for ourselves—He helped us discover what He is really like. During Jesus' earthly ministry, Jesus refused to trust people's hearts and intentions, even after some "believed in His name." John records that Jesus "was [still] not entrusting Himself to them, for He knew all men, and because He did not need anyone to testify concerning man, for He Himself knew what was in man."[6]

Jesus knows the true motives of people's hearts. And He understands that left to our own flawed imaginations, we'll usually get it wrong when describing, understanding, or explaining God. He knows we have a crippling disability when it comes to finding Him and understanding Him on our own. Our natural minds are darkened as it relates to comprehending His truth.[7] Even after coming to faith, we are still desperately dependent on the Holy Spirit's illuminating ministry, as we are prone to misinterpret and subtly twist God's Word.

But that's exactly why He gave us the Bible. As we engage it, the Author reveals His truth; our minds are opened to understand it. The Holy Spirit "turns on the lights," allowing us to see clearly and understand fully.[8]

Without God's divine revelation, we may end up believing in Him for all the wrong reasons. Or equally disastrous, the "Jesus" we choose to embrace may stem from a faulty, self-generated perception of who He actually is. One unintended result of this is that our expectations of Him can become unrealistic or unbiblical due to our own unbiblical understanding or conclusions. Instead of responding to and worshiping the Christ of Scripture, we would project an insufficient replica of Him onto our faith experience. We see this happening in these last days, not only as false Christs have appeared but also with the previously mentioned warped depictions of Him.[9]

As believers, we must guard against embracing a Savior who simply suits our spiritual taste buds or fits our theological, social, moral, and political constructs. Though it's human nature to do so, it becomes intrinsically defective and dysfunctional.

It's also sinful.

So one of the dangers of apostasy that we face right now is a "Jesus" who is both inaccurate and incomplete. Because many today have molded Him into whatever they want or need Him to be, He has become a "conjured-up Christ": loosely biblical but with all the practical details filled in by the human imagination. He is a god of our own making, a creation borne out of fantasy rather than reality. Tragically, failing to understand who Jesus is and what He came to accomplish leads to a false conclusion about the nature of the gospel itself. Emergent theologian Brian McLaren is one of those who paints an inaccurate portrait of Christ. In his book, *A New Kind of Christianity*, he writes,

> Instead, [Jesus] came to announce a new kingdom, a new way of life, a new way of peace that carried good news to all people of every religion. A new kingdom is much bigger than a new religion, and *in fact it has room for many religious traditions within it.* This good news wasn't simply about a new way to solve the religious problems of ontological fall and original sin (problems, remember once more, that arise centuries later and within a different narrative altogether). It wasn't simply information about how individual souls could leave earth, avoid hell, and ascend to heaven after death. No, it was about God's will being done on earth as in heaven for all people. It was about God's faithful solidarity with all humanity in our suffering, oppression, and evil.[10]

This redefining of Christianity is not a new understanding but simply an unbiblical one. McLaren's misunderstanding of Jesus and His substitutionary atonement makes it clear that in these last days, we need a passionate return to God and His Word in order to form and transform our understanding of His Son.

SO . . . ANSWER THE QUESTION

One of the pleasant ironies of truth is that the sovereign, exalted Christ doesn't have a problem relating to mortals like us. On the contrary He identifies with all of humanity, including people from every race, tribe, tongue, and nation. He understands our struggles because He actually "became flesh, and dwelt among us."[11]

Hebrews reminds us,

> Since the children share in flesh and blood, He Himself likewise also partook of the same. . . . He had to be made like His brethren in all things, so that He might become a merciful and faithful high priest in things pertaining to God, to make propitiation for the sins of the people. For since He Himself was tempted in that which He has suffered, He is able to come to the aid of those who are tempted.[12]

And again, "We do not have a high priest who cannot sympathize with our weaknesses, but One who has been tempted in all things as we are, yet without sin."[13]

Jesus understands what it's like to walk the earth. Like us, He worked, sweat, grew hungry, and became tired. He felt the wide range of emotions we feel—joy and peace, along with sadness, disappointment, and the dark night of the soul. He experienced the hurt of being abandoned by those He loved the most, and He identifies with our mental stress and physical abuse. He bled and died. He was 100 percent human.

In fact, this was one of the reasons He came down from heaven and took on human flesh: to let us know that He really does get what it's like to be one of us. This is what qualifies Him to be a sympathetic Savior.[14]

But He also came to reveal the Father to us, to accomplish redemption, and to become our sin substitute. In doing so, He now represents us to the Father.[15] And though His identification with us doesn't allow us to perpetually morph Him into a fantasy of who we wish Him to be, it does tell us He *understands*.

The issue today isn't really, "Does Jesus get *us*?" but rather "Do we get *Him*?"

That's precisely the question the Lord asked His disciples toward the end of His earthly ministry: "Who do people say that the Son of Man is?" And after they reported what they had heard from the "social media" of their day, Jesus got more personal: "But who do *you* say that I am?"

Peter, the resident blurter of the Twelve, correctly responded, "You are the Christ, the Son of the living God."[16]

Good answer, Peter. You've been paying attention.

But Jesus didn't ask them this question so He could know how to more effectively relate to them or somehow accommodate their preferred image of Him. (These Jewish disciples expected the Christ to deliver them from Roman oppression and to set up His earthly kingdom in their lifetime.) Rather, He quizzed them so they could reveal whether or not they had developed an accurate and authentic concept of Him in their minds, to show whether or not *they* had received and processed the truth He had been teaching them. In forming their perception and understanding of Jesus Christ, it was imperative that they see the whole picture and not just the bits that accommodated their preconceived ideas. Their conclusion?

He was 100 percent God.

And He still is. There is, and will only ever be, one Jesus. He doesn't adapt, evolve, or change but is the same "yesterday and today and forever."[17] And His Word—not our emotional needs, cultural trends, church-growth fads, missional philosophies, or theological preferences—is our source of authority regarding Him.

Jesus is who Scripture says He is. Period. To augment that definitive biblical declaration is to create a "Frankenstein" god, pieced together with parts we've dug up and stitched together along our spiritual journey. Therefore, we dare not transform the Jesus who turned water to wine into a watered-down version of Himself. This is why we check every thought, belief, and teaching, sifting it through the filter of Scripture to see if it holds up as true. And if not, we reject it, no matter how attractive it may appear to be.

EXPERIENCING GOD

Fortunately, the Lord doesn't bypass our minds in order to reach our hearts. Even in the most basic, infantile decision to trust Christ, there must first be some existing knowledge of who that Christ is and what He has done. Therefore, *experiencing* Jesus doesn't happen unless we first *know* something about Him. God designed and made us, intricately crafting humanity in body, mind, and spirit.[18] And He created us to respond to Him based on His revelation. Our experience of Him grows out of receiving and believing what He says is true about Himself. Any other experiential claim is unbiblical and heretical.

That's one reason Jesus, on His last night before being crucified, filled His high priestly prayer with language that was heavy on content and high on life change. Consider what He prayed for His disciples (and for you) in John 17:

> "That they may *know* You" (verse 3).
> "I have *manifested Your name* to the men whom You gave Me" (verse 6).
> "They have kept Your *word*" (verse 6).
> "The *words* which You gave Me *I have given* to them" (verse 8).
> "They *received them* [the words] and truly *understood* that I came forth from You" (verse 8).
> "These things I *speak in the world*, so that they may have *My joy made full*" (verse 13).
> "I have given them *Your word*" (verse 14).
> "Sanctify them in *the truth*; *Your word is truth*" (verse 17).

> "I have *made Your name known* to them . . . that the love with which You loved Me may be in them" (verse 26).

So even the joy and love we all long for begins with understanding and embracing God's revelation about Jesus! Apart from Scripture, we can know virtually nothing about Jesus Christ.[19]

So what do you believe about Jesus Christ? What's He like? What did He do? What theological truths did He teach? Further, what did He do for your sin? How can you know how to walk with Him daily? What do you need to know about God, the Christian life, Satan, the world, your sin nature, and how sanctification works? What do you do when you sin, and why don't you lose your salvation? *All* of these—and countless other topics—are a part of doctrine and theology. And they are all found within the pages of your own Bible.

You can rest in the confidence that yours is a God who is as holy as He is loving, as wrathful as He is gracious. The humble Jesus of the Gospels is the same exalted coming, conquering Christ of Revelation. The same Jesus who proclaimed, "Blessed are the poor in spirit" in Matthew 5:3 also prophesied in Matthew 7:23 concerning the day when He would say, "I never knew you; depart from Me, you who practice lawlessness." The same Jesus who beckoned, "Come to Me, all who are weary and heavy-laden, and I will give you rest" also predicted that some will "be cast into the outer darkness; in that place there will be weeping and gnashing of teeth."[20] The same Christ who comforts a grieving Mary and Martha in John 11 also offended thousands of followers in John 6. We cannot have one Jesus without the other.

He is all this and much more. He is one and the same—a complete Christ, not a cafeteria version of Himself.

Know that in these last days, there will be a continued assault on this biblical Jesus. As we are already seeing, He will be depicted as a

Savior who winks at wickedness; who simply makes people feel good about themselves; who promises health, happiness, and prosperity; and who promotes tolerance and unity over discernment and doctrine. This makeshift Savior is heavy on sentimentality and light on sovereignty. Today's Jesus welcomes everyone into heaven regardless of religion. Some have made fantastical claims of visiting this heaven and have described Jesus Christ differently than Scripture does. And though millions swallow their syrupy tales and emotion-tugging lies, don't you be one of them.[21]

The lord of deception is a master at distorting the truth about the One who will one day cast him into the lake of fire.[22]

Many erroneous things will be said, preached, blogged, written, and sung about Jesus in the days to come. But we must hold fast to God's truth and not be swayed by false teachers and phony images of Christ. With Scripture as our anchor and rudder, we won't be "tossed and blown about by every wind of new teaching . . . [or] be influenced when people try to trick us with lies so clever they sound like the truth."[23]

Marry your mind and heart to God and His Word. And watch the Real Jesus stand *up* and stand *out* in your life.

CHAPTER 9

ACTS OF THE APOSTATES

Be on guard for yourselves and for all the flock.

ACTS 20:28

Meandering through the beautiful Welsh countryside are endless arteries of narrow, hedgerow-lined lanes. These tiny roads are so narrow it's a wonder two cars can pass each other without colliding. While I (Jeff) was speaking in England a few years ago, my host pastor took my wife and me on a day trip into the Black Mountains of Wales. Winding our way through the back roadways of that ancient land, we crested a hill and came upon a shepherd herding his sheep across our path. Coming to a stop, we rolled down our windows to get a better look. The old farmer, outfitted with a wooden staff, wellies, a tweed jacket, and a hat to match, dutifully guided his flock across the rural lane.

Accompanied by a loyal border collie, the man glanced in our direction, then suddenly whistled, and the entire flock began scurrying across the road. He whistled again, this time with a slight variation, and the whole herd turned through a gate and into a fenced pasture, with the border collie assisting. I remember being amazed at how easy and effortless it all seemed. Just a whistle, the slightest sound from the man's mouth, and dozens of ewes, lambs, and rams obediently navigated their way to greener meadows.

One of the most picturesque ways Jesus describes Himself is as a shepherd. Once again He displays His brilliance in effective communication. Jesus' generation understood well the world of shepherds and sheep, as they were plentiful in His day and culture. And so, drawing upon that familiar way of life, the Lord beautifully illustrates the pastoral role He plays in our lives. After describing Himself as the "door of the sheep" (i.e., the only way to God), He continues, "I am the good shepherd; the good shepherd lays down his life for the sheep."[1] And later, "I am the good shepherd, and I know My own and My own know Me. . . . My sheep hear My voice, and I know them, and they follow Me."[2] But instead of whistling at His flock, our Lord personally "calls his own sheep *by name*, and leads them out."[3]

What a Savior!

This intimate connection Jesus has with us has so many facets to it, and all of them are for our benefit. As shepherd, He is Protector, even to the point of laying down His life for us, which He willingly did at the Cross.[4] But He is also our Provider, leading us to still waters and rich, green pastures, giving us a life that, according to John 10:10, is truly *abundant* and satisfying. That is, in part, why He is the Good Shepherd. He desires only what is best for us because He knows us and loves us. Jesus Christ is the "Great Shepherd of the sheep."[5]

However, according to Scripture, we sheep have other shepherds as well—"undershepherds," if you will—those to whom God has entrusted the care of His people. We call them pastors.[6] A pastor (or elder) is one to whom a certain responsibility of oversight in the church is given. Implicit within that role and responsibility is a duty to preach and teach the Word of God. In fact, this is the primary way a pastor shepherds his flock, the church, which Paul describes as *the* "pillar and foundation of the truth."[7] In a fallen world, the church is what primarily upholds, supports, and defends God's revelation to mankind, and her godly presence and influence, via the indwelling Holy Spirit, are currently preventing a tidal wave of sin, depravity, and chaos from hitting earth's shores.[8] Being a pastor is a sobering responsibility, and those who are called to pastor must understand what an honorable yet serious task it is to lead God's people.

Paul reminded young pastor Timothy of both the gravity and necessity of this duty, urging the young minister to:

> Be "constantly nourished on the words of the faith and of the sound doctrine."[9]
> Make sure Scripture was read publicly to the church, along with "exhortation and teaching."[10]
> "Take pains with these things; be absorbed in them."[11]
> "Pay close attention to yourself and to your teaching."[12]

In his final letter to Timothy, Paul further strengthens his exhortation, writing,

I solemnly urge you in the presence of God and Christ Jesus, who will someday judge the living and the dead when he comes to set up his Kingdom: Preach the word of God. Be prepared, whether the time is favorable or not. Patiently correct, rebuke, and encourage your people with good teaching.

For a time is coming when people will no longer listen to sound and wholesome teaching. They will follow their own desires and will look for teachers who will tell them whatever their itching ears want to hear. They will reject the truth and chase after myths.

But you should keep a clear mind in every situation. Don't be afraid of suffering for the Lord. Work at telling others the Good News, and fully carry out the ministry God has given you.[13]

Paul's words make it clear that you have to be crazy or called by God to be a pastor! Clearly the apostle believed the study, understanding, and communication of God's truth was to be a high priority in the church. And even more so considering the context of his earlier words: "But the Spirit explicitly says that *in later times* some will *fall away* from the faith, paying attention to deceitful spirits and doctrines of demons."[14] "Later times" here refers to the time between Christ's first coming and when He returns for His bride.[15] This time period is where we currently find ourselves.

And like other signs of the end times, this falling away will increase dramatically the closer we get to Revelation's day.[16] The Greek word translated "will fall away" is related to our word *apostasy*. And how does Paul say these people will desert the faith? By "paying attention to deceitful spirits and doctrines of demons." Satisfying self and luring humanity away from God and His truth have long been two of Satan's top strategies. He is known in Scripture as the one who "deceives the whole world" in the end times.[17] He is the "father of lies," the "god of this age," and the "ruler of demons," who themselves also rule over the darkness.[18]

Satan's deceptiveness is further seen in his ability to transform into an "angel of light," meaning he regularly masquerades as a messenger of truth. It is then no surprise that his servants impersonate "servants of righteousness." Paul says these messengers are, in reality, "false apostles" and "deceitful workers."[19] The men Paul writes about here desired the authority, respect, and influence that came with being an apostle of Christ, and they used self-made, artificial credentials to undermine Paul's ministry and mission. And while there are no living apostles today, this fact has in no way deterred Satan from his efforts to lead God's people astray through subtle, demonically inspired deception and doctrines. And even through some who claim to be "apostles."

THE NEW APOSTATES

But heretics don't fly into churches on brooms, maniacally mocking Scripture and terrorizing the flock. They don't show up sporting horns and sinister smiles. Rather, they gain entrance into the fold through persuasive words, self-help principles, and charismatic personalities. They enter via slick, well-designed websites and blogs, bringing promises of personal utopia for their followers. They are well groomed, attractive, smiling, likable, inspiring, convincing, and most of all *marketable*. Their mission is to make you happy; to make you feel good about yourself. They want to help you make the world a place of "Justice. Peace. Love. Equality."[20] Of course, each of those virtues is redefined to accommodate and conform to an ever-evolving worldly value system.[21] Their portrayal of Jesus' love is like a magic blanket that somehow mutes other, more disturbing attributes of God or uncomfortable truths found in the Bible.

Though these teachers often reference Christ and selected Scripture, it's a new image of Christianity they're peddling, one not bound to the archaic, restrictive, narrow beliefs and practices of your grandparents' faith. (We're more enlightened now.) The world has changed. Rachel Held Evans, for example, has unashamedly doubted "the Bible's exclusive authority, inerrancy, perspicuity, and internal consistency."[22] Even the government has woken up to the plight of the morally and sexually oppressed, passing legislation and declaring edicts to ensure that anyone standing in the way of "social progress" and "equality" will be squeezed out of the marketplace, kicked to culture's curb, and silenced.

Naturally, as disciples of Jesus, we are convinced that *Scripture alone*, not attractive teachers in whatever form they come, is the final word on truth, history, and where it's headed. As such, those who follow Christ are the ones who will end up on the right(eous) side of history, right beside Him when He comes in glory.[23] In the meantime, the waters of apostasy continue to rise. And what's at stake is the very nature and definition of Christianity itself. But it's not simply the *institution* of Christianity that is at risk here. It's the *soul* of our faith.

What makes the Christian faith distinct from every other religion, belief system, and personal philosophy is the person of Jesus Christ. Detract from who He is in even the most minute way, and you have just veered onto the apostasy on-ramp. Because He alone accomplished salvation and rose from the dead, He definitively proved His deity. Therefore, every word He uttered, whether recorded in the Old Testament, spoken by Him while on earth, or inspired by His Spirit in the New Testament, becomes undeniable and unchangeable. And every prophetic word of His will be fulfilled, all the way down to the last and smallest letter. As Jesus Himself claimed, "Do not think that I came to abolish the Law or the Prophets; I did not come to abolish but to fulfill. For truly I say to you, until heaven and earth pass away, not the *smallest letter or stroke* shall pass from the Law until *all* is accomplished."[24] That's quite a declaration, rich with dramatic prophetic implications.

Still, today's apostates, and those who flirt with heresy, carry on with their smooth-talking doublespeak. They can talk for hours and say nothing yet leave you with the impression they know what they're talking about. Subtly, yet clearly, they subvert, sabotage, and deny core doctrines and beliefs of the Christian faith such as these:

> The deity of Jesus Christ
> His substitutionary atonement on the cross
> Jesus as the only way to salvation and heaven
> Salvation by grace through faith
> The inerrancy and infallibility of Scripture
> The triune nature of God—Father, Son, and Holy Spirit
> The existence of a literal hell and eternal, conscious torment
> The supernatural creation of the universe, earth, and man as described in Genesis 1–2
> The prophetic nature of Scripture
> The return of Jesus Christ to earth[25]

And they do it all in the name of God and, of course, "love."

Some of those who are currently departing from the faith are fueled by a reliance on "impressions" and internal voices giving direction and declaring truth about God. This is not the same as the Holy Spirit's inner witness and guidance every believer enjoys. Rather, these voices and impressions are definitively described as an authoritative "word from the Lord."

John MacArthur writes,

Does the Spirit of God move our hearts and impress us with specific duties or callings? Certainly, but He works through the Word of God to do that. Such experiences are in no sense prophetic or authoritative. They are not *revelation*, but the effect of *illumination*, when the Holy Spirit applies the Word to our hearts and opens our spiritual eyes to its truth. We must guard carefully against allowing our experience and our own subjective thoughts and imaginations to eclipse the authority and the certainty of the more sure Word.[26]

So yes, God does guide us internally. However, we believe direct, divine, authoritative revelation ended with the conclusion of the canon of Scripture. The book of Revelation was God's final revelation.[27] Therefore, claims of "new truth" or revelations from God must come from another source, be it fallibly human or deceptively demonic.[28] Again, our thoughts must be grounded in Scripture and dependent upon the illuminating ministry and witness of the Holy Spirit.[29]

Unfortunately, in our "direct feed" culture, yesterday's truth is seen as outdated. Every morning we awaken to a fresh Twitter feed. Online news and social-media sites like Facebook constantly provide new content, updating themselves in a never-ending supply of pictures and posts. So why shouldn't God give us fresh, up-to-the-minute revelation as well? After all, our generation demands it, right?

Because of our culture's conforming and persuasive influence in our thinking, Scripture no longer is "enough." This is why, for many professing Christians, opening the Bible is like scrolling through outdated Instagram pictures. They may evoke a warm, sentimental feeling but still be (subconsciously) viewed as "old news." And yet what these people fail to realize is that the Word of God is "living and active and sharper than any two-edged sword, and piercing as far as the division of soul and spirit, of both joints and marrow, and able to judge the thoughts and intentions of the heart."[30]

The concept of living, perpetual truth from God's Word has become lost in an age of fresh, fluid social-media interaction. We open our phones, and virtually everything has changed since two minutes ago. But we open our Bible, and it reads the same as it did two days, two months, two years, or two centuries ago! It all boils down to how we understand the nature of God's Word and its life-changing power. Almost every professing Christian owns a Bible, but how many have been adequately equipped and inspired to dive into it? Or perhaps we have become products of a generation that is either too busy, too lazy, or too distracted to take the time and energy necessary to study it.

In reality, the Bible is *more* up-to-date and relevant than your Twitter feed—and many times over, since God's Word not only evaluates what is currently happening in the world but also tells us what is going to happen *before* it happens! That's relevance on a whole new, fresh level.

We must guard ourselves from drifting away from the "sola scriptura" (Scripture alone) championed by the Protestant reformers. Today's Christian motto is more like "*sometimes* Scriptura" (accompanied by wherever my emotions, pursuit of happiness, and self-fulfillment lead me). Without an intentional return to the primacy of God's Word on a large scale, the church will succumb to apostasy and be plunged into lethargy, apathy, impurity, and spiritual slumber.[31] We are quickly becoming a church culture of activity, presentation, self-help, and sermonettes. Our love affair with self must end and a rekindled love for Jesus be put in its place. *This* is the revival you can pray for!

Because we live in an age of instant media gratification and shallow interaction, we must retrain our minds to engage Scripture and understand its amazing daily relevance and fresh application to our lives.

A DIFFERENT KIND OF DRIFTING

For others, this departure from the faith is more difficult to spot. In fact, read the doctrinal statements of many church pastors and leaders today, and you'll have a hard time finding points of disagreement. They all seem biblical and legit.

But there is much more to orthodoxy and integrity than doctrinal statements.

Not long ago, I (Jeff) was standing in line to board a plane on my way to a speaking engagement. Just ahead of me in line was a middle-aged man accompanied by a much younger man, around college age. The older gentleman was dressed in black from head to toe—black leather shoes, black slacks, black knit sweater, and slick black hair. The younger man accompanying him carried a large backpack that appeared full. The older fellow carried only a cell phone. I couldn't help but overhear their conversation, which was heated. Well, only one of them was actually talking. The college boy just stood there. It soon became clear, due to the nature of the older man's rebuke, that the younger guy was his personal assistant and had committed a grievous mistake. As he repeatedly pointed his finger at the younger man, the boss's face grew more and more red.

I remember thinking, *Any second now he's going to punch that kid.*

Finally, we boarded the plane, and the (very public) verbal flogging ended. Making my way to my seat, I was disheartened to discover that I would be flying near the man in black. The college kid was seated in the row behind him and across from me.

No worries, I thought. *I'll be asleep in five minutes anyway.*

And that's when I heard a woman's voice call out to the man.

"Well, hello, Pastor! I didn't know you were on this flight. What a coincidence. I just have to tell you how much I *loved* your message last week . . ." These introductory remarks were followed by a long string of compliments, platitudes, and praises.

The man in black's face brightened, and he smiled, immediately transitioning to "minister mode." The tone of his voice became soft as he nodded his head, acknowledging the woman's adulation. Meanwhile, the college boy was on the phone, presumably talking to the church office. Overhearing his conversation, I was able to ascertain that the "unpardonable sin" this young man had committed was forgetting to arrange for the church van to pick them up on their arrival at the airport. Completing his call, the whipped and defeated young man slumped in his seat and stared out the window.

This pastor may subscribe to the same essential beliefs and doctrines as I do. And I'm quite sure he would claim to be a committed follower of Jesus. Sadly, though, his character that day didn't get the memo.

Now, I don't pretend to know this man's heart. And it's possible he could have simply been having a very bad day, or there might have been other extenuating circumstances. I could have observed him at the one time all year when he lost his temper in public. It's God's job to sort that out.

But what I can say with confidence is that there are people, according to Jesus, who don't just have "snapshot moments" where they drift off the narrow road. Instead, they've left the map altogether, as their entire lives betray what they say they believe. For them, it's not just an isolated scene out of the movie but rather the entire film that reveals their true character and where their allegiance lies.

Jesus, after explaining to His followers the narrow road concept and the "few who find it," stated,

> Not everyone who says to Me, "Lord, Lord," will enter the kingdom of heaven, but he who does the will of My Father who is in heaven will enter. Many will say to Me on that day, "Lord, Lord, did we not prophesy in Your name, and in Your name cast out demons, and in Your name perform many miracles?" And then I will declare to them, "I never knew you; depart from Me, you who practice lawlessness."[32]

When the lost are called to stand before Christ at the Great White Throne Judgment, the full extent of apostasy will be revealed.[33] And among those He will reject are individuals *within* the church who will profess to have been Christians. While on earth, they professed Christ, even claiming to have participated in supernatural acts and experiences—prophesying, casting out demons, and performing miracles. Impressive religious résumé material, to be sure. But to this particular group of people, Christ will utter the most terrifying words ever heard by human ears.

"I NEVER KNEW YOU; DEPART FROM ME"

Salvation is all about a *relationship* with Jesus Christ. By definition, a Christian is one who knows Christ and is known by Him.[34] In the Matthew 7 passage quoted above, Jesus is saying that because of their departure from genuine faith,[35] they give evidence of having never experienced genuine salvation. They never had an actual relationship with Him, even though they appeared to do great Christian things. A facade of faith existed but not the reality behind it. As a result, He will cast them out of His presence. Similar warnings are given to those who have been "enlightened" and who have "tasted" the Word of God but who have subsequently "fallen away."[36]

These are the "tares among the wheat."[37] Wolves among the sheep. Weeds in the garden. They may look like disciples and even believe as the rest do. They are almost indistinguishable from other Christians as they seamlessly blend into the body of Christ now. But they are separated from any association with Him at the judgment. These are the *Judases*. False converts. Pretenders. Fakes. Counterfeits.[38]

And the saddest thing of all is that they don't even realize it.

Chief among these are the false teachers who lead thousands of others astray. They posture and position themselves as teachers of the truth and sometimes even as prophets, but Jesus says they are nothing more than "blind guides."[39] So blind, in fact, that they can neither see the truth nor admit their own failure to abide by it. Far from holding anything back, Jesus also calls these spiritual gurus and guides "sons of hell," "fools," "hypocrites," "whitewashed tombs," "serpents," and "sons of vipers." He also told them they would not enter the Kingdom of Heaven.[40]

So Jesus, tell us what You *really* think!

In his prophetic epistle, Jude also warns us about these false teachers:

> When these people eat with you in your fellowship meals commemorating the Lord's love, they are like dangerous reefs that can shipwreck you. They are like shameless shepherds who care only for themselves. They are like clouds blowing over the land without giving any rain. They are like trees in autumn that are doubly dead, for they bear no fruit and have been pulled up by the roots. They are like wild waves of the sea, churning up the foam of their shameful deeds. They are like wandering stars, doomed forever to blackest darkness.[41]

Harsh language. Stinging speech. But the truth can be like that sometimes. That's because much is at stake when guarding the purity of Jesus' precious bride.

Among the top priorities of today's apostate teachers is to gather large numbers of followers, creating national and international ministries. And this is by design. Some high-profile celebrity pastors even persuade their churches to purchase thousands of copies of their books, costing in the hundreds of thousands of dollars, in order to artificially inflate sales to give a false impression of the book's success. This is a marketing/sales technique used to "prime the pump" and boost *individual* sales to guarantee the book a spot on the *New York Times* Best Seller List. It's a "play" sometimes used today in the world of megachurch pastors. Though it's not illegal, it's nevertheless deceptive and evidences an absence of godly integrity.

One of the by-products of this Christian celebrity cult and culture is that it preys (and depends) upon there being an ample supply of untrained and ill-equipped churchgoers. In other words, unsuspecting, innocent sheep. And sadly, this supply never runs out. When those in leadership roles or those in influential writing, speaking, or pastoral positions drift into the error of apostasy, they drag masses of gullible followers out to sea with them. And because many sincere pastors fail to actually equip their own people in biblical discernment, this tragic phenomenon is only growing. False teachers are smooth talkers and expert performers. They are adept at presentation, persuasion, entertainment, and psychological manipulation . . . for "Kingdom purposes," they would say. Many know exactly what they're doing, having meticulously planned out and structured their messages to massage the minds and emotions of those in attendance. They are very skilled at what they do. Sadly, their delivery and "demonstration of power" is often mistaken for a "movement of the Spirit."

Like their secular celebrity counterparts, they love (and crave) the attention and praise of people, with the bottom line often being the accumulation of wealth—lots of it. For some of these fame-seeking teachers, ministry equals money.[42] Unfortunately, they are often the very personalities at ministry or denomination conferences who are paraded up front and put on display as "successful." They use descriptors like "mega," "multi," and "massive" to describe their ministries. Though church size is no indicator of the Spirit's work or blessing, it is often a primary qualification for fulfilling such speaking roles. Sadly, the church has bought into the "bigger is better" philosophy of the world. Though there is nothing intrinsically spiritual about a small church or inherently heretical about a big one, there is a value and *currency* being exchanged here. "Big" more and more often equals "success" and "God's favor." As a result, you won't likely see many small-church pastors, no matter how gifted or godly, speaking at these events.

Neglected and almost forgotten at such conferences are words like *faithful*, *sacrifice*, *suffering*, *disciple*, and *servant*. The one success these false teachers have achieved for certain is that they have augmented the Word of God to fit and facilitate a last-days generation—one that values above all the unholy trinity of Self, Size, and Silver.

But Jesus calls such people thieves, robbers, and hired hands. And they are assuredly *not* shepherds.[43]

THANK GOD FOR THE REAL DEAL

What a stark contrast these forgeries of faith are to authentic ministers. And thankfully, authentic ministers do exist. Look at 1 Thessalonians 2:1-9, and see how Paul's refreshing example compares to some of the self-obsessed Christian communicators today:

> You yourselves know, brethren, that our coming to you was not in vain, but after we had already suffered and been mistreated in Philippi, as you know, we had the boldness in our God to speak to you the gospel of God amid much opposition. For our exhortation does not come from error or impurity or by way of deceit; but just as we have been approved by God to be entrusted with the gospel, so we speak, not as pleasing men, but God who examines our hearts. For we never came with flattering speech, as you know, nor with a pretext for greed—God is witness—nor did we seek glory from men, either from you or from others, even though as apostles of Christ we might have asserted our authority. But we proved to be gentle among you, as a

nursing mother tenderly cares for her own children. Having so fond an affection for you, we were well-pleased to impart to you not only the gospel of God but also our own lives, because you had become very dear to us.

For you recall, brethren, our labor and hardship, how working night and day so as not to be a burden to any of you, we proclaimed to you the gospel of God.

To the Corinthians, Paul proclaimed, "You see, we are not like the many hucksters who preach for personal profit. We preach the word of God with sincerity and with Christ's authority, knowing that God is watching us."[44]

Hucksters and peddlers, like the carnival barkers of old. Spiritual "snake oil salesmen."

Not Paul. His message and ministry were marked by humility, simplicity, and a true demonstration of the Spirit's power. And why? So that the Corinthians' faith would not rest on the wisdom, persuasion, and personality of a man but rather on the power of God.[45]

Paul was a man whose life was transformed by the risen Christ. And his faithful example is still being followed by godly people today. Those whom Jesus calls and equips to shepherd and speak, whether it be within the church or at large, are marked by a distinguishing characteristic—a burning passion to promote *Jesus'* name, not their own.[46] It is His fame they seek as they preach, teach, and serve. They subscribe to John the Baptist's motto: "He must increase, but I must decrease."[47]

They are men and women of the Word who possess a commitment to both doctrinal and personal integrity. They care nothing for people's praise but are content to please God alone with reverential honor. They don't "sweet talk" their audiences for contributions.

They don't minister for awards, recognition, or human glory but for a future crown.[48] They are far more concerned with the health of the church than they are the size of it and more focused on faith than finances. And no matter the particulars of their church or ministry, they simply desire to be good *custodians* of it. Their joy is found in being faithful.

In heaven, those receiving the greatest rewards from Christ just may be men and women you've never heard of. What do you think?

No matter what our areas of service in God's Kingdom, we must all see ourselves as stewards, loyal servants managing the influence, authority, and platform given us by God.[49] We must be mindful to never use that authority to dominate others or lead them astray.

That's because God's true leaders are gentle. Like nursing mothers, they treat people and their needs with tenderness. They understand the biblical balance of imparting both truth *and* life through real relationships. And if necessary, they are even willing to make costly personal sacrifices for the sake of the gospel and for those to whom they minister. Their motivation is a compelling call and a consuming love for their Lord Jesus Christ. And they are well aware that there is a "stricter judgment" for those who teach.[50]

This then is the antithesis of the self-serving doctrines and practices of today's apostasy.

I thank God for those who choose biblical integrity over popularity and expediency. They are authentic, dedicated disciples of Jesus, and the banner of faithfulness flies strong over them. Choose such people as your mentors, pastors, and teachers. These godly few. These servants of the Most High.

And strive to *be* one yourself.

CHAPTER 10

SURVIVING
THE LAST DAYS
OF APOSTASY

Several years ago, Tommy Nelson, pastor of Denton Bible Church, wrote an article in a publication from Dallas Theological Seminary titled "'Classic' Christianity." In the article he notes that "for several generations leading up to the 1960s, Coca-Cola was clearly the dominant soft drink in America." In a savvy marketing move, Pepsi decided to target the younger generation and let Coke continue to dominate the market for the older generations.

By the 1980s, Coke was losing market share to Pepsi, so in an effort to regain ground against Pepsi with the younger generation, Coca-Cola reformulated its flagship drink, branding it "New Coke." New Coke was sweeter and introduced as the "new taste of Coca-Cola." Coke's move was hailed as the biggest risk in consumer goods history. And if you're old enough to remember New Coke, you'll know that it was undoubtedly one of the greatest marketing missteps ever.

A fierce backlash from loyal Coke drinkers ensued. Angry calls and letters poured into Coke headquarters. The fans of Coke liked the old formula and didn't want it to change.

The day New Coke was announced, PepsiCo gave their employees the day off, saying, "By today's action, Coke has admitted that it's not the real thing." Pepsi was confident they were poised to dominate the market. Coke had compromised and changed.

Nelson describes what happened next: "But then Coke made what was called the greatest stroke of marketing genius in history. They apologized nationally, saying they realized that Coke was an American institution. They pulled New Coke off the shelves and brought back the original formula under the name of Classic Coke.

Nelson writes, "That name was not only a signal to the soft drink market that the familiar Coke had come back, *but it was also a recognition of the fact that when you have a classic, you don't change it just because of the pressure of a new generation.*"[1]

I (Mark) love that last sentence because that's the basic message of this book. Again and again, from different angles, we've highlighted the authority and sufficiency of the truth in God's Word and the centrality and exclusivity of the gospel of Jesus Christ. We have the classic. We have the real thing. Any attempt to distort, dilute, or deny it will lead to the spiritual equivalent of Coke's marketing catastrophe.

Our calling is to stick to the classic.

HEY, JUDE

In the final New Testament book before the unfolding of the book of Revelation, Jude, the half brother of Jesus, calls all followers of Jesus to cling to "classic Christianity" and contend for it:

Dear friends, I had been eagerly planning to write to you about the salvation we all share. But now I find that I must write about something else, urging you to defend the faith that God has entrusted once for all time to his holy people. I say this because some ungodly people have wormed their way into your churches, saying that God's marvelous grace allows us to live immoral lives. The condemnation of such people was recorded long ago, for they have denied our only Master and Lord, Jesus Christ.[2]

The book of Jude has been called the "Acts of the Apostates" by some. He soberly warns that apostates will mingle with God's people, pretending to be true believers. In light of this ever-present danger, followers of Jesus are to "defend" or "contend" for the faith. The word Jude uses for *defend* in the original language carries the idea of the strenuous, intense struggle expended in a wrestling match. Every believer in Christ is to contend for "the faith," that is, the orthodox body of truth and doctrine contained in God's Word.[3] Notice how the faith was delivered. It was entrusted and delivered to us by God with certainty and finality—"once for all time"—in His Word. No addition or alteration is ever needed. We have the classic.

Contending for the faith doesn't mean we have to be contentious or angry, but it does mean we must stand up for it. Yet far too many today are caving, not contending. The siren song of our culture is to water down the truth or simply omit the parts that may not go down smoothly.

I'm reminded of the young preacher who began his ministry at a new church. He preached the first Sunday on the dangers of drinking alcohol. After the service, one of the deacons approached him and said, "One-third of our people raise barley and distill alcohol, so I would be careful if I were you."

The next Sunday, the young pastor preached against smoking. The same deacon came up after the service and told him, "One-third of our members grow tobacco, so you'd better be careful."

The third Sunday, the sermon was on the perils of gambling. Again, after the service the same deacon pulled him aside. "One-third of our people raise thoroughbred horses, so you need to be more sensitive."

The following Sunday, the sermon title was "The Danger of Deep-Sea Diving in International Waters." He got the message loud and clear. But we must not cave to the pressures from our culture; we must contend for the faith.

Jude has often been described as the foyer or vestibule to the book of Revelation. Jude vividly describes the conditions that will prevail in the professing church in the final days before the events of the end times commence. His letter is another witness that the rise of apostasy is a sign of the times, portending the arrival of the end of days.

After his brief introduction in verses 1-3, verses 4-16 issue a strong denunciation of apostate false teachers who have wormed their way into the churches Jude addresses. To underscore those churches' danger, Jude gives three corporate examples of past apostasy (the wilderness generation, angels who sinned, and the cities of Sodom and Gomorrah) and three individual illustrations of apostasy from the Old Testament (Cain, Balaam, and Korah). Jude leaves no doubt about the disobedience and doom of all who turn from the truth and attempt to pull others into their wake.

HOW SHOULD WE THEN LIVE?

Beginning in verse 17, Jude shifts suddenly from the false teachers to the true followers. He sharply contrasts his readers with the apostates he's been describing and denouncing in verses 4-16. Jude 1:17 begins, "But you, beloved." The same words are found again in verse

20. He's telling us our duty in days of apostasy. As a loving pastor, Jude isn't just concerned with denouncing apostates. He wants to support and strengthen believers surrounded by apostasy. If we want to know how to survive in the last days of apostasy, Jude 1:17-25 gives us clear instruction. In these verses, Jude lays out four simple directives to equip his readers and us.

REMEMBER

The first thing Jude tells us to do in days of apostasy is *remember*: "But you, beloved, ought to remember the words that were spoken beforehand by the apostles of our Lord Jesus Christ, that they were saying to you, 'In the last time there will be mockers, following after their own ungodly lusts.'"[4] Jude is telling us that apostasy shouldn't surprise us. Apostasy was predicted by all the apostles.[5] While departure from the truth should sadden us, it shouldn't surprise us. We need to remember the apostles told us it would come.

REMAIN

Along with remembering, believers must also *remain* or stand firm in our own spiritual growth: "But you, beloved, building yourselves up on your most holy faith, praying in the Holy Spirit, keep yourselves in the love of God, waiting anxiously for the mercy of our Lord Jesus Christ to eternal life."[6] These verses contain four things every believer must do to stand strong in the midst of the falling away.

First, we are to continually build ourselves up in the most holy faith. How do we do this? By faithful study of God's Word, which contains the truth of "the faith." The pure truth of God's Word builds us up spiritually and strengthens us to stand in difficult days.

Second, believers must pray in the Holy Spirit. Our prayer life must be consistent and must be prompted, controlled, and guided by the Holy Spirit who indwells us.[7]

Third, we must keep ourselves in the love of God. This does not mean we must keep God loving us. God loves His children and will never stop. Nothing can separate us from His love for us.[8] However, when we sin, we can keep ourselves from experiencing and enjoying His love. The love of God is like sunshine that never ends, but our sin is like an umbrella we put up in our lives that keeps us from fully enjoying the love of God. We abide in God's love by obeying Him.[9]

Fourth, as we witness the widespread departure around us, we're to anxiously anticipate the coming of Jesus Christ. As someone said years ago, "The darker the outlook, the brighter the uplook!" God's people are not defeatists. We are the ultimate optimists. Jesus may be coming soon. All the signs we see around us are like runway lights signaling the approach of our Savior. Our task as we wait for the end times to arrive is to live for Christ in the meantime, committed to a life of studying, praying, obeying, and looking as we await our Lord's coming.

REACH OUT

After we secure our own spiritual health and stability, Jude calls us to lovingly *reach out* to those around us who are the victims of the false teachers. Jude highlights three groups of people that need help.

The first group is the *doubters*. Verse 22 states, "Have mercy on some, who are doubting." In days of falling away and departure from the truth, we are surrounded by believers who are confused, wavering, and hesitating. False teachers prey upon the weak. I meet professing Christians regularly who struggle with all sorts of doubts about the truth of the Bible, the exclusivity of Jesus, the nature of God, and the meaning of life. For those drowning in doubt and confusion, we're to meet them with compassion and mercy.

Second, we need to reach out to the *deceived*. Verse 23 says, "Save others, snatching them out of the fire." The only other time Jude uses the word "fire" is in verse 7, which refers to the fire of judgment, so I believe the same meaning is intended here. These are people in great spiritual peril. When sound doctrine is under siege, as it is today, we need to be on the lookout for those who are deceived and to allow God to use us to share the gospel with them so they can be snatched out of the fire. Their false ideologies must be confronted and exposed by the power of God's truth.[10]

The final group who needs the touch of God's people is the *defiled*. Verse 23 tells us, "On some have mercy with fear, hating even the garment polluted by the flesh." These are people who have been overcome, contaminated, and polluted by the filth of this world. As moral standards, even within churches, continue to slide, moral apostasy will hold more and more people in its clutches. The sins of the culture inevitably become the sins of the church. For those over-taken by sin, we're to have mercy on them with compassion. But Jude adds this caveat: "hating even the garment polluted by the flesh." The "garment polluted by the flesh" literally refers to undergarments soiled by human excretions. This means we're to have an aversion or loathing for the sin in other people's lives just as we would hate to handle someone else's dirty underwear. We're to have a healthy fear of sin and maintain a wariness of getting too close to prevent our own defilement. Dealing with sin requires caution and a healthy fear.

REST

The final condition for surviving the last days of apostasy is for us to *rest*. I love this. Jude ends this dark, stormy letter with a calming doxology of our safety and security in Christ: "Now to Him who is able to keep you from stumbling, and to make you stand in the presence of His glory blameless with great joy, to the only God our Savior, through Jesus Christ our Lord, be glory, majesty, dominion and authority, before all time and now and forever. Amen."[11] Like bookends, Jude begins and ends his letter highlighting our security in Christ.[12]

No true believer can apostatize from the faith. A believer may be confused, struggle with sin, and even believe some wrong things, but we can never lose our standing before God. He has the power to keep us from falling. He will see us through all the way to the end, when we stand in His glorious presence. But you are only secure if you have a personal relationship with God through faith in His Son, Jesus Christ.

KNOWN TO BE SAVED

In 1912, when the *Titanic* sank in the North Atlantic, 1,517 people met their demise in a watery grave. Once word of the tragedy got out, everyone wanted to know whether their loved ones had been saved. To aid those who had gathered to find news of their loved ones' fate, the White Star Line office in Liverpool, England, put up a big board divided in two with a heading on each side: "Known to Be Saved" and "Known to Be Lost." Hundreds watched with bated breath as each news report was recorded on the board.

The *Titanic*'s passengers had registered as first, second, or third class, but after the shipwreck, only two categories had any meaning: the living and the dead. The same will be true someday when the Lord comes. In the end, there will be only two classes: the saved and the lost—those who turned from self to Jesus Christ for salvation and those who did not. First John 5:12 draws the line of demarcation clearly: "He who has the Son has the life; he who does not have the Son of God does not have the life."

In spite of a rash of modern denials about the existence of hell, there are only two eternal destinations—heaven or hell. Jesus, the loving Savior who died for a world of sinners, unequivocally spoke of hell as the final destiny of those who reject Him.

Above all else, make sure you are among those "known to be saved." Make sure you have received Jesus as your Savior from sin. Make sure you know your final destination.

John 1:12 puts this as simply as possible. "As many as received Him, to them He gave the right to become children of God, even to those who believe in His name." Eternal life, forgiveness, and entrance into God's family come through simple faith and trust in Jesus Christ, the One who died in your place on the cross and rose again from the dead.[13]

You can trust Jesus now by calling upon Him to save you from your sins and by receiving the free gift of eternal life.

ORDERS REMAIN UNCHANGED

Of all the landmarks to see in our nation's capital, the Tomb of the Unknown Soldier in Arlington National Cemetery is one of the most profound. This is due in part to the constant, watchful guard that a platoon of thirty soldiers undertakes. Each day since 1937, every hour of the day, through all weather (including hurricanes) and every holiday, a single soldier has walked exactly 21 steps, then paused for 21 seconds before doing it again. The precision of the number 21 corresponds to the 21-gun-salute, the highest honor a soldier can receive. When the guard's watch is finished and a new guard comes on duty, the orders pass in three simple words: "Orders remain unchanged."

As the storm clouds gather and grow darker and the coming of Christ nears, these words—"orders remain unchanged"—should echo in our hearts and minds. We have our final marching orders from our Savior as we await His return:

Jesus came up and spoke to them, saying, "All authority has been given to Me in heaven and on earth. Go therefore and make disciples of all the nations, baptizing them in the name of the Father and the Son and the Holy Spirit, teaching them to observe all that I commanded you; and lo, I am with you always, even to the end of the age."[14]

Many things will change in our lives and in our ministries over the years. But one thing must never change—our commitment to the classic. We must never waver in our allegiance to Jesus and our dedication to spread His gospel and teach people all that He commanded. Our world doesn't need "New Coke." It needs the one thing that only God's Word can give it—the unchangeable, unchanging truth of God.

NOTES

INTRODUCTION

1. The exact etymology of the term *sabotage* is uncertain. This is one view.
2. See David Jeremiah, *God in You* (Sisters, OR: Multnomah, 1998), 73–74.
3. Genesis 3:1.
4. Jeremiah, *God in You*, 75.
5. Ibid.

CHAPTER 1: GOD AND GHOST SHIPS

1. "Shock Poll: Startling Numbers of Americans Believe World Now in the 'End Times,'" Religion News Service, September 11, 2013, http://pressreleases .religionnews.com/2013/09/11/shock-poll-startling-numbers-of-americans-believe -world-now-in-the-end-times.
2. Aamer Madhani, "Several Big U.S. Cities See Homicide Rates Surge," *USA Today*, July 10, 2015, http://www.usatoday.com/story/news/2015/07/09/us-cities-homicide -surge-2015/29879091/.
3. "Number of Abortions—Abortion Counters," *US Abortion Clock.org*, accessed August 10, 2016, http://www.numberofabortions.com.
4. See Isaiah 5:20; Judges 21:25.
5. Bob Unruh, "Psychiatrists Seek to Destigmatize Adult-Child Sex," *WND*, August 22, 2011, http://www.wnd.com/2011/08/336869.
6. "Global Risks 2014 Insight Report," World Economic Forum, http://reports .weforum.org/global-risks-2014.
7. Kim Hjelmgaard, "Ten Greatest Threats Facing the World in 2014," *USA Today*, January 16, 2014, http://www.usatoday.com/story/news/world/2014/01/16/wef -biggest-risks-facing-world-2014/4505691.
8. See Revelation 13:16-17.
9. "2015 World Hunger and Poverty Facts and Statistics," *World Hunger Education Service*, http://www.worldhunger.org/articles/Learn/world%20hunger%20facts%20 2002.htm#Number_of_hungry_people_in_the_world.

10. "New ILO Global Estimate of Forced Labour: 20.9 Million Victims," *International Labour Organization*, June 1, 2012, http://www.ilo.org/global/topics/forced-labour /news/WCMS_182109/lang--en/index.htm.
11. Joshua Teitelbaum and Michael Segall, "The Iranian Leadership's Continuing Declarations of Intent to Destroy Israel, 2009-2012," *The Jerusalem Center for Public Affairs*, http://jcpa.org/wp-content/uploads/2012/05/IransIntent2012b.pdf.
12. This war, commonly called "The Battle of Gog and Magog," will involve a massive invasion of Islamic nations aligning themselves with Russia and its leader. Their objective will be to annihilate Israel. However, God will supernaturally intervene, rescuing his covenant people for his glory. See Ezekiel 38–39.
13. For a more detailed examination of this, see Mark Hitchcock, *Iran and Israel* (Eugene, OR: Harvest House, 2013).
14. Greg Botelho, "Police: FBI Probing Past of Suspect in Oklahoma Beheading," *CNN*, September 27, 2014, http://www.cnn.com/2014/09/26/us/oklahoma-beheading.
15. Catherine Herridge, "Army Warns US Military Personnel on ISIS Threat to Family Members," *Fox News*, October 2, 2014, http://www.foxnews.com/politics/2014/10 /02/army-warns-us-military-personnel-on-isis-threat-to-family-members.
16. "Military Experts: With ISIS in El Paso, Ft. Bliss in Danger of Terrorist Attack," *Judicial Watch* (blog), September 4, 2014, http://www.judicialwatch.org/blog/2014 /09/military-experts-isis-el-paso-ft-bliss-danger-terrorist-attack.
17. "Terrorist Training Camps in the US," *Military.com*, February 18, 2009, http://www .military.com/video/operations-and-strategy/domestic-terrorism/terrorist-training -camps-in-the-us/660940716001.
18. Douglas Ernst, "ISIL to U.S.: 'We will raise the flag of Allah in the White House,'" *Washington Times*, August 8, 2014, http://www.washingtontimes.com/news/2014 /aug/8/isil-us-we-will-raise-flag-allah-white-house. In October of 2015, FBI Director James Comey stated that there were at least nine hundred active investigations into jihadist (ISIS-related) activity on American soil. The FBI is investigating ISIS-related activity in all fifty US states, meaning that ISIS has a network of supporters and sympathizers in every state in the union. See Kevin Johnson, "Anxiety Grows over ISIL Recruits in U.S.," *USA Today*, November 14, 2015, http://www.usatoday .com/story/news/2015/11/14/isil-recruits-in-us-worry-officials/75774094.
19. 2 Corinthians 13:5. See also 1 Corinthians 10:12.
20. 2 Peter 1:10-11. All the important qualities Peter refers to in this opening chapter (verses 5-9) stem from a believer's authentic experience with the Word of God (verses 3-4).
21. See Acts 27:27-44; 2 Corinthians 11:25-26.
22. 1 Timothy 1:18-20, emphasis added.
23. See Hebrews 12:4-11.
24. See Matthew 7:21-27.
25. 1 John 2:4.
26. See Revelation 2:4.
27. See Ephesians 2:1-3.
28. Matthew 6:33. See also Psalm 37:4; Proverbs 3:5-6.
29. See 2 Corinthians 11:1-3; Ephesians 4:3.

30. 2 Timothy 3:16, emphasis added.
31. Matthew 16:18.
32. See Philippians 1:6.
33. See John 18:2.
34. John 17:15-16. See 2 Corinthians 4:4.
35. John 17:17.
36. See Galatians 1:6-9; 3:1-4; 5:1, 7-12.

CHAPTER 2: THE FIFTH COLUMN

1. George Sweeting, "Betrayal in the Church," *Moody* (April 1992): 74.
2. A.W. Tozer, *Man: The Dwelling Place of God* (Camp Hill, PA: WingSpread, 2008), 118.
3. Andy Woods, "The Last Days Apostasy of the Church (Part 1)," *Bible Prophecy Blog*, November 19, 2009, http://www.bibleprophecyblog.com/2009/11/last-days-apostasy-of-church-part-1.html.
4. Examples of personal apostasy are found in the serious warnings of Hebrews 6:4-8 and 10:26-31.
5. Titus 1:16.
6. See Revelation 13:1-18; 17:11-15.
7. See Genesis 11:1-9; Revelation 13:4.
8. See Daniel 9:27; Ezekiel 38:8, 11.
9. See 1 Thessalonians 5:1-3; Revelation 6:1-4.
10. Woods, "Last Days."
11. See Acts 18:1-11.
12. 2 Thessalonians 2:1-2, ESV.
13. See 1 Thessalonians 1:9-10; 4:17; 5:1-9.
14. That the Thessalonians were so upset by the teaching that they were in the Day of the Lord indicates this was not something they were expecting. This lends support to the pre-Tribulation timing of the Rapture. If the Thessalonians believed they would have to endure the Tribulation before Christ's coming, then why would they have been so upset to receive a letter telling them the Day of the Lord had come? They would have been excited, not shaken and afraid. This would mean that what Paul had taught them was being fulfilled. They would have faced the Tribulation with hope and endurance, knowing that the coming of the Lord was less than seven years away. But their response was the exact opposite. They were "shaken from their composure" and "disturbed." The spurious letter they had received contradicted what Paul had taught them in 1 Thessalonians 4–5. It either meant that Paul had lied to them before about the pre-Trib Rapture, they had totally misunderstood what he said, or the Rapture had already come and they had been left behind. Any of these scenarios was devastating. The only logical conclusion from 2 Thessalonians 2:1-2 is that from Paul's previous teaching in 1 Thessalonians, the Thessalonians must have believed that the Rapture would occur before the beginning of the Tribulation. Paul went on in 2 Thessalonians 2:3-11 to show the believers that the teaching that they were already in the Day of the Lord was false doctrine and that their fears of being

in this awful period were groundless. For a thorough discussion of the timing of the Rapture, see Mark Hitchcock, *The End* (Carol Stream, IL: Tyndale, 2012).

15. Charles R. Swindoll, *Steadfast Christianity: A Study of Second Thessalonians*, Bible Study Guide (Anaheim, CA: Insight for Living, 1986), 23.

16. 2 Thessalonians 2:3, esv.

17. Since the word *apostasia* means "departure," some have understood the term "the apostasy" to be the physical departure of the church itself—that is, the Rapture, since the Rapture will be a physical departure of believers from the earth. If this view were correct, it would definitely place the Rapture before the Tribulation, which would be a slam dunk for the pre-Tribulation Rapture position. While this is attractive to pretribulationalists, there are six main reasons to reject a physical departure as the meaning of *apostasia* in this context: (1) In classical Greek, *hē apostasia* ("the apostasy") was used to denote a political or military rebellion. (2) In the Septuagint (the Greek translation of the Old Testament), this term was used of rebellion against God (see Joshua 22:22; Jeremiah 2:19). (3) In 2 Maccabees 2:15 (a noncanonical book written in the time between the Old and New Testaments), it is used of apostasy to paganism. (4) In Acts 21:21, the only other use of the noun in the New Testament, it refers to apostasy or spiritual departure from Moses. (5) The Rapture is not an act of departure by the saints; the saints are passive not active participants. (6) In 2 Thessalonians 2:1, Paul refers to the Rapture as "our gathering together to Him." It seems strange to use this unlikely term ("the apostasy") for the same thing in the immediate context. (These six points are from D. Edmond Hiebert, *1 & 2 Thessalonians* (Chicago: Moody, 1971), 331. For these reasons, most expositors have understood "the rebellion" (apostasy) not as the physical departure of the church at the Rapture but rather as doctrinal, theological, and moral departure from the truth.

18. F. F. Bruce, *1 & 2 Thessalonians*, Word Biblical Commentary, gen. ed. David A. Hubbard and Glenn W. Barker, vol. 45 (Waco, TX: Word Books, 1982), 166. See also Leon Morris, *1 and 2 Thessalonians*, Tyndale New Testament Commentaries, rev. ed. (Grand Rapids, MI: Eerdmans, 1989), 127.

19. John Calvin, *1 & 2 Thessalonians,* Crossway Classic Commentaries, ed. Alister McGrath and J. I. Packer (Wheaton, IL: Crossway, 1999), 86–87.

20. G. K. Beale, *1-2 Thessalonians*, IVP New Testament Commentary Series, ed. Grant R. Osborne (Downers Grove, IL: InterVarsity Press, 2003), 204. Beale provides several convincing points to support his view.

21. 2 Thessalonians 2:4, esv.

22. John R. W. Stott, *The Message of 1 & 2 Thessalonians* (Downers Grove, IL: InterVarsity Press, 1991), 158.

23. Charles Ryrie, *First and Second Thessalonians* (Chicago: Moody, 1959), 103–104.

24. Homer A. Kent, Jr., *The Pastoral Epistles*, rev. ed. (Chicago: Moody, 1986), 143.

25. Mal Couch, gen. ed., *A Biblical Theology of the Church* (Grand Rapids, MI: Kregel, 1999), 110.

26. John Phillips, *Exploring the Future: A Comprehensive Guide to Bible Prophecy* (Grand Rapids, MI: Kregel, 2003), 225, 269.

27. John F. Walvoord, *The Church in Prophecy* (Grand Rapids, MI: Zondervan, 1964), 66.

28. Ibid., 50.
29. J. Dwight Pentecost, *Will Man Survive?* (Grand Rapids, MI: Zondervan, 1980), 58.
30. John Harold Ockenga, quoted in "Apostasy," Paul Lee Tan Prophetic Ministries, http://www.tanbible.com/tol_ill/apostasy.htm.
31. Donald Grey Barnhouse, *Thessalonians: An Expository Commentary* (Grand Rapids, MI: Zondervan, 1977), 98.
32. John Horsch, *Modern Religious Liberalism* (Scottdale, PA: Fundamental Truth Depot, 1921), 322.

CHAPTER 3: FAITH OF OUR FATHERS

1. Genesis 3:5.
2. 2 Timothy 3:16-17, NLT.
3. See John 15:18-27.
4. In an interview on Oprah Winfrey's *Super Soul Sunday*, Bell said, "We're moments away. I think the culture is already there. And the church will continue to be even more irrelevant when it quotes letters from 2,000 years ago as their best defense." See "Rob Bell Suggests Bible Not Relevant to Today's Culture," *CBN News*, February 19, 2015, http://www1.cbn.com/cbnnews/us/2015/February/Rob-Bell-Suggests-Bible-Not-Relevant-to-Todays-Culture.
5. Jim Hinch, "Evangelicals Are Losing the Battle for the Bible. And They're Just Fine with That," *Los Angeles Review of Books*, February 15, 2016, http://lareviewofbooks.org/article/evangelicals-are-losing-the-battle-for-the-bible-and-theyre-just-fine-with-that.
6. Hebrews 5:14.
7. See 2 Peter 3:18.
8. See Titus 1:10–2:1.
9. See 1 Timothy 4:6.
10. See 2 Timothy 4:2-3.
11. See Titus 1:9; 1 Timothy 6:3-5.
12. John 4:22-24, NLT.
13. See Genesis 1:26. Being created in God's image involves possessing intellect (being able to think and reason), emotion (the capacity for feeling), and will (the ability to choose). It also means we are *spiritual* beings. Though we spiritually died in Adam's fall, we are made alive once again through Christ at salvation (see Ephesians 2:1, 5; Colossians 2:11-13; Titus 3:5).
14. See Romans 1:18-20; 2:14-15 concerning general revelation. See also Colossians 1:15-19; Hebrews 1:1-4 regarding special revelation through Jesus Christ.
15. John 4:23.
16. See Exodus 20:1-8. See also Exodus 32:1-6, where Israel portrayed its God as a golden calf. This false image of God not only insulted His glory but also led to all sorts of sin and debauchery.
17. 2 Corinthians 10:3-5.
18. See Matthew 4:1-11.
19. See 1 Corinthians 8:1.

20. Romans 1:21-22, emphasis added.

21. Romans 11:36.

22. Philippians 1:9-11, NIV, emphasis added.

23. Colossians 1:9-10, emphasis added.

24. John 17:3.

25. The word most often used to describe this knowledge is *ginóskó*, whose primary meaning is to know through personal experience. This experience begins with the mind and is translated to practical living.

26. See 1 Corinthians 13:12; 1 John 3:2-3.

27. See Ephesians 4:11-16.

28. Jude 1:3, emphasis added.

29. 1 Timothy 6:20; 2 Timothy 1:13, NLT.

30. 2 Timothy 1:14, NLT, emphasis added.

31. Jude 1:4.

32. "Theology" refers to the study of God. Specifically, the study of salvation is referred to as "soteriology," and the study of Christ, "Christology." These are terms used to help systematize and categorize Christian doctrine and teaching. Generally speaking, most systematic theologies break down as follows: prolegomena (introduction to general theology, how God reveals himself, etc.), bibliology (the study of the Bible), theology proper (the study of the doctrine of God), Christology (the study of Jesus Christ), pneumatology (the study of the Holy Spirit), anthropology (the study of humankind), soteriology (the study of salvation), ecclesiology (the study of the church), angelology (the study of angels and demons), and eschatology (the study of the end times).

33. See Proverbs 1:7.

34. See John 17:3, 17; Romans 3:4; Titus 1:2.

35. See John 14:26; 16:13-16.

36. See Ephesians 6:11, 14.

37. See 1 Peter 3:15.

38. Matthew 7:15-16, NLT.

39. See John 1:17-18; 14:6.

40. Here is an excellent list of Scriptures dealing with false teachers and our response to them: https://www.openbible.info/topics/exposing_false_teachers.

41. See Acts 17:11.

42. See Matthew 7:24-27.

CHAPTER 4: CULTURE OF COMPROMISE

1. Paul W. Powell, *Thee Old Time Religion* (Waco, TX: Paul W. Powell, 2001), 9.

2. Francis A. Shaeffer, *The Great Evangelical Disaster* (Wheaton, IL: Crossway, 1984), 64.

3. "Americans: My Faith Isn't the Only Way to Heaven," Associated Press, June 24, 2008, http://www.foxnews.com/story/2008/06/24/americans-my-faith-isnt-only-way -to-heaven.html.

4. See Romans 12:2.

5. A. W. Tozer, *Man: The Dwelling Place of God*, reprint (Camp Hill, PA: WingSpread, 2008), 188.
6. See Daniel 1:3-20.
7. See 2 Timothy 4:10.
8. See Hebrews 2:1-4.
9. See Hebrews 3:12.
10. See John 6:60, 66.
11. John Shore, "The Inevitability of the Rise of Progressive Christianity," *Patheos*, September 19, 2011, http://www.patheos.com/blogs/johnshore/2011/09/the-inevitability-of-the-rise-of-liberal-christianity.
12. 2 Timothy 4:1-4.
13. Tim LaHaye and Jerry B. Jenkins, *Are We Living in the End Times?* (Carol Stream, IL: Tyndale, 1999), 71.
14. Rachel Held Evans, *A Year of Biblical Womanhood* (Nashville: Thomas Nelson, 2012), 54.
15. J. Carl Laney, *John* (Chicago: Moody, 1992), 156–57.
16. Trillia Newbell, "Biblical Womanhood and the Problem of the Old Testament," *Desiring God*, October 15, 2012, http://www.desiringgod.org/articles/biblical-womanhood-and-the-problem-of-the-old-testament.
17. See John 8:11.
18. John 7:7, NLT.
19. John 15:18-23, NLT.
20. Glennon Doyle Melton, "Are You Waiting for Heaven or Working for It?" *Momastery* (blog), March 29, 2016, http://momastery.com/blog/2016/03/29/waiting-or-working.
21. See Matthew 7:13-14; John 3:36; 8:24.

CHAPTER 5: WHEN TOLERANCE IS INTOLERABLE

1. Jeremiah 17:9, NLT.
2. C. S. Lewis, *The Case for Christianity* (Nashville: Broadman and Holman, 2000), 32.
3. 1 John 3:16, NLT.
4. John 3:16, NLT.
5. Romans 5:8, NLT.
6. See 1 John 4:7-8.
7. See 1 John 4:19.
8. See Ephesians 5:25, 28-29.
9. 2 Peter 3:18.
10. "For the First Time, Starbucks Raises the Pride Flag atop Its Headquarters," *Starbucks Newsroom*, June 23, 2014, https://news.starbucks.com/news/for-the-first-time-starbucks-raises-the-pride-flag-atop-its-headquarters.
11. See John 1:9; 3:19-20; 8:12.
12. Isaiah 5:20.
13. Romans 1:24-28.
14. Romans 1:29-32, NLT.

15. See John 15:18-25.
16. John 6:37, NLT. See Mark 2:13-17; Luke 7:36-50; 19:1-10.
17. See Genesis 9:9-17.
18. See Genesis 6:1-13; Romans 1; 3:1-12, 23. For a more detailed explanation of the Flood judgment, Noah's generation, and their relationship to end-times prophecy, see Jeff Kinley, *As It Was in the Days of Noah: Warnings from Bible Prophecy about the Coming Global Storm* (Eugene, OR: Harvest House, 2014).
19. *The Safe Space Network*, http://safespacenetwork.tumblr.com/Safespace.
20. See Ephesians 4:32; Philippians 4:5.
21. Matthew 23:23, ESV. See also Matthew 9:13.
22. See 2 Corinthians 10:5.
23. See Romans 14.
24. Revelation 2:2, NLT. See Revelation 2:20.
25. Revelation 2:24.
26. See Romans 6:1-2, 15; Galatians 2:17-21; 5:13; 1 Peter 2:16.
27. Matthew 15:9.
28. Mark 7:6, NIV.
29. Matthew 23:27-28. See also Isaiah 29:13; Matthew 6:1-2; 23:24; Luke 16:15; Galatians 4:10-11; 5:2-4.
30. John 14:15.
31. See 2 Timothy 4:3-5; 2 Corinthians 4:4; Ephesians 2:2; 6:11; John 8:44.
32. Habakkuk 1:13, NIV.
33. God has a plan and a purpose for everything, even the existence of evil and evil men (see Romans 9:15-22; Proverbs 16:4; Deuteronomy 29:29). It is impossible to know all His reasons for allowing evil to exist, but we do know that He can turn sinful actions into good things for us and glory for Him (see Genesis 50:20; Acts 2:23; 4:27-28; Romans 8:28).
34. 2 Peter 3:9, NIV.
35. See Acts 14:15-17; Romans 3:24-25.
36. See Acts 17:24-25; 2 Corinthians 6:1-2.
37. Ephesians 5:16.
38. See 2 Timothy 2:2.
39. Greek *koinonia*—meaning a partnership or sharing together, a joint participation.
40. See Ephesians 2:20. 1 Peter 2:5; Hebrews 10:23-25.

CHAPTER 6: MORAL FREEFALL

1. This is adapted from John MacArthur's "The Conscience, Revisited," Grace to You, http://www.gty.org/resources/Articles/A273/The-Conscience-Revisited.
2. This joke is adapted from "100 Mile an Hour Goat," November 9, 2009, http://www.ebaumsworld.com/jokes/read/80809499.
3. A. W. Tozer, *Man: The Dwelling Place of God* (Camp Hill, PA: WingSpread, 2008), 181.
4. Read 2 Peter 2 and the Epistle of Jude, and you will see this pattern vividly illustrated.
5. 2 Timothy 3:1-5.

6. See Acts 2:17; Hebrews 1:1-2; 1 Peter 1:20; 1 John 2:18 ("the last hour").

7. Homer A. Kent Jr., *The Pastoral Epistles*, rev. ed. (Winona Lake, IN: BMH Books, 1986), 272.

8. John F. MacArthur, *1 & 2 Timothy*, in The MacArthur New Testament Commentary (Chicago: Moody, 1995), 107.

9. Ray C. Stedman, *The Fight of Faith: Studies in the Pastoral Letters of Paul, I and II Timothy and Titus* (Grand Rapids, MI: Discovery House, 2009), 238.

10. Don Carson, *From the Resurrection to His Return: Living Faithfully in the Last Days* (Tain, Scotland: Christian Focus, 2010), 18.

11. K. Edward Copeland, "Shadowlands: Pitfalls and Parodies of Gospel-Centered Ministry," in *Entrusted with the Gospel: Pastoral Expositions of 2 Timothy*, ed. D. A. Carson (Wheaton, IL: Crossway, 2010), 93–94.

12. This illustration is borrowed from Doug McIntosh, *Life's Greatest Journey: How to Be Heavenly Minded AND of Earthly Good* (Chicago: Moody, 2000), 13–14.

13. Philip DeCourcy, "You Don't Get to Write the Rules," *Know the Truth*, January 23, 2015, http://www.ktt.org/pages/page.asp?page_id=153644&articleId=47346.

14. Ibid.

15. See 1 Thessalonians 1:9-10.

16. See 2 Thessalonians 2:2-3.

17. 2 Timothy 3:14-17, esv.

18. See 2 Timothy 2:1; 3:10, 14; 4:5.

19. Every main passage in the New Testament on apostasy and false teaching is followed closely with a statement about God's Word. Here are a few examples: 1 Timothy 4:13-16; 2 Timothy 3:16-17; 2 Peter 1:21 (here the statement about Scripture precedes the warning about false teachers); 2 Peter 3:1-2; Jude 1:17.

20. Philip Graham Ryken, *He Speaks to Me Everywhere: Meditations on Christianity and Culture* (Phillipsburg, NJ: P & R Publishing, 2004), 17-18.

CHAPTER 7: THE WATERSHED MOMENT FOR THE CHURCH

1. Obergefell v. Hodges, 576 S. Ct. at 22 (2015).

2. The Associated Press, "Presbyterian Church Leaders Declare Gay Marriage Is Christian," *NBC News*, June 20, 2014, http://www.nbcnews.com/news/us-news /presbyterian-church-leaders-declare-gay-marriage-christian-n136256.

3. "Tony Campolo's Gay Marriage Support Highlights Divide," *CBN News*, June 12, 2015, http://www1.cbn.com/cbnnews/us/2015/June/Campolos-Gay-Marriage -Support-Highlights-Divide.

4. "Rob Bell Suggests Bible Not Relevant to Today's Culture," *CBN News*, February 19, 2015, http://www1.cbn.com/cbnnews/us/2015/February/Rob-Bell-Suggests-Bible -Not-Relevant-to-Todays-Culture.

5. Rachel Held Evans, "For the Sake of the Gospel, Drop the Persecution Complex," *Rachel Held Evans* (blog), July 15, 2015, http://rachelheldevans.com/blog /persecution-complex.

6. In one recent example, an influential blogger among evangelicals posted this message on Facebook: "After our beautiful, beautiful event today, a woman walked up to me

and said: 'I have been waiting my entire life for someone in church to say the words you said today.' . . . I said . . . that it is high time Christians opened wide their arms, wide their churches, wide their tables, wide their homes to the LGBT community. So great has our condemnation and exclusion been, that gay Christian teens are SEVEN TIMES more likely to commit suicide. Nope. No. No ma'am. Not on my watch. No more. This is so far outside the gospel of Jesus that I don't even recognize its reflection. I can't. I won't. I refuse. So whatever the cost and loss, this is where I am: gay teens? Gay adults? Mamas and daddies of precious gaybees? Friends and beloved neighbors of very dear LGBT folks? Here are my arms open wide. . . . You matter so desperately and your life is worthy and beautiful. There is nothing 'wrong with you,' or in any case, nothing more right or wrong than any of us, which is to say we are all hopelessly screwed up but Jesus still loves us beyond all reason and lives to make us all new, restored, whole." Posted April 23, 2016, https://www.facebook .com/permalink.php?story_fbid=946752262090436&id=203920953040241.

7. Christian Smith, *Soul Searching: The Religious and Spiritual Lives of American Teenagers* (New York: Oxford University Press, 2009), 171.

8. Ibid.

9. See 1 Peter 4:12-19.

10. See Romans 1:26-27.

11. See James 2:10-11.

12. See Genesis 19 (Sodom is catastrophically wiped out for its sin); Leviticus 18:22 (it's called an "abomination"); Leviticus 20:13 (it's punishable by death).

13. "Campolo's Gay Marriage Support," *CBN News*.

14. Glenn R. Kreider and Thomas M. Mitchell, "Kindness and Repentance: Romans 2:4 and Ministry to People with Same-Sex Attractions," *Bibliotheca Sacra* 173 (January–March 2016): 60.

15. See John Stott, *Same-Sex Partnerships? A Christian Perspective* (Grand Rapids, MI: Revell, 1998), 18.

16. Ibid., 22.

17. See Jude 1:6-7.

18. Kevin DeYoung, *What Does the Bible Really Teach about Homosexuality?* (Wheaton, IL: Crossway, 2015), 55.

19. Ibid., 63–65.

20. Ibid., 77.

21. Thomas E. Schmidt, *Straight & Narrow? Compassion & Clarity in the Homosexuality Debate* (Downers Grove, IL: InterVarsity Press, 1995), 64.

22. Peter Coleman, *Christian Attitudes to Homosexuality* (London: SPCK, 1980), 101.

23. Rod Dreher, "What If Rachel Held Evans Is Wrong?" *Real Clear Religion*, May 15, 2012, http://www.realclearreligion.org/articles/2012/05/15/what_if_rachel_held _evans_is_wrong_106490.html.

24. Stott, *Same-Sex Partnerships?*, 54.

25. Ibid., 54–55.

26. See John 14:15; Romans 13:8.

27. Stott, *Same-Sex Partnerships?*, 57.

28. Stott, *Same-Sex Partnerships?*, 58.

29. See Leviticus 18:22; 20:13.
30. See Matthew 10:14-15; 11:23-24; Luke 10:10-12; 17:26-30.
31. Romans 1:32.
32. Thomas R. Schreiner, *Romans*, Baker Exegetical Commentary on the New Testament, ed. Moses Silva (Grand Rapids, MI: Baker Books, 1998), 99–100.
33. C. E. B. Cranfield, *The Epistle to the Romans*, The International Critical Commentary, gen. ed. J. A. Emerton and C. E. B. Cranfield, vol. 1 (Edinburgh: T&T Clark, 2006), 135.
34. Robert H. Mounce, *Romans*, The New American Commentary, gen. ed. E. Ray Clendenen, vol. 27 (Nashville: Broadman & Holman, 1995), 86.
35. Russell Goldman, "Here's a List of 58 Gender Options for Facebook Users," *ABC News*, February 13, 2014, http://abcnews.go.com/blogs/headlines/2014/02/heres-a-list-of-58-gender-options-for-facebook-users.
36. Luke 17:28-30.
37. Chelsen Vicari, "Jen Hatmaker, Blurry Lines, and Transformative Truth," *Faith & Chelsen* (blog), Patheos, April 26, 2016, http://www.patheos.com/blogs/faithchelsen/2016/04/jen-hatmaker-blurry-lines-and-transformative-truth. For an excellent presentation of our response to those with same-sex attraction, see Glenn R. Kreider and Thomas M. Mitchell, "Kindness and Repentance: Romans 2:4 and Ministry to People with Same-Sex Attractions," *Bibliotheca Sacra* 173 (January–March 2016): 57–79.

CHAPTER 8: WILL THE REAL JESUS STAND UP?

1. This version of "One Solitary Life" is adapted from James Allan Francis, "Arise Sir Knight!" in *The Real Jesus and Other Sermons* (Philadelphia: The Judson Press, 1926), 123–24.
2. Kenneth Humphreys, *Jesus Never Existed: An Introduction to the Ultimate Heresy* (Charleston, WV: Nine-Banded Books, 2014). This is, of course, a minority view, as very few credible secular historians actually doubt or deny the historicity of Jesus.
3. Warren Cole Smith, "A Conversation with Bart Ehrman," *World*, January 9, 2015, https://world.wng.org/2015/01/a_conversation_with_bart_ehrman.
4. "What Do Americans Believe about Jesus?" Barna Group, April 1, 2015, https://www.barna.org/barna-update/culture/714-what-do-americans-believe-about-jesus-5-popular-beliefs#.VyJyHmPwB20.
5. See Revelation 1:4-18.
6. John 2:23-25. Their belief in Jesus could have been merely intellectual and not a volitional trust in Him. As a result, though they "believed" in Him, Jesus did not "believe" (same Greek word) in *them*.
7. See Isaiah 55:8-9; Romans 3:10-12; Ephesians 2:1-3. See also Romans 1:21; 1 Corinthians 2:14.
8. See John 14:16-17, 26; 16:13-14. See also Ephesians 1:17-18; 1 Corinthians 2:10-16.
9. Nicola Menzie, "5 False 'Messiahs' and Why Their Claims to Be Christ Contradict

the Bible," *Church & Ministry*, The Christian Post, June 6, 2013, http://www
.christianpost.com/news/5-false-messiahs-and-why-their-claims-to-be-christ
-contradict-the-bible-97059.

10. Brian D. McLaren, *A New Kind of Christianity: Ten Questions That Are Transforming the Faith* (San Francisco: HarperOne, 2011), 139, emphasis added.
11. John 1:14. See also Romans 8:3; Philippians 2:7.
12. Hebrews 2:14, 17-18.
13. Hebrews 4:15.
14. See Romans 8:3; Hebrews 2:17; 4:14-16.
15. See John 1:14, 18; 2 Corinthians 5:21; Titus 2:14; Hebrews 7:25-27; 9:15.
16. Matthew 16:13-16, emphasis added.
17. Hebrews 13:8.
18. See Psalm 139:13-16.
19. Through "general revelation" (creation and conscience), we can understand that God is a divine being who is eternal, powerful, moral, and creative. But the specifics regarding the incarnate Christ we can know authoritatively only through Scripture.
20. Matthew 11:28 and Matthew 8:12.
21. For more on this topic, see Mark Hitchcock, *Visits to Heaven and Back: Are They Real?* (Carol Stream, IL: Tyndale, 2015).
22. See Revelation 12:9; 20:10.
23. Ephesians 4:14, NLT.

CHAPTER 9: ACTS OF THE APOSTATES
1. John 10:7, 11.
2. John 10:14, 27.
3. John 10:3, emphasis added.
4. See John 10:11.
5. Hebrews 13:20. See also 1 Peter 2:25.
6. Though the English word *pastor* (in its plural form) is translated as such only once in the New Testament (see Ephesians 4:11), the Greek word (*poimen*) is otherwise rendered "shepherd" seventeen times. In verb form, it is used three times to refer to leadership and overseeing God's people (see John 21:16; Acts 20:28; 1 Peter 5:2).
7. 1 Timothy 3:15, NIV. See 1 Timothy 5:17.
8. See 2 Thessalonians 2:6-7.
9. 1 Timothy 4:6.
10. 1 Timothy 4:13.
11. 1 Timothy 4:15.
12. 1 Timothy 4:16.
13. 2 Timothy 4:1-5, NLT.
14. 1 Timothy 4:1, emphasis added.
15. See Hebrews 1:1-2; 9:26; 1 Peter 1:20; 1 John 2:18.
16. See Matthew 24:37; 2 Thessalonians 2:3-12; Hebrews 3:12; 5:11–6:8; 10:25; 2 Peter 3:3; Jude 1:18.
17. Revelation 12:9.

18. John 8:44; 2 Corinthians 4:4; Luke 11:15; Ephesians 6:12.
19. 2 Corinthians 11:13-15.
20. Glennon Doyle Melton, "Are You Waiting for Heaven or Working for It?" *Momastery* (blog), March 29, 2016, http://momastery.com/blog/2016/03/29/waiting-or -working.
21. This is precisely the kind of worldliness Paul warns the Roman believers about in Romans 12:1-2. It's an external pressure that forces us into a certain way of thinking and acting. It involves both values and behavior. And in a religious context, it often means "rethinking" the long-held historical beliefs of Christianity.
22. Rachel Held Evans, "Loving the Bible for What It Is, Not What I Want It to Be," *Rachel Held Evans* (blog), January 2, 2012, http://rachelheldevans.com/blog/bible -series.
23. See Revelation 19:11-16.
24. Matthew 5:17-18, emphasis added.
25. There are other dangerous doctrinal aberrations that do not directly call into question Christ's identity or the foundations of Christianity but that nevertheless deviate and depart from orthodox Christian belief. These "second tier" aberrations include beliefs and practices such as the prosperity gospel, the social gospel, the "second blessing," the word of faith movement, "name it and claim it," faith healers, the laughing movement, and the veneration of Mary and "saints."
26. John MacArthur, "False Prophets and Lying Wonders," Grace to You, accessed August 29, 2016, https://www.gty.org/resources/print/blog/B100111.
27. See Hebrews 1:1-2; Jude 1:3; Revelation 22:18-19.
28. There is no shortage today of these types of claims—from supposed visits to heaven to sensationalized revelations regarding prophecy and the end times. Some of these "words from God" are relatively trivial in nature, while others border on the bizarre.
29. See John 14:16-17, 26; 15:26; 16:13-14; Romans 8:9, 16.
30. Hebrews 4:12.
31. See Revelation 3:1-2.
32. Matthew 7:21-23.
33. See Revelation 20:11-15.
34. See John 10:14; 17:3; Philippians 3:8; 1 John 2:3; 5:20.
35. The word for "depart from" that Jesus uses in Matthew 7:23 is distinct from yet similar to the Greek word for *apostasy.* ἀποχωρέω comes from two words, *apo* ("from" or "away from") and *choreo* (to leave or go away, depart).
36. See Hebrews 6:4-6.
37. See Matthew 13:24-30.
38. See 1 John 2:19; Jude 1:20-24.
39. See Matthew 23:16, 17, 19, 24, 26.
40. See Matthew 23:13-36; Luke 11:52.
41. Jude 1:12-13, NLT.
42. See 1 Timothy 6:10.
43. See John 10:1-16.
44. 2 Corinthians 2:17, NLT.
45. See 1 Corinthians 2:1-5.

46. See Psalm 115:1; 2 John 1:7.
47. John 3:30.
48. See 1 Peter 5:2-4.
49. See 1 Corinthians 4:1-5.
50. James 3:1.

CHAPTER 10: SURVIVING THE LAST DAYS OF APOSTASY

1. Tommy Nelson, "'Classic' Christianity: Teaching and Living the Unchanging Truth of God's Word," *Veritas* (January 2008), http://www.dts.edu/download/publications/veritas/veritas-2008-january.pdf, emphasis added.
2. Jude 1:3-4, NLT.
3. See 1 Timothy 1:9; 4:1; 5:8; 6:10, 21; 2 Timothy 4:7.
4. Jude 1:17-18.
5. See 1 Timothy 4:1; 2 Timothy 3:1-13; 4:3; 1 John 2:18-19; 4:1-3; 2 Peter 2:1-2; 3:3-4.
6. Jude 1:20-21.
7. See also Ephesians 6:18.
8. See Romans 8:38-39.
9. See John 15:9-10.
10. See 2 Corinthians 10:3-5.
11. Jude 1:24-25.
12. See Jude 1:1.
13. See Romans 10:9.
14. Matthew 28:18-20.

RUSSIA RISING

MARK HITCHCOCK

CHAPTER I

THERE IS A BEAR IN THE WOODS

A bear will not ask anyone for permission.

VLADIMIR PUTIN

During the 1984 presidential campaign, candidate Ronald Reagan used a television commercial that's become known for its compelling opening line—"There is a bear in the woods."

The ad featured a grizzly bear wandering menacingly through a forest while the narrator said, "There is a bear in the woods. For some people, the bear is easy to see. Others don't see it at all. Some people say the bear is tame. Others say it's vicious and dangerous. Since no one can really be sure who's right, isn't it smart to be as strong as the bear? If there is a bear."

A man appears in the closing scene, and the bear takes a step back. The captivating ad concludes with a picture of Reagan and the tagline "President Reagan: Prepared for Peace." Reagan took the Bear seriously, and in December 1991, the Soviet Union collapsed, no longer dominating Eastern Europe.

Fast-forward almost thirty years, and no one doubts there's a bear in the woods. Russia is back. The Russian bear has roared out of hibernation and into the headlines. The Bear is back—but what does that mean for our world?

The movie *The Revenant* depicts one of the most savage, vicious scenes in cinematic annals. Not far into the movie, frontiersman and fur trapper Hugh Glass (played by Leonardo DiCaprio) unwittingly gets between a mother grizzly bear and her cubs. Without warning, he's slammed to the ground by the charging grizzly. It happens so quickly he doesn't have time even to turn and raise his rifle. The ferocious mauling is so brutal and unrelenting, it's difficult to watch. Glass's broken, lacerated body is left near death. The lesson is clear: get between a mother grizzly and her cubs, and the result won't be pretty.

BACK TO THE USSR

Since 1991 and the collapse of the Soviet Union, Vladimir Putin and others of his ilk have felt like a mother bear robbed of her cubs, willing to maul anyone who stands in the way of restoring Soviet greatness. Putin, a former KGB lieutenant colonel, became Russian prime minister in August 1999 and president in May 2000. He was reelected in 2004, then bowed out for his pupil Dmitry Medvedev to assume the presidency. But Putin ran successfully again in 2012. There's no sign now that he will ever step down again. *Forbes* ranked Putin as the world's most powerful person for the fourth year in a row in 2016.[1]

During his 2005 State of the Nation address to parliament, Putin lamented that the demise of the Soviet Union was "the greatest geopolitical catastrophe" of the century.[2] Ukrainian foreign minister Pavlo Klimkin wrote in the *Guardian*, "Reversing the breakup of the Soviet Union and restoring the Russian empire have now become an obsession for the Kremlin."[3]

RUSSIA RISING

The obsession has gone so far that the Kremlin is commissioning new statues of Joseph Stalin, one of the twentieth century's worst mass murderers.[4] This is certainly a chilling window into the current Russian psyche.

Putin seizes every opportunity to stoke smoldering resentment within Russia and to draw attention to the perceived threats against his nation in order to take more and more aggressive actions to reestablish the empire. With every passing day, the Bear gets more bellicose. Putin has launched a crusade to rebuild the empire that fell along with the Berlin Wall.

President Obama promised a Russian reset in 2009 when he took office, but the opposite has occurred. US-Russian relations have relapsed into a Cold War 2.0, and some say the current situation is even worse than the Cold War. Slowly and subtly Europe and the West have sleepwalked into a new era of danger and instability. In just a little more than a decade, "the unthinkable has become a reality. Russia, seemingly finished after its defeat in the Cold War, now is emerging as a prospective great power challenging the West."[5]

Russia is on the march. General Sir Richard Shirreff, the former Deputy Supreme Allied Commander of NATO, said of Vladimir Putin, "[he] is calling the shots at the moment."[6]

That the Russian bear is on the prowl is clearly evidenced by the steady stream of world headlines:

"RUSSIA'S RISING EMPIRE"

NATIONAL REVIEW, AUGUST 9, 2016

"THE RUSSIAN BEAR IS RISING"

HUFFINGTON POST, SEPTEMBER 2, 2016

"BEWARE: THE RUSSIAN BEAR IS GETTING BOLDER"

WASHINGTON POST, DECEMBER 1, 2016

"RUSSIA'S RISING ROLE IN THE WORLD"

FOREIGN POLICY NEWS, DECEMBER 30, 2016

Russian aggression has moved into a new phase that threatens international order and stability. General James Mattis, the US defense secretary, has called Russia the world's top threat, and Senator John McCain agrees, calling Vladimir Putin "the premier and most important threat, more so than ISIS.[7] In all the Bear's bluster, we sometimes forget that Russia possesses the world's largest stockpile of nuclear weapons, with more than seven thousand nuclear warheads.[8]

Putin's grand goals are to destroy the West by breaking up the European Union, dividing NATO, frustrating and unnerving the United States, and expanding Russia's global influence. On all fronts Russia seems to be succeeding.

The Bear is on the move, leaving its footprints across the globe. First, it was Georgia in 2008. Next, the Bear invaded and annexed Crimea in 2014 and supported separatists in eastern Ukraine. In 2015, Russia, working in tandem with Iran, sent armed forces and especially air power into Syria to prop up Bashar al-Assad's crumbling regime. We're facing a new "Red Dawn." Russia is pulling the strings in the Middle East. Putin is trying to break NATO. He yearns to bring Eastern Europe and the Baltic States back into the Russian orbit.

Despite that Russia is the world's largest nation,[9] the Bear is hungry for more. Putin is busily canvassing the globe in search of weak prey and willing allies. And he's finding no shortage on either front. The Kremlin, with assistance from Iran, is arming the Taliban in Afghanistan. There are reports of Russian activity in Nicaragua. Putin's territory grab extends even to the Arctic Circle, which holds more than one-quarter of the world's undiscovered oil and gas. He visited the area in 2017, and plans are under way to construct a massive military base there. The top of the world is a top Russian priority.

FANCY BEAR AND COZY BEAR

While many Americans may not be fully aware of all that Russia is doing around the world, Russia has dominated US headlines in 2017 because of its meddling in the 2016 US presidential election. By now everyone is well aware Russia has perfected cyber-terrorism and cyber-espionage. Global technological dependence has been weaponized.

The computer-hacking scheme and interference in the US elections has been directly tied to Russian spy agencies and was part of a larger strategy that included hacking computers of the Democratic National Committee. Nearly twenty thousand e-mails hacked by the Russians were dumped by WikiLeaks on July 22, 2016—just three days before the Democratic National Convention—and embarrassed many Democratic Party leaders.

The cyber-security firm CrowdStrike gave these Russian cyber-criminals names—"Fancy Bear" and "Cozy Bear":

Traditionally, Cozy Bear targets potential victims with phishing attacks—email messages that appear to be from a legitimate, trusted friend or associate. Those messages may contain malicious software that scans a machine for antivirus software, then plants malware on the target machine that make it possible for attackers to monitor keystrokes, communications, documents and other sensitive material on target computers. Fancy Bear is known for stealing targets' usernames and passwords by setting up dummy websites that appear real enough to convince users to input their email and password information.[10]

Russian attempts to influence American politics are nothing new. In the 1960s "Soviet intelligence officers spread a rumor that the U.S. government was involved in the assassination of Martin Luther King, Jr." In the 1980s "they spread the rumor that American intelligence had 'created' the AIDS virus, at Fort Detrick, Maryland. They regularly lent support to leftist parties and insurgencies."[11] Russian intelligence services have been sifting through computer networks in the United States for more than a decade.

One of Russia's strategies is known as *dezinformatsiya*, "false information intended to discredit the official version of events, or the very notion of reliable truth."[12] We know this strategy better today as "fake news." Due to the increasing polarization in the American political landscape and the fractured media environment, Russia views the United States as a ripe target for this tactic.

Former Director of National Intelligence James Clapper testified before the Senate regarding "an unprecedented Russian effort to interfere in the U.S. electoral process. The operation involved hacking Democrats' e-mails, publicizing the stolen contents through WikiLeaks, and manipulating social media to spread 'fake news.'"[13] The e-mail hacks are part of a much larger strategy to damage American confidence and undermine Western power and alliances. Again, Russia's meddling in other nations' elections is nothing new. Just ask the Europeans. Russia's "Red Web," as its espionage efforts have been called, has worked to exert influence on German and French elections as well.

The best term to describe Russia's strategy, according to historian Angus E. Goldberg, "is the Russian word 'bespredel,' which means 'absence of limits,' or 'anything goes.'"[14] What we see today is "bespredel" on steroids—a dangerous new game of Russian roulette.

Russian meddling in US elections combined with Russia's growing international aggression has pushed US-Russian relations to a troubling low point. Sergey Rogov, academic director of the Institute for US and Canadian Studies in Moscow, says that hostility between the United States and Russia is deeper than it has been in years. He adds, "I spent many years in the trenches of the first Cold War, and I don't want to die in the trenches of the second. We are back to 1983. . . . It's frightening."[15] The world has descended into a Putin-led Cold War 2.0. Consider these current headlines:

"TRUMP, PUTIN, AND THE NEW COLD WAR"

NEW YORKER, MARCH 6, 2017

"COLD WAR 2.0?"

MSNBC, SEPTEMBER 29, 2016

"VLADIMIR PUTIN'S OUTLAW STATE"

NEW YORK TIMES, SEPTEMBER 29, 2016

"RUSSIAN HACKING AND THE 2016 ELECTION"

CNN, DECEMBER 16, 2016

In addition to its cyber-espionage, Russia is constantly testing US patience and resolve with pinprick provocations. Russian bombers are flying off the coast of Alaska. Russian spy ships are loitering off the east coast of the United States. Russia's acts appear to be carefully calculated and measured. Putin doesn't want to cross the line and spark open confrontation with the United States, but he knows that microaggressions will be tolerated—to a point. Russia may also be testing the waters to see how far its intimidations can go without incurring a response from the US, or these may just be Putin's attempts to constantly remind the world that Russia is relevant again. Whatever the Russian motivation for these actions may be, one thing is clear: the Bear is working on all fronts to let the US and the world know that there is a bear in the woods.

DESERT BEAR

As the Kremlin is combing the world for soft spots to exert its influence, the Middle East and North Africa are key targets. Putin is taking advantage of the unrest, instability, and chaos in these places to promote his expansionist agenda. The disarray in the Middle East and North Africa has proved to be fertile soil for Putin's unbridled ambition to bring back the Russian empire. Russia is working to bring Libya, Sudan, Turkey, and Iran under its umbrella. But the linchpin in Russia's push into the Middle East is Syria, where the Kremlin has thrown in with the devil, supporting the diabolical tyrant Bashar al-Assad. Russian troops and aircraft poured into Syria in 2015. Russian air power combined with Iranian ground support is propping up the Assad regime. Russia is entrenched in Syria, even establishing a naval port in Tartus, giving Russia the warm-water port it has coveted.

The United States is already engaged in a proxy war with Russia in Syria that's been going on for several years with both powers supporting different sides in the Syrian civil war. After the US Tomahawk missile strike of a Syrian air base on April 6, 2017, Russia and Iran warned the US of crossing "red lines" and raised the prospect of war. Without a doubt, Syria is a dangerous flash point. With Russian and Iranian troops stationed there and the United States launching missile strikes, the potential for a serious misstep is ever present.

Any wrong move there could push the world to the brink of disaster. The Russian-Iranian alliance in Syria has put troops from these two nations ominously on Israel's northern border. Russia's new allies would love nothing more than to drive the Jewish state into the sea.

All of this forces us to reckon with some serious questions. Is what we're witnessing just geopolitical coincidence, or could there be a hidden hand behind it all? Is it possible that the rise of Russia and the alliances that the Bear is forming are part of something bigger? Could it be the buildup for the fulfillment of ancient prophecies from Scripture? Is this another prophetic signpost that the world is racing toward the end of days?

CODE RED

On January 26, 2017, the Science and Security Board for the *Bulletin of the Atomic Scientists* moved the minute hand on the Doomsday Clock ahead thirty seconds, bringing it to two minutes and thirty seconds to midnight. This is "the closest the clock has been to midnight since 1953."[16] Among the reasons for the move were the rise of nationalism and the possibility of a renewed arms race between the United States and Russia.

People everywhere seem to sense that world events are moving toward an apocalyptic showdown. According to a recent poll, "41% of all U.S. adults, 54% of Protestants and 77% of Evangelicals believe the world is now living in the biblical end times."[17]

A Pew Research poll found that

> 72 percent of Americans expect the world to face a major world energy crisis,
> 58 percent think it "definite or probable" that there will be another world war, and
> 41 percent believe Jesus Christ will return by the year 2050.[18]

Additionally, a 2004 *Time*/CNN poll found that 59 percent of Americans believe the prophecies of the book of Revelation will come to pass.[19] Similar polls have revealed the following:

> 55 percent of Americans believe "that before the world ends the religiously faithful will be saved."
> 46 percent of Americans agree with this statement: "The world will end in the Battle of Armageddon between Jesus and the Antichrist."[20]

Similarly, "research conducted by the Brookings Institute's Center for Middle East Policy on Americans' attitudes toward the Middle East and Israel found that 79 percent of Evangelicals say they believe 'that the unfolding violence across the Middle East is a sign that the end times are nearer.'"[21]

Concerning the terrible civil war in Syria, "almost one in three Americans see Syria's recent conflict as part of the Bible's plan for the end times. One in four thinks that a U.S. military strike in Syria could lead to Armageddon. One in five believes the world will end in their lifetime."[22]

These statistics reveal that people everywhere have serious questions—searching questions—about how recent events, including the rise of Russia, relate to the ancient prophecies of the Bible.

And the Bible is certainly the best place to look for answers. The Bible is a book of prophecy. Almost 30 percent of the Bible was prophecy at the time it was written. Scripture contains about one thousand prophecies, and about five hundred of them have been literally fulfilled with 100 percent accuracy. That's quite a track record, setting the Bible far apart from any other holy book. Unlike the predictions of astrologers, mystics, and mediums, the prophecies of the Bible aren't vague and general predictions that can be altered to accommodate any situation. The prophecies recorded in the Bible are detailed and intricately interwoven. The specificity of the Bible's prophecies and its stellar track record continue to draw people to its pages for insight into the future. Even the most skeptical person can put the prophecies of Scripture to the test. In light of current events, prophecies formerly brushed aside as incredible or speculative are now being carefully examined again.

We must never forget that while the prophecies of the Bible never change, world events are constantly in flux. The Bible, not cable news, is our prophetic plumb line, the standard by which we measure everything else. Nevertheless, today's headlines are increasingly aligning with ancient biblical prophecies that describe an end-times scenario not unlike what we see today.

FUTURE SHOCK

The Jewish prophet Ezekiel, writing more than 2,500 years ago, foretold a Russian-led invasion of Israel in the end times. Russia's allies in this predicted offensive are a group of Islamic nations that are forming closer ties with the Bear as you're reading these words. Russia is rising right on schedule and is expanding its influence in the Middle East just as the Bible predicts. That's precisely what we should expect if the coming of Christ is drawing near.

When we track the Bear in biblical prophecy, we discover its footprints lead to the Middle East—and ultimately to the land of Israel. Israel is ground zero for the events of the end times.

But why Israel? As David Jeremiah comments, "Israel is one of the smallest nations on earth. It is one-nineteenth the size of California and roughly the size of New Jersey. Russia is 785 times larger than Israel. Israel measures approximately 290 miles at its longest, 85 miles at its widest, and 9 miles at its narrowest."[23] Charles Dyer and Mark Tobey offer some explanation:

From a human perspective Israel ought to occupy nothing more than a minor supporting part in any worldwide drama. In terms of geographical size, Israel ranks 148th among the nations of the world, nestled between Belize and El Salvador. Her standing improves slightly when ranked by population. At just over eight million, Israel breaks the top 100, coming in 98th between Switzerland and Honduras. And when comparing gross domestic product (GDP), Israel is ranked between 34th and 37th, depending on which organization is doing the measuring. Still, that puts Israel in with countries such as Malaysia, Singapore, and Hong Kong with barely one-quarter the GDP of a country like Mexico.

God, however, uses a different standard of measurement. And in His eyes Israel ranks at the top of the list in terms of national significance.[24]

God made unconditional promises to the descendants of Abraham, Isaac, and Jacob that have not been fulfilled—promises involving the land of Israel. But before these promises are fulfilled, Scripture tells us that the people of Israel must go through a time of trouble and tribulation that will turn them to the Lord. Consistent with these ancient prophecies, the modern state of Israel exists, is under constant pressure by the international community, and is surrounded by a sea of enemies who will play a role in the tribulation Israel will endure. The tiny nation of Israel is at the center of world attention, just as we should expect if the end of the age is drawing near. At the same time, Russia is the new power broker in the Middle East. The convergence of these events and many more that we see in the headlines every day strikingly foreshadows the ancient prophecy of Ezekiel 38–39. What we see today in light of this passage in Ezekiel raises many questions:

> Is the rise of Russia in the end times *really* predicted in the Bible, or is this just "headline theology"?
> Who are Russia's end-times allies?
> Does the Bible say anything about Russia's ties with Iran?
> What events will precipitate the Russian invasion of Israel?
> Will Israel survive?
> How soon could the Bear make its final push to the south?
> Does the United States play any role in these events?
> What does it all mean?

We'll answer these questions, and many more, as we track the Bear through the pages of Bible prophecy. Our spiritual GPS for tracking the Bear is primarily found in the ancient prophecies of Ezekiel 38–39. You will find these chapters at the end of this book in appendix 1 (page 503). I recommend that you read these chapters from God's inspired Word now to prepare you for the rest of this book.

I, and many others, believe Russia's rising in current events reveals a trajectory that points toward the ultimate fulfillment of Ezekiel's prophecy . . . maybe very soon!

CHAPTER 2

THE FINAL GAME
OF THRONES

It all looks as if the world is preparing for war.
MIKHAIL GORBACHEV IN *TIME* MAGAZINE (2017)

When you play a game of thrones you win or you die.
GEORGE R. R. MARTIN, *A GAME OF THRONES*

Just days before his crucifixion, Jesus led his disciples from the Temple down through the Kidron Valley and up the Mount of Olives, which overlooks the Temple precincts. From that vantage point he pulled back the prophetic curtain and laid out a stunning, yet simple, blueprint for the end of days. This sermon, known as the Olivet discourse, begins with a list of signs that will portend his return to earth. Jesus likened these events to birth pains that will intensify in severity and get closer and closer together:

> Don't let anyone mislead you, for many will come in my
> name, claiming, "I am the Messiah." They will deceive many.
> And you will hear of wars and threats of wars, but don't
> panic. Yes, these things must take place, but the end won't
> follow immediately. Nation will go to war against nation,

and kingdom against kingdom. There will be famines and earthquakes in many parts of the world. But all this is only the first of the birth pains, with more to come.

MATTHEW 24:4-8

After talking about false messiahs, Jesus mentions the second birth pain: "wars and threats of wars" and "nation [going] to war against nation, and kingdom against kingdom." This prophecy is mirrored by the apostle John in Revelation 6:3-4, which predicts the outbreak of wars during the end times using the symbol of a rider with a sword on a blood-red horse. The fragile, relative sense of peace the world experiences today will be shattered and suddenly stripped from the earth (see 1 Thessalonians 5:1-3).

While "wars and threats of wars" have always been part of human history, international strife and conflict will mushroom and proliferate in the end times to levels never seen before. I think we can sense the foreshocks of that today. Peace is tentative. Threats of wars are rumbling. The Middle East is like a powder keg ready to explode—fueled by ISIS, Syria, Iran, the Israeli-Palestinian standoff, Hezbollah, Hamas, and Al-Qaeda. Some small yet reckless act could unleash total chaos.

Bad actors all over the world seem ready to spin out of control at any time. North Korea and its loony leader are conducting ballistic and nuclear weapons tests. The Russian bear is on the prowl all over the globe. Other hot spots could ignite suddenly. The winds of war are blowing.

How much longer can this all be kept in check?

How much longer until the lid blows off?

THE FINAL FOUR

In the strife between nations and kingdoms that will crest during the end times, the Bible highlights four "kings" or leaders who will ascend to power. While the world of the last days will be engulfed with "wars and threats of wars . . . nation . . . against nation, and kingdom against kingdom," four key leaders will emerge from the pack, locking themselves and their allies in a final, deadly game of thrones. Scripture speaks of this final game of thrones as nations and kingdoms jockeying for power and preeminence. In the end times, four kings will take center stage in a dramatic geopolitical death struggle.

These leaders and their power blocs will rise and fall at different times. This book is primarily about the rise of Russia—which, as we'll see, the Bible identifies as the king of the north. We don't want to get too far ahead of ourselves, but for us to understand the rise of Russia and the northern confederacy, it's helpful to get an overview of the end-times alignments of nations.

In the scramble for power and resources, the world will divide into four main power blocs:

> The king of the west (see Daniel 7:8; Revelation 13:1-10)
> The king of the south (see Daniel 11:40)
> The king of the north (see Ezekiel 38; Daniel 11:40)
> The kings of the east (see Revelation 16:12)

The directional location of each of these powers is given in relation to Israel, which from God's perspective is the center, or "navel," of the earth (see Ezekiel 38:12, NASB). Pointing to these four power blocs of the end times, Bible prophecy scholar J. Dwight Pentecost says,

In studying the alignments of Gentile nations at the time of the tribulation period we find there will be: (1) a ten kingdom federation of nations that has become the final form of the fourth kingdom or the Roman empire under

the leadership of the Beast [Antichrist] (Rev. 13:1-10);
(2) a northern confederacy, Russia and her allies; (3) an
eastern or Asiatic confederacy; and (4) a north African
power. The movements of these four allied powers against
Palestine [Israel] in the tribulation period are clearly stated
in Scripture and constitute one of the major themes of
prophecy.[1]

The two main objectives of these four kings will be the same—
dominate the world and destroy Israel. The common goals they seek
will pit them against one another. The ultimate prize in this final
game of thrones is the tiny land of Israel, which means all of this was
set in motion by the rebirth of the modern state of Israel in 1948,
as predicted in Ezekiel 37. The stage is being set for the rise of these
kings.

Of course, the Bible doesn't mention every nation on earth in the
end times, so we can't be sure exactly which nations will be part of
these blocs. Also, it's impossible to say that all nations will be part of
one of these coalitions. But when the dust settles, these four will be
key players according to Scripture.

THE KING OF THE WEST

The first king who will appear on the world scene is a leader often
called the "king of the west," although the Bible never gives him that
designation. This title is fitting, however, because he will lead the
reconstituted, revived, and reunited Roman empire or Western alliance of nations. The world knows him best as the Antichrist.

Daniel 2 and 7 reveal that a group of ten Western leaders will
come to power sometime after the church is raptured to heaven.
These ten leaders will serve as a kind of ruling committee or oli-
garchy over the Western confederacy of nations. In Daniel 2 they're

represented by the ten toes on the metallic image, while in Daniel 7 they're pictured by ten horns on the fourth beast. They represent the final form of the Roman empire. I like to call them the "Group of Ten" or "G-10." The European Union could be an embryonic form of this final alignment of nations or simply the first stage of some greater alliance of nations. Either way, the Bible is clear that when the end times arrive, these ten kings or leaders will have control over the Western nations.

At some point, one ruler—the final Antichrist—will emerge, and he will grab control over the reunited Roman empire. He is depicted by Daniel as a "small horn" that rises up among the ten horns (Daniel 7:8). With the rule of this leader, the revived Roman empire will mimic the historical Roman empire that transitioned from a republic to an empire—from the rule of a body of leaders to rule by one caesar. As the Antichrist seizes control of the Western federation, the Bible says he will consolidate and expand his power, ultimately ruling the entire world for the final three and a half years before the return of Christ.

The Western leader is the subject of more than one hundred Bible passages. The Bible paints a vivid portrait of this end-times dictator:

> - He will be a Gentile, not a Jew (see Revelation 13:1).[2]
> - He will burst onto the world scene as a peacemaker, forging a seven-year agreement or peace treaty with Israel, solving (albeit temporarily) the Middle East crisis (see Daniel 9:27; Revelation 6:1-2).[3]
> - He will break the seven-year treaty at its midpoint, double-crossing the Jewish people (see Daniel 9:27). At this point, his mask of moderation will come off.
> - As the final great anti-Semite, he will unleash a reign of terror against the Jewish people (see Daniel 7:25).

> He will declare himself to be God and will demand worship (see Daniel 11:37; 2 Thessalonians 2:4; Revelation 13:4, 12).[4]
> He will defile the rebuilt Jewish Temple in Jerusalem by establishing an image of himself in the Holy of Holies (see Matthew 24:15; 2 Thessalonians 2:4).
> He will have a lieutenant and propaganda minister known as the "false prophet" (see Revelation 13:11-15; 16:13-14; 19:20).
> He will force people to bear his "mark" to participate in the world economic system he establishes (see Revelation 13:16-18). He will control the one-world economic system of the end times.

The final king of the west is identified in Scripture by many different names and titles that shed light on his character and career:

> The small horn (see Daniel 7:8)
> A king, insolent and skilled in intrigue (see Daniel 8:23)
> The prince who is to come (see Daniel 9:26)
> The one who makes desolate (see Daniel 9:27)
> The king who does as he pleases (see Daniel 11:36-45)
> The man of destruction (see 2 Thessalonians 2:3)
> The man of lawlessness (see 2 Thessalonians 2:8)
> The Antichrist (see 1 John 2:18)
> The rider on the white horse (see Revelation 6:2)
> The beast out of the sea (see Revelation 13:1-2)

The Western king will be nothing short of a satanic masterpiece—a satanic superman.

Human history begins with the sin of man and ends with the man of sin.

THE KING OF THE SOUTH

Another end-times king will rise from North Africa, probably Egypt, and he is called the king of the south (see Daniel 11:40). Daniel 11:1-35a discusses the past kings of the south who ruled Egypt, but in Daniel 11:35b, the text jumps from the past to the future—from history to prophecy. The leap to the end times is signaled by the words, "until the time of the end, for the appointed time is still to come." Daniel 11:40 also places these verses in an end-times setting—"at the time of the end."

J. Dwight Pentecost identifies this last-days leader: "Evidently this King of the South is allied with the King of the North, for they simultaneously invade Palestine (Dan. 11:40). There is general agreement among interpreters that the King of the South has reference to Egypt, inasmuch as Egypt is frequently referred to as the land to the south in Scripture."[5] This alliance will probably include other nations from the area such as Libya and Sudan, referenced in Ezekiel 38, and possibly Algeria and Tunisia.

A North African alliance will be part of the end-times scenario. The king of the south will be in league with the king of the north. We will look at this alliance more in depth in chapter 4.

THE KING OF THE NORTH

Russia is identified as the king of the north in Daniel 11:40 and is further described in Ezekiel 38–39. Daniel 11:5-35 describes the back-and-forth struggle between Egypt (the king of the south) and the ancient Seleucid empire centered in Syria (the king of the north). Israel was caught between these two ancient powers for centuries.

Daniel 11:40 refers to a king of the north who will rise in the end times. This leader, like the ancient Seleucids, will control a vast swath of territory north and east of Israel. The prophetic counterpart to the historical Seleucid monarchs is Russia. Russia's identification as the king of the north is confirmed by the parallel passage in Ezekiel 38, which describes a northern alliance that invades Israel in the end times.

We'll discuss Russia's role much more in the pages to come, but there's one final human king who's part of the end-times game of thrones.

THE KINGS OF THE EAST

This is the only one of the four power blocs whose leader's title is plural—"kings," not "king." The kings of the east are specifically referenced just one time in Scripture. Revelation 16:12 says, "Then the sixth angel poured out his bowl on the great Euphrates River, and it dried up so that the kings from the east could march their armies toward the west without hindrance."

The specific nations in this coalition are not listed. All we know is that they come from east of the Euphrates River, since the river must be dried up for their march into the land of Israel.

John Walvoord notes,

The most simple and suitable explanation is to take the passage literally. The Euphrates River then becomes the geographic boundary of the ancient Roman Empire. The kings of the east are kings from the east or "of the sunrising," that is, monarchs who originated in the Orient. . . . If the drying of the Euphrates River is to be taken literally, then what can be understood by the reference to "the kings of the east"? Here again the literal view is to be preferred. Inasmuch as it would be most natural in a world war culminating in the Middle East to have the Orient represented, the interpretation that views the kings of the east as the political and military leaders of Asiatic forces east of the Euphrates is a satisfactory solution.[6]

Revelation 16:14 reveals that the movement of the kings of the east into Israel is part of a worldwide gathering of the "rulers of the world . . . for battle against the Lord on that great judgment day of God the Almighty." According to Revelation 16:16, the geographical focal point of the gathering is Armageddon (Mount Megiddo in northern Israel).

This army from the east in Revelation 16 is often connected with the army of 200 million in Revelation 9:16. Some take a further step and associate this massive army with China. If this view is correct, it's astounding, because when the apostle John wrote these words, 200 million would have been close to the population of the entire world. My view is that the army of 200 million in Revelation is a demonic horde that will come forth in the end times.[7]

Either way, a great army from east of the Euphrates will be a key part of the wars of the end times.

PUTTING THE PIECES TOGETHER

I hate puzzles and am terrible at assembling them, but early on I discovered a very simple guideline—the key to putting together a puzzle is the picture on top of the box. The assembled pieces must look like the picture. I also learned that you have to begin with the edge pieces to frame the picture. What's true of putting together a cardboard puzzle is also true of putting together the prophetic picture in Scripture. As we look at our world today, the picture we see is steadily looking more and more like the picture we see in the Bible. The edges seem to be taking form, and some of the picture is beginning to fill in. The rise of the four kings is part of the picture.

THE FINAL FOUR KINGS	
The king of the west	Western powers under the rule of the Antichrist; the reunited Roman empire
The king of the south	North African coalition
The kings of the east	Grouping of nations from east of the Euphrates River
The king of the north	Russian-led alliance

Today, many key Western nations are allied in the agreements of NATO. The European Union is a further cementing of Western interests. Radical Islam has ignited the Muslim nations of North Africa, and we can see how they could form into a southern coalition. Russia is emerging and establishing alliances with other nations north and east of Israel. To the east of the Euphrates River are a host of nations that could coalesce into the predicted kings of the east. Certainly, many twists and turns will occur in the days ahead, reshaping and reforming current headlines, but the edges of the puzzle appear to be taking shape.

Putting this final game of thrones together, we see that sometime after the rapture of all believers in Christ to heaven, the first move is made by the king of the west, who will begin the seven-year Tribulation by forging some kind of peace agreement or treaty with Israel. At some point, the kings of the north (Russia and its Islamic allies) and south (likely Egypt and the nations of North Africa) will invade Israel. Their attack will have two objectives: 1) wiping out the Jewish people and stealing their land, and 2) challenging the authority of the Western king (who has a treaty with Israel). Charles Ryrie describes their attack on Israel as a pincer move: "A pincer is an instrument with two claws used to grab something. . . . The King of the South is situated perfectly: right on the southern doorstep of the land that is up for grabs. Russia will form the northern claw, Egypt the southern claw; put them together . . . and you have the pincer. The attack will be launched on both fronts simultaneously."[8]

After the kings of the north and south are destroyed by God, the king of the west (the Antichrist) will surge to global ascendancy. Finally, at the end of the seven-year Great Tribulation, the kings of the east will make their move as they cross the Euphrates River and pour into the land of Israel along with the remainder of the armies from around the world. The armies will muster at Armageddon in northern Israel. With the kings of the east and the Antichrist gathered in the land, there's one final King who will make his move.

THE FIFTH KING

To make sure we have the full story, the final move in the end-times game of thrones is the return of the King of kings to take back planet Earth. His move will occur at Armageddon when he crushes the forces of the king of the west and the kings of the east, as well as the remaining armies from around the globe. Recently, the United States dropped a bomb on ISIS in Afghanistan called MOAB (the mother of all bombs). Revelation 19 describes the final MOAB—the mother of all battles. Revelation 19:11-21 describes the King who comes to take his rightful throne in a righteous bloodbath. The second coming of Christ will be as different as one can imagine from his first coming as a baby in Bethlehem.

There's an often-told story that Vernon Grounds relates. When a friend of Grounds's was in seminary, he would play basketball at a public school because there was no gym at the seminary. Each week as he and some other seminarians played, an elderly janitor would wait patiently until they were finished. He always sat in the stands reading his Bible. One day Grounds's friend approached the custodian. "What are you reading?" he asked. The janitor answered, "The book of Revelation." Grounds's friend was surprised. "Do you understand what you're reading?" "Oh, yes," the janitor replied. The seminarian was even more surprised and asked, "What does it mean?" The janitor answered him, "It means that Jesus is gonna win." Grounds writes, "That's the best commentary I have ever heard on that book. Jesus is going to win."[9]

Jesus wins the final game of thrones. None can stand against him. All will wither under his mighty hand.

It's great to get the big picture in mind and know up front who the key players are and how the story ends. But we've gotten way ahead of ourselves. Now that we have a broad overview of some of the events of the end times, we're going to slow down, back up a bit, and look in detail at key prophecies that must be fulfilled before Jesus comes, including the rise and fall of Russia.

Let's zero in on the king of the north and track the Bear in Bible prophecy.

CHAPTER 3

IS RUSSIA *REALLY* IN THE BIBLE?

Ezekiel says that . . . the nation that will lead all the other powers into darkness against Israel will come out of the north. What other powerful nation is to the north of Israel [besides Russia]? None.

RONALD REAGAN[1]

Ezekiel 38 is the biblical entry point for any discussion of Russia in biblical prophecy. All agree the names *Russia* and *Moscow* do not appear in this chapter or anywhere else in the Bible. Yet as you will see, many reputable scholars believe that the ancient prophet refers to the nation we know today as Russia. Ezekiel 38:1-2 is the beginning of a list of nations that will join together, forming a northern storm in the end times: "The word of the LORD came to me saying, 'Son of man, set your face toward Gog of the land of Magog, the prince of Rosh, Meshech and Tubal, and prophesy against him'" (NASB).

Two key words in this verse have been associated with Russia—*Rosh* and *Magog*. Some claim that any attempt to associate these ancient places with modern Russia is speculative and sensationalistic.[2] Others believe the ancient prophet identified the ruler of the modern nation of Russia as the final king of the north described in Daniel 11:40. To discover which view carries more weight, we have to examine the evidence. But before we look at Ezekiel 38, let's briefly consider one other biblical passage that some have associated with Russia.

THE RISING BEAR IN DANIEL 7

Because of the symbolism of a bear, some believe Daniel 7:5 is a reference to modern Russia: "Then I saw a second beast, and it looked like a bear. It was rearing up on one side, and it had three ribs in its mouth between its teeth. And I heard a voice saying to it, 'Get up! Devour the flesh of many people!'" Those who believe this refers to Russia in the last days place undue emphasis on the modern designation of Russia as the Bear, which would have been foreign to the original audience. Those who hold this view usually interpret the lion with wings of an eagle in Daniel 7:4 as a reference to Great Britain (the lion) and her offspring the United States (the eagle).

However, interpreting ancient prophecies based on modern national symbols is misguided. I, as well as an overwhelming number of Bible commentators, believe the lion in Daniel 7 refers to the ancient Babylonian empire while the bear refers to the ancient Persian empire. The basis for this interpretation is simple. In Daniel 2, four empires are symbolized by four metals in a great statue that King Nebuchadnezzar sees in a dream. The four metals are gold, silver, bronze, and iron. Daniel reveals that the first empire (represented by the head of gold) is Babylon (see Daniel 2:38). Then he says that Babylon will be succeeded by another empire. We know from history that the Medo-Persians followed Babylon, overtaking the city of Babylon in 539 BC. The Persians were followed by Greece and then Rome. Commentators are almost unanimous that the four metals of the statue in Daniel 2 refer to Babylon, Medo-Persia, Greece, and Rome.

The four beasts in Daniel 7:1-7 are parallel to the four metals in Daniel 2, which means the bear in Daniel 7 is not Russia but the ancient Persian empire. We know this because the entire section from Daniel 2–7 is structured as a chiasm, an intentional literary device in which a sequence of ideas is repeated in reverse order, mirroring the original sequence in order to focus attention and highlight the center of the chiasm. Items in a chiasm are parallel, working toward the central point. The chiastic structure reveals that Daniel 2 and 7 cover the same ground, employing different images for the same empires.

CHIASTIC STRUCTURE OF DANIEL 2–7
Daniel 2—World empires symbolized by four metals of a statue
Daniel 3—Three young men delivered from the fiery furnace
Daniel 4—Nebuchadnezzar humbled
Daniel 5—Belshazzar humbled
Daniel 6—Daniel delivered from the lion's den
Daniel 7—World empires symbolized by four wild beasts

Daniel 2 presents the four world empires from man's perspective as a great metallic man, while Daniel 7 views the same empires from God's perspective as wild, ravenous beasts. The bear in Daniel 7:5 is ancient Persia, not Russia.

THE MAGOG CONNECTION

The first place mentioned in Ezekiel 38 is Magog (see Ezekiel 38:2; 39:6).[3] Besides its mention in Ezekiel, the name *Magog* is found in the Bible only in Genesis 10:2 and 1 Chronicles 1:5—where he is listed as a son of Japheth (one of Noah's three sons)—and in Revelation 20:8, a connection we'll examine in chapter 8.[4]

Flavius Josephus, the Jewish historian, says the ancient Scythians inhabited the land of Magog.[5] The Scythians were ruthless northern nomadic tribes who inhabited a large swath of territory encompassing Central Asia and the southern steppes of modern Russia. Magog today includes five former Soviet republics: Kazakhstan, Kyrgyzstan, Uzbekistan, Turkmenistan, and Tajikistan. Afghanistan could also be part of this territory. These nations, with a combined population of more than sixty million, are all Islamic.

Many believe ancient Magog also includes what today is Russia. *The Nelson Study Bible* describes Magog as "usually understood to be in the area near the Black Sea or the Caspian Sea. Magog is one of the sons of Japheth, whose descendants occupied lands from Spain to Asia Minor, the islands of the Mediterranean to southern Russia."[6]

Charles Ryrie says, "*Magog* was identified by Josephus as the land of the Scythians, the region N and NE of the Black Sea and E of the Caspian Sea (now occupied by three members of the Commonwealth of Independent States: Russia, the Ukraine, and Kazakhstan)."[7] Referring to Magog, Rosh, Meshech, and Tubal, Arnold Fruchtenbaum says, "These tribes of the ancient world occupied the areas of modern day Russia."[8] John MacArthur, referring to Ezekiel 38:2, says, "The names of ancient peoples are given who lived in northern Mesopotamia and the Caucasus region of modern Russia."[9]

Ancient Magog included land that today is in Russia.

THE ROSH REFERENCE

After Gog and Magog, the third proper name in Ezekiel 38:2 is Rosh. It's referred to again in Ezekiel 38:3 and 39:1. Because of the obvious similarity of Rosh with Russia, many have equated them. This view was popularized in the note on Ezekiel 38:2 in *The Scofield Reference Bible*: "That the primary reference is to the northern (European) powers, headed up by Russia, all agree. . . . The reference to Meshech and Tubal (Moscow and Tobolsk) is a clear mark of identification."[10]

Scofield seems to base his correlation on the similarity in sound and pronunciation of Rosh, Meshech, and Tubal with Russia, Moscow, and Tobolsk. Linking Rosh in Ezekiel 38:2 and 39:1 with Russia simply because the two words sound similar, however, is not a valid method of interpretation. There is no justification to equate an ancient word with a modern location just because they sound the same. Yet the evidence that Ezekiel was thinking of the land that is now Russia is based on much more than just a similar sound. Three lines of evidence point toward Rosh as Russia.

THE GRAMMAR

The language in Ezekiel 38 favors equating Rosh with Russia. The word *rosh* in Hebrew simply means "head, top, summit, or chief." It is a very common word found in all Semitic languages. In the Old Testament alone it appears more than six hundred times. Many English translations of *rosh* render it as the word *chief*, not as the proper name of a geographical location. The King James Version, the Revised Standard Version, the English Standard Version, the New American Bible, and the New International Version all adopt this translation. However, the translation is not unanimous. The Jerusalem Bible, the New English Bible, and the New American Standard Bible all translate *rosh* as a proper name indicating a geographical location.

The preponderance of the evidence supports taking *rosh* as a proper name in Ezekiel chapters 38 and 39. Four main points support this reading. First, the eminent Hebrew scholars C. F. Keil and Wilhelm Gesenius both hold that the superior translation of *rosh* in Ezekiel 38:2-3 and 39:1 is as a proper noun denoting a specific geographical location.[11] Support from these two scholars from the nineteenth century is significant. G. A. Cooke translates Ezekiel 38:2 "the chief of Rosh, Meshech and Tubal." He believes this is "the most natural way of rendering the Hebrew."[12] Nevertheless, many modern translations and commentators translate *rosh* as the adjective "chief," modifying the word "prince." The main reason seems to be that they aren't aware of a place in Ezekiel's day called Rosh. Old Testament scholar John B. Taylor admits that "if place-name Rosh could be vouched for," then Rosh would be the best translation.[13] As we'll discover shortly, a place known as Rosh did exist in Ezekiel's day, thus removing this obstacle to translating *rosh* as a proper name.

Second, in the Septuagint—the Greek translation of the Hebrew Old Testament—*rosh* is translated as the proper name "Ros." While not conclusive, this evidence is weighty in light of the close proximity of the Septuagint to Ezekiel's day. The Septuagint was translated within three centuries of the writing of the book of Ezekiel.[14] The Hebrew Masoretic Text, the basis for most English translations of the Old Testament, also supports taking *rosh* as the name of an ethnic group.[15]

Third, several standard Bible dictionaries and encyclopedias support taking *rosh* as a proper name in Ezekiel 38: *New Bible Dictionary*, *Wycliffe Bible Dictionary*, *Jones' Dictionary of Old Testament Proper Names*, and *Baker Encyclopedia of the Bible*.

Fourth, *rosh* occurs for the first time in Ezekiel 38:2. It appears again in Ezekiel 38:3 and 39:1. C. F. Keil notes that *rosh* must be a proper name since it appears several times because titles are generally abbreviated in Hebrew.[16] If *rosh* were the adjective "chief," it wouldn't reappear two more times.

The biblical evidence strongly supports taking *rosh* as a proper noun referring to a geographical location. But that's only half of the issue. The next question is—which geographical location? Wilhelm Gesenius, the father of modern Hebrew lexicography, believed Rosh in Ezekiel is a proper name referring to Russia. He wrote in 1846 that Rosh is "undoubtedly the Russians, who are mentioned by the Byzantine writers of the tenth century, under the name Ros, dwelling to the north of Taurus [in Turkey]."[17] Clearly, Gesenius did not base his view on current events or any theological predisposition to favor this view. As author Joel Rosenberg observes,

> What is interesting to me about this assessment is that it was written in 1846, long before the Communist revolution or the subsequent rise of the Soviet Union as a nuclear superpower. In this case, Gesenius was not using a political or economic lens to reach his conclusions. He was using *only* the third lens of Scripture, and the evidence pointed him to Russia more than 160 years ago.[18]

The compelling evidence from biblical scholarship concerning the grammar and language of Ezekiel 38:2 indicates that *rosh* be understood as a proper name, the name of a specific geographic area. Rosh refers to Russia.

THE GROUP OF PEOPLE

One of the arguments against equating Rosh with Russia is that no ancient nation named Rosh existed. However, a growing body of evidence points toward a group of people in the sixth century BC identified as "Rash," "Reshu," or "Ros," who inhabited territory that today is in southern Russia.[19] While the word has a variety of forms and spellings, it is clear that the same people are in view.

Egyptian inscriptions indicate that Rosh existed as early as 2600 BC. A place called Reshu, located north of Egypt, is mentioned in an Egyptian inscription from around 1500 BC.[20] Many other ancient documents mention the place-name *Rosh* in upwards of twenty instances.[21] Rosh was apparently a well-known place in Ezekiel's day. In the sixth century BC, when Ezekiel wrote his prophecy, many of the Rosh people lived in a region north of the Black Sea. After providing extensive evidence of the origin and early history of the

Rosh people and then tracing them through the centuries, Clyde Billington concludes,

> As early as 438 A.D., Byzantine Christians placed Gog, Magog, Meshech, Tubal and Ros peoples to the north of Greece in the area that today is Russia. . . . Historical, ethnological, and archaeological evidence all favor the conclusion that the Rosh people of Ezekiel 38–39 were the ancestors of the Rus/Ros people of Europe and Asia. . . . The Rosh people who are mentioned in Ezekiel 38–39 were well-known to ancient and medieval writers by a variety of names which all derived from the names of Tiras and Rosh. . . . Those Rosh people who lived to the north of the Black Sea in ancient and medieval times were called the Rus/Ros/Rox/Aorsi from very early times. . . . From this mixture with Slavs and with the Varangian Rus in the 9th century, the Rosh people of the area north of the Black Sea formed the people known today as the Russians.[22]

All agree that there is no geographical place today named Rosh. Our task is to identify where the Rosh people lived in Ezekiel's day and then determine what nation occupies that territory today. Arnold Fruchtenbaum writes, "While the names of these geographical areas have changed over the centuries . . . and may change again, the geography itself remains intact. Regardless of what names they may carry at the time of this invasion, it is these very geographical areas that are involved. Although the leading nation may have once been called the Soviet Union, and more recently the Commonwealth of Independent States, and traditionally Russia, it is this territory—by whatever name it may be called at that time—that will lead this invasion."[23]

THE GEOGRAPHY

The third main line of evidence for identifying Rosh as Russia is based on location. Ezekiel chapters 38 and 39 emphasize repeatedly that at least part of this last-days' invading force will come "from the distant north" (38:6, 15; 39:2). Biblical directions are usually given in reference to Israel, which on God's compass is the "center" (or "navel") of the earth (see Ezekiel 38:12, NASB). This valuable textual clue points to Russia. If you draw a line directly north from Israel on a map, only five nations are in line: Lebanon, Syria, Turkey, Ukraine, and Russia. But the one farthest north is Russia.[24] John Walvoord says, "One cannot escape Russia if he goes north of the Holy Land. On the basis of geography alone, it seems quite clear that the only nation which could possibly be referred to as coming from the far north would be the nation Russia."[25]

Paul Enns notes, "These enemies come from the 'remote parts of the north' (vv. 6, 15), modern Turkey and southern Russia—the nations surrounding the Black and Caspian Seas."[26]

Walter Kaiser is unsure if Rosh in Ezekiel 38 is Russia, but he sees the geographical reference to the far north as unmistakable. "They are depicted by Ezekiel as 'coming from [their] place in the far north' (15). The allusion to the 'far north' also points to a Russian-led confederation, for Moscow is almost directly north of Jerusalem on a modern map."[27]

Based on geography, Scripture indicates Russia will be the leader of the northern coalition of the end times.

THE BEAR NECESSITY

To further support the presence of Russia in Ezekiel 38, I thought it would be helpful to briefly quote a few other reliable sources who have studied this issue extensively. Charles Dyer and Mark Tobey say, "Most Bible students with even cursory understanding of biblical prophecy suspect that Russia will play some strategic role in end-time events."[28] Charles Dyer, in his commentary on Ezekiel, is even more specific: "Some of the countries named by Ezekiel were located in what is now Russia."[29] Speaking of Ezekiel 38, Lamar Cooper says, "The geographical area would today include . . . southern provinces of Russia."[30] Theologian Charles Ryrie says, "The land of Russia looms large and menacing in Ezekiel's prophetic picture."[31] Dr. David Jeremiah writes, "Approximately twenty-five hundred years ago, Ezekiel predicted Russia's return to power in the latter days."[32]

Popular Bible teacher J. Vernon McGee describes how he came to his view:

> When I first entered the ministry, I took the position that these two chapters of Ezekiel could not possibly speak of the modern nation of Russia under any circumstances. Even when I began seminary work on my Th.M. and Th.D., I did not accept that interpretation. I began to study on my own and attempt to arrive at a decision—whether or not this could possibly be Russia. Now I am convinced beyond a shadow of a doubt that chapters 38 and 39 refer to Russia.[33]

J. Dwight Pentecost, a preeminent prophecy scholar, authored his classic work *Things to Come* in 1958 and noted, "The identification of Rosh as modern Russia would seem to be well authenticated and generally accepted."[34] Joel Rosenberg concludes,

> The words *Russia, Moscow, Soviet Union,* and *czar* never appear in these passages [Ezekiel 38–39]. Nor do they appear anywhere in the book of Ezekiel. Nor are they ever mentioned anywhere in the Bible. But there is no doubt

that the ancient prophet was referring to the nation we now know as Russia. . . . Based on the textual, linguistic, and historical evidence, we can . . . conclude with a high degree of confidence that Ezekiel is speaking of Russia and the former Soviet Union in chapters 38 and 39.[35]

These authors and scholars are far from alone in their assessment. Many, many more well-respected scholars, pastors, commentators, and popular Bible teachers could be cited who believe Ezekiel 38 refers to Russia and its allies. Of course, their support for this view doesn't prove it's correct, but it should demonstrate that this is not a fringe, fanatical view.

HISTORY, NOT HEADLINES

Contemporary writers aren't the only ones who believe Ezekiel chapters 38 and 39 refer to Russia. This view has a long line of support. I make this point because one repeated objection to identifying Magog or Rosh with Russia is that this is nothing more than "sensationalistic end-time speculation" based on the current headlines.[36] While there is certainly unwarranted speculation and newspaper exegesis by some prophecy teachers, contemporary scholars are not alone in their appraisal that Rosh and Magog in Ezekiel 38 refer to Russia.

Here's a brief list of scholars from previous generations who identified Rosh or Magog with Russia:

> Matthew Henry, in his famous commentary written in the early 1700s, was aware of some who identified Russia with Ezekiel 38. He says, "Some think they find them afar off, in Scythia, Tartary, and Russia."[37] Henry doesn't say he agrees with the view, but his awareness of it demonstrates that it at least was not uncommon.

> Patrick Fairbairn, a Scottish Presbyterian preacher, in his 1842 commentary on Ezekiel, notes that Rosh is a reference to Russia.[38]

> Jamieson, Fausset, and Brown, commenting on Rosh in Ezekiel 38 in 1871, says, "The Scythian Tauri in the Crimea were so called. The Araxes also was called 'Rhos.' The modern Russians may have hence *assumed* their name" (emphasis added).[39]

> William Kelly, a Plymouth Brethren scholar, writing in 1876, identifies Gog (the leader of the invasion in Ezekiel 38) by noting, "He is autocrat of all the Russias, prince of Rosh, Meshech, and Tubal."[40] He writes, "Next follow two chapters which contain a prediction of God's judgment to fall in the last days, when Israel is restored, on a great north-eastern chief with his vast array of satellites and allies on the mountains of the Holy Land. . . . Who can deny that the rapid and immense development of the Russian empire bears its unmistakable witness to the judgment that is coming, as here declared so long before?"[41]

> Arno Gaebelein, writing in the early twentieth century, says, "The leader is the prince of Rosh. . . . And here we call attention to the prince, this northern leader, or king, who is the head of all these nations. He is the prince of Rosh. Careful research has established the fact that the progenitor of Rosh was Tiraz [Genesis 10:2], and that Rosh is Russia. All students of prophecy are agreed that this is the correct meaning of Rosh. The prince of Rosh, means, therefore, the prince or king of the Russian empire."[42]

Studying the Word of God, not current events or headlines, formed the views of these scholars. We seek to follow their example.

God's Word must be our guide. The fact that current events are aligning with what Scripture says does not render this view sensationalism. Rather, it demonstrates the truth of Scripture and points toward the coming of Christ.

CONCLUSION

Ezekiel 38 reveals that Russia will rise in the last days as a formidable global power. Whether or not one sees Rosh or Magog as Russia, the far northern geographical notation is clear. The rise of Russia today is no coincidence; it's divine providence. Events happening in Russia today strikingly foreshadow Ezekiel's ancient prophecy. Russian tentacles reach around the world. The buildup toward a Middle East war is accelerating. The Bear is rising to take its place among the cast of characters in the final drama of the ages. But Russia will not rise alone. Ezekiel lists a group of allies who will conspire with Russia's leader for a final push into the Middle East—into the land of Israel. These nations dominate today's headlines and are presently forming alliances with Russia.

Who are these allies?

The *Who's Who* of Middle Eastern bad actors.

CHAPTER 4

EZEKIEL'S PROPHETIC INTELLIGENCE BRIEFING

You will come from your homeland in the distant north
with your vast cavalry and your mighty army.

EZEKIEL 38:15

As we saw in the last chapter, when we carefully examine the text of Ezekiel 38, we can see that in the end times a Russian leader will spearhead an attack on Israel. But Ezekiel 38 also reveals that Russia will not mount this attack alone. Who will join them? Ezekiel "provides us extraordinarily precise intelligence," Joel Rosenberg writes. "Though he wrote more than 2,500 years ago, the Hebrew prophet was able to tell us what to watch for."[1] Incredibly, all the way back in 586 BC, Ezekiel peered into the future and gave us an intelligence briefing for who will join Russia in their anti-Israel assault.

The first thing Ezekiel does is give a detailed list of the participants in the Russian-led coalition:

1. Gog
2. Magog
3. Rosh
4. Meshech
5. Tubal
6. Persia
7. Ethiopia (Cush)
8. Libya (Put)
9. Gomer
10. Beth-togarmah

Pause for a moment and read these verses to get the context in view:

> This is another message that came to me from the LORD:
> "Son of man, turn and face Gog of the land of Magog, the
> prince who rules over* the nations of Meshech and Tubal,
> and prophesy against him. Give him this message from
> the Sovereign LORD: Gog, I am your enemy! I will turn
> you around and put hooks in your jaws to lead you out
> with your whole army—your horses and charioteers in full
> armor and a great horde armed with shields and swords.
> Persia, Ethiopia, and Libya will join you, too, with all their
> weapons. Gomer and all its armies will also join you, along
> with the armies of Beth-togarmah from the distant north,
> and many others.
>
> "Get ready; be prepared! Keep all the armies around you
> mobilized, and take command of them."
>
> EZEKIEL 38:1-7

---

* The New Living Translation translates the Hebrew *rosh* as "who rules over." See the discussion in the last chapter, where I make the case that the better translation is "Rosh," a proper noun/nation (as in NASB).

Before we examine the location names listed in Ezekiel 38:1-6, I want to briefly comment on the principle of interpretation we'll employ. More and more scholars and commentators today opt for a general or even spiritualizing approach to the prophecy of Ezekiel 38 and many other prophetic Scriptures.[2] Interestingly, those who adopt this approach usually take the geographical references in Ezekiel 1–32 to refer to literal places and people, yet when they come to the final chapters of Ezekiel, they shift to a spiritualizing approach, claiming that these chapters are "apocalyptic" and justify a shift in interpretive method. Much could be said about this practice, but at the very least it's inconsistent. Nothing in Ezekiel chapters 38 and 39 signals these chapters are to be understood in any way other than literal. The method of interpretation is the same for the whole book of Ezekiel. Charles Feinberg spotlights an important interpretive guideline:

> Some suggest a "generally literal" interpretation where the details are not necessarily so. The writer cannot allow himself such liberties in interpreting the plain statements of the prophetic Scriptures. It is either the grammatical, literal, historical interpretation or we are adrift on an uncharted sea with every man the norm for himself. There is not a syllable at the beginning of this chapter to alert us to explain the passage in any other than the literal method.[3]

The best approach, in my opinion, is to understand these chapters as referring to actual places and people that will appear on the world scene in the last days, just as the text says.

Ezekiel 38 describes a coalition of nations, listing each of the nations by its ancient place-name in Ezekiel's day. But before he unveils the nations that will join Russia in this military offensive, Ezekiel identifies the commander of this horde.

THE COMMANDER

The leader of the first great war of the end times is called "Gog of the land of Magog, the prince of Rosh, Meshech and Tubal" (Ezekiel 38:2, NASB). The name *Gog*, which occurs ten times in the New Living Translation of Ezekiel 38–39, is the name or title of the leader of the invasion. We know this because he is directly addressed by God (see 38:14; 39:1), called a prince (see 38:2; 39:1), and repeatedly referred to by the use of personal pronouns. Also, he is "of the land of Magog," indicating he is an individual. The word *Gog* is likely not the leader's name but serves as a title like "pharaoh," "president," or "czar."

In the Old Testament, the word *Gog* appears only one time outside Ezekiel 38–39—in 1 Chronicles 5:4—but clearly in reference to a different person. *Gog* may mean "high" or "supreme," or it may represent a height, possibly emphasizing this leader's elevated position and pride. The word *Gog* may come from the Sumerian word *gug*, meaning "darkness."

The name *Gog* has been identified with many personages both ancient and modern. Here are some of the more common views:

> Gog is Gugu or Gyges, a Lydian king in the seventh century BC. (Lydia is part of the modern nation of Turkey.)
> Gog is a cryptogram or code name for Babylon.
> Gog is another name for the end-times Antichrist.
> Gog is a symbolic term for any enemy of God.

I don't believe Gog and the Antichrist should be equated. According to Daniel 7 and Revelation 13, the final Antichrist will lead the Western confederacy of nations, reunited out of the old Roman empire, while Gog is from Russia and leads a primarily northern force. Daniel 11:40 calls the Russian leader "the king of the north." Gog and the Antichrist are two different leaders who are in opposition to each other.

The best view seems to be that Gog is a title for the ruler of Russia derived from a recent ruler in Ezekiel's day (Gyges or Gugu) that Ezekiel employs to describe the character of the final Russian ruler. Charles Dyer and Mark Tobey hold this view. They believe Gog is "most likely an allusion to an ancient king named Gyges who died about seventy years before Ezekiel delivered his prophecy. By identifying this still-future ruler as 'Gog,' Ezekiel was using someone from his recent past to paint a one-word portrait of this future ruler. It is similar to someone today identifying the future Antichrist as the next 'Hitler' or 'Stalin'—men who also died several decades ago but whose evil legacy is still fresh on people's minds."[4] Whatever specific view one takes of the meaning of Gog, Ezekiel is clear that he will be the northern commander of this last-days coalition.

THE COALITION

The name *Gog* is followed by nine ancient place-names. Our task is to decode these ancient locations and identify their modern counterparts.

The Table of Nations in Genesis 10 helps us with this task because all the names in Ezekiel 38 (save Rosh) are listed there as the descendants of Noah's sons Shem, Ham, and especially Japheth. In locating these places today, we need to remember that Ezekiel used the names for these places that were familiar in his day (ca. 593–570 BC). The names of these places have changed many times over the millennia and may change again before this prophecy is fulfilled. Nevertheless, these are the geographical locations, whatever their names may be, that will be part of this massive Russian-led incursion into Israel in the last days. Paul Enns observes, "The names *Gog, Rosh, Meshech,* and *Tubal* were historic names that should be understood *representatively* or *eschatologically*. Ezekiel prophesied concerning a future invasion against Israel, but used names of nations during his day because the future invaders would be from the same geographical places."[5]

In the last chapter we looked at the evidence that identifies Rosh as Russia, so we won't go over that same ground again, but we'll identify the other eight places Ezekiel pinpoints.

MAGOG

Magog was the second son of Japheth and the grandson of Noah. The name *Magog* is found elsewhere in Scripture in Genesis 10:2, 1 Chronicles 1:5, Ezekiel 39:6, and Revelation 20:8. We discussed Magog in the last chapter in some detail and discovered that many identify Magog as Russia and/or the Islamic nations of Central Asia, possibly including Afghanistan. Again, Charles Ryrie notes that Magog "was identified . . . as the land of the Scythians . . . now occupied by . . . Russia, the Ukraine, and Kazakhstan."[6] Magog is the land of the ancient Scythians and encompasses the Central Asian nations that formed the underbelly of the Soviet Union. These predominantly Muslim nations have a combined population of more than sixty million. Robbed of these nations and longing for a return to the Soviet empire, Russia is working to woo them back under its umbrella. The Eurasian Economic Union is strongly supported by Russia to extend its influence in Central Asia.

MESHECH AND TUBAL

Meshech and Tubal are normally mentioned together in Scripture (see Ezekiel 27:13; 32:26). C. I. Scofield identifies Meshech and Tubal as the Russian cities of Moscow and Tobolsk.[7]

Over the years many others have followed Scofield's identification. The names of these places do sound alike, but as I mentioned in the last chapter, this by itself is not a proper method of identifying the current locations of these ancient places. The context of the book of Ezekiel rules out any association of these places with Moscow or Tobolsk. Meshech and Tubal are mentioned as trading partners with ancient Tyre, which is modern Lebanon (see Ezekiel 27:13). Ezekiel 32:26 records their recent defeat by their enemies. Ancient records provide no credible evidence that Tyre was trading with places as remote as Moscow and the Siberian city of Tobolsk. Also, Ezekiel would certainly not have been aware of any defeat of armies that distant from Israel.

The more reliable identification is that Meshech is the ancient *Moschoi* in Greek writing and *Musku* in Assyrian inscriptions, while Tubal is *Tibarenoi* and *Tabal*. Both of these locations are in present-day Turkey, a nation that is strengthening ties with Russia and Iran.

GOMER

Like Magog, Meshech, and Tubal, Gomer was a son of Japheth. He was the first son of Japheth and the grandson of Noah (see Genesis 10:2-3). Many have identified Gomer as Germany. Arnold Fruchtenbaum says, "Gomer . . . [is] located in present-day Germany. This too was the rabbinic view. The *Midrash* calls Gomer *Germania* and that is also the way the *Talmud* refers to Gomer."[8] In the days of the Cold War and the Iron Curtain, when Eastern Europe was under Soviet control, Gomer was often identified with East Germany. John Phillips believes Gomer refers to Germany and speculates, "What if a united and anti-Semitic Germany were to seek its future fortunes while allied to an anti-Semitic Russia?"[9] If true, that would be a formidable partnership.

While Gomer could refer to modern Germany, since the ancient Gomerites migrated from their original home in the area of modern Turkey to other locations, the more likely connection is with Turkey. That's where the Gomerites resided in Ezekiel's day.

Ancient Gomer was referred to by the Assyrians as the *Gimirrai* and by the Greeks as the *Cimmerians*. They emerged in the eighth century BC in the area of Asia Minor, or modern Turkey. Later, in the first century AD, the Jewish historian Josephus connected the Gomerites with the Galatians, who inhabited what today is central Turkey.[10]

Turkey is an Islamic nation, and under the influence of President Erdoğan it is throwing off its secular leanings and embracing its Islamic roots from the days of the Ottoman empire. With growing ties to Russia and Iran, Turkey exerts a growing political and military influence on events in the Middle East.

PERSIA

After the mention of the northern threat from Russia and Turkey, the next future member of the Russian coalition in the War of Gog and Magog is Persia. The words *Persia*, *Persian*, or *Persians* are found more than thirty times in the Old Testament. In Ezekiel 38:5, Persia is best understood as modern-day Iran. The ancient land of Persia became the modern nation of Iran in March 1935, and then the name was changed to the Islamic Republic of Iran in 1979. Walter Kaiser states, "It is interesting to note that the nation of Iran (which includes present-day Pakistan and Afghanistan as well) gets first mention and that most of Gog's allies are countries that are today predominantly Islamic."[11]

Iran's present population is almost eighty million. Iran's mullah regime is the world's number-one sponsor of terror and is making its bid for regional supremacy at the same time it is pursuing nuclear weapons. Iran's venomous hatred of Israel is no secret.

The agreement with Iran brokered by the United States appears to be a bad deal. The deal does delay Iran getting its hands on nukes, but only for ten years. After ten years, all bets are off, and Iran will be free to cross the nuclear finish line. Time will tell whether the Iran deal was successful. But we do know that Iran is now out from under crippling sanctions and had more than $100 billion returned to its coffers to further fund its terrorist proxies.

Iran is a nuclear-threshold state with a breakout capacity of less than one year. Iran's compliance with the US agreement is not always easy to verify, so the likelihood of cheating is ever present. All the while, Iran is conducting ballistic missile tests and has three underground ballistic missile factories. Nuclear capability in Iran combined with ballistic missiles raises a sum-of-all-fears scenario. Clearly, modern Iran is a country hostile to Israel and the West. We'll deal more in depth with Iran in the next chapter.

ETHIOPIA (CUSH)

Two North African nations are listed in Ezekiel 38. The first is Ethiopia, which translates the Hebrew word *Cush*. Ancient Cush was called *Kusu* by the Assyrians and Babylonians, *Kos* or *Kas* by the Egyptians, and *Nubia* by the Greeks. Secular history locates Cush directly south of ancient Egypt, extending down past the modern city of Khartoum, which is the capital of modern Sudan. Modern Sudan inhabits the ancient land of Cush.

Sudan was locked in a deadly struggle between the Islamic north and Christian south for decades, culminating with South Sudan announcing its independence in July 2011. Since then, Sudan has been split into two sovereign nations. Northern Sudan, known simply as "Sudan" or officially as "the Republic of the Sudan," is a militant, radical Islamic nation that supported Iraq and its leader Saddam Hussein in the Gulf War. The Sudanese government invited Osama bin Laden and his deputy Ayman al-Zawahiri to Sudan and became a safe haven for jihadists. Osama bin Laden was sheltered there from 1991 to 1996. It should be no surprise that Sudan appears in this list of Russian allies against Israel and the West in the end times. Sudan would jump at the opportunity to take its place with Russia in the coming Gog alliance, just as Ezekiel predicted.

LIBYA (PUT)

Put was a son of Ham (see Genesis 10:6). Josephus identified Put as Libya. The ancient *Babylonian Chronicles* reveal that *Putu* was the distant land to the west of Egypt, which we know as Libya and could possibly include nations farther west, such as modern Algeria and Tunisia. The Greek translation of the Old Testament renders the word *Put* as *Libues*.

Modern Libya remains a hardened Islamic state that hates Israel and despises the West. Strongman Muammar al-Qaddafi exercised a reign of terror over Libya from 1969 until he was killed in 2011 in an Arab Spring eruption that spread to Libya. After the collapse of his government and his death, Libya fragmented and quickly fell into disarray, with various fighting factions vying for power. ISIS seized the opportunity and moved in to fill some of the vacuum. Many fear Libya may end up in a morass like Somalia, which is a dangerous, chaotic land of pirates and warlords. A steady stream of desperate refugees is fleeing the chaos.

In recent days, Russia has begun to exert greater influence in Libya. Russia has deployed troops near the Libyan border. Recent headlines unveil the strengthening ties between Russia and Libya:

"GLOBAL INSIGHTS: RUSSIA'S LIBYA STRATEGY"

WORLD POLITICS REVIEW, APRIL 12, 2011

"RUSSIA ENLARGES MILITARY FOOTPRINT IN LIBYA"

UPI.COM, MARCH 20, 2017

"RUSSIA MAKES PLAY FOR LIBYA"

LIBERTY UNYIELDING, MARCH 18, 2017

"HAS MOSCOW FOUND ITS NEW GADHAFI IN LIBYA?"

REAL CLEAR WORLD, MARCH 24, 2017

"RUSSIAN WARSHIP HOSTS LIBYA'S HAFTAR AS PUTIN COURTS NEW ALLY"

BLOOMBERG, JANUARY 11, 2017

A crucial result of the Syrian war is that Russia is now emboldened. Russia has an increasing military presence in Libya, supporting Libyan Field Marshal Khalifa Haftar in the ongoing civil conflict that has engulfed that nation.[12] Haftar is a former colonel in the army of Libyan leader Muammar al-Qaddafi. "While testifying to the Senate's foreign relations committee, the chief of the Pentagon's Africa command, General Thomas D. Waldhauser, said, 'Russia is trying to exert influence on the ultimate decision of who and what entity becomes in charge of the government inside Libya.'"[13]

Libya is in place for the coming Middle East war led by Russia.

BETH-TOGARMAH
Togarmah was the third son of Gomer, who was a son of Japheth (see Genesis 10:3). Ezekiel 38:6 states that the armies of Beth-togarmah, from the distant north, will join the Russian alliance.

Beth-togarmah is referenced in Ezekiel 27:14 as a trading partner of Tyre (modern Lebanon). Ancient Beth-togarmah was called *Til-garamu* by the Assyrians and *Tegarma* by the Hittites. Both the Assyrians and Hittites located Beth-togarmah in what is modern-day Turkey, along with Meshech, Tubal, and Gomer.

THE COMING COALITION

Thomas Constable puts the pieces of this coalition together, showing how the players come from every direction:

> Persia lay to Israel's northeast, Ethiopia to her southwest, Put to her southeast (on the African coast of the southern Red Sea), Gomer to her northwest (in the Taurus mountains of Anatolia and possibly farther northwest in modern western Europe), and Beth-togarmah to her northwest (southeast of the Black Sea). Thus peoples all around Israel would unite against her under Gog's leadership. As Babylonia sought to destroy Israel in the past, so this latter-day Babylon will seek to destroy her in the future.[14]

THE GOG COALITION	
ANCIENT NAME	**MODERN LOCATION**
Rosh	Russia
Magog (Scythians)	Central Asia and possibly Afghanistan
Meshech	Turkey
Tubal	Turkey
Persia	Iran
Ethiopia (Cush)	Sudan
Libya (Put)	Libya
Gomer	Turkey
Beth-togarmah	Turkey

Ezekiel 38–39 predicts a Russian-led invasion of the land of Israel in the last days by an alliance of nations collapsing on Israel from every direction. Russia will be joined by five main allies: Turkey, Iran, Libya, Sudan, and the Islamic nations of the former Soviet Union. Increasingly, these nations are hotbeds of radical Islam and

are either forming or consolidating their bonds with Russia and each other. This list of nations could be taken from the headlines of any newspaper or Internet news source. Envisioning these nations coming together under Russian leadership to attack Israel and trigger a Middle East war is not far-fetched.

Seven times throughout Ezekiel 38–39 the words "thus says the Lord God" appear.[15] Ezekiel's prophecy claims to be the very word of God himself. The detail of this ancient prophecy is also an ironclad proof that this claim is true. Think about it. More than 2,500 years ago, the prophet Ezekiel named each of these specific nations that we read about in the news every day. This degree of detail and specificity validates the uniqueness of the Bible as the Word of the living God.

Ezekiel 37 predicts the regathering and restoration of the Jewish people to their ancient homeland, which began in 1948 with the rebirth of the modern state of Israel. This astounding prophecy is being fulfilled before our eyes. God's Word is coming to pass. Immediately after Ezekiel 37, the prophet predicts the rise of the Gog coalition. The consolidation of these nations will be literally fulfilled, just like Ezekiel 37, and we're already seeing its foreshadowing. The convergence of these events is no happenstance. No one but an all-knowing, all-powerful God could make predictions like this.

MISSING IN ACTION

As we've made our way through this list of nations, you might be asking, "What about the other Middle East nations not included here—nations like Egypt, Syria, Jordan, Lebanon, Saudi Arabia, and Iraq? Do we know anything about their future? Could they play some role in the events of Ezekiel 38?"

Ezekiel's list focuses on Israel's remote enemies, the outer ring of nations from every direction—Russia, Central Asia, Iran, Turkey, Sudan, and Libya. The near enemies or inner ring of nations that encircle Israel are conspicuously absent from the litany of nations for the War of Gog and Magog. Two plausible answers for this omission have been suggested.

First, these near nations may not be mentioned because they have suffered defeat at some earlier point and been neutralized. That's the thesis of prophecy teachers who posit a "Psalm 83 war" that they believe precedes the War of Gog and Magog. Psalm 83 describes the nations surrounding Israel "sign[ing] a treaty as allies against [God]" (verse 5), with the psalmist asking God to intervene, to "utterly disgrace them until they submit to your name, O LORD" (verse 16). During this war, these prophecy teachers contend that Israel will defeat its near enemies and emerge from the war with renewed military prowess and peace, setting the stage for Ezekiel 38–39.

While this view is certainly a possible explanation, the main drawback for a Psalm 83 war is that the Jewish prophets are silent about it. A Psalm 83 war would be a momentous event on God's prophetic calendar, and it seems strange to me that any mention of it would be missing from the prophets. Moreover, Psalm 83 is a lament psalm, lacking any chronological specifics concerning when it will be fulfilled. Any suggestion for when it will be fulfilled is based on speculation, not the psalm itself. In contrast, the War of Gog and Magog contains several chronological indicators.[16] For these reasons, I reject the idea of a separate Psalm 83 war.

The second possibility, and in my view a better explanation, is that the inner ring of nations around Israel could be part of the invasion but not specifically mentioned. At the very end of Ezekiel 38:6, after listing the specific allies in this assault force, Ezekiel adds, "and many others." I believe this general statement refers to the closer nations surrounding Israel that are not specifically mentioned by Ezekiel. The nations mentioned in Ezekiel 38:1-6 are distant, remote enemies of Israel from every direction. Ezekiel's addition of the words "and many others" at the end of his list includes the near enemies of Israel that live within the outer circle of far enemies. Walter Kaiser supports this view: "There seems also to be many other nations not mentioned, but who are fully allied with Gog."[17]

The mountains of Israel are mentioned three times (see Ezekiel 38:8; 39:2, 4). While forming a spine down its middle, Israel's mountains are mainly found in the north, near Israel's border with Syria and Lebanon. This area is known as the Golan Heights. The Russian-led invasion will come primarily from the north and seems to be focused on the mountains of Israel, so it's not hard to imagine that Syria and Lebanon could participate in this invasion.[18]

Egypt, the end-times king of the south, will probably be a part of this invasion as well. Egypt's inclusion is derived from Daniel 11:40, which predicts a coalition between the king of the north (Russia and the northern allies) and the king of the south, which points to an end-times leader of Egypt joined by the other North African nations in Ezekiel 38. The reason Ezekiel 38 omits Egypt from its list is probably because Ezekiel 38 focuses on the far enemies. The parallel passage in Daniel 11:40 fills in the total picture.[19]

Egypt has enjoyed peaceful relations with Israel since 1978, when Menachem Begin and Anwar Sadat signed the Camp David Accords. But Egypt must turn against Israel for Daniel 11:40 to be fulfilled. Years ago Henry Kissinger said that no war in the Middle East is possible without Egypt.[20] While Kissinger's statement may not always hold true, Egypt will lead the North African contingent in the end times.

As you can see, Russia will pull together a colossal coalition in the end of days.

THE DISSENTERS

All signs in our world today point toward the fulfillment of Ezekiel 38–39. Russia and its allies seem to be far down the road that eventually leads to Israel. But not every nation in the end times will support this invasion. Ezekiel highlights a group of nations that will lodge a protest, albeit a lame one, to this military offensive. The opposition is described in Ezekiel 38:13: "Sheba and Dedan and the merchants of Tarshish will ask, 'Do you really think the armies you have gathered can rob them of silver and gold? Do you think you can drive away their livestock and seize their goods and carry off plunder?'"

Notice that these nations don't *do* anything; they just question what's happening. Their mild protest doesn't change anything. They question the motivation and purpose of the invasion. This looks frighteningly similar to the passive reaction we often see from the United Nations and nations in the West to international aggression.

Three specific places are listed as the source of the opposition—Sheba, Dedan, and Tarshish. Sheba and Dedan are easy to identify. They refer to nations on the Arabian Peninsula and along the Persian Gulf. Walter Kaiser notes that Sheba and Dedan are usually identified with people "living in the Arabian peninsula, including Saudi Arabia, Yemen, Oman, Kuwait, and the United Arab Emirates."[21] Most of these nations are under moderate Sunni Arab regimes who oppose the more militant strains of Islam.[22]

Tarshish is more difficult to identify with precision. The identification is complicated by the mention of "all its villages" (NASB) or "all the young lions" (KJV). Arnold Fruchtenbaum notes, "This phrase is a Hebrew idiom meaning nations that have come out of Tarshish."[23] But the real issue is the location of Tarshish itself. Two places in the ancient world are identified as Tarshish—Spain and England. If Tarshish is Spain, the nations that came from it include "Central and South America, except for Brazil."[24] If the location is England, it would include the United States, Canada, Australia, and New Zealand.

The name *Tarshish* was used in ancient times to denote the farthest lands to the west, so it's probably best to identify Tarshish as the western nations of Europe and possibly even the United States, although the US connection is more tenuous.

The lack of any mention of international support for Israel, other than this weak protest, means that by the time of the Russian invasion, the United States will be either unwilling or unable to do anything to help. There are many plausible scenarios that could explain US absence in Bible prophecy, but clearly the Rapture—the instantaneous vanishing of all believers as they are taken up to heaven (recorded in 1 Thessalonians 4:15-17)—would leave the United States severely weakened and possibly a second-rate world power.

Regardless of the exact location of Tarshish or of what role, if any, the United States will play, these nations in Ezekiel 38:13 will resist Russia and its allies but only with words. Israel's only help will come from God.

THE CLOCK IS TICKING

The pieces of Ezekiel's prophecy seem to be moving into place. Russia and the allies outlined in Ezekiel 38 are identifiable nations with the intent and incentive to join together and attack Israel. Even the nations that will object to this foray are viable nations with competing interests against Russia and its radical partners.

The rise of Russia under Vladimir Putin and the formation of new alliances is another sign indicating the Lord's coming may be very soon. As Joel Rosenberg says,

> Whether he realizes the prophetic implications of his actions
> or not, Putin has clearly embarked upon an aggressive
> and systematic effort to build new alliances with countries
> specifically cited in Ezekiel 38–39, as well as with those

countries that could be involved in the War of Gog and Magog but are not clearly defined in the text. And the clock is ticking.

So watch closely, for such efforts will only intensify as the time of Ezekiel's vision comes to fulfillment.[25]

I like the story about a bunch of sailors who were returning from a long voyage away from home. As the boat approached shore, the men were all looking eagerly for their wives and girlfriends on the dock. As the men scanned the crowd of women lining the railing, the air of excitement and expectancy grew. One man, however, was all alone as he watched all the other men find their wives and girlfriends, and they all embraced. But his wife was nowhere to be found. Worried, he hurried home and found a light on in his house. As he entered he was relieved to see his wife. She quickly turned and said, "Honey, I've been waiting for you." His response displayed his deep disappointment. "The other men's wives and girlfriends were *watching* for them!"

Are we just *waiting* for Jesus, or are we *watching* for him? Are we watching closely?

The clock is ticking.

Live looking!

CHAPTER 5

TRIPLE THREAT: RUSSIA, IRAN, AND TURKEY

*A tectonic shift has occurred in the balance of power
in the Middle East. . . . Turkey and Iran are simultaneously moving toward
Russia, while Russia is expanding its global military and strategic reach. . . .
This will have a major impact across the region, potentially
leaving U.S. ally Israel isolated to face a massive
hostile alliance armed with nuclear weapons.*

KENNETH R. TIMMERMAN

As we saw in the last chapter, Ezekiel 38:1-6 lists ten proper names, identifying the leader and the nations that will launch an offensive against Israel in the latter years. At least seven, and possibly eight, of the ten names refer to the leader of Russia and the modern nations of Russia, Turkey, and Iran. These three nations form the central core of the northern coalition led by the king of the north.

All three of these nations are emerging at the same time and forging stronger ties to one another. Any news watcher, no matter how casual, knows that these three countries find themselves in the headlines almost every day.

In the case of Russia, the Kremlin has accused Americans of

having an "emotional obsession" with Russia in light of US allegations of election hacking and meddling and collusion.[1]

Iran's open pursuit of nuclear weapons, numerous ballistic missile tests, and the Obama administration's controversial Iran nuclear deal keep it front and center.

Turkey's controversial referendum vote in April 2017, which gives President Erdoğan almost unilateral control over his country, has perplexed and worried the world.

The horrible Syrian conflict and the rise of ISIS have put the Russia-Iran-Turkey axis in the daily news.

The rise of a Russian-Iranian-Turkish triumvirate is a hugely significant development both historically and prophetically. Historically, these nations share a fascinating, common feature: "All three were empires long before they became nation-states."[2] Each had its turn dominating the region and basking in glory, but each has lost much of the territory it previously controlled:

> Persian empire (550–331 BC)
> Ottoman empire (AD 1299–1923)
> Russian empire created by Peter the Great (1721–1917)
> Soviet empire (1917–1991)

In its own way, each of these nations seems to be driven to recover its former glory. To one degree or another, each also feels snubbed by Western powers and holds a smoldering resentment against them. Their shared historical experience, while not the sole explanation for their ties, may play some role in their sharing headlines.

Russia and Iran are already in Syria, right on Israel's northern border. Turkey is in the mix in the Syrian civil war and the war on ISIS. World news takes notice of the growing alignment of these three allies, especially in relation to the war in Syria.

"AN INEVITABLE TRIUMVIRATE: SYRIA, RUSSIA, AND IRAN"

FOREIGN POLICY IN FOCUS, OCTOBER 15, 2015

"WHY RUSSIA, TURKEY AND IRAN ARE NATURAL ALLIES"

THE CONVERSATION, JANUARY 5, 2017

"SYRIA AND THE COMPLEX GEOSTRATEGIC GAME OF RUSSIA-TURKEY-IRAN"

MIDDLE EAST BRIEFING, JANUARY 12, 2017

"RUSSIA, IRAN, TURKEY TO ENFORCE CEASE-FIRE IN SYRIA"

UPI, JANUARY 24, 2017

"SYRIAN SAFE ZONES PLAN GOES INTO EFFECT AFTER DEAL BY RUSSIA, TURKEY, IRAN"

CHICAGO TRIBUNE, MAY 5, 2017

"RUSSIA, IRAN AND TURKEY MEET FOR SYRIA TALKS, EXCLUDING U.S."

NEW YORK TIMES, DECEMBER 20, 2016

Russia, Iran, and Turkey inhabit the same neighborhood and share many common interests, yet the Syrian conflict that began in 2011 has pulled them closer than ever. At the same time that Turkey is becoming more distanced from the West and Iran's alienation has pushed them further into the Russian orbit, the Syrian civil war is a driving force in uniting these nations. Russia and Iran both support the brutal regime of Syrian president Bashar al-Assad against the US-supported rebels.

Russia, Iran, and Turkey are getting closer to one another in Syria and very close to Israel's northern border. The framework for ending the Syrian conflict, known as "the Moscow Declaration," was accepted by Russia, Iran, and Turkey. Christian Caryl of the *Washington Post* writes, "While Moscow, Ankara and Tehran plot their own 'peace process' for the Syrian civil war, the United States is conspicuous in its absence."[3] Washington's reticence has created a vacuum, and these powers are all too willing to fill it.

RUSSIAN RESURGENCE

We've discussed current events in Russia and Russia's future quite a bit already, so let's just touch on a couple of ways Russia is allying itself with Iran and Turkey.

In spite of past differences and disagreements, Russia and Turkey are finding an alliance to be in their mutual interest. The growing ties between Turkey and Russia are to the point that Turkey may be buying advanced defense systems from Russia.

Concerning Iran, "Russia launched a fleet of bombers bound for Syria . . . from an Iranian air base, becoming the first foreign military to operate from Iran's soil since at least World War II."[4] Putin has praised Iran's leader as a "reliable and stable partner."[5]

Putin announced that trade between Russia and Iran rose 70 percent from 2016 to 2017. Russia and Iran "signed more than a dozen agreements on economics, tourism, diplomacy and other issues" in March 2017. Speaking of the Russian-Iranian alliance, Putin said, "Russia and Iran share many years, if not centuries, of bilateral cooperation." He went on to say that "Iran and Russia have maintained diplomatic relations for more than 500 years."[6] Russia began delivering S-300 missile systems to Iran at the end of 2016, which Iran will use to defend its nuclear facilities from attack.

Douglas E. Schoen summarizes the ties between Russia and Iran:

> What unites Russia and Iran today . . . are three common concerns: first, a shared goal of protecting Bashar al-Assad's regime in Syria, a mission that places them firmly against the United States and its Western allies; second, a common general interest in opposing radical Sunni Islamist movements, today exemplified by ISIS . . . and third, a common interest in smashing internal dissent in their own countries and quelling secessionist movements—whether from the Chechens in Russia or from the Kurds in Iran. Undergirding it all, however, is a common foe: the United States.[7]

History could soon give way to prophecy.

PERSIA—PRESENTLY AND PROPHETICALLY

No nation today is more dangerous than Iran—especially for Israel. Iran is the world's number-one sponsor of terror. Iran has spread its tentacles to other nations in its attempt to pave the way for the coming of its messiah, the Twelfth Imam. (More on this in a moment.) Iran's messianic ideology fuels its expansionist strategy. Through its own military and its surrogates, Iran now holds sway over five Arab nations: Lebanon, Yemen, the Palestinian territories, Syria, and Iraq. Iranian troops are just north of Israel in Syria. Iran's proxy Hezbollah in Lebanon is lying in wait on Israel's northern border, ready to strike at any time.

The term "Shiite crescent" was coined in 2004 by Jordan's King Abdullah. He noted that an Iranian-fueled "Shiite alliance was being

formed from Tehran to Damascus and passing through Baghdad."
Iran's sights are now set even higher. Iran's leaders speak not just of a
"Shiite crescent" but of a "Shiite full moon."[8] Iran seeks a land corri-
dor to the Mediterranean to anchor its territorial ambitions, allowing
it to move people and supplies from Tehran to the sea.[9] The leader of
the prominent Iran-supported Shiite group Asaib Ahl al-Haq says that
"an alliance of Shiite forces across the region would be ready to achieve
that goal by the time the hidden Shiite Imam Mahdi reappears." He
adds that "the Shiite force will include the Islamic Revolution Guards
Corps (I.R.G.C.) in Iran, the Lebanese Hezbollah, the Houthi movement in Yemen, the Popular Mobilization Forces (P.M.F) and other
Shiite militant groups operating in Syria and Iraq."[10]

Time and again, Iran has taken advantage of chaos in nearby
nations to promote its hegemonic agenda and ambitions. The success
Iran has enjoyed in Iraq, Yemen, Lebanon, and Syria has emboldened
its leaders. The *Guardian*'s Martin Chulov observes, "That should
trouble every western leader and our regional allies because this will
further embolden Iran to continue expanding, likely into the Gulf
countries next, a goal they have explicitly and repeatedly articulated.
Why should we expect them to stop if they've been at the casino,
doubling their money over and over again, for a decade?"[11]

Middle East activist group Naame Shaam outlines Iran's support
of its proxies in other nations:

> *Lebanon:* "From the 1980s to the beginning of the Arab
> Spring, Hezbollah received between $100m and $200m
> annually from Iran. Domestic economic decline and the
> increasing intervention in Syria led to this number . . . being
> cut to around $50m to $100m per year from 2010 onwards."
> *Iraq:* "From the 2003 invasion of Iraq until the end of Bush's
> presidency, Iran provided a range of Iraqi Shia militias with

$10m to $35m a year, a number which skyrocketed after 2009 to $100m to $200m a year."

> *Palestine:* "From its consolidation of power in 2007 to the start of the Arab Spring in Syria and elsewhere in 2011, Hamas received approximately $100m to $250m per year from Iran. Hamas's refusal to back Assad led to a dramatic decline in funding."

> *Yemen:* "The Houthis have received anywhere between $10m and $25m a year since 2010."

> *Syria:* "Assad government forces and its allied militias received between $15bn and $25bn over the first five years of the conflict, amounting to between $3bn and $5bn per year."[12]

Despite Iran's strong influence in the region, commentator Alireza Nader writes, "One thing is clear: while Iran may appear to have the upper hand in Syria and perhaps the Middle East, Russia appears to be pulling the real strings."[13] This is exactly what we should anticipate if the Russian-led coalition of Ezekiel 38 is on the horizon.

Iran's game plan may be a "Shiite full moon" across the Middle East—a clear path to the Mediterranean—but Iran's main ambition is the destruction of the Jewish state. Israel fears Iran much more than it fears ISIS. Iran has a sophisticated military and a large army and is pursuing the nuclear prize. The Iran nuclear deal has temporarily frozen Iran's nuclear pursuits, yet the restrictions are only temporary. In exchange for placing a hold on its nuclear program, Iran received more than $100 billion to build up its military machine and support its surrogates.

Iran agreed to freeze its nuclear development in return for lifted sanctions, but these restrictions disappear after ten years. Moreover, there's always the risk of Iranian covert activity in the meantime. In violation of a UN resolution, Iran has an active ballistic missile program, which is useful for only one thing—delivering a nuclear payload. Iran is waiting but also working. The growing connection between North Korea and Iran is troubling.

The clock is ticking.

No nation has expressed its hatred of the Jewish state more vehemently and viciously than Iran. With rabid regularity, Iran calls for Israel's annihilation. If there's any doubt that Iran still despises Israel and wants to see Israel wiped off the face of the earth, their military hardware tells the tale:

> Iran displayed various missile systems in a military parade in Tehran on Tuesday, many of which were emblazoned with slogans calling for the death of Israel. . . .
>
> "Some of the trucks carrying weapons were adorned with banners showing a fist punching through a blue Star of David and the slogan 'Death to Israel' in Persian," Agence France-Presse reported. Another truck at the event had "Death to Israel" emblazoned on its side in both Persian and Arabic, as well as "Down with Israel" in English and an image of the Israeli flag on fire.[14]

If this were not bad enough, Iran is propelled by its "Twelver" brand of Shiite Islam, which focuses on the coming of the Twelfth Imam—Imam Muhammad al-Mahdi. Twelvers believe that in the ninth century he disappeared in the mosque of Samarra as a young boy without leaving any descendants. They believe that since that time he has been hidden by God—thus his alternate title "Hidden Imam." He's also known as the Mahdi (Arabic for "rightly guided one").

For centuries Shiites have been waiting for the Mahdi to emerge from hiding to bring global victory and usher in an era of righteousness. Their eschatological view teaches that the Mahdi will return near the end of the world. Joel Rosenberg gives a helpful synopsis of the eschatological ideology that fuels Iran:

> Shias believe the Mahdi will return in the last days to establish righteousness, justice, and peace. When he comes, they say, the Mahdi will bring Jesus with him. Jesus will be a Muslim and will serve as his deputy, not as King of kings and Lord of lords as the Bible teaches, and he will force non-Muslims to choose between following the Mahdi or death. . . .
>
> One thing that is fairly well agreed upon among devout "Twelvers" is that the Mahdi will end apostasy and purify corruption within Islam. He is expected to conquer the Arabian Peninsula, Jordan, Syria, "Palestine," Egypt and North Africa, and eventually the entire world. During this time, he and Jesus will kill between 60 and 80 percent of the world's population, specifically those who refuse to convert to Islam.[15]

Based on this ideology, and Iran's obsession with wiping out Israel, Rosenberg has rightly called Iran's mullah regime an "apocalyptic, genocidal death cult."[16]

Certainly Iran's Twelver ideology is a game changer. Iranian politics and aspirations cannot be divorced from this ideology. They believe the United States is the "Great Satan" and Israel is the "Little Satan."[17] Both are considered obstacles that need to be removed for the Mahdi's return. Added to all this, Twelvers believe it is their duty to hasten the Mahdi's coming, which they believe will occur in a time of chaos and turmoil. They believe they can put out the "welcome mat" for the Mahdi.

These views can be puzzling to Western minds, but even other Muslims are perplexed by Iran's ideology. The crown prince of Saudi Arabia expressed his inability to dialogue with Iran due to its belief in the coming of the Twelfth Imam:

> The prince said that dialogue with Iran was impossible because of its belief in the Imam Mahdi, the so-called hidden imam, who many Shiites believe is a descendant of the Prophet Muhammad who will return to save the world from destruction. "Their stance is that the awaited Mahdi will come, and they need to create a fertile environment for the arrival of the awaited Mahdi, and they need to take over the Islamic world," he said. "Where are the common points that we might be able to reach an understanding on with this regime?"[18]

If fellow Muslims can't reason with Iran due to its apocalyptic views, how can Israel or the West ever hope to reach any common ground? Iran is driven by a dogma that seeks to overrun the Islamic world—and annihilate Israel.

What we're witnessing in Iran strikingly sets the stage for the events in Ezekiel 38–39.

LET'S TALK TURKEY

The Ottoman empire, centered in Turkey, lasted for more than six hundred years and occupied the land of Israel for four hundred years. In the wake of World War I, Mustafa Kemal Atatürk founded the Republic of Turkey and served as its first president from 1923 until his death in 1938. For almost a hundred years, while dominated by Islam, Turkey has remained a secular republic ruled by a parliament.

In the last decade, much has changed with the ascent of President

Recep Tayyip Erdoğan. He has dominated Turkish politics since 2002. Erdoğan served as mayor of Istanbul (elected in 1994), as prime minister (beginning in 2003), and as president (since August 2014). Erdoğan towers over Turkey's political landscape. Since his rise to power, many have feared that he's an Islamist with ambition for greater power. Under Erdoğan, Turkey has been on the road to authoritarianism for several years. Years ago, Erdoğan likened democracy to "a train that you get off once you reach your destination."[19] We've learned a great deal recently about the destination he had in mind.

Erdoğan leveraged an attempted coup in July 2016 to purge the police force and military, strengthening his grip on the nation. Some have questioned whether the coup was secretly orchestrated by Erdoğan to justify his subsequent power grab. There's no way to know, but the result is the same: more power for the president.

A controversial referendum vote on April 16, 2017, narrowly passed (51.4 percent), giving sweeping new powers to President Erdoğan. The referendum promised to bring these (and other) changes:

> "Abolish the post of prime minister and transfer executive power to the president."
> "Allow the newly empowered president to issue decrees and appoint many judges and officials responsible for scrutinizing his decisions."
> "Limit the president to two five-year terms, but give the option of running for a third term if Parliament truncates the second one by calling for early elections."
> "Allow the president to order disciplinary inquiries into any of Turkey's 3.5 million civil servants, according to an analysis by the head of the Turkish Bar Association."[20]

The referendum is a watershed event in Turkish history.

At the same time Erdoğan is grabbing power, Turkey's ties with Russia and Iran are strengthening, and relations between Turkey and Israel have taken a major turn for the worse.

Erdoğan's true colors are on full display when he talks about Jerusalem. His ultimate ambition to return Jerusalem to Muslim rule is clear. In a speech in Istanbul before millions who appeared to celebrate 562 years since the capture of Constantinople from European Christians, Erdoğan spoke these inflammatory words: "Conquest is Mecca, conquest is Saladin, it's to hoist the Islamic flag over Jerusalem again; conquest is the heritage of Mehmed II and conquest means forcing Turkey back on its feet."[21] Speaking of Jerusalem, Erdoğan said, "It's a symbol that unites us. All those who claim that Jerusalem is the Jew's holy city should be ashamed. We chose the name Saladin in order to send a message with the help of Allah that Jerusalem will always belong to the Kurds, to Turkey, to Arabs, to Muslims." As Erdoğan spoke, the IHH—an Islamist organization—marched in Istanbul "calling for the 'liberation of Jerusalem.'"[22]

On May 15, 2015, President Erdoğan spoke these chilling words: "Unfortunately we the Muslims lost our aim to head towards Jerusalem. The water of our eyes froze, making us blind, and our hearts that were destined to beat for Jerusalem are now instead conditioned for rivalry, in a state of war with each other." In his analysis of this statement, commentator Burak Bekdil says, "In other words, Erdogan is calling the *ummah* [the Muslim community] to end its conflicts in order to unite behind a jihad march toward Jerusalem."[23]

About two years later, Erdoğan ratcheted up the rhetoric even further, delivering an anti-Semitic rant issuing a call for Muslims to swarm the Temple Mount in Jerusalem. The tirade "called on Muslims from around the world to flood the Al-Aqsa Mosque," which sits on the Temple Mount. He said, "Every day that Jerusalem is under occupation is an insult to Muslims."[24] He called on Muslims to "join forces to protect Jerusalem from Israel's Judaization attempts."[25]

Some believe Erdoğan considers himself a twenty-first-century Saladin, who, like the Muslim leader during the Crusades, will similarly rally the forces of Islam to reassert control over Israel and Jerusalem. Events in Turkey, accelerated by Erdoğan's emergence, are shifting suddenly and point toward the fulfillment of the invasion of Israel prophesied in Ezekiel 38.

WHAT DOES IT MEAN?

The war in Syria, the rise of ISIS, and at the same time a withdrawal, or at least a weakening, of US influence has sparked a Russian-Iranian-Turkish triumvirate that is gaining momentum. While the advance of this trio raises all kinds of geopolitical considerations that give Western leaders headaches, the prophetic implications are even more significant.

Writing almost forty years ago about world events in light of Bible prophecy, Charles Ryrie said,

> Turkey will move out of the orbit of Western influence and cooperation, and move into the sphere of Russian domination. What will trigger this, we do not know. But eventually Turkey will align herself with Russia and her other allies. It says the same for Iran, since Persia will also be a Russian ally in the coming war.[26]

How did Dr. Ryrie know these things back in 1981? Because he based his view on the Bible, not current events. With forty years of hindsight, we're now seeing what Ryrie knew was coming.

As all these developments converge, Israel sits at the epicenter of the region in the middle of the bull's-eye, just a few miles south of the

Syrian war zone. What's happening seems to be part of the buildup for the fulfillment of biblical prophecy. Major tremors are moving the pieces into place.

The three-nation axis of Russia, Iran, and Turkey could quickly morph into the full coalition the prophet Ezekiel predicted long ago. In the increasingly volatile atmosphere in the world, not much would have to happen for these nations to conspire against Israel and challenge the West. We can all imagine a host of events that could trigger this offensive.

Time will tell whether the convergence of these three allies is part of the near trajectory that leads to the War of Gog and Magog or whether they're part of a longer orbit. Either way, as we'll see throughout this book, we can be sure that God is at work behind the scenes, ruling and overruling in the affairs of humanity.

CHAPTER 6

VLADIMIR PUTIN, RISING CZAR

It's Putin's World

HEADLINE IN THE *ATLANTIC*

DOUGLAS SCHOEN'S *PUTIN'S MASTER PLAN*

"Putin's Russia is clearly the biggest and most dangerous threat facing the world today."[1] So laments Russian chess grand master Garry Kasparov in his book *Winter Is Coming*.

He's right.

"Putinism" is mushrooming in Russia and spreading throughout the world. Putin rules over a neo-Czarist Russia. *Forbes* has named Vladimir Putin the world's most powerful person four years in a row, saying, "From the motherland to Syria to the U.S. presidential elections, Russia's leader continues to get what he wants."[2] In 2014 Vladimir Putin was chosen as Russia's "Man of the Year," the fifteenth time (in a row) he was given that honor.[3] Putin is the leading candidate for *Time* magazine's "Person of the Year" in 2017, as he was named in 2007.

441

Putin has fashioned what he calls a "vertical of power," which means "the entire structure of Russian political power rests on one man."[4] According to former Soviet leader Mikhail Gorbachev, Putin views himself as "second only to God."[5]

LORD OF THE RING

A bizarre story from June 2005 illustrates Putin's belief that he's a law unto himself and takes what he wants. Putin was hosting a group of businessmen in a palace in Petersburg, Russia, including Robert Kraft, owner of the New England Patriots, whose team had won the Super Bowl in February. When the meeting ended, the executives gathered around Putin to greet him and pose for photographs. It was all smiles. One of the executives asked Kraft, "Why don't you show the president your ring?" Kraft didn't normally wear his Super Bowl ring but kept it in his suit pocket. The ring was laced with 124 diamonds and engraved with Kraft's name (and valued at $25,000). Kraft fished the ring from his pocket and handed it to Putin, who put it on his finger and said, "I could kill somebody with this."

As the gathering broke up, Kraft held out his hand for the ring, but Putin put it in his pocket and abruptly left. Putin evidently assumed it was a gift, but Kraft was astonished by Putin's actions. Kraft appealed to the chairman of Citigroup, who helped arrange the meeting, and even to the White House. He was told it would be best to say it was intended as a gift. Kraft objected strenuously that it was not a gift. He was told repeatedly that it would be best if he gave the ring as a present. Kraft eventually acquiesced and four days later issued a public statement that the ring was a "symbol of the respect and admiration that I have for the Russian people and the leadership of President Putin."[6] Putin's actions gnawed at Kraft for years. "Kraft had another ring made, and the original went into the Kremlin library, where gifts to the head of state are collected."[7]

Few believe there was any misunderstanding. Putin stole the ring. His open, unapologetic theft of a Super Bowl ring is a microcosm of his brash, thuggish inclination to grab what he wants without fear. Whether a ring or a realm, Putin takes what he wants and gets away with it.

Putin's success in his raw expansionist aggression has emboldened him to keep moving forward. Putin invaded Georgia and "took Crimea with barely a shot fired. He flooded Eastern Ukraine with agents and weaponry."[8] When he annexed Crimea, protests in Russia against him stopped, and his personal approval ratings shot up from 60 percent to 80 percent. Putin seems to have a sense of invincibility and destiny. In September 2014, Putin boasted, "If I wanted, in two days I could have Russian troops not only in Kiev, but also in Riga, Vilnius, Tallinn, Warsaw and Bucharest."[9]

Putin knows that military power is key. In a Russian documentary in 2015, Putin said, "A well-known person once said, 'You can get much farther with a kind word and a Smith & Wesson than you can with just a kind word.'"[10] In keeping with that philosophy, he's arming Russia to the teeth.

While Western European nations are busy slashing military budgets, Russia is spending more than ever. Russian military spending increased 25.6 percent from 2014 to 2015, an increase of $20 billion in just one year. Since he took power in 2000, Putin has boosted military spending twentyfold.[11] Uniformed manpower has declined in every Western European nation since 2011, while Russian personnel increased 25 percent to more than 850,000. Putin's goal is one million combat-ready troops by 2020.[12]

Douglas Schoen, an influential Democratic campaign consultant, writes, "Over the next decade, Putin plans to acquire and develop four hundred new intercontinental ballistic missiles (ICBMs); more than two thousand next-generation tanks; six hundred modernized combat aircraft; eight nuclear ballistic submarines; fifty warships; . . . and about 17,000 new military vehicles."[13] Russia already has the world's largest nuclear arsenal but "added thirty-eight nuclear missiles in 2014 and another forty in 2015."[14] Russia's nuclear storehouse is staggering.

Putin wants military parity, if not superiority, to the United States, and the gap is closing. If Putin serves three full terms as president, as he's allowed by law, he can rule until 2024. He has many years left to achieve his goals. And who knows if he will relinquish power in 2024? If he does step down, he may simply hand the reins over to a puppet to serve on his behalf, as he did in 2008 with Dmitry Medvedev. Putin's grasp on Russia is strong, his reach immense, and his ambition boundless.

"A SENSE OF HIS SOUL"

When President George W. Bush met with Putin for the first time (in 2001), he said he "looked the man in the eye" and "was able to get a sense of his soul."[15] Bush has been chided, even mocked, for this remark, but he had the right idea. There's something in Putin's soul, as with every person, that drives him. What powers Putin?

Vladimir Vladimirovich Putin was born on October 7, 1952, in Leningrad. The city was still scarred by the German siege in World War II and languishing in deprivation and fear. Putin's father sustained injuries in the war that left him limping in pain the rest of his life. Putin grew up in cramped communal quarters, mesmerized by the power of the Soviet state. He fulfilled his dream in 1975, joining the KGB. Since that time, Putin has been a Soviet man.

The Soviet empire dissolved on December 25, 1991. Vladimir Putin has never gotten over it. The *New Yorker* article "Trump, Putin, and the New Cold War" captures the essence of Putin's humiliation over the fall of the Soviet Union and his drive to bring back the glory days:

> Putin's resentment of the West, and his corresponding ambition to establish an anti-Western conservatism, is rooted in his experience of decline and fall—not of Communist ideology, which was never a central concern of his generation, but, rather, of Russian power and pride. . . .
>
> Posted [as a KGB agent] in one of the grayest of the Soviet satellites [East Germany], Putin entirely missed the sense of awakening and opportunity that accompanied perestroika, and experienced only the state's growing fecklessness. At the very moment the Berlin Wall was breached, in November, 1989, he was in the basement of a Soviet diplomatic compound in Dresden feeding top-secret documents into a furnace. As crowds of Germans threatened to break into the building, officers called Moscow for assistance, but, in Putin's words, "Moscow was silent." Putin returned to Russia, where the sense of post-imperial decline persisted. The West no longer feared Soviet power; Eastern and Central Europe were beyond Moscow's control; and the fifteen republics of the Soviet Union were all going their own way. An empire shaped by Catherine the Great and Joseph Stalin was dissolving.[16]

Fareed Zakaria adds,

> To understand Putin, you have to understand Russia. The last hundred years for that country have seen the fall of the monarchy, the collapse of democracy, the great depression, World War II with its tens of millions of Russians dead,

Stalin's totalitarian brutalities, the collapse of communism, the breakup of the Soviet Union, and Boris Yeltsin's years of chaos and corruption.[17]

Many events have played a formative role in Putin's view of the world, but the collapse of the Soviet Union seems to have scarred and shaped him more than anything else. In 2005, in his annual state of the nation address to parliament, referring to the dissolution of the Soviet Union, he said, "First and foremost it is worth acknowledging that the demise of the Soviet Union was the greatest geopolitical catastrophe of the century."[18]

Putin is bent on rebuilding the Soviet Union and restoring the glory of imperial Russia. He wants Russia to regain lost territory and dominate the nations that brought about the Soviet dissolution. Part of restoring this greatness is securing allies. In his efforts to restore the greatness of mother Russia, Putin is tirelessly scouring the globe in search of willing allies. He's obsessed with elevating Russia's international influence.

Putin has spearheaded the formation of a Eurasian Economic Union (EAEU). The main goal is to merge the former Soviet republics into a unified economic and political confederation. Many believe this is Putin's attempt to restore the Soviet Union. Thus far, the union includes just five states: Armenia, Belarus, Kazakhstan, Kyrgyzstan, and Russia. Russia is trying to create an alternative and counterbalance to the European Union. Commentator Areg Galstyan writes, "In other words, Moscow is trying to institutionalize its influence in the Eurasian space, collecting fragments of the collapsed Soviet empire."[19] Once again, Putin's desire to restore the empire is his driving motivation.

Former Secretary of State Condoleezza Rice warns that "Russian President Vladimir Putin is trying to re-establish 'Russian greatness' with his assertiveness and aggressiveness abroad." She further cautions that this is a "dangerous time with the Russians."[20]

VLADIMIR PUTIN: KEY DATES[21]
1975—Joins the KGB.
1992—Departs the KGB.
1992–1994—Serves as deputy mayor of St. Petersburg.
1997–1998—Works in the administration of President Boris Yeltsin.
August 9–December 31, 1999—Serves as acting prime minister of Russia.
May 7, 2000—Inaugurated as second president of the Russian Federation.
May 7, 2004—Begins second term as president.
December 19, 2007—Named *Time* Person of the Year.
May 7, 2008—Not permitted to serve a third consecutive term; relinquishes power to his puppet Dmitry Medvedev. Medvedev is inaugurated as president and appoints Putin as his prime minister.
May 7, 2012—Begins his third term as president (presidential terms are now six years).
September 1, 2016–present—Accused of hacking and influencing US presidential elections and collusion with Donald Trump but denies any Russian involvement.

KREMLIN, INC.

During Putin's time in office, the lines between Russian oil interests and the Kremlin have been blurred to the point of no distinction. Affairs of state and business are fused. Where they diverge is difficult to discern. Putin has learned how to take advantage of privatized Russian assets to enrich himself. Putin's ties to business are so extensive, Russians sometimes refer to the Putin regime as "Kremlin, Inc." and call Putin the CEO.

Putin oversaw the dissolution of major Russian oil interests that have been sold to shadowy figures. Yukos Oil was dismantled and sold at an auction. The "auction" was all theatrics. Only one person put in a bid, and the entire auction lasted ten minutes. No one outside the Kremlin knew who purchased these interests, although Russian oligarchs certainly control them with Putin's hand in their pockets.[22] Since he assumed the presidency in 2000 (with a break from 2008 to 2012), Putin has raked in billions from business deals mainly within the energy sector.

Estimates of Putin's personal wealth vary wildly. According to official reports he owns a small apartment, a shared garage, and a few cars. His income in 2014 was reported as a modest 7.65 million rubles ($119,000). However, Putin has amassed a vast fortune, enriching himself and his close friends and allies. His palace on the Black Sea cost $1 billion. His net worth has been estimated at between $70 billion and $200 billion.[23] Putin may be the richest man in the world. Bill Gates is worth around $80 billion, so Putin is either close to the world's richest person or more than twice as rich.

The CEO of Kremlin, Inc., is doing quite well.

MAN WITH A PLAN

From the outside, Putin's actions may seem haphazard or disjointed. Much of the time he may seem like an "unpredictable tyrant, obsessed with power, violence, and conquest, who lashes out at neighboring countries impulsively and spasmodically."[24] But these characterizations are far off the mark. There's no doubt he possesses a clear vision of his objectives.

Douglas Schoen summarizes Putin's global master plan: "Putin is a calculating master of geopolitics with a master plan to divide Europe, destroy NATO, reestablish Russian influence in the world, and, most of all, marginalize the United States and the West in order to achieve regional hegemony and global power. And his plan is working."[25]

As you can see, Putin is not a wild-eyed tyrant. He has a specific plan.

The West faces a greater threat from Russia today than at any point during the Cold War. Douglas Schoen continues:

> Vladimir Putin is many things—KGB officer, master politician, multibillionaire, ruthless autocrat—but, above all, Vladimir Putin is a man with a plan. His plan is to unmake the world order that has stood since the end of the Cold War, especially in Europe, and replace it with one where Russia has the power, influence, and military strength to get its way on any issue. This means subjugating Russia's immediate neighbors and integrating them into a Russia-centric political and economic system, neutralizing Europe and ending the transatlantic relationship with America, and seeding an endless series of global crises that drain the West's ability and desire to influence global affairs while promoting the interests of Russia and its allies. In short, Putin plans to make the twenty-first century the Russian century.[26]

At the same time Putin is implementing his master plan by invading neighboring nations and building ties with Syria, Iran, and Turkey, he's also employing a global strategy of all-out cyber-warfare. Russian hackers have meddled in the 2016 US presidential election as well as elections in France and Germany. They've compromised the US State Department, the Pentagon, and the White House and have even gained access to at least some of former president Barack Obama's e-mails.[27] Grave concerns abound concerning Russian hacking of elections and the undermining of democracy. This is another prong in Putin's global strategy to weaken the West. All the energy the US press and Congress have expended on Russia and Putin in the wake of the US presidential election are evidence that Putin's strategy has already worked, at least to some degree. The cover of *Time* dated May 18, 2017, is a graphic depiction of the White House overtaken by Russia. Inside that issue of *Time*, Massimo Calabressi notes, "By raising doubts about the validity of the 2016 vote and the vulnerability of future elections, Russia has achieved its most important objective: undermining the credibility of American democracy."[28]

One thing is sure: Putin has a global strategy, and on all fronts, he seems to be getting what he wants.

THE MAIN QUESTION

In light of Putin's actions, many have speculated whether he could be the Russian leader known as Gog in Ezekiel 38–39. Speaking at churches and prophecy conferences, I've been asked this question many times. Is Putin the Russian leader that Ezekiel foretold—the one who will marshal an attack against Israel in the latter years?

While it's possible he *could* be, we must always avoid irresponsible attempts to identify any current world leader with an end-times figure. Many have fallen into this trap. Any form of date setting, identifying the Antichrist with a contemporary person, or pinpointing someone as Gog or as any other person mentioned in end-times prophecy must be soundly rejected.

Having said that, we sometimes see people from the past or present who demonstrate the same characteristics as end-times figures. The Bible foretold the rise of Seleucid ruler Antiochus Epiphanes, for example, and uses him as a type or prefigure of the final Antichrist (see Daniel 8). Other dictators from the past like Alexander the Great, Pharaoh, Nebuchadnezzar, Napoleon, Hitler, and Stalin serve as adumbrations of the final Antichrist.

Keeping this in mind, Putin is forging economic, political, and military ties with the nations outlined in Ezekiel 38:1-6. He also possesses some of the traits (military aggression, pride, and greed) that Gog possesses. Joel Rosenberg gives his assessment about any connection between Putin and Gog:

> Over the years, people have asked me if Putin might be the Russian dictator referred to as "Gog" in the Biblical prophecies of "Gog and Magog" in Ezekiel 38–39. I suspect as Putin continues to re-emerge, those questions will begin to be asked again. Here's my quick answer: It's too soon to draw such a conclusion. There's much more that would have to happen to indicate that Putin was the "Gog" of Bible prophecy. But there's no question in my mind that Putin is *Gog-esque*. He is dangerous, and both Israel and the West should keep a close and wary eye on him, especially given all that Putin has done to build a strategic alliance between Russia and Iran and the other countries mentioned in the "Gog and Magog" prophecies.[29]

Time will tell. What we can say is that Putin can be neither definitively identified as Gog nor conclusively ruled out. He may be responsible for the invasion of Israel foretold in Ezekiel, or he may be setting the stage for another leader waiting in the wings. But at a minimum Putin is showing us a faint foreshadowing of what's coming. Make no mistake—Gog will come, but only in God's time.

Maybe very soon!

CHAPTER 7

RED DAWN: THE WAR OF GOG AND MAGOG

You and all your allies—a vast and awesome army—will roll down on them like a storm and cover the land like a cloud.

EZEKIEL 38:9

I grew up during the height of the Cold War in the 1960s and 1970s. The Soviet Union was the rival superpower to the United States. The Soviet hammer and sickle loomed large. Communism was the dark threat hanging over the world. At school we ran through drills preparing us to take cover in the event of a nuclear detonation nearby (although I always wondered what good it would do to get under my desk). Deep down, every American's worst nightmare was a nuclear exchange with the Soviets or a Russian invasion of our homeland. We prayed it would never happen but knew it was possible.

In 1984, a movie that tapped into this foreboding fear hit the big screen. *Red Dawn* instantly became a favorite for me and my friends. It became an overnight classic. The movie depicts a surprise Russian invasion of the United States set in a small town in Colorado.

Red Dawn opens with a gripping, surreal scene. A group of high school students are sitting in class when suddenly one student looks out the window and sees foreign paratroopers dropping from the sky. As the students struggle to make sense of what's happening, they begin to flee, and pandemonium breaks out. The plotline focuses on a group of teenagers who escape into the mountains and use guerilla tactics to disrupt their Russian and Cuban occupiers.

After the fall of the Soviet empire in 1991, and the end of the Cold War, fear of a "red dawn" receded into the history books . . . or did it?

Russia's rise has reawakened old fears—both at home and abroad. These concerns appear to be justifiable, especially in light of biblical prophecy. According to Scripture, the fictional surprise attack on the United States depicted in *Red Dawn* will someday become fact in the land of Israel when Russia and its allies spring a shocking surprise attack.

Russia's aggressive posture shows no signs of relaxing and is even tightening, and it could lead in the near future to the "red dawn" invasion of Israel predicted in Ezekiel 38–39. Since this war could be on the horizon, we need to understand what will happen and how events today could point toward its fulfillment. Referring to these chapters in Ezekiel, David Jeremiah says, "In these two chapters, God gave to Ezekiel the most detailed prophecy concerning war in the entire Bible."[1]

Let's examine some of those details.

THE RUSSIAN AIM

When Russia's forces invade the Holy Land, they will have four main motivations.

First, they desire to *steal* the Promised Land from Israel (see Ezekiel 38:12). Jewish presence in the land has been a global issue since 1948. A string of wars have been waged against Israel by its Muslim neighbors over the mere presence of the Jewish people in their ancient homeland. Added to that, the third most holy site in Islam, the Dome of the Rock and Al-Aqsa Mosque, sits on the Jewish Temple Mount in Jerusalem. Taking permanent possession of the Temple Mount in Jerusalem could be motivation for the Islamic invaders listed in Ezekiel 38. Prophecy expert Randall Price writes, "Orthodox Jews in the Temple movement in Israel generally agree that the war of Gog and Magog is to be the next of Israel's wars, and believe that it will be fought over possession of Jerusalem and the Temple Mount."[2] The presence of the massive Islamic contingent in the Russian coalition, and their desire to steal land, supports this idea.

Second, the invaders will come to *seize* the assets of Israel. What spoil or plunder will they seek? We can't say for sure, but recent discoveries of vast oil and gas reserves in the Golan Heights and Israel's coastal waters could figure into Russia's calculations. The Tamar and Leviathan fields are massive and virtually untapped. Currently, the world is experiencing an oil bonanza, but that could change quickly. Black gold could play a part in end-times events.

Third, driven by anti-Semitism, the Russian-led invaders will come to *slaughter* the Jewish people and wipe them off the face of the earth (see Ezekiel 38:10, 16). This is in keeping with the hatred of the Jewish people by their Muslim neighbors that we see today. They would love nothing more than to destroy the Jewish people and the Jewish state. They've attempted several times to bring this to pass. Russia also has a long, ugly history of anti-Semitism.

Fourth, the Russian assault force will attack to *scare* the West and *stifle* the influence of the Antichrist, the king of the west, who will be Israel's ally as a result of the treaty referenced in Daniel 9:27. In a bold power grab, the invasion of Israel will be considered an attack against Israel's ally and protector, the Western confederacy, attempting to test their mettle or even tempting them to launch a Middle East counterattack. The constant threats of Vladimir Putin against

Europe and NATO are consistent with this strategy to intimidate and threaten the West.

The Russian leader will be driven by his own agenda, with a desire to *steal* the land of Israel, *seize* its assets, *slaughter* the Jewish people, and *stifle* the power of the West or suck them into a war in the Middle East.

HOOKS IN THE JAWS

Ezekiel leaves no doubt that the Russian leader will come into Israel for his own nefarious reasons; however, Ezekiel doesn't want the human element to overshadow the sovereign plan of God. Ezekiel graphically depicts the Russian invasion as the result of God putting hooks in the jaws of the Russian leader and drawing him out. Ezekiel wants us to know above all else that God is in control of all that's happening. He is sovereign—even over evil. Nothing occurs outside his prophetic plan.

Over the years there's been speculation about what event God will use to hook the Russians and draw them into the land of Israel. The hooks could be Russia's alliances with Islamic nations like Iran that want to wipe Israel off the map. Randall Price says, "Russia could easily fulfill the role of Gog, for its current economic hardships and political instability have led Russia to forge military alliances with Islamic powers that continually call for Israel's destruction."[3]

Another possible scenario is that the Antichrist's move to forge or enforce a peace treaty with Israel and her neighbors will be interpreted as a threat to Russia's power and will precipitate a disastrous countermove by Russia and its Islamic allies.

Thomas Ice presents another possibility:

For over fifteen years I have speculated that the "hook in the jaw" of Gog that God could use to bring a reluctant

Russia down upon the land of Israel could be some thing like the following scenario that I articulated to Hal Lindsey on a National television show in 1991 on the day the first Gulf War ended: I could see the Muslims approaching the Russians and telling them that America has set a precedent for an outside power coming into the Middle East to right a perceived wrong. (America has done it again in recent years by going into Afghanistan and Iraq.) On that basis, Russia should help her Muslim friends by leading them in an overwhelming invasion of Israel in order to solve the Middle East Conflict in favor of the Islamic nations. Will this be the "hook in the Jaw" of Gog? Only time will tell. But something is up in the Middle East and Russia appears to have her fingerprints all over things.[4]

There will be many twists and turns in the days ahead, but Russia's increased involvement in the Middle East will certainly play a key role in pulling them into invading Israel. Whatever the hooks in the jaws may be, Russia will fulfill this prophecy according to God's sovereign will and on his timetable.

THE RUSSIAN ANNIHILATION

When the Russian-led horde descends on Israel, it will look like Israel is finished. Surprised and surrounded, the Israelites will be seized by unimaginable panic. Nothing in Israel's modern history will compare. Not the Six-Day War in 1967. Not the Yom Kippur War in 1973. Yet in a stunning reversal of fortunes, the invincible invaders who come to possess the mountains of Israel will perish on those same mountains. God will come down to rescue his people. Almighty God will intervene to win the battle. Those who come to loot Israel will themselves be looted by Israel.

Ezekiel 38–39 describes an overwhelming, sudden destruction when the forces of Gog meet God. What looks like a massive mismatch between Russia and Israel now becomes an infinitely greater mismatch as Gog faces the living God. Here's how Ezekiel graphically describes the bloodbath:

> This is what the Sovereign LORD says: When Gog invades the land of Israel, my fury will boil over! In my jealousy and blazing anger, I promise a mighty shaking in the land of Israel on that day. All living things—the fish in the sea, the birds of the sky, the animals of the field, the small animals that scurry along the ground, and all the people on earth—will quake in terror at my presence. Mountains will be thrown down; cliffs will crumble; walls will fall to the earth. I will summon the sword against you on all the hills of Israel, says the Sovereign LORD. Your men will turn their swords against each other. I will punish you and your armies with disease and bloodshed; I will send torrential rain, hailstones, fire, and burning sulfur!
>
> EZEKIEL 38:18-22

God will rise up in his fury to annihilate the invaders, employing four catastrophes to totally destroy Russia and its Islamic allies:

> *Shaking—a great earthquake (verses 19-20).* God will use a massive tremor with its epicenter in Israel to spread fear and confusion throughout the ranks of the Russian military machine. God will defeat and disorient the invading forces.
> *Slaughter—infighting among the troops of the various nations (verse 21).* In the chaos of the battle and the shaking of the earth under their feet, the Russian forces and their allies

will turn against each other, resulting in a massive body count by friendly fire. Charles Dyer pictures the scene: "In the pandemonium, communication between the invading armies will break down and they will begin attacking each other. Every man's sword will be against his brother. Fear and panic will sweep through the forces so each army will shoot indiscriminately at the others."[5] God will repeat what he did on previous occasions in the Old Testament to deliver his people, turning the enemies upon themselves (see Judges 7:22; 1 Samuel 14:20; 2 Chronicles 20:22-25).

> *Sickness—disease and plagues (verse 22a).* The ruin of the invaders will be accelerated by additional supernatural disasters. God will unleash a lethal epidemic, adding to the misery and devastation already inflicted.

> *Storms—torrential rain, hailstones, fire, and burning sulfur/ brimstone (verse 22b).* Reminiscent of Sodom and Gomorrah, God will rain fiery destruction from on high on the invading army. There will be no place to hide. "The rain will combine with dirt and debris from the earthquake to produce massive mud slides and floods. Large hailstones will pelt the survivors, killing many. The 'burning sulphur' might be volcanic ash."[6]

Old Testament scholar Walter Kaiser summarizes the results of this war:

Things will not end well for the nations that press their attack against Israel, for in the end, what they are doing is nothing less than an attack on God and his plan for time and eternity. In one great push, an axis of nations from that part of the world will make one huge incursion into the land of Israel, but that will call for the response of God himself.

The carnage, bloodshed, and loss of life and power will be unrivaled up to that point in history. This will be at once one of the darkest, and yet also one of the brightest, days of all history, as God settles the issue in a startling way. Such is the predicted fortunes of the War of Gog and Magog against Israel in the end of the days of history's ongoing time line.[7]

The King James Version of Ezekiel 39:2 says, "I will turn thee back, and leave but the sixth part of thee," which indicates one-sixth of the invading army will be left alive. There's uncertainty about the meaning of the second Hebrew verb in Ezekiel 39:2. This is the only time this verb is found in the Hebrew Bible. Some believe it was derived from the Hebrew *shisha*, which means "to leave a sixth part."[8] According to this understanding, only one in six (or around 17 percent) of the invading army will remain alive. But I prefer the reading that the entire invading army will be destroyed.[9] Most modern translations, including the New King James Version, omit any reference to the sixth part surviving and translate the verb as "to lead" or "to drive" (as in the New Living Translation: "I will turn you around and drive you toward the mountains of Israel").

Ezekiel 39:4 reveals the utter destruction of the invading army: "You and your army and your allies will all die on the mountains. I will feed you to the vultures and wild animals." If the destruction of the armies in the land of Israel were not bad enough, according to verse 6, there's another devastating dimension to the Russian invasion: "I will rain down fire on Magog and on all your allies who live safely on the coasts. Then they will know that I am the LORD." As we've seen, Magog includes territory in Russia as well as the nations of Central Asia, so not only will the invading forces be wiped out in Israel, but the Russian homeland will also suffer catastrophic collateral damage. God will wreak havoc by unleashing fire. The "fire" probably refers to devastation and military destruction (see Ezekiel 30:8, 14, 16). The "coasts" refers to "the farthest reaches of the known world," which certainly fits a description of the Russian motherland.[10] The raining of brimstone will inflict heavy casualties in the nation itself. The devastation will be so widespread, it "will cause Russia to cease being a political force in world affairs."[11]

THE WAR OF GOG AND MAGOG IN ISLAM

The Koran mentions Gog and Magog twice, calling them Yajuj and Majuj (18:96; 21:94). In Islam, there are ten major signs that portend the end of the age and the final resurrection. As with Christian eschatology, there are different opinions about the sequence of these signs, but the War of Gog and Magog is often the number four sign that the end is near.

The Islamic identity of Gog and Magog is quite strange. Muslims believe they are two groups of evil Turks who spread corruption through the earth during the days of Abraham. In order to restrain their evil, they were quarantined behind a great barrier. For centuries they have been trying to escape their prison. Finally, when the time is right, Allah will act, and the barrier will crumble, unleashing Gog and Magog. The horde will flood into the land of Israel to attack the Muslims residing there. According to Islamic teaching, Jesus will pray against Gog and Magog, and Allah will destroy them by sending a fatal plague.[12] The disease is depicted as either deadly boils or a malady that consumes the flesh from their bones.

Of course, this sounds very similar to the account in Ezekiel 38, except the players are different. Muhammad, who wrote the Koran more than one thousand years after Ezekiel prophesied, adapted and distorted this prophecy to fit his worldview. However, in a twist of prophetic irony, the prophecy of Gog and Magog will not be fulfilled by Allah on behalf of Muslims living in Israel but by the true

God against the army (composed of Russians and Muslims) that will invade the Holy Land in the last days.

THE RUSSIAN AFTERMATH

In the wake of the stunning supernatural decimation of the invading army, Ezekiel tells us four things that will happen in Ezekiel 39:9-24.

BURNING OF THE WEAPONS

Ezekiel 39:9-10 describes the fate of the weaponry that will be strewn throughout the land:

> Then the people in the towns of Israel will go out and pick up your small and large shields, bows and arrows, javelins and spears, and they will use them for fuel. There will be enough to last them seven years! They won't need to cut wood from the fields or forests, for these weapons will give them all the fuel they need. They will plunder those who planned to plunder them, and they will rob those who planned to rob them, says the Sovereign LORD.

Think of all the small arms, artillery, and so on that will be present after the invaders are wiped out. To finish burning all these weapons will take seven years! Are these weapons literal spears, clubs, and bows, or are they representative of their modern counterparts? We will discuss the meaning of the weapons listed in Ezekiel 39 in the next chapter. Either way, the weapons will be incinerated.

BURYING OF THE DEAD

The brash, bold offensive against Israel to steal land will result in the possession of only one piece of real estate for the invaders—their burial plots:

I will make a vast graveyard for Gog and his hordes in the Valley of the Travelers, east of the Dead Sea. It will block the way of those who travel there, and they will change the name of the place to the Valley of Gog's Hordes. It will take seven months for the people of Israel to bury the bodies and cleanse the land. Everyone in Israel will help, for it will be a glorious victory for Israel when I demonstrate my glory on that day, says the Sovereign LORD.

After seven months, teams of men will be appointed to search the land for skeletons to bury, so the land will be made clean again. Whenever bones are found, a marker will be set up so the burial crews will take them to be buried in the Valley of Gog's Hordes. (There will be a town there named Hamonah, which means "horde.") And so the land will finally be cleansed.

EZEKIEL 39:11-16

The bodies will be so numerous that they will block the normal travel routes. The Russian-Iranian axis will set out to bury Israel, but God will bury the invaders instead. Seven months will be required to cleanse the land of all the dead bodies.

BANQUETING OF THE BIRDS AND BEASTS

The gory, grisly result of the battle is described in Ezekiel 39:17-20:

Now, son of man, this is what the Sovereign LORD says: Call all the birds and wild animals. Say to them: Gather together for my great sacrificial feast. Come from far and near to the mountains of Israel, and there eat flesh and drink blood! Eat the flesh of mighty men and drink the blood of princes as though they were rams, lambs, goats, and bulls—all fattened animals from Bashan! Gorge yourselves with flesh until you are glutted; drink blood until you are drunk. This is the sacrificial feast I have prepared for you. Feast at my banquet table—feast on horses and charioteers, on mighty men and all kinds of valiant warriors, says the Sovereign LORD.

God calls the gathering of the birds and the beasts to feed upon the carnage a "sacrificial feast." "Usually people slaughtered and ate sacrificed animals. Here, however, the men of Gog's armies will be sacrifices; they will be eaten by animals."[13] A similar scene will follow the final great campaign of Armageddon in Revelation 19:17-18.

BLESSING OF SALVATION

The final result of the War of Gog and Magog will be a great spiritual awakening. In the book of Ezekiel the phrase "that you may know I am the LORD" or its equivalent occurs more than sixty times. This phrase recurs again and again in Ezekiel 38–39: "I will demonstrate my glory to the nations. Everyone will see the punishment I have inflicted on them and the power of my fist when I strike. And from that time on the people of Israel will know that I am the LORD their God" (Ezekiel 39:21-22; see also Ezekiel 38:16, 23; 39:6).

God will use the demonstration of his power and might to show the world who he really is. Many will shake it off and go on in their wicked ways. But many other Jews and Gentiles will turn to the Lord, acknowledging his power. Even in the dark days of the Great Tribulation, our merciful God will still be seeking and saving the lost, bringing about great spiritual revival.

Only God can save Israel then; only God can save us now.

CONCLUSION

There are five points to take away regarding the War of Gog and Magog:

1. The Gog-Magog War against Israel will be a Russian-Islamic axis of nations bent on wiping Israel off the face of the earth. Specifically, they will come to *steal* land, *seize* spoil, *slaughter* the Jews, and *stifle* the Antichrist's growing power.

2. God will dramatically intervene, routing the invaders in a devastating defeat of a magnitude never seen in military history. Even Russia's homeland and headquarters will face devastating destruction.

3. The war will radically reorder world power. Here are a few of the more important ways this war will shape prophetic events:

   It will *cripple* Islamic influence in the Middle East. Many Muslims live outside the Middle East, even the most populous nations such as Indonesia, but the annihilation of armies from Iran, Turkey, Central Asia, Libya, Sudan, and probably the near nations around Israel will deal a debilitating blow to Muslim power, effectively neutralizing this power bloc.

   It will *crush* Russian aggression. The end-times king of the north will fall, never to rise again.

   It will *create* a giant power vacuum. With the Russian-Islamic coalition taken out, the Western leader, whom we know as the Antichrist, will catapult onto the world scene. I've often wondered if the Antichrist might take credit for the destruction of the Russian horde, claiming possession of some secret weapon that enabled him to wipe them out. However events unfold, we know that by the middle of the Tribulation, the Antichrist will seize control of the world economically and politically (see Revelation 13). The destruction of the Russian-Islamic coalition will propel Antichrist's rise to global domination.

4. Through this victory, God will demonstrate his greatness and holiness to such an extent that all nations will be forced to acknowledge he alone is King of kings and Lord of lords. God will use this war to bring many Gentiles to faith in himself.

5. Likewise, the nation of Israel will come to a turning point, recognizing there is no one like the Lord their God.[14] The ultimate result of this war will be the national repentance and restoration of the Jewish people under the reign of their Messiah in the Kingdom.

We can learn many lessons for our lives today from the War of Gog and Magog, but two stand out: God is sovereign. And God is our only Savior.

Nothing is more important for us to hold on to than these two truths.

CHAPTER 8

HOW CLOSE ARE WE?

The book of Ezekiel predicts that a large force, identified as "Magog,"
from the north of Israel will attack the nation. . . . There is a lot going on in
our current headlines that leads me to believe it could happen at any time.
And when it does, it will transpire in rapid succession,
like dominoes closely stacked together.

GREG LAURIE

The Russian bear continues to flex its muscle against its neighbors and in the Middle East. The Bear's footprint is expanding with a swelling presence in Syria, an increasing alliance with Iran, and strengthening ties with Turkey. As we've seen, all of this is headed toward a colossal conflict in the Holy Land led by Russia. One of the principal questions concerning this coming Middle East war is, When will it occur? How much longer until the first great war of the end times breaks out? Ezekiel 38 sheds light on the all-important timing question:

> Get ready; be prepared! Keep all the armies around you
> mobilized, and take command of them. A long time from
> now you will be called into action. In the distant future

you will swoop down on the land of Israel, which will be enjoying peace after recovering from war [NASB, "the sword"] and after its people have returned from many lands to the mountains of Israel. You and all your allies—a vast and awesome army—will roll down on them like a storm and cover the land like a cloud.

This is what the Sovereign LORD says: At that time evil thoughts will come to your mind, and you will devise a wicked scheme. You will say, "Israel is an unprotected land filled with unwalled villages! I will march against her and destroy these people who live in such confidence!" . . .

Therefore, son of man, prophesy against Gog. Give him this message from the Sovereign LORD: When my people are living in peace in their land, then you will rouse yourself. You will come from your homeland in the distant north with your vast cavalry and your mighty army, and you will attack my people Israel, covering their land like a cloud. At that time in the distant future, I will bring you against my land as everyone watches, and my holiness will be displayed by what happens to you, Gog. Then all the nations will know that I am the LORD.

EZEKIEL 38:7-11, 14-16

The mention of swords and cavalry in Ezekiel 38 has led some commentators to conclude that this battle occurred sometime in the distant past. The weapons mentioned in Ezekiel chapters 38 and 39 are ancient weapons made out of wood such as bows, arrows, shields, war clubs, and spears (see 39:9). The means of transportation is horses (see 38:15). So how do we account for these ancient weapons if this invasion is in the end times? There are two plausible solutions to this problem.

First, it could be that by the time this event is fulfilled, nations will have reverted to archaic weapons and means of transportation due to oil shortages and other wars that have depleted these nations' resources, or possibly there will be some comprehensive disarmament treaties. Albert Einstein reportedly said, "I know not with what weapons World War III will be fought, but World War IV will be fought with sticks and stones." He could be right. John Walvoord favors this view of Ezekiel 38:

> [One possible] solution is that the battle is preceded by a disarmament agreement between nations. If this were the case, it would be necessary to resort to primitive weapons easily and secretly made if a surprise attack were to be achieved. This would allow a literal interpretation of this passage. . . . Whatever the explanation, the most sensible interpretation is that the passage refers to actual weapons pressed into use because of the peculiar circumstances of that day.[1]

A second interpretation is that Ezekiel spoke, inspired by the Holy Spirit, in language that the people of his day could understand. If he had spoken of planes, missiles, tanks, and rifles, this text would have been nonsensical to everyone until the twentieth century. As Paul Enns notes, "It is not necessary to suggest the final battle will be fought with horses. How would Ezekiel describe future warfare? Since he had no terminology for modern warfare, he would use the terminology of his time—horses and swords."[2] Walter Kaiser notes, "No doubt, we must understand here perhaps the modern equivalent for the use of horses, such as tanks and the like, for they would otherwise have had no meaning to those of Ezekiel's day. There is, however, the possibility that weather conditions and strategic reasons may force the use of horses where mechanized equipment would be impossible."[3]

Either way, the main point of Ezekiel's great prophecy is that a specific group of nations will attack Israel intent on completely destroying it. The emphasis is not on the specific weapons that will be used by these invaders. The point Ezekiel is making is that the invaders will wield weapons of destruction and that there will be all-out warfare. Understanding the weapons in light of their modern counterparts is not symbolic interpretation but rather situating God's Word in its historical context as understood by the original audience. The Holy Spirit speaks to people in their own context and culture in ways that communicate God's truth meaningfully and understandably.

Accounting for all the details of Ezekiel 38 and 39 leads to the conclusion that these chapters cannot have been fulfilled at any point in the past. No invasion of Israel even remotely similar to Ezekiel 38 has ever occurred in Israel's history, despite the claims of some who place the fulfillment of all or most biblical prophecy in the past.[4] John Walvoord states the issue accurately and succinctly: "There has never been a war with Israel which fulfills the prophecies of Ezekiel 38–39."[5]

Orthodox Jews view these chapters as a future event, referring to Ezekiel 38–39 as the "Wars of Gog" and seeing them as a series of three future invasions that will be the next of Israel's wars before the Messiah's appearance.[6] Eminent biblical scholar F. F. Bruce believes the events of Ezekiel 38–39 are located in the end times: "In Ezekiel 38:16 Gog's invasion of the land of Israel is to take place 'in the latter days'; here the original intention is eschatological."[7]

The War of Gog and Magog will occur in the end of days. That much seems clear. But is it possible to narrow the time frame down more specifically? What hints do we have in Ezekiel chapters 38 and

39 about the specific timing of this invasion? Numerous opinions have been offered by capable Bible scholars on this point, and every view is beset with weaknesses. The invasion has been placed at almost every key point in the end times. Let's look carefully at Ezekiel 38 and see if we can unravel some of the mystery.

IT'S ABOUT TIME

A group of authors and prophecy teachers place the Ezekiel invasion before the rapture of believers to heaven (this is the view depicted in the fictional Left Behind series); others believe it will occur between the time of the Rapture and the beginning of the seven-year Tribulation; others maintain it will transpire during the first half of the Great Tribulation; others believe it will take place in connection with the Battle of Armageddon at the end of the Great Tribulation. Many place it at the end of the Millennium, since there is a reference to Gog and Magog in Revelation 20:8. Others maintain that it will unfold in phases over the entire period of the Tribulation.[8] As you can see, this is among the most debated issues concerning the coming Russian invasion.

FOUR MAIN VIEWS OF THE TIMING OF THE RUSSIAN INVASION
Before the Rapture (or between the Rapture and the beginning of the Tribulation)
First half of the Tribulation (some put it close to the midpoint)
End of the Tribulation (equates Ezekiel 38–39 with Armageddon)
End of the Millennium (parallel with Revelation 20:8)

To simplify the process, we can reduce the scope of the problem by considering the textual hints or internal markers within Ezekiel 38 and the surrounding context that suggest when this battle will take place.[9] There are four chronological keys that narrow down the time when the events in Ezekiel 38–39 will come to pass.

THE PLACEMENT

The most general clue rises from the broader context of Ezekiel's prophecy. The battle in Ezekiel 38–39 is placed between the regathering of Israel in Ezekiel 37 and the restoration of the Jewish people as they worship in the millennial Temple in Ezekiel 40–48. In Ezekiel 37 the Jewish people are regathered to the land *physically*, while in Ezekiel 40–48 they are restored to the Lord *spiritually* in the millennial kingdom. Ezekiel 38–39 falls between these two events.

EZEKIEL 37	EZEKIEL 38–39	EZEKIEL 40–48
Jewish people regathered	War of Gog and Magog	Jewish people restored to the land physically, Lord spiritually

The regathering of the Jewish people to their land before this invasion is essential because, obviously, the Jewish people cannot be invaded if they aren't in their land.

As John Phillips notes, "The prophet put it between a discussion of the physical rebirth of the nation of Israel (chap. 37) and a long description of Israel's spiritual rebirth (chaps. 40–48). In other words, Russia's brief day of triumph lies somewhere between those two crucial events. . . . The prophet deliberately sandwiched Russia's 'date with destiny' between Israel's political and spiritual rebirths."[10]

This narrows the time frame for the Ezekiel 38 invasion down to the period between 1948, the year of the birth of the modern state of Israel, and the beginning of the thousand-year reign of Christ. We're now about seventy years after Israel's rebirth. Currently more than six million of the world's fourteen million Jews reside in Israel. This piece of the end-times puzzle is firmly in place.

THE PROSPERITY

At the time this invasion occurs, Israel not only will be back in their land, but they also will be prosperous and thriving: "See, I care about you, and I will pay attention to you. Your ground will be plowed and your crops planted. I will greatly increase the population of Israel, and the ruined cities will be rebuilt and filled with people. I will increase not only the people, but also your animals. O mountains of Israel, I will bring people to live on you once again. I will make you even more prosperous than you were before" (Ezekiel 36:9-11). Russia and her allies will be lured into Israel to seize the nation's great wealth, indicating that Israel will be thriving in the latter years. Russia will come to Israel to "capture vast amounts of plunder, for the people are rich with livestock and other possessions now" (Ezekiel 38:12).

Massive gas reserves have been discovered in Israel in recent years, the most impressive being the Leviathan field, which contains around 20 trillion cubic feet of gas. This is a stunning economic game changer for Israel. Other gas reserves such as the Tamar field are so plentiful that they will meet Israel's needs for the next twenty-five years, leaving the Leviathan reserves available for export.

In May 2013, Secretary of State John Kerry told reporters, "I think there is an opportunity [for peace], but for many reasons it's not on the tips of everyone's tongue. People in Israel aren't waking up every day and wondering if tomorrow there will be peace because there is a sense of security and a sense of accomplishment and of prosperity."[11] Kerry's statement, as well as leading economic indicators, shows that the second prerequisite for this invasion is in place.

THE PERIOD

Another chronological indicator is found in the phrases "latter years" (Ezekiel 38:8, NASB) and "last days" (38:16, NASB; NLT, "distant future" in both instances). We need to make a distinction between the last days for Israel in the Old Testament and the last days for the church in the New Testament. The "last days" in the New Testament refers to the last days of the church, which is the entire age between the two comings of Christ (see Hebrews 1:1-2). We currently live in the last days of the church.

"Last days" or "latter years" in the Old Testament refers to the last days for Israel, which are the seven years of Tribulation, culminating with the second coming of Christ and the setting up of his Kingdom on earth (see Deuteronomy 4:30; Isaiah 2:2; Jeremiah 30:24; Ezekiel 38:8, 16; Micah 4:1).

The reference to the "latter years" and "last days" in Ezekiel 38 eliminates any past fulfillment for these events. This could also render any time before the Tribulation unlikely, depending on how loosely one interprets the last days for Israel. I believe the Tribulation begins the "latter years" for Israel, but others are more expansive in their view of Israel's last days and believe this invasion could occur at any time. Either view is possible. If we're currently in the last days for Israel, this condition has also been met.

THE PEACE

Three times Ezekiel tells us that Russia will swoop into Israel when the people are dwelling securely and are at rest (see Ezekiel 38:8, 11, 14). Israel will be a "land filled with unwalled villages" when the surprise attack is launched (38:11). In ancient language this speaks of peace and safety, with little concern for protective measures.

There are not many occasions in God's prophetic program when Israel is secure and at rest. The Jewish people have been scattered and persecuted over the face of the earth, and not even in the future will Israel have many periods of rest and security.

Some believe this state of affairs is present in Israel today, so this condition could be fulfilled. We'll look at this issue as we briefly survey the four basic views of when the Russian invasion will transpire.

VIEW #1—EZEKIEL 38–39 IS THE SAME AS REVELATION 20:8

The simplest view for many scholars is to equate the only two biblical references to Gog and Magog in the Bible, found in Ezekiel 38 and Revelation 20. While this view is attractive in connecting the biblical dots, the different settings for these two passages to me eliminates this view from serious consideration.

	GOG AND MAGOG IN EZEKIEL 38	GOG AND MAGOG IN REVELATION 20:8
The Period	Before or during the Tribulation	After Christ's thousand-year reign (Revelation 20:1-6)
The Participants	Specific list of nations	Worldwide enemies of Christ

The only things these battles have in common are the terms *Gog* and *Magog* and the total annihilation of the enemy.[12] But if we view these two events as distinct, the question arises—how do we explain the identical names used for them? One common explanation is that the apostle John was simply using "Gog and Magog" as a kind of shorthand, the way we might use "Waterloo" to describe the final battle in Revelation 20. Rather than giving all the details of what will happen, John employs a well-known biblical allusion to communicate that nations will invade Israel and be wiped out by God just like what is described in Ezekiel 38–39. John is telling us in the briefest way possible that this will be another Gog and Magog, even though the two events are separated by more than a thousand years. In the same way that we speak of World War I and World War II, this will be Gog and Magog I and Gog and Magog II.

VIEW #2—THE WAR CAN HAPPEN AT ANY TIME

An impressive array of scholars and commentators believe all the preconditions for the fulfillment of Ezekiel 38–39 are currently in place, including Israel's prosperity and security. For them, this war can happen at any time. Walter Kaiser believes the Russian-led invasion of Israel will occur before the Tribulation begins. "It appears that before the final seven years begin, a Russian-Iranian confederation along with most Arab states will decide to act against Israel in the Gog-Magog plot."[13] Randall Price favors this view: "There is nothing in the description of Israel in Ezekiel 38–39 that does not fit the reality of the modern State of Israel today."[14]

Joel Rosenberg believes conditions in Israel today are ripe for this invasion to occur at any time: "The point here is that never before in her modern history has Israel been so secure, so prosperous, so eager to give up land for peace."[15] He adds,

> For the first time since the book of Ezekiel was written more than 2,500 years ago, it is now possible that the two prerequisites of relative peace and rising prosperity in Israel are already checked off God's to-do list, and that the rest of the prophecies will soon come true as well.
>
> Israel has been reborn as a country. Millions of Jews have poured back into the Holy Land. The deserts have bloomed. The economy is booming. The ancient ruins are being rebuilt. Israel has signed peace treaties, truces, cease-fire agreements, and/or other diplomatic and economic accords with all of its immediate neighbors. It has all happened just as Ezekiel told us it would happen, and all of it begs the question: What will happen next?[16]

Those who hold this view believe that the War of Gog and Magog will happen before the Tribulation, thus eliminating the Islamic threat and allowing the Jewish people to rebuild the Temple in Jerusalem as required by Scripture (see Matthew 24:15; 2 Thessalonians 2:4).

Others are quick to point out that Israel today, while secure in one sense, is far from what is described in Ezekiel 38. David Jeremiah says,

> This is clearly one condition that has not yet occurred. There has never been a time in Israel's existence, ancient or modern, when it has not been concerned about defense. Israel has always been surrounded by enemies. Even today Israel is constantly threatened from all sides by extremely hostile neighbors many times its size. It has already fought three major wars in its brief modern history, and Israel's close neighbor Iran is rabidly eager to annihilate it.
>
> There is no country on earth as massively armed for its size and as constantly vigilant as Israel. Every young Israeli man is required to undergo three years of military training, and every young woman trains for two years. Visit Israel today and you will see its readiness for war on display everywhere. Armed soldiers are stationed in every strategic location, and security is the highest priority. One cannot enter a shop or restaurant without going through a metal detector. No, Israel is not at peace or anywhere close to it.[17]

Israel today is an armed camp, living under a tenuous truce with only two of its Arab neighbors—Egypt and Jordan—and both of those agreements could be in dire jeopardy with current events in the Middle East. The rest of its neighbors would love nothing more than to drive every Israelite into the Mediterranean Sea if they could. The reason they do not is because Israel possesses a formidable military machine that is more than a match for its neighbors.

To me, the prerequisite for peace does not seem to be fully in place, but it could be soon.[18]

VIEW #3—THE WAR IN EZEKIEL 38–39 IS THE SAME AS THE CAMPAIGN OF ARMAGEDDON

This view equates Ezekiel 38–39 with Revelation 19:11-21. One point in favor of this view is that both of these battles are great end-times conflagrations in the land of Israel, and both mention the birds feeding on the carnage (see Ezekiel 39:17-19; Revelation 19:17-18). While there are undoubtedly some similarities between the two passages, here are a few of the significant differences between these two events that demonstrate they are two separate end-times wars:

GOG AND MAGOG	ARMAGEDDON
Leader is Gog	Leader is Antichrist
Israel is at rest/living securely	No mention of Israel's security
Specific nations: Russian-Islamic coalition	All nations
Nations know that the Lord is God	Nations are destroyed

Additionally, at the end of the Great Tribulation, Israel will not be at rest and living securely as Ezekiel 38 requires. The Jewish people will be scattered and pursued by the Antichrist (see Revelation 12:13-17). Therefore, the invasion described by Ezekiel could not be a part of the Battle of Armageddon at the end of the Great Tribulation.

VIEW #4—THE WAR WILL TRANSPIRE DURING THE FIRST HALF OF THE TRIBULATION

While I hold open the possibility that view #2 might be correct, I favor placing this invasion in the first half of the coming Tribulation because it best explains the security requirement. I don't believe what we see in Israel today meshes with the description of rest and security in Ezekiel 38. However, Scripture tells us the day is coming when Israel will be secure and at rest. So how will this come about? Charles Dyer and Mark Tobey suggest, "Perhaps a treaty [will be] forged by an outside power that is strong enough to enforce the treaty's conditions and compromises."[19] The prophet Daniel tells us how this peace will come to pass: "The ruler [the Antichrist] will make a treaty with the people for a period of one set of seven [years]" (Daniel 9:27).

Daniel reveals that in the end times, a group of ten leaders will spearhead a coalition of countries that will reunite the Roman empire (the Western confederacy). Out of this Group of Ten, which I call the G-10, a strong man will rise to power. He is the final Antichrist, who will take control of the G-10. This regional leader will emerge on the world stage as a peacemaker, accomplishing what no one else has been able to do—crafting a seven-year treaty of protection and peace with the people of Israel that will solve the Middle East crisis. One can only imagine the accolades he will receive for pulling off this agreement. He will receive the Nobel Peace Prize and be *Time's* "Person of the Year." The perpetual, thorny Middle East crisis will appear to be solved.

With this guarantee of peace and protection, Israel will be able to relax and let its guard down for the first time in its modern history. Lulled into a false sense of security, Israel will direct its energies toward increased wealth rather than defense—only to have the peace treaty shattered in less than four years when the Russian-led assault force will strike the unsuspecting nation, fulfilling Ezekiel's prophecy.[20]

John Phillips summarizes the timing of this invasion in relation to other end-times events: "Only one period fits all the facts. When the Beast first comes to power in Europe, he will quickly unify the West, impose his totalitarian will on the nations under his control, and begin to prepare for world conquest. The major obstacle to his future plans will be a revitalized Russia." And, I might add, a radical Islamic presence. Phillips continues: "The invasion, then, takes place *after* the Rapture of the church, *after* the rise of the Beast in the West, *after* the signing of the pact with Israel, and just *before* the Beast takes over the world. Indeed it is the collapse of Russia [and its Islamic allies] that makes his global empire possible."[21]

David Jeremiah pinpoints the timing of this invasion: "To summarize, it will come after Israel returns to its homeland, after it has become highly prosperous, and after the implementation of the seven-year peace treaty with the Antichrist."[22]

THE RUSSIANS *ARE* COMING

Whatever view one holds of the timing of the coming Russian invasion, one thing is certain—it will happen. It may happen *soon* if the Rapture comes quickly and the Antichrist appears to bring peace to Israel, or even *sooner* if all the conditions in Ezekiel 38 are currently in place, as some believe.

The *timing* of Russia's offensive may be debated, but the *truth* of it is not up for discussion. God has spoken. And we see signs all around us that it could be very soon. The Jewish people are back in their land living in prosperity. Russia is taking its place on the world stage right on cue. World leaders continue to pursue a road map to Middle East peace. The signs are lighting up like runway lights signaling the coming of Jesus Christ.

As John Walvoord says, "The world today is like a stage being set for a great drama. The major actors are already in the wings waiting for their moment in history. The main stage props are already in place. The prophetic play could begin at any time. . . . Russia is poised to the north of the Holy Land for entry in the end-time conflict. . . . Each nation is ready to play out its role in the final hours of history."[23]

The time is at hand.

CHAPTER 9

WHAT DOES THE FUTURE HOLD?

The board is set, and the pieces are moving.

GANDALF, *THE RETURN OF THE KING*

There's a famous story from Russian history about Grigory Alexandrovich Potemkin. He lived from 1739 to 1791 during the reign of Catherine the Great. He was a brilliant statesman and successful field marshal, conquering several new territories, creating new armies, and building up the Russian fleet. But he had one fatal flaw in his character—he exaggerated nearly everything he did. This trait reached its peak when he boasted incessantly to Catherine the Great about the construction projects he had undertaken in the outlying regions of Russia, especially in Crimea. He painted such a lavish picture of all the beautiful buildings that had been constructed that she decided she had to go see it all for herself.

Of course, this put Potemkin in quite a spot because it was all a lie. He left the city as quickly as possible, traveled to Crimea, and gathered thousands of people to build entire pasteboard villages—hollow facades of villages, like Hollywood props, along the desolate banks of the Dnieper River. Potemkin had people there walking up and down the streets at the time of the queen's visit. As the queen and her entourage passed by and were quickly paraded down the streets, they didn't notice that it was not a real city at all. It was all just a facade. Potemkin's standing was greatly enhanced in the eyes of Catherine the Great. To add even more intrigue to the story, most believe that even the story itself is a myth.

Nevertheless, there arose an expression—"Potemkin Village." A Potemkin Village is a facade, something that appears to have substance but has no reality. Since that time, the term Potemkin Village has come into our language to express that which is supposed to be something but is really nothing, something that appears elaborate and impressive but is a sham.

The prophecies of God's Word, including the prophecies about Russia in Ezekiel 38–39, are no Potemkin Village. They're not a myth. They're not imagination. They're not speculation. As David Jeremiah says, "We have good reason to believe the Russian threat is real. In fact, we have evidence that, at some point, Russia will ignite a pivotal world war like none ever seen or imagined. According to the prophet Ezekiel, this is a sure thing. Russia's aggressive moves today cast a long shadow into a future explicitly described in Ezekiel's prophecy."[1]

TIMES OF THE SIGNS

As we've seen, recent trends bear a remarkable correspondence to what Ezekiel predicted more than 2,500 years ago. Events are unfolding just as we should expect in light of Ezekiel's prophecy. As Charles Dyer and Mark Tobey say, "The parallels between Ezekiel's prophecy and events today are compelling, almost frighteningly so."[2]

The starting point for the prophetic panorama of events is Ezekiel 37, which predicts the regathering of the Jewish people to their land.

Since 1948, the world has watched this prophecy come to fruition. Against all odds, after almost two thousand years of dispersion, the Jewish people are in the process of being regathered to their ancient homeland. About six million Jews reside in the Promised Land, sitting in the middle of a sea of enemies.

Ezekiel 37 forms the foundation for all that will follow. The regathering and restoration of the Jews to the Promised Land was a kind of "super sign" that set many gears in motion. Israel is God's timepiece—his clock. When we want to know where we are on God's prophetic timetable, the first place we need to look is Israel.

The presence of the Jewish people in their ancient land is the prerequisite for the unfolding of the end times. The event that commences the final seven years of Tribulation is the signing of a covenant between the final Antichrist and the Jewish people (see Daniel 9:27). For that to occur, there must be a nation of Israel. The rebirth of Israel in 1948 set the prophetic sequence in motion.

As Joel Rosenberg says, "Today, for the first time in two thousand years, we are seeing all of these signs come true, and the rebirth of Israel is the most dramatic sign of them all. We can, therefore, have confidence that Jesus' return is closer than ever. . . . It is true that Jesus cautions us not to speculate on the exact day and hour of his return. But we are encouraged to watch current events closely and know when the clock is running out."[3]

In addition to the rebirth of Israel, many other developments point toward the end-times scenario in Scripture. Globalism is paving the way for a one-world government and economy of the end times predicted in Revelation 13.

The Middle East is a hotbed of radicalism and turmoil. The attention of the world is focused there, just as we should anticipate if the end of days is getting close.

The Russian bear has roared out of hibernation suddenly and

dramatically and dominates world headlines every day. The Bear's footprints continue to leave their mark all over the world.

Iran, the world's number-one sponsor of terrorism, is testing ballistic missiles at the same time it continues down the path toward nuclear capability. The Iran nuclear deal has temporarily stalled its nuclear development but only for a few years. Iran is Israel's most dangerous enemy. Its leaders make no effort to hide their malice toward Israel. Iran's Mahdi mentality fuels its expansionist ambitions as it works to hasten the coming of its messiah.

Turkey is descending into a dictatorship led by an Islamist and is cozying up to Russia and Iran. President Erdoğan's rhetoric against Israel is heating up. Four of the ancient allies named in Ezekiel 38 are located in modern Turkey.

The rise of ISIS and the civil war in Syria, while not the direct fulfillment of any biblical prophecies, are keeping the world focused on the Middle East. Syria is a flashpoint that is aligning Russia, Iran, and Turkey into a fearsome triumvirate. Russia and Iran have seized the chaos in Syria as an opportunity to bring in troops and air power, putting them just north of Israel.

Libya and Sudan are radical Islamic nations with deep animus toward Israel. The deepening turmoil and instability in these nations has provided an opening for greater Russian influence. These nations, too, are mentioned by Ezekiel.

The world desperately yearns for peace in the Middle East, primarily in Israel. The Bible says Israel will be at rest and secure when the Russian-led invasion occurs. The ongoing Middle East peace process could be a harbinger of the peace treaty the Antichrist will negotiate or at least confirm with Israel and her near enemies.

Never before have so many signs converged so quickly in such a short span of time that correspond to the matrix of end-times events predicted in Scripture. The pieces are moving.

The words of J. Vernon McGee are fitting: "I am seeing a stage being set for Russia's move against Israel. I do not know how close we are. I see not only one sign but the multiplication of all these signs about us and believe they are setting the stage. It looks as if God is getting ready to move again in the affairs of this earth."[4] Current events in Russia and the Middle East trace the trajectory that points toward the gathering storm of the Russian invasion of Israel—the War of Gog and Magog.

A PROPHETIC CHECKLIST

With all we've seen thus far, I thought it might be helpful to bring together all the key events and players in a simple chronology. The list below is a succinct summary of significant past and present world events that are part of the buildup to the end of days, a preview of what's next, and a forecast of where it's all headed.[5]

1. The modern state of Israel was established on May 14, 1948.
2. The Soviet Union, led by Russia, became a world superpower and an ally of the Islamic world.
3. The Middle East became the most significant trouble spot in the world and the hub of global terror.
4. The Iron Curtain fell in 1991, removing a major barrier to the revival of the Roman empire and the rise of the king of the west.
5. The 9/11 attacks on the United States began the war on terror, setting in motion a chain of events and bringing major realignment in the Middle East.
6. The world clamors for peace as continued turmoil, terror attacks, chaos, and instability plague the Middle East.
7. Russia has reemerged as a global force.

8. Ten leaders (the "Group of Ten") will emerge from a European and Mediterranean coalition, commencing the last phase of the final world empire.

9. In a bold power play, a new Mediterranean strongman (aka the Antichrist) will seize control of the powerful ten-leader group.

10. The Western leader will negotiate what appears to be a "final" peace settlement in the Middle East. The duration of the agreement will be seven years. Israel will feel secure and relax its defenses.

11. While all these events are transpiring, the king of the north—the Russian head of an alliance including Turkey and Iran—will emerge as a challenger to the Antichrist.

12. The king of the south—who will lead a North African coalition consisting of Egypt, Libya, Sudan, and possibly other nations—will come on the scene, allying his forces with the king of the north.

13. While Israel is at rest, Russia will ignite a surprise invasion to wipe out the Jewish people and challenge the king of the west. The Western nations and moderate Arabs will raise a weak protest that's all words but no action. No one will come to Israel's defense, not even the United States.

14. When all looks lost for Israel, God will intervene, miraculously destroying the invaders. Russia's coalition will go up in smoke.

15. With the northern and southern alliances out of the way, the king of the west will take center stage, proclaim himself world dictator, break his peace agreement with Israel, and declare himself to be God.

16. The terrible judgments of the Great Tribulation will be poured out on the nations of the world as outlined in

Revelation 6–18. The world will be plunged into a terrible time of wrath.

17. As the Antichrist's hold on power begins to slip, armies from throughout the world, including the kings of the east, will converge on the Middle East for the final world war. The armies will gather in northern Israel at Armageddon and spread all the way to Jerusalem.

18. Jesus Christ, the fifth and final King of the end times, will return to earth with his armies from heaven. He is the Word of God, the King of kings and Lord of lords, the Alpha and Omega, the Beginning and the End.

19. The armies of the world gathered at Armageddon will unite to resist Christ's coming and will be obliterated in the Battle of Armageddon. Jesus will speak a word, and they will all wither under his presence.

20. Christ will establish his thousand-year reign on earth, and after his reign, God will create a new heaven and a new earth where God will dwell with his people forever.

What a forecast! What a future! That's where it's all headed. What's the world coming to? It's coming to the feet of Jesus. History is headed toward the feet of Jesus. Since everything is headed toward the feet of Jesus, we should humbly live our lives there now and keep looking for his coming.

THE BLESSED HOPE

In the days ahead, there will undoubtedly be many sudden, unexpected turns in world events. Headlines will come and go. Events will ebb and flow. Nations and leaders will rise and fall. Real news and fake news will continue to clarify and confuse. The drumbeat of wars and rumors of wars will quicken. But the Word of God will not change. What God has prophesied will come to pass, just as surely as hundreds of biblical prophecies have already been fulfilled. For this reason, as time runs out, our focus must always remain on the unchanging Word of the living God and the hope of Christ's coming. A. W. Tozer says it well:

> Let us be alert to the season in which we are living. It is the season of the Blessed Hope. . . . It is imperative that we stay fully alert to the times in which we live. . . . All signs today point to this being the season of the Blessed Hope. . . . All around us, we have the evidence of Jesus' soon return. Each day our focus should be on the Coming One. Our focus on the Blessed Hope is the most important discipline of our Christian life.[6]

That's quite a statement. "The most important discipline of our Christian life" is to focus on the coming of Jesus Christ. That's humbling. How true is this in the lives of most followers of Christ? How true is this in your life . . . and in mine? With all we see happening today, we have more reason than any previous generation to observe this discipline and to keep our focus on the Blessed Hope. No previous generation has seen anything compared to what we're witnessing every day.

Professor and prophecy expert Ed Hindson reminds us of the urgency of our times: "God's clock, the clock of history, is ticking away. It never speeds up and never slows down. It just keeps on ticking, continually and relentlessly, moving us closer and closer to the end of the age. How close we are to the end will only be revealed by time itself. Don't gamble with your eternal destiny. Time may very well be running out."[7]

Time *is* running out. The return of Christ could be very soon. But how soon?

CHAPTER 10

IT'S ALWAYS SOON

He who is the faithful witness to all these things [Jesus] says,
"Yes, I am coming soon!"
REVELATION 22:20

In C. S. Lewis's *The Voyage of the Dawn Treader,* Aslan, the lion who is the Christ figure in the story, tells Lucy that he will have to go away. He reassures her by saying, "Do not look so sad. We shall meet soon again."

Lucy, concerned about when she will next see him, asks, "Please, Aslan, what do you call *soon*?"

And Aslan replies, "I call all times soon."[1]

Jesus is coming soon. He can come back at any time—any moment. Let those words sink in. Do we really believe he's coming? Do we believe he could come today? Do we live like we believe that? Is the truth of meeting him at any moment transforming your life and my life?

As I write and speak about end-times prophecy, I try to remind myself often of the wise words of Warren Wiersbe: "The purpose of Bible prophecy is not for us to make a calendar, but to build character."[2]

We've looked at Scripture's forecast for Russia's part in the end times. We've seen how God has set the stage for Russia to rise right on cue. This book is evidence that I believe in discerning legitimate signs of the times, but I believe even more strongly that we must never get so consumed with the signs that we forget the Savior. Christ must be our consuming passion. Meeting him must be our motivation. We're waiting for a person. We must never allow ourselves to get so focused on what will happen and when it will happen that we forget how it must change us to be more like him. We must never get so enamored with *timing* that we neglect *transformation*.

Studying the truth of Bible prophecy was never intended just to stir our emotions, satisfy our curiosity, or fill our heads with knowledge. The prophetic Scripture is given to fill us with hope and move us to a sense of urgency and action as we watch and wait for Jesus to come. Over the years, I've been surprised to hear many people demean the study of Bible prophecy, calling it impractical, unrelated to everyday life, or simply a scare tactic. This attitude is unfounded. A. W. Tozer reminds us, "The point of Bible prophecy is not to alarm us but to alert us to the circumstances leading up to the Lord's return. This alertness is to spur us on to be ready; and the Bible says a lot about how we can be ready for His return."[3]

Every time the New Testament gives any substantial teaching about the end times, it is always accompanied by practical application of that truth to our daily lives. Few things are more practical than prophecy. Paul Benware shares this sentiment:

Does this doctrinal area of Bible prophecy make a difference? Yes, emphatically yes! God wants us to know many truths about what is going to take place in the future, and He wants those truths to change us right now in the present. He desires that prophetic truth change the way we think, the way we behave, and the way we view Him.[4]

God wants us to know the prophetic Scripture. The sheer volume of prophecy makes that clear. Almost 30 percent of the Bible was prophecy at the time it was written. If God didn't want us to study prophecy and know the future, he would have omitted that 30 percent. However, our knowledge of prophecy, like all biblical knowledge, must transform us. We must be faithful doers of the Word (see James 1:22-25).

There are many positive effects that result from anticipating Christ's coming, but I want to leave you with five simple points to apply to your life.

LET THE EXPECTATION OF CHRIST'S COMING CONVERT YOU

If you have never accepted Jesus Christ as your Savior, that's the first life-changing step you need to take. Everything begins here. You need the forgiveness of sins and new life that Jesus offers more than you've ever needed anything else. God's gracious answer to mankind's desperate plight is found in the death and resurrection of Jesus Christ. At the cross, Jesus, who is without sin, bore the sin of all humanity. He took your sins. He took my sins. The Bible says, "God made Christ, who never sinned, to be the offering for our sin, so that we could be made right with God through Christ" (2 Corinthians 5:21).

In taking our place on the cross, Jesus exhausted God's just wrath against human sin, leaving God free to extend his grace and mercy to all who will come in simple, childlike faith to trust and receive Jesus. Speaking of Jesus, Scripture says, "To all who believed him and accepted him, he gave the right to become children of God" (John 1:12). We become God's children by receiving his Son, Jesus.

In *Fresh Illustrations for Preaching and Teaching,* there's a great story about the mighty Niagara Falls, where the Niagara River plummets some 180 feet at the American and Horseshoe Falls. "Before the falls, there are violent, turbulent rapids. Farther upstream, however, where the river's current flows more gently, boats are able to navigate. Just before the Welland River empties into the Niagara, a pedestrian walkway spans the river. Posted on this bridge's pylons is a warning sign for all boaters: 'Do you have an anchor?' followed by, 'Do you know how to use it?'" The author concludes, "Faith, like an anchor, is something we need to have and use to avoid spiritual cataclysm."[5]

That's true for every person—including you and me. Without Christ, we're all in a boat helplessly headed for the falls. Our only hope is an anchor. Jesus is our anchor, and faith is how we access that anchor. The questions for every reader are simple: Do you have an anchor? Do you know how to use it?

Make sure you have faith in Jesus Christ as your Savior from sin. Let the truths of what lies ahead move you to accept Christ. If you have never accepted the grace of the Lord Jesus, you can do so right now by calling upon the Lord to save you. There are no magic words that bring salvation. It's the attitude of the heart and mind that really matters. But a simple prayer like this one can serve as an expression of faith in Christ. Why not pray these words if you've never done so before?

Father, I know I'm a sinner. I know I cannot save myself.
I need a Savior, and I believe Jesus is the Savior I need. I
believe he died for me and rose from the dead. I trust in him
alone to wash away my sins and give me eternal life. Amen.

If you prayed that prayer and it expresses the desire of your heart, the Bible says you've become a child of God. You have an anchor that will never fail you. Find a loving church that teaches the Bible, get baptized, read your Bible every day, and begin to serve the Lord in whatever way you can.

For those who already know the Lord, there are other effects the study of Bible prophecy and Christ's coming should have on our daily lives.

LET THE EXPECTATION OF CHRIST'S COMING COMFORT YOU

An Arab proverb says, "Death is a black camel that kneels at every door." Sorrow is no respecter of persons. It comes to every person on earth at one time or another. Our only hope when the grim reaper strikes is the hope of Christ's resurrection and second coming. Jesus is our supreme comfort and encouragement when death hits close to home. The apostle Paul reminds us that while we may weep at the grave, we don't have to fear the grave. Death doesn't have the last word:

> Now, dear brothers and sisters, we want you to know what will happen to the believers who have died so you will not grieve like people who have no hope. For since we believe that Jesus died and was raised to life again, we also believe that when Jesus returns, God will bring back with him the believers who have died.
>
> We tell you this directly from the Lord: We who are still living when the Lord returns will not meet him ahead of those who have died. For the Lord himself will come down from heaven with a commanding shout, with the voice of the archangel, and with the trumpet call of God. First, the believers who have died will rise from their graves. Then,

together with them, we who are still alive and remain on the earth will be caught up in the clouds to meet the Lord in the air. Then we will be with the Lord forever. So encourage each other with these words.

1 THESSALONIANS 4:13-18

The Lord's coming comforts and consoles us with the assurance of ultimate resurrection and reunion with our loved ones. When a believer dies, we don't say "good-bye," just "good night."

I had the privilege of knowing Tim LaHaye, coauthor of the best-selling Left Behind series. Several times I've heard him tell the story of his father's death, when Tim was only nine years old. As you can imagine, the sudden loss of his father had a lasting impact on his life. Tim was in despair, but the pastor officiating the funeral delivered a message that gave young Tim hope: "This is not the end of Frank LaHaye; because he accepted Jesus Christ, the day will come when the Lord will shout from heaven and descend, and the dead in Christ will rise first and then we'll be caught up together to meet him in the air." Tim often recounted how, once he heard these words, "all of a sudden, there was hope in my heart I'd see my father again."

That's the comforting hope Christ brings.

LET THE EXPECTATION OF CHRIST'S COMING CALM YOU

On many fronts, our world today seems to be spinning out of control. Fear and anxiety about the future is mounting. People are searching for ways to cope. The night before he died on the cross, Jesus spoke these words to his closest followers, but they apply to our lives today just as much:

Don't let your hearts be troubled. Trust in God, and trust also in me. There is more than enough room in my Father's home. If this were not so, would I have told you that I am going to prepare a place for you? When everything is ready, I will come and get you, so that you will always be with me where I am.

JOHN 14:1-3

What a challenge in our world today. "Don't let your hearts be troubled." Jesus is telling us that we can remain calm and stable in the midst of troubled times, knowing where everything is headed and knowing that he can come at any moment to take us home.

LET THE EXPECTATION OF CHRIST'S COMING CONTROL YOU

After an extended section describing the any-moment rapture of believers to meet Jesus, the apostle Paul concludes with this challenge: "So, my dear brothers and sisters, be strong and immovable. Always work enthusiastically for the Lord, for you know that nothing you do for the Lord is ever useless" (1 Corinthians 15:58). Knowing that Jesus can come at any time serves as a powerful, pressing motivation and incentive to sacrificially serve him. We know that what we do for him won't be in vain because his coming for us is sure.

Allow the hope of Christ's coming to control your life. Get involved in a local church that preaches the gospel and teaches the Bible. Find a place to serve there. The Bible tells us that every believer has at least one spiritual gift, that is, a divine enablement to carry out some function with ease and effectiveness to serve others (see Romans 12:6-8; 1 Corinthians 12:8-10, 28-29; Ephesians 4:11-12). Read these passages in your Bible, and ask the Lord to guide you into a place of effective, empowered service. Listen to others who will affirm and confirm what you're gifted to do.

Jesus is coming. Your sacrifice and service won't be in vain. "Work enthusiastically for the Lord." It will be worth it.

LET THE EXPECTATION OF CHRIST'S COMING CLEANSE YOU

To borrow a phrase from Judge Robert Bork, our culture today is "slouching towards Gomorrah." We see it on every front. Morality is sliding, and decadence—even outright depravity—seems more and more to be accepted and even applauded. Everywhere we turn, it seems our culture is coarsening and corroding. Sadly, even in the lives of many professing Christians, there seems to be a major disconnect between what is professed and what is practiced. Moral malaise surrounds us.

None of us are perfect in our efforts no matter how hard we try. We all fail far more than we would like. Our lack of faithfulness is humbling. Yet in spite of our frailty, our goal is to please the Lord in what we do, what we say, and what we think. The hope of Christ's coming is a powerful yet often neglected incentive to live as a pure vessel. You might be surprised what a close connection exists between prophecy and practical living in the New Testament. Here are four texts that underscore the purifying power of prophecy. Please read them thoughtfully.

> We are instructed to turn from godless living and sinful pleasures. We should live in this evil world with wisdom, righteousness, and devotion to God, while we look forward with hope to that wonderful day when the glory of our great God and Savior, Jesus Christ, will be revealed. He gave his life to free us from every kind of sin, to cleanse us, and to make us his very own people, totally committed to doing good deeds.
> TITUS 2:12-14

Dear friends, we are already God's children, but he has not yet shown us what we will be like when Christ appears. But we do know that we will be like him, for we will see him as he really is. And all who have this eager expectation will keep themselves pure, just as he is pure.

I JOHN 3:2-3

Since everything around us is going to be destroyed like this, what holy and godly lives you should live, looking forward to the day of God and hurrying it along. On that day, he will set the heavens on fire, and the elements will melt away in the flames. But we are looking forward to the new heavens and new earth he has promised, a world filled with God's righteousness.

And so, dear friends, while you are waiting for these things to happen, make every effort to be found living peaceful lives that are pure and blameless in his sight.

2 PETER 3:11-14

This is all the more urgent, for you know how late it is; time is running out. Wake up, for our salvation is nearer now than when we first believed. The night is almost gone; the day of salvation will soon be here. So remove your dark deeds like dirty clothes, and put on the shining armor of right living. Because we belong to the day, we must live decent lives for all to see. Don't participate in the darkness of wild parties and drunkenness, or in sexual promiscuity and immoral living, or in quarreling and jealousy. Instead, clothe yourself with the presence of the Lord Jesus Christ. And don't let yourself think about ways to indulge your evil desires.

ROMANS 13:11-14

The close connection in these passages between anticipating the coming of the Lord and holy living is striking. What this means is that any believer who gets up in the morning thinking Jesus could come today will strive to please the Lord. It's a fail-safe formula. Yet the opposite is also true. Failure to live expectantly makes us far more vulnerable to temptation and sin.

Charles Haddon Spurgeon, the eminent English pastor, cites the any-moment expectancy of Christ's coming as an energizing force:

> I feel rebuked, myself, sometimes, for not watching for my Master when I know that, at this very time, my dogs are sitting against the door, waiting for me—and long before I reach home, there they will be and, at the first sound of the carriage wheels, they will lift up their voices with delight because their master is coming home! Oh, if we loved our Lord as dogs love their masters, how we should catch the first sound of His Coming—and be waiting, always waiting—and never happy until at last we should see Him! Pardon me for using a dog as a picture of what you ought to be, but when you have attained to a state above that, I will find another illustration to explain my meaning.[6]

Spurgeon puts us in our place, but he also gives this impassioned plea:

> Oh, Beloved, let us try, every morning, to get up as if that were the morning in which Christ would come! And when we go up to bed at night, may we lie down with this thought, "Perhaps I shall be awakened by the ringing out of the silver trumpets heralding His Coming. Before the sun arises, I may be startled from my dreams by the greatest of

all cries, 'The Lord is come! The Lord is come!'" What a check, what an incentive, what a bridle, what a spur such thoughts as these would be to us! Take this for the guide of your whole life—act as if Jesus would come during the act in which you are engaged—and if you would not wish to be caught in that act by the Coming of the Lord, let it not be your act.[7]

Jesus is coming. Only the time is uncertain. As J. Dwight Pentecost encourages us, "May the joy of looking for Him produce in us a holy life so that we will not be ashamed when we see Him."[8]

LIVE LOOKING

In his excellent book *Is This the End?* David Jeremiah issues this challenge from the past to the current generation:

I have heard it said that when first-century Christians traveled from city to city, they would stop at every crossroads and look in all directions, always anticipating the possibility that they might see Christ returning. The ensuing centuries seem to have dulled that imminent expectation, but they should not. We must ever be aware that the Rapture could occur at any moment.[9]

The current rumblings in Russia and the Middle East can spark terror, but they can also spark a hunger for Christ's return. We know that God is in control, and we know that Jesus is coming back for his church. He tells us, "Yes, I am coming soon!" (Revelation 22:20). Remember: with Jesus, it's always soon!

May he find us focused and faithful when he comes.

EZEKIEL 38–39

The following text is chapters 38 and 39 of the biblical book Ezekiel. What follows is the New Living Translation, the translation I've used in most of the book. In a few places where my interpretation differs from the New Living Translation, I've left notes to this effect. I hope this passage of Scripture will help you to understand what I've written in this book about Russia's rise in the end times.

CHAPTER 38
A Message for Gog

¹ This is another message that came to me from the LORD: ² "Son of man, turn and face Gog of the land of Magog, the prince who rules over* the nations of Meshech and Tubal, and prophesy against him. ³ Give him this message from the Sovereign LORD: Gog, I am your enemy! ⁴ I will turn you around and put hooks in your jaws to lead you out with your whole army—your horses and charioteers in full armor and a great horde armed with shields and swords. ⁵ Persia, Ethiopia, and Libya will join you, too, with all their weapons.

---

* See chapter 3, where I discuss the term *rosh*. The NLT translates the Hebrew word *rosh* as "who rules over." NASB has "of Rosh," which, as I discuss in chapter 3, is the name of a place currently occupied by Russia. The word *rosh* also occurs in 38:3 and 39:1.

⁶ Gomer and all its armies will also join you, along with the armies of Beth-togarmah from the distant north, and many others.

⁷ "Get ready; be prepared! Keep all the armies around you mobilized, and take command of them. ⁸ A long time from now you will be called into action. In the distant future you will swoop down on the land of Israel, which will be enjoying peace after recovering from war and after its people have returned from many lands to the mountains of Israel. ⁹ You and all your allies—a vast and awesome army—will roll down on them like a storm and cover the land like a cloud.

¹⁰ "This is what the Sovereign Lord says: At that time evil thoughts will come to your mind, and you will devise a wicked scheme. ¹¹ You will say, 'Israel is an unprotected land filled with unwalled villages! I will march against her and destroy these people who live in such confidence! ¹² I will go to those formerly desolate cities that are now filled with people who have returned from exile in many nations. I will capture vast amounts of plunder, for the people are rich with livestock and other possessions now. They think the whole world revolves around them!' ¹³ But Sheba and Dedan and the merchants of Tarshish will ask, 'Do you really think the armies you have gathered can rob them of silver and gold? Do you think you can drive away their livestock and seize their goods and carry off plunder?'

¹⁴ "Therefore, son of man, prophesy against Gog. Give him this message from the Sovereign Lord: When my people are living in peace in their land, then you will rouse yourself. ¹⁵ You will come from your homeland in the distant north with your vast cavalry and your mighty army, ¹⁶ and you will attack my people Israel, covering their land like a cloud. At that time in the distant future, I will bring you against my land as everyone watches, and my holiness will be displayed by what happens to you, Gog. Then all the nations will know that I am the Lord.

[17] "This is what the Sovereign LORD asks: Are you the one I was talking about long ago, when I announced through Israel's prophets that in the future I would bring you against my people? [18] But this is what the Sovereign LORD says: When Gog invades the land of Israel, my fury will boil over! [19] In my jealousy and blazing anger, I promise a mighty shaking in the land of Israel on that day. [20] All living things—the fish in the sea, the birds of the sky, the animals of the field, the small animals that scurry along the ground, and all the people on earth—will quake in terror at my presence. Mountains will be thrown down; cliffs will crumble; walls will fall to the earth. [21] I will summon the sword against you on all the hills of Israel, says the Sovereign LORD. Your men will turn their swords against each other. [22] I will punish you and your armies with disease and bloodshed; I will send torrential rain, hailstones, fire, and burning sulfur! [23] In this way, I will show my greatness and holiness, and I will make myself known to all the nations of the world. Then they will know that I am the LORD.

CHAPTER 39
The Slaughter of Gog's Hordes

[1] "Son of man, prophesy against Gog. Give him this message from the Sovereign LORD: I am your enemy, O Gog, ruler of the nations of Meshech and Tubal. [2] I will turn you around and drive you toward the mountains of Israel, bringing you from the distant north. [3] I will knock the bow from your left hand and the arrows from your right hand, and I will leave you helpless. [4] You and your army and your allies will all die on the mountains. I will feed you to the vultures and wild animals. [5] You will fall in the open fields, for I have spoken, says the Sovereign LORD. [6] And I will rain down fire on Magog and on all your allies who live safely on the coasts. Then they will know that I am the LORD.

7 "In this way, I will make known my holy name among my people of Israel. I will not let anyone bring shame on it. And the nations, too, will know that I am the LORD, the Holy One of Israel. 8 That day of judgment will come, says the Sovereign LORD. Everything will happen just as I have declared it.

9 "Then the people in the towns of Israel will go out and pick up your small and large shields, bows and arrows, javelins and spears, and they will use them for fuel. There will be enough to last them seven years! 10 They won't need to cut wood from the fields or forests, for these weapons will give them all the fuel they need. They will plunder those who planned to plunder them, and they will rob those who planned to rob them, says the Sovereign LORD.

11 "And I will make a vast graveyard for Gog and his hordes in the Valley of the Travelers, east of the Dead Sea. It will block the way of those who travel there, and they will change the name of the place to the Valley of Gog's Hordes. 12 It will take seven months for the people of Israel to bury the bodies and cleanse the land. 13 Everyone in Israel will help, for it will be a glorious victory for Israel when I demonstrate my glory on that day, says the Sovereign LORD.

14 "After seven months, teams of men will be appointed to search the land for skeletons to bury, so the land will be made clean again. 15 Whenever bones are found, a marker will be set up so the burial crews will take them to be buried in the Valley of Gog's Hordes. 16 (There will be a town there named Hamonah, which means 'horde.') And so the land will finally be cleansed.

17 "And now, son of man, this is what the Sovereign LORD says: Call all the birds and wild animals. Say to them: Gather together for my great sacrificial feast. Come from far and near to the mountains of Israel, and there eat flesh and drink blood! 18 Eat the flesh of mighty men and drink the blood of princes as though they were rams, lambs, goats, and bulls—all fattened animals from Bashan!

[19] Gorge yourselves with flesh until you are glutted; drink blood until you are drunk. This is the sacrificial feast I have prepared for you. [20] Feast at my banquet table—feast on horses and charioteers, on mighty men and all kinds of valiant warriors, says the Sovereign LORD.

[21] "In this way, I will demonstrate my glory to the nations. Everyone will see the punishment I have inflicted on them and the power of my fist when I strike. [22] And from that time on the people of Israel will know that I am the LORD their God. [23] The nations will then know why Israel was sent away to exile—it was punishment for sin, for they were unfaithful to their God. Therefore, I turned away from them and let their enemies destroy them. [24] I turned my face away and punished them because of their defilement and their sins.

RESTORATION FOR GOD'S PEOPLE

[25] "So now, this is what the Sovereign LORD says: I will end the captivity of my people; I will have mercy on all Israel, for I jealously guard my holy reputation! [26] They will accept responsibility for their past shame and unfaithfulness after they come home to live in peace in their own land, with no one to bother them. [27] When I bring them home from the lands of their enemies, I will display my holiness among them for all the nations to see. [28] Then my people will know that I am the LORD their God, because I sent them away to exile and brought them home again. I will leave none of my people behind. [29] And I will never again turn my face from them, for I will pour out my Spirit upon the people of Israel. I, the Sovereign LORD, have spoken!"

APPENDIX 2

THE KING OF THE NORTH: THE NORTHERN CONFEDERACY

BY DR. JOHN F. WALVOORD

In my books I like to expose the readers to some of the scholars and giants of Bible prophecy who have influenced my thinking and shaped my own views. Dr. John Walvoord was one of those men. His book The Nations in Prophecy *was first published in 1967. I read it for the first time in 1985, and it had a formative impact on my understanding of Ezekiel 38–39.*

I've quoted this book a few times in Russia Rising, *but I thought it would be helpful to include Dr. Walvoord's chapter on Ezekiel 38–39 for you to read. Some of the material goes over ground I've covered but does so in a different way. Also, I often find that reading something stated in different words can reinforce its meaning.*

I hope you enjoy reading this chapter as much as I have over the years.

In the warfare that characterizes the end of the age, the Scriptures predict a great world conflict which eventually involves all the nations of the earth. In the Scriptures that portray these stirring events, three major crises may be observed. First, a crisis in the Mediterranean area leads to the formation of the revived Roman Empire composed of a ten-nation confederacy. This is occasioned by the rise of the Roman "prince that shall come" (Daniel 9:26) who subdues three of the kings and secures the submission of the seven remaining rulers. His successful conquest of these ten kingdoms, outlined in Daniel 7:23-26, makes the Roman ruler supreme in his control of this revived form of the ancient Roman Empire.

The second phase of the struggle is recorded in Ezekiel 38 and 39. The great battle there described may be the forerunner of the expansion of the Roman Empire from domination of the Mediterranean area to the role of a world empire embracing all nations of the earth (cp. Daniel 7:23; Revelation 13:7, 8). The third phase of the world struggle is at the end of the great tribulation period just before the second coming of Christ, when major sections of the world rebel against the Roman ruler as their leader. A gigantic world war ensues with the Holy Land as its focal point (Daniel 11:40-45; Revelation 16:12-16).

Expositors are by no means agreed as to the precise details of these events or their place in the sequence. It is possible, however, to be sure about such facts as the geographic origination of military forces which converge upon the Holy Land, described as coming from the north, the east, and the south. All of these forces seem to be in opposition to the Roman ruler who may be called the king of the west, although the Scriptures never assign him this title.

The prophet Daniel in his summary of the world struggle which ends the age declares: "And at the time of the end shall the king of the south push at him: and the king of the north shall come against him like a whirlwind, with chariots, and with horsemen, and with many ships; and he shall enter into the countries, and shall overflow and pass over" (Daniel 11:40). The reference to the king of the north in this passage raises the question concerning Russia and other countries to the north of the Holy Land which figure in this final world struggle. A major contribution to this subject is found in the prophecies of Ezekiel concerning a great invasion of the Holy Land from the north in the end time.

THE RISE OF RUSSIA IN THE TWENTIETH CENTURY

One of the significant aspects of modern life which all have observed in the last quarter of a century is the remarkable rise of Russia to a place of world prominence. At the close of World War II, Russia as a nation was crushed, its manpower destroyed, its cities in ruin. It was a nation that would have been utterly defeated if it had not been for American help. Since World War II, Russia has recovered and has become a prominent nation with world-wide influence which few nations have ever achieved. Today, Russia is one of the principal competitors of the United States of America for world fame and world leadership. Through the instrument of communism and nations which share Russia's convictions on communism, almost half of the world's population is in some sense or other in the Russian orbit. Such a phenomenal rise of a nation so godless and blasphemous must have some prophetic significance.

DOES THE BIBLE CONTAIN PROPHECY ABOUT RUSSIA?

In the study of prophecy, care must be taken not to create doctrine without proper Scriptural support. Many aspects of prophecy in the Bible may be understood only partially. There are great themes of prophecy, however, which do not rest on isolated texts, but upon extended portions of the Word of God. As these Scriptures are studied, some settled conclusions can be reached regarding the main movements of God in the prophetic future.

The word *Russia* is not found in the English Bible, and at first glance it would seem that there is nothing in the Bible that would give any information about Russia. A more careful investigation, however, reveals that there are two long chapters in the Bible which seem to concern themselves with the nation Russia, with certain other portions of Scripture which cast added light upon the subject. Not only has the Bible something to say about Russia, but what it reveals is of tremendous significance in God's prophetic program.

In Ezekiel 38 and 39, a description is given of a war between Israel and a nation which many have identified as Russia. The two chapters mentioned describe the invasion of the land of Israel by the armies of Russia and the nations that are associated with her. The Scriptures are plain that this is a military invasion and reveal many details about the situation existing at the time of that invasion. The dramatic outcome of the battle is the utter destruction of the army that invades the land of Israel. Written by the prophet Ezekiel, who himself was in exile from the land of Israel, this prophecy was inspired by the Spirit of God. A natural question can be raised, however, inasmuch as this was written some twenty-five hundred years ago, whether this passage has already been fulfilled.

The land of Israel has been the scene of many wars, and invasions have come from various parts of the world, north, east, and south. Many times the march of soldiers' feet has been heard crossing the little nation of Israel. The Bible records some of these wars and some of them have occurred since the canon of Scripture was closed. It would be difficult to examine the details of all these wars; however, if one did, he would find that none of them correspond to this prophecy. There never has been a war with Israel which fulfills the prophecies of Ezekiel 38 and 39. If one believes that the Bible is the Word of God and that it is infallible and must be fulfilled, the only logical conclusion is that this portion of Scripture, like many others, is still due a future fulfillment.

THE IDENTIFICATION OF RUSSIA

In beginning the study of this chapter, it is necessary to establish beyond any question that this passage deals with the nation Russia, inasmuch as the term itself does not occur. There are a number of important factors which lead to the conclusion that the only nation which could possibly fulfill the specifications of these two chapters is the nation Russia. In the study of this chapter the American Standard Version will be used because of its clarification of certain difficult passages.

First of all, it is important to note the geographic description which is given. The terms "king of the north" and "king of the south" were used in Daniel 11:5-35 to describe the rulers to the north and south of Palestine who engaged in constant warfare in the second and third centuries B.C. This is now fulfilled prophecy. The king of the north and king of the south of Daniel 11:40-45, however, are future rulers involved in warfare in the end time. This is still unfulfilled prophecy. Ezekiel 38 and 39 fit into this future picture.

According to Ezekiel, the invading armies come to the land of Israel from "the uttermost part of the north" or as we would put it from the far north. In the Authorized Version the expression is translated merely "from the north," but in the more literal translation of the Hebrew found in the American Standard Version it is rendered, "the uttermost parts of the north," i.e., the extreme north. The important point is that it designates not merely the direction from which the army attacks Israel, but specifies the geographic origination of the army from a territory located in the far north. The house of Togarmah, one of the nations that is associated with Russia in this invasion, also comes from "the uttermost parts of the north" (Ezekiel 38:6).

A similar statement concerning the invader is made in verse 15, "Thou shalt come from thy place out of the uttermost parts of the north, thou, and many peoples with thee, all of them riding upon horses, a great company and a mighty army" (ASV). Again in Ezekiel 39:2, God says to them, "I will turn thee about, and will lead thee on, and will cause thee to come up from the uttermost parts of the north; and I will bring thee upon the mountains of Israel" (ASV). Three times in these chapters this army is stated to come from the extreme north.

If one takes any map of the world and draws a line north of the land of Israel he will inevitably come to the nation Russia. As soon as the line is drawn to the far north beyond Asia Minor and the Black Sea it is in Russia and continues to be in Russia for many hundreds of miles all the way to the Arctic Circle. Russia today spreads east and west some 6,000 miles, and one cannot escape Russia if he goes north of the Holy Land. On the basis of geography alone, it seems quite clear that the only nation which could possibly be referred to as coming from the far north would be the nation Russia. The suggestion that the nation is ancient Assyria revived is rendered improbable by the geographic description.

As the Scriptures are further examined, not only geographic data but also some confirming linguistic evidence is discovered. In the opening portion of Ezekiel 38, in verses 1 through 6, some names are mentioned which identify the invaders. This portion indicates that the Word of the Lord came to Ezekiel saying,

> Son of man, set thy face toward Gog, of the land of Magog, the prince of Rosh, Meshech, and Tubal, and prophesy against him, and say, Thus saith the Lord Jehovah: Behold, I am against thee, O Gog, prince of Rosh, Meshech, and Tubal: and I will turn thee about, and put hooks into thy jaws, and I will bring thee forth, and all thine army, horses and horsemen, all of them clothed in full armor, a great

company with buckler and shield, all of them handling swords: Persia, Cush and Put with them, all of them with shield and helmet; Gomer, and all his hordes; the house of Togarmah in the uttermost parts of the north, and all his hordes; even many peoples with thee (ASV).

Most of the terms in this portion of Scripture are quite strange to us and do not immediately connote anything relating to Russia. Certain facts are discovered as the passage is examined more particularly. This portion of Scripture is a message from God delivered by the prophet Ezekiel, directed to a person whose name is Gog, who is described as of the land of Magog and apparently the ruler of this land. The term "Magog" is mentioned in Genesis 10:2. There we learn that Magog was the second son of Japheth, the son of Noah.

Magog is best identified with the Scythians, a people descended from Magog. The ancient historian Josephus makes that identification and we have no reason to question it. The Scythians apparently lived immediately to the north of what was later to be the land of Israel, then some of them emigrated north, going all the way to the Arctic Circle. In other words, their posterity was scattered precisely over the geographical area that today is called Russia.

In Ezekiel 38 Gog is described as "the prince of Rosh" (ASV). The Authorized Version expresses it as the "chief prince." The translation, "the prince of Rosh," is a more literal rendering of the Hebrew. "Rosh" may be the root of the modern term, Russia. In the study of how ancient words come into modern language, it is quite common for the consonants to remain the same and the vowels to be changed. In the word "Rosh," if the vowel "o" is changed to "u" it becomes the root of the modern word, Russia, with the suffix added. In other words, the word itself seems to be an early form of the word from which the modern word, Russia, comes. Gesenius, the famous lexicographer, gives the assurance that this is a proper identification, that is, that Rosh is an early form of the word from which we get Russia.

The two terms, "Meshech" and "Tubal," also correspond to some prominent words in Russia. The term "Meshech" is similar to the modern name Moscow, and "Tubal," obviously, is similar to the name of one of the prominent Asiatic provinces of Russia, the province of Tobolsk. When this evidence is put together, it points to the conclusion that these terms are early references to portions of Russia, and therefore, the geographic argument is reinforced by the linguistic argument and supports the idea that this invading force comes from Russia.

As the prophecy is examined further it becomes obvious that the invaders utterly disregard God, because any nation that attacks the nation of Israel by so much is disregarding the Word of God. The godlessness of the invading army attacking Israel also points the finger to the nation Russia. On the basis of these three arguments, the geographic argument, the linguistic argument, and what might be called the theological argument, it may be concluded that the reference is to the nation Russia. In fact, there is no other reasonable alternative. Russia is today the only nation which seems to fit the picture.

A number of nations are associated with Russia in the invasion, but not too much is known about them. Persia, of course, is in that general area. Cush is another name for Ethiopia, which poses a problem because today Ethiopia is to the south. The term *Cush* may have been applied to other geographic areas, including that to the north of the land of Israel. The term, "Put," is a difficult expression about which little is known. In verse 6 the term, "Gomer," is identified by most as referring to the ancient Cimmerians, a portion of whom lived in what today is called southern or western Germany. Togarmah is commonly recognized as referring to the Armenians, who at one time lived immediately north of the land of Israel, and they, too, to some extent emigrated to the north. The nations which accompany Russia, for the most part, fit properly into the picture of assisting Russia in this invasion of the land of Israel.

THE PREDICTED INVASION OF ISRAEL

The actual invasion is described in Ezekiel 38:8-12. Some of the distinctive facts mentioned about the particular situation which will exist when this war begins are of utmost significance in the light of the world situation today. In this passage the "thou" refers through-out to Russia or to Gog. The term "they" is used to refer to Israel. Beginning in verse 8 and continuing through verse 16, the passage reads as follows:

> After many days thou shalt be visited: in the latter years thou shalt come into the land that is brought back from the sword, that is gathered out of many peoples, upon the mountains of Israel, which have been a continual waste; but it is brought forth out of the peoples, and they shall dwell securely, all of them. And thou shalt ascend, thou shalt come like a storm, thou shalt be like a cloud to cover the land, thou, and all thy hordes, and many peoples with thee.
>
> Thus saith the Lord Jehovah: It shall come to pass in that day, that things shall come into thy mind, and thou shalt devise an evil device: and thou shalt say, I will go up to the land of unwalled villages; I will go to them that are at rest, that dwell securely, all of them dwelling without walls, and having neither bars nor gates; to take the spoil and to take the prey; to turn thy hand against the waste places that are now inhabited, and against the people that are gathered out of the nations, that have gotten cattle and goods, that

dwell in the middle of the earth. Sheba, and Dedan, and the merchants of Tarshish, with all the young lions thereof, shall say unto thee, Art thou come to take the spoil? hast thou assembled thy company to take the prey? to carry away silver and gold, to take away cattle and goods, to take great spoil?

Therefore, son of man, prophesy, and say unto Gog, Thus saith the Lord Jehovah: In that day when my people Israel dwelleth securely, shalt thou not know it? And thou shalt come from thy place out of the uttermost parts of the north, thou, and many peoples with thee, all of them riding upon horses, a great company and a mighty army; and thou shalt come up against my people Israel, as a cloud to cover the land: it shall come to pass in the latter days, that I will bring thee against my land, that the nations may know me, when I shall be sanctified in thee, O Gog, before their eyes (ASV).

INVASION AFTER ISRAEL'S REGATHERING

Some highly significant facts are given in the above passage concerning the precise situation existing when the invasion takes place. There are a number of references to the fact that the people of Israel are back in their ancient land. This of course is of tremendous importance because it is only in our generation that the people of Israel have gone back to their ancient land. In A.D. 70, Titus, the Roman general, conquered Jerusalem, utterly destroyed it, and killed up to a million of the Jews. Roman soldiers later systematically went throughout the entire land of Israel destroying every building, sawing down or uprooting every tree, and doing everything they could to make the land totally uninhabitable. The result was that the land of Israel lay in waste for several generations. The children of Israel from that day to this have been scattered over the face of the earth.

At the close of World War II the children of Israel began to return to their ancient land in large numbers. Some had gone earlier, but they were few in number. They built up their strength and numbers until finally they were recognized as a nation in May, 1948. At that time one million Jews were back in their ancient land, the largest return since the days of the Exodus. In the years since, their number has doubled, and today there are two million Israelites under their own flag, speaking the Hebrew language, and reviving and restoring their ancient land to a scene of fertility, wealth, and prosperity. These facts are tremendously significant, for the return of Israel has occurred in our generation.

Ezekiel's prophecy obviously could not have been fulfilled prior to 1945, for the nation Israel was not regathered to their ancient land. Until our generation, Israel's situation did not correspond to that which is described in Ezekiel's passage. Ezekiel's prophecy of twenty-five hundred years ago seems to have anticipated the return of Israel to their ancient land as a prelude to the climax of this present age.

INVASION AFTER REBUILDING OF CITIES

Another important aspect of the prophecy is found in verse eleven where it states that the people of Israel will be dwelling "securely, all of them dwelling without walls, and having neither bars nor gates." It was customary in ancient times, whenever a city prospered, to build a wall around it. One can go to ancient lands and see the ruins of walls around most important cities. They would, at least, have a fortress with a wall around it to which they could retire if the houses themselves were scattered and a wall about the houses was impracticable. In other words, it was customary to build walls about cities. In our modern day, this custom has been discontinued for the obvious reason that a wall is no protection against modern warfare.

If one goes to Israel today, though one can see many fabulous cities being built and marvelous developments taking place, one will not find a single new city with a wall built around it. They are cities without walls. How did Ezekiel know that at a future time the war situation would be such that cities would be built without walls? Of course, the answer is a simple one. He was guided by the inspiration of God, and it was not a matter of his own wisdom. But in this scene he is describing a modern situation, something that could not and would not be true back in the days of old, before Christ. This detail is very important because un-walled villages point to Israel's situation today.

INVASION AT A TIME OF ISRAEL'S PROSPERITY

A third feature may also be observed. This portion of Scripture is explicit that one of the reasons why Russia wants to conquer the land of Israel is that it had become a land of great wealth. Russia comes to take a prey, to take silver and gold, and the wealth that has been accumulated (cp. Ezekiel 38:12, 13). Until our generation, the geographic area of the land of Israel was anything but something to be prized. It did not have any wealth; it was a land that was strewn with stones; a land that was backward as far as civilization is concerned. Many of the areas that at one time were fruitful in Bible times were unused prior to Israel's reclamation. The land was eroded and useless as far as agriculture is concerned.

Since the Israelites have gone back to their ancient land, they have done fabulous things. They have taken rocky fields, gathered the stones in piles along the edge, and cultivated and irrigated the ground and made it to bring forth abundantly. They have reclaimed swamps where mosquitoes and malaria made civilization impossible before. In fact, the first people that tried to do something about it lost their lives because of the unhealthy situation. These former swamps are today one of the richest areas of farm land in the entire world. It is almost incredible what has occurred there since 1948. They have spent money, they have put forth extreme effort, and from one end of Israel to the other tremendous progress is in evidence. The result is today that Israel is beginning once again to be a nation that has wealth. A great deal is being exported to other countries, and money is beginning to flow back to the little nation of Israel.

In addition to agricultural wealth, there are some factors that Ezekiel did not know which we know today. One factor is that to the east of the land of Israel are tremendous oil reserves. One of the largest and richest oil fields in the entire world is in the Middle East. It is outside the present geographic area of Israel, but the nation that wants to control that oil land must control the nation Israel. It is obvious that the tremendous oil reserves of the Middle East are one of the prizes that Russia wants to secure.

Another aspect of wealth which has come to light in modern times is the chemical value of the Dead Sea area, where water has evaporated for centuries, leaving its mineral deposit. Israel has established a plant at the south end of the Dead Sea and is reclaiming the chemicals. Millions of dollars of those chemicals are being shipped, and they have just begun to tap this wealth. Ezekiel anticipated the time when the land of Israel would be fabulously wealthy.

MILITARY IMPORTANCE OF ISRAEL

In addition to all these factors, it is obvious that the geographic location of the Middle East, being as it is a hub between three major continents—Europe, Asia, and Africa—is of tremendous strategic importance to any nation that wants to dominate the world. The geographic significance of the Middle East alone would be worth a real effort on the part of Russia to have this portion of the world under its control. Again Ezekiel anticipates today's situation.

THE DESTRUCTION OF THE INVADING ARMY

When the Russian army comes down upon this land they are met with complete and utter destruction. Strange to say, as we examine the Scriptures, we do not find them being destroyed by an opposing army, but rather it seems to be by divine intervention. Somehow God by His own power destroys the army. In Ezekiel 38:19, 20 a description is given of earthquakes, mountains falling, and other disturbances which hinder their progress.

Then God declares:

> And I will call for a sword against him unto all my mountains, saith the Lord Jehovah: every man's sword shall be against his brother. And with pestilence and with blood will I enter into judgment with him; and I will rain upon him, and upon his hordes, and upon the many peoples that are with him, an overflowing shower, and great hailstones, fire, and brimstone. And I will magnify myself, and sanctify myself, and I will make myself known in the eyes of many nations; and they shall know that I am Jehovah (Ezekiel 38:21-23, ASV).

The army's destruction is portrayed in Ezekiel 39:4ff. God declares: "Thou shalt fall upon the mountains of Israel, thou, and all thy hordes, and the peoples that are with thee: I will give thee unto the ravenous birds of every sort, and to the beasts of the field to be devoured." In other words, the army is completely destroyed, and the means used are earthquakes, hailstones, fire and brimstone. It seems also that parts of the army begin to fight each other, so that every man's sword is against his brother.

Some natural questions are raised about this. Some have suggested that the description of hailstones, fire and brimstone might be

Ezekiel's way of describing modern warfare, such as atomic warfare. There is a possibility that Ezekiel was using terms that he knew to describe a future situation for which he did not have a vocabulary. The language of Scripture indicates, however, that the victory over this invading horde is something that God does. It is God, Himself, who is destroying the army.

In any case, regardless of the means, the army is completely destroyed and chapter 39 goes on to describe the aftermath. For months thereafter they have the awful task of burying the dead. For a long period after that men are given full-time employment as additional bodies are discovered, and the process of burial continues. Attention is also directed to the debris of the battle. It is used as kindling wood for some seven years. The general character of this battle and its outcome seems to be quite clear, even though we may have some questions and problems about the details.

TIME OF THE INVASION

One of the principal questions one could ask about this battle is, When is the battle going to occur? It has not occurred in the past. What indication do we have in this portion of Scripture that the battle will occur at a specific time? Unfortunately, varying opinions have been offered by capable Bible scholars on this point, and there has been considerable disagreement. Some have felt that the battle will take place before the rapture, others believe it will take place in connection with the battle of Armageddon, or the battle of the Great Day of God Almighty, at the end of the great tribulation. Some place it at the beginning of the millennium, as an act of rebellion against Christ. Some find it at the end of the millennium, for there is a reference to Gog and Magog in Revelation 20. Others put it in the earlier part of Daniel's seventieth week, just before the great tribulation.

It will not be possible to consider all these views in detail, but there are some hints that provide a good clue as to when this battle will take place. One of the hints given is that the battle takes place at a time when Israel has been regathered into their ancient land, and are dwelling securely and at rest. There are not too many times when Israel is at rest in God's prophetic program. They have been scattered and persecuted over the face of the earth, and not even in the future will Israel have many periods of rest.

Certainly Israel is not at rest today. Israel is an armed camp, living under a truce with their Arab neighbors about them. Their enemies would drive every Israelite into the Mediterranean Sea and kill them if they could. The reason that they do not is because, humanly speaking, Israel has a good army which is more than a match for its neighbors. Today an armed truce and a no-man's land separate Israel from their enemy.

Every young Israeli man is required to have two and one-half years of military training and every young woman two years of military training. While the women are trained for jobs that are not necessarily of combatant type, they also learn to use weapons, so that if they need to fight, they can. After military training, many of them are settled in villages near the border, where they can serve a double purpose—following their occupation, whatever it is, and serving as guards for the border of Israel. Israel's state of unrest does not correspond to Ezekiel's prophecy. If Russia should invade the Middle East today, it would not be a fulfillment of this portion of Scripture. That has to take place when Israel is at rest.

One point at which Israel will be at rest is in the millennial kingdom. But we are told expressly that, in the millennial kingdom, there will be no war (Isaiah 2:4), and only when the rebellion occurs at the end of the millennium when Satan is let loose (Revelation 20:7-9) does war break out. Certainly Israel is not going to be at rest under these circumstances either, once Satan is let loose.

Some have suggested that Israel will be at rest in the period of great tribulation, and that the prophecy of Russia will be fulfilled at that time. In the time of great tribulation, Israel will not be at rest, for Christ told them to flee to the mountains to escape their persecutors. Therefore the invasion described by Ezekiel could not be a part of the battle of Armageddon, or the battle of the Great Day of God Almighty.

There is only one period in the future that clearly fits this description of Ezekiel, and that is the first half of Daniel's seventieth week of God's program for Israel (Daniel 9:27). After the church has been raptured and saints have been raised from the dead and the living saints have been caught up to be with the Lord, a confederacy of nations will emerge in the Mediterranean Sea. Out of that confederacy will come a strong man who will become its dictator (discussed in previous chapters). He is described in Daniel 9:26 as "the prince that shall come." He will enter into a seven-year covenant of protection and peace with the people of Israel (Daniel 9:27).

Under that covenant, Israel will be able to relax, for their Gentile enemies will have become their friends, apparently guaranteed their borders and promised them freedom. During that first three and one-half years, we have the one time when regathered Israel is at rest and secure. Apparently Russia will invade the land of Israel during that period, possibly toward its close, and the Scripture will then be fulfilled.

PROBLEMS OF INTERPRETATION

There are some other problems in the passage which merit study. A reference is made to bows and arrows, to shields and chariots, and to swords. These, of course, are antiquated weapons from the standpoint of modern warfare. The large use of horses is understandable as Russia today uses horses a great deal in connection with their army. But why should they use armor, spears, bows and arrows? This certainly poses a problem.

There have been two or more answers given. One of them is this that Ezekiel is using language with which he was familiar—the weapons that were common in his day—to anticipate modern weapons. What he is saying is that when this army comes, it will be fully equipped with the weapons of war. Such an interpretation, too, has problems. We are told in the passage that they used the wooden shafts of the spears and the bow and arrows for kindling wood. If these are symbols, it would be difficult to burn symbols. However, even in modern warfare there is a good deal of wood used. Possibly this is the explanation. We are not in a position today to settle this problem with any finality.

A second solution is that the battle is preceded by a disarmament agreement between nations. If this were the case, it would be necessary to resort to primitive weapons easily and secretly made if a surprise attack were to be achieved. This would allow a literal interpretation of the passage.

A third solution has also been suggested based on the premise that modern missile warfare will have developed in that day to the point where missiles will seek out any considerable amount of metal. Under these circumstances, it would be necessary to abandon the large use of metal weapons and substitute wood such as is indicated in the primitive weapons. Whatever the explanation, the most sensible interpretation is that the passage refers to actual weapons pressed into use because of the peculiar circumstances of that day.

THE FUTURE OF RUSSIA

The general character of the passage, the nature of the war, the invasion when it comes, and the outcome is, however, perfectly clear. What significance does it have to the modern scene? First of all, if we understand the passage correctly, Russia, instead of being a nation which is going to dominate the whole world, is headed for a tremendous military defeat. It is not possible to predict what is going to happen between now and the time this battle takes place, but the Bible seems quite clear that there is no room for a Russian-dominated world empire. The Bible prophesies only four world empires. The empire of the great tribulation period which will come as a form of the revived Roman Empire, is the final form of the fourth empire of Daniel, not a Russian Empire. This, in turn, will be succeeded by the millennial reign of Christ.

The passage seems to confirm that Russia, instead of becoming a world power that is going to dominate the whole world, is instead headed for an awful defeat, a judgment from God because of its blasphemy and ungodliness. If this becomes true during the time of the seventieth week of Daniel, it may explain something that otherwise might be difficult.

THE EMERGENCE OF A WORLD EMPIRE

We know that in the last half of Daniel's seventieth week there will be a world government headed by the ruler of the Mediterranean confederacy. The question is, how does he forge this world empire so quickly and so easily, and apparently without fighting for it? We learn in Revelation 13:4 that the question is asked, "Who is able to make war with him?" i.e., with the Beast. The answer is that nobody is able to make war with him. It should be obvious that if Russia and her satellites are destroyed as military powers, the other side of the balance of power, represented by the Mediterranean confederacy, is then in a position to dominate the whole world. Nobody is able, for at least a time, to contest their right to rule.

The destruction of the Russian army may be the preface to the world government which will sweep the world during the last half of

Daniel's seventieth week and be in power at the time Christ comes back to establish His millennial kingdom. These two portions of Scripture, while they concern themselves with a future war, are of tremendous significance as we face the present world scene and the dominance of Russia as a military power. We can trust that God, in due time, and perhaps sooner than we think, will bring these Scriptures to their sure conclusion and fulfillment.[1]

APPENDIX 3

COMMON QUESTIONS RELATED TO RUSSIA, THE MIDDLE EAST, AND THE END OF DAYS

1. DOES THE BIBLE PREDICT A WAR BETWEEN THE UNITED STATES AND RUSSIA?

Just days before he died on the cross Jesus said that the end times will be punctuated by military conflict: "You will hear of wars and threats of wars, but don't panic. Yes, these things must take place, but the end won't follow immediately. Nation will go to war against nation, and kingdom against kingdom" (Matthew 24:6-7).

Since the United States and Russia are the two most powerful military machines in the world and have engaged in a seventy-year standoff, it's reasonable to wonder whether these two powers will come to blows in the future. Inquiring minds want to know.

We've seen in this book that Russia is referenced in Scripture in Ezekiel 38–39. Russia will be a part of the first main war of the end times—the War of Gog and Magog. America, on the other hand, is not mentioned in the Bible, at least explicitly. All agree that the words *America* or *the United States* are absent from Scripture, but some believe they've discovered symbolic references to the US in three main texts: the unnamed nation in Isaiah 18:1-2, Babylon in

Revelation 17–19, or "the merchants of Tarshish, with all the young lions" (KJV) in Ezekiel 38:13. One other view is that America is the ten lost tribes of Israel.

Ezekiel 38:13 and its reference to "the merchants of Tarshish, with all the young lions" (KJV) is the only one of the four views that could possibly refer to the United States. The others are tenuous at best.

The words "young lions" are employed in Scripture to refer to energetic rulers, so this could refer to leaders or the nations that have come out of Tarshish.[1]

Tarshish in Ezekiel's day was in the most distant western region of the known world. In Jonah 1:1-3, when God called the prophet Jonah to go east to preach to Nineveh, Jonah went as far as he could to the west, to Tarshish, a Phoenician colony likely in what today is Spain.

We discussed this briefly in chapter 4. The young lions and the merchants of Tarshish could be a reference to the lands that emerged from Spain, including the nations of South and Central America. Some contend that ancient Tarshish was actually in England. If this view is correct, the "young lions" could represent "the United States, Canada, Australia, New Zealand, and other present-day western democracies."[2] This would be a clear biblical reference to the role of America in the end times.

In any event, nothing in this passage refers to a war between the United States and Russia. Ezekiel 38:13 presents Tarshish and the young lions as sitting on the sidelines when Russia attacks Israel, not engaging in battle. So even if the merchants of Tarshish is a veiled reference to the United States, it points toward Russia and the US once again avoiding an all-out showdown of forces.

Russia and the United States may square off militarily at some point in the future, but the Bible doesn't speak to this issue one way or the other.

2. DOES THE BIBLE PREDICT THE USE OF NUCLEAR WEAPONS IN THE END TIMES?

The dawn of the nuclear age in the 1940s ushered in a staggering new reality—humanity's ability to blow up this planet. Since that time, fears have mounted that the world will end in a nuclear nightmare. This fear was palpable during the tense days of the Cold War. Anyone growing up in the 1950s through the 1970s remembers the tangible threat of nuclear war. Russia has the world's largest stockpile of nukes, followed closely by the United States. During the Cold War, the threat of a nuclear exchange was a sum-of-all-fears scenario.

In the last twenty years, the proliferation of nuclear weapons has changed everything. Pakistan, India, and China have nuclear weapons. North Korea and its bizarre leader have the bomb, and the world watches as Kim Jong-un conducts ballistic missile tests in an effort to obtain a missile that can deliver a nuclear payload to the United States. Terrorist states like Iran are waiting in the wings to join the nuclear club.

With this many nuclear players on the scene, and with Russia as the leader of the pack, many people want to know if the Bible predicts the use of nuclear weapons in the end times. In today's volatile international environment, it's reasonable to wonder whether the Bible addresses this critical question.

Three main biblical passages are cited in support of the view that a nuclear exchange is prophesied in the latter years:

The LORD will send a plague on all the nations that fought against Jerusalem. Their people will become like walking corpses, their flesh rotting away. Their eyes will rot in their sockets, and their tongues will rot in their mouths.

ZECHARIAH 14:12

By the same word, the present heavens and earth have
been stored up for fire. They are being kept for the day of
judgment, when ungodly people will be destroyed. . . . But
the day of the Lord will come as unexpectedly as a thief.
Then the heavens will pass away with a terrible noise, and
the very elements themselves will disappear in fire, and
the earth and everything on it will be found to deserve
judgment. . . . On that day, he will set the heavens on fire,
and the elements will melt away in the flames.

2 PETER 3:7, 10, 12

The first angel blew his trumpet, and hail and fire mixed
with blood were thrown down on the earth. One-third of
the earth was set on fire, one-third of the trees were burned,
and all the green grass was burned.

Then the second angel blew his trumpet, and a great
mountain of fire was thrown into the sea. One-third of the
water in the sea became blood, one-third of all things living
in the sea died, and one-third of all the ships on the sea were
destroyed.

Then the third angel blew his trumpet, and a great star
fell from the sky, burning like a torch. It fell on one-third of
the rivers and on the springs of water. The name of the star
was Bitterness. It made one-third of the water bitter, and
many people died from drinking the bitter water.

Then the fourth angel blew his trumpet, and one-third
of the sun was struck, and one-third of the moon, and one-
third of the stars, and they became dark. And one-third of
the day was dark, and also one-third of the night.

REVELATION 8:7-12

Each of these passages describes devastating destruction. Revelation 8 even mentions objects falling from the sky that contaminate the planet, much like a nuclear explosion would.

In each of these passages I believe the context is clear that the destruction comes from the hand of God, not nuclear detonation. Even in Revelation 8, the ecological disasters are explicitly traced to God as the source of these judgments, not some madman. The seven seal judgments in Revelation 6 are opened and unleashed by Jesus, and the seventh seal judgment in Revelation 8:1 contains the seven trumpets. Therefore, it follows that the trumpets are also divine judgments. This point is further strengthened in that the trumpet judgments are very similar to the Egyptian plagues in the book of Exodus. They are even called plagues in Revelation 9:20. The Egyptian plagues were not natural occurrences or man-made; they were direct judgments from God.

Nuclear weapons may be used in the near future or during the end times. As weapons of mass destruction mushroom, it's difficult to see how they can be kept out of the hands of unstable leaders or terrorists. However, I don't believe the Bible says anything about nuclear weapons. When the Bible is silent, we're wise not to go beyond what's written.

3. DOES THE BIBLE PREDICT THE DESTRUCTION OF SYRIA IN THE END TIMES?

Since the founding of the modern state of Israel in 1948, Syria has remained an entrenched enemy of Israel. The two nations have faced off in three bloody wars: the War of Independence (1948), the Six-Day War (1967), and the Yom Kippur War (1973). The loss of the Golan Heights to Israel in 1973 was a major blow to the Syrians.

Since early 2011, and the outbreak of civil war, Syria has been a major international flash point. The brutality of Bashar al-Assad has been on full display for the world to see. More than four hundred thousand Syrians have died in the bloody civil war. Russia and Iran have propped up the Assad regime, sending troops and air power. For Iran, Syria is part of the strategy for a "Shiite full moon" across the region. For Russia, presence in Syria expands Russian influence, and many believe Russia is using the chaos to flood Europe with refugees, further stretching and weakening European financial resources and increasing the threat of terror in Europe.

About five million Syrian refugees have fled the country, and more than six million within the nation have been displaced. Most Syrian refugees have relocated in the Middle East, but more than half a million have come to the shores of European nations. With mounting deaths and displacement, the Syrian refugee crisis has been called "the worst human security disaster of the twenty-first century."[3]

Added to all this misery, ISIS has focused much of its effort in Syria primarily because Dabiq, Syria, "is where the Prophet Mohammed is supposed to have predicted that the armies of Islam and 'Rome' would meet for the final battle that will precede the end of time and the triumph of true Islam."[4]

Questions about Syria are closely related to Russia because the chaos in Syria has afforded Russia a unique opportunity to accomplish many of its goals and has brought Russia, Iran, and Turkey into closer alliance.

With all these factors converging in Syria, many prophecy teachers believe the world focus on Syria in the last few years points toward the fulfillment of Isaiah 17 in the near future. Isaiah 17:1-2 prophesies the destruction of Damascus, Syria's capital: "Look, the city of Damascus will disappear! It will become a heap of ruins. The towns of Aroer will be deserted. Flocks will graze in the streets and lie down undisturbed, with no one to chase them away."

Many who believe the fulfillment of this prophecy is imminent hold that Israel will take out Damascus, possibly by a nuclear attack, while others believe the destruction will be supernatural. Often only the first two verses of Isaiah 17 are quoted, yet if we continue reading the passage, we find it also predicts the destruction of northern Israel at the same time. In Isaiah's day, Ephraim was the name for the Northern Kingdom of Israel. Notice that at the same time Damascus is destroyed, Israel is too:

"The fortified towns of Israel [NASB, "Ephraim"] will also
    be destroyed,
    and the royal power of Damascus will end.
All that remains of Syria
    will share the fate of Israel's departed glory,"
    declares the LORD of Heaven's Armies.

"In that day Israel's glory will grow dim;
    its robust body will waste away.
The whole land will look like a grainfield
    after the harvesters have gathered the grain.
It will be desolate,
    like the fields in the valley of Rephaim after the harvest.
Only a few of its people will be left,
    like stray olives left on a tree after the harvest.
Only two or three remain in the highest branches,
    four or five scattered here and there on the limbs,"
    declares the LORD, the God of Israel.

Then at last the people will look to their Creator
    and turn their eyes to the Holy One of Israel.
They will no longer look to their idols for help
    or worship what their own hands have made.
ISAIAH 17:3-8

In light of the overall context of Isaiah 17, I believe the best interpretation sees the fulfillment of this passage in the eighth century BC, when both Damascus, the capital of Syria (732 BC), and Samaria, the capital of Israel (722 BC), were pounded by the Assyrians. In the Assyrian invasion of Syria and Israel, there's a clear point in time when both Damascus and Samaria were destroyed, just as Isaiah 17 predicts.

The past fulfillment of Isaiah 17 finds further confirmation in Isaiah 17:12-14, which was fulfilled in 701 BC, when 185,000 Assyrians under the command of Sennacherib were destroyed in one night by God (see Isaiah 37:36-38).

As the fuse on the Middle East powder keg continues to burn, Syria, although not specifically singled out in Scripture, seems to be a key player in setting the stage. The chaos in Syria has created the vacuum for Russia and Iran to fill. Their presence in Syria on Israel's northern border foreshadows the future invasion of Israel by these nations and their allies in Ezekiel 38.

4. WHY IS IT TAKING SO LONG FOR JESUS TO RETURN?

Three times in the final chapter of the New Testament, Jesus promises to come back "soon" or "quickly" (see Revelation 22:7, 12, 20). As early as about thirty years after the death, resurrection, and ascension of Jesus, people were beginning to question and even mock the truth of Christ's return because it had not happened. The promise of his soon coming seemed to be fading away. They mistakenly believed that the delay of his coming equaled nonfulfillment. The apostle Peter challenged these first-century mockers and their erroneous thinking:

> Most importantly, I want to remind you that in the last days
> scoffers will come, mocking the truth and following their
> own desires. They will say, "What happened to the promise

that Jesus is coming again? From before the times of our ancestors, everything has remained the same since the world was first created."

2 PETER 3:3-4

If people within three decades of Christ's ascension were wondering why it was taking so long for Jesus to return, then certainly people must be wondering the same thing almost two thousand years later.

A general answer to this question is found in the first coming of Jesus. God had a perfect time for his Son to come to earth the first time. Galatians 4:4 says, "But when the right time came, God sent his Son, born of a woman, subject to the law." The world stage was perfectly arranged for the coming of Jesus and the spread of the gospel: the Roman peace (*Pax Romana*) had brought relative stability to the world, Greek was a common language for the writing of the New Testament, and the Roman road system was a powerful means for taking the gospel all over the world of that day.

In the same way, we can rest assured that a sovereign God has a perfect time, known only to him, for the return of his Son. The Bible is clear that "God keeps his own calendar."[5]

More specifically, while we don't know every reason behind God's timing, he has told us at least two reasons for this apparent delay in his coming in 2 Peter 3:8-15. First, "God's calendar is a *heavenly* calendar."[6] As we read in 2 Peter 3:8, "You must not forget this one thing, dear friends: A day is like a thousand years to the Lord, and a thousand years is like a day." This refers to God's relationship to time. God views time differently than we do. "God's 'delay' is not really a delay at all in the dimensions of his existence. . . . We see the movement of time as a sequential series of still frames, passing one-by-one, as in a motion picture, but God sees the entire movement at once."[7]

D. Edmond Hiebert explains: "The point is not that time has no meaning for God but rather that His use of time is extensive, so that He may use a thousand years to do what we might feel should be done in a day, as well as intensive, doing in a day what we might feel could only be done in a thousand years."[8] One way to understand the passage of time before Christ's coming is God's heavenly calendar, viewing time from his vantage point.

Second, "God's calendar is an *evangelistic* calendar."[9] This deals with God's use of time. Second Peter 3:9, 15 says, "The Lord isn't really being slow about his promise, as some people think. No, he is being patient for your sake. He does not want anyone to be destroyed, but wants everyone to repent. . . . And remember, our Lord's patience gives people time to be saved."

The extended time between Christ's two comings serves a redemptive purpose and underscores the patience and longsuffering of God. "God guides all human history as salvation history, moving nations and people groups to meet the appointments for redemption made for those who will hear the gospel and receive the Savior."[10] The "slowness" in Christ's coming is not the result of divine indifference, powerlessness, or distraction, but rather the gracious patience of God toward sinners in need of salvation.

Michael Green says, "It is not slowness but patience that delays the consummation of all history, and holds open the door to repentant sinners, even repentant scoffers. Not impotence but mercy is the reason for God's delay."[11] The character of God moves him to patiently wait to send his Son.

Since one of the reasons for the apparent delay of Christ's coming is God's mercy for sinners, believers should be alert to opportunities God gives us to be part of the "hastening" of his coming by sharing the Good News with those around us. Rather than wondering or worrying about the delay, may we be moved by God to keep working in light of his mercy and patience.

NOTES

CHAPTER 1: THERE IS A BEAR IN THE WOODS

1. "Vladimir Putin," *Forbes*, accessed May 5, 2017, https://www.forbes.com/profile
/vladimir-putin/.
2. "Putin Deplores Collapse of USSR," *BBC News*, April 25, 2005, http://news.bbc
.co.uk/2/hi/4480745.stm.
3. Pavlo Klimkin, "Putin's Desire for a New Russian Empire Won't Stop with Ukraine,"
Guardian, March 25, 2017, https://www.theguardian.com/commentisfree/2017
/mar/25/putin-new-russian-empire-ukraine.
4. Jana Bakunina, "In Russia, Stalin Is Back," *NewStatesman*, October 6, 2015,
http://www.newstatesman.com/world/europe/2015/10/russia-stalin-back.
5. Jonathan Adelman, "Thinking the Unthinkable: Russia Has Re-Emerged as a Great
Power," *Huffington Post*, April 19, 2016, http://www.huffingtonpost.com/jonathan
-adelman/thinking-the-unthinkable-_2_b_9720304.html.
6. Allan C. Brownfeld, "The Putin-Trump Alliance Threatens Europe, America,"
Communities Digital News, March 5, 2017, http://www.commdiginews.com/politics
-2/the-putin-trump-alliance-threatens-europe-america-84910/.
7. Olivier Knox, "Defense Secretary Pick Mattis Calls Russia Top Threat, Says Iran
Deal Will Be Enforced," Yahoo News, January 12, 2017, https://www.yahoo
.com/news/defense-secretary-pick-mattis-says-russia-top-threat-will-enforce-iran
-deal-185357939.html; Paul Karp, "Vladimir Putin Is a Bigger Threat than ISIS,
John McCain Says," *Guardian*, May 29, 2017, http://www.theguardian.com/us
-news/2017/may/29/vladimir-putin-is-bigger-threat-than-isis-john-mccain-says.
8. Only nine nations are believed to currently have nuclear weapons. Russia has the
world's largest stockpile of nuclear warheads (7,300), followed by the US (around
7,000). Russia and the US hold 90 percent of the world's nuclear arms. The rest of
the world's nuclear powers are as follows: France (300), China (260), Britain (215),
India (130), Pakistan (120), Israel (80), North Korea (fewer than 10). Kiersten
Schmidt and Bill Marsh, "Which Countries Have Nuclear Weapons and How Big

Their Arsenals Are," *New York Times*, December 23, 2016, https://www.nytimes .com/interactive/2016/12/23/world/nuclear-weapon-countries.html.

9. Fareed Zakaria writes, "Russia is the largest country on the planet—48 times larger than Germany and encompassing 11 time zones that straddle Europe, Asia, and the Middle East." Fareed Zakaria, "Why Putin Is World's Most Powerful Man," *CNN*, March 14, 2017, http://www.cnn.com/2017/03/13/opinions/putin-most-powerful -man-world-zakaria/.

10. Jeff Stone, "Meet Fancy Bear and Cozy Bear, Russian Groups Blamed for DNC Hack," *Christian Science Monitor*, June 15, 2016, http://www.csmonitor.com/World /Passcode/2016/0615/Meet-Fancy-Bear-and-Cozy-Bear-Russian-groups-blamed-for -DNC-hack.

11. Evan Osnos, David Remnick, and Joshua Yaffa, "Trump, Putin, and the New Cold War," *New Yorker*, March 6, 2017, http://www.newyorker.com/magazine/2017/03 /06/trump-putin-and-the-new-cold-war.

12. Ibid.

13. Ibid.

14. David Ignatius, "Russia May Be Wounded, but It Can Still Bite," *Washington Post*, November 3, 2016, https://www.washingtonpost.com/opinions/russia -may-be-wounded-but-it-can-still-bite/2016/11/03/ec2287c0-a205-11e6-a44d -cc2898cfab06_story.html?tid=a_inl&utm_term=.1114581528bb.

15. Osnos, Remnick, and Yaffa, "Trump, Putin, and the New Cold War."

16. W. J. Hennigan and Tracy Wilkinson, "Scientists Move Doomsday Clock Closer to 'Midnight.' Trump's Comments on Nuclear Weapons Are a Big Reason Why," *Los Angeles Times*, January 26, 2017, http://www.latimes.com/politics/la-na-pol -trump-nuclear-weapons-20170126-story.html.

17. "Shock Poll: Startling Numbers of Americans Believe World Now in the 'End Times,'" Religion News Service, September 11, 2013, http://religionnews.com /2013/09/11/shock-poll-startling-numbers-of-americans-believe-world-now-in-the -end-times/.

18. "Public Sees a Future Full of Promise and Peril," Pew Research Center, June 22, 2010, http://www.people-press.org/2010/06/22/public-sees-a-future-full-of-promise -and-peril.

19. Jeff Brumley, "Global Events, Prophecy Stir Talk of 'End Times' Beliefs," *Florida Times-Union*, July 16, 2010, http://jacksonville.com/news/metro/2010-07-16/story /global-events-prophecy-stir-talk-end-times-beliefs.

20. Douglas Todd, "We Need to Bring End-Times Beliefs Out of Their Closet," *Vancouver Sun*, November 8, 2008, www.canada.com/vancouversun/news/editorial /story.html?id=ac308456-5493-4756-8ad6-68d.

21. Walter Einenkel, "New Survey Shows That about 80% of Evangelicals Believe the 'End Times' Are Near," *Daily Kos*, December 7, 2015, http://www.dailykos.com /story/2015/12/7/1457887/-New-survey-shows-that-about-80-of-Evangelicals -believe-the-end-times-are-near.

22. Jeremy Weber, "Survey Surprise: Many Americans See Syria as Sign of Bible's End Times," *Christianity Today*, September 13, 2013, http://www.christianitytoday .com/gleanings/2013/september/syria-survey-end-times-armageddon-lifeway.html.

23. David Jeremiah, *Is This the End? Signs of God's Providence in a Disturbing New World* (Nashville: W Publishing Group, 2016), 221.

24. Charles Dyer and Mark Tobey, *Clash of Kingdoms: What the Bible Says about Russia, ISIS, Iran, and the End Times* (Nashville: Nelson Books, 2017), 61–62.

CHAPTER 2: THE FINAL GAME OF THRONES

1. J. Dwight Pentecost, *Things to Come: A Study in Biblical Eschatology* (Grand Rapids, MI: Zondervan, 1964), 332.

2. Revelation 13:1 calls the Antichrist the "beast rising up out of the sea," which pictures the Gentile nations—see Revelation 17:15.

3. Revelation 6:1-2 describes the Antichrist as a rider on a white horse—a false messiah—who brings a brief window of peace to the earth. We know he brings peace because the next rider (in Revelation 6:3-4) destroys that peace.

4. Some today believe the Antichrist will be a Muslim, possibly even the Islamic Mahdi, but 2 Thessalonians 2:4 says the Antichrist will declare himself to be God. The central tenet of Islam is that there is one god, who is Allah. No practicing Muslim could take this step. The Islamic Mahdi could never do this.

5. Pentecost, *Things to Come*, 331–32.

6. John F. Walvoord, *The Nations in Prophecy* (Grand Rapids, MI: Zondervan, 1967), 139, 141.

7. In the previous verses (Revelation 9:1-12) a demonic invasion is described, so taking the army in Revelation 9:13-21 in the same light is consistent. Also, the way the army is described fits the demonic view. "Fire and smoke and burning sulfur" (Revelation 9:17) are associated with hell in the book of Revelation.

8. Charles C. Ryrie, *The Best Is Yet to Come* (Chicago: Moody, 1981), 69.

9. Vernon Grounds, "Jesus Is Going to Win," *Morning Glory*, January 4, 1994, 9, https://bible.org/illustration/jesus-going-win.

CHAPTER 3: IS RUSSIA *REALLY* IN THE BIBLE?

1. Reagan said this when he was governor of California. See Joel C. Rosenberg, "Ronald Reagan & Book of Ezekiel," IOM America Resources, July 11, 2011, http://archive .constantcontact.com/fs086/1101261534859/archive/1106145003521.html.

2. Douglas Stuart, for example, claims Ezekiel 38–39 is widely misinterpreted. He says, "Many people who know little about how apocalyptic prophecy is properly interpreted have tried to equate Gog with some modern 'northern' nation. . . . No modern nation is mentioned in the Bible. . . . The history of any particular modern nation is not a subject that God has chosen to cause to be incorporated into His Word." Douglas Stuart, *Ezekiel*, Mastering the Old Testament, gen. ed. Lloyd J. Ogilvie, vol. 18 (Dallas: Word Publishing, 1988), 351. Stuart doesn't take any of the nations in Ezekiel 38 literally, but he does take all the nations in Ezekiel 25–32 literally. He makes the distinction based on his designation of Ezekiel 38–39 as "apocalyptic." Yet there is nothing in the text that indicates the places in Ezekiel 38 are to be taken in any way other than literally. I agree that modern nations aren't mentioned per se in Scripture; however, I believe that the places in Ezekiel 38 are

ancient locations that represent the nations in the end times that will reside in those places.

3. Gog is mentioned before Magog, but Gog is the leader of this invasion. We will discuss the meaning of Gog in the next chapter.

4. Daniel I. Block, *The Book of Ezekiel, Chapters 25–48*, The New International Commentary on the Old Testament, gen. ed. R. K. Harrison and Robert L. Hubbard Jr. (Grand Rapids, MI: Eerdmans, 1998), 433.

5. Josephus, *Antiquities*, 1.6.1. Block places Magog in ancient Lydia in western Anatolia (modern Turkey). Block, *Book of Ezekiel*, 434.

6. *The Nelson Study Bible* (Nashville: Thomas Nelson, 1997), 1396, note on Ezekiel 38:2.

7. Charles C. Ryrie, *Ryrie Study Bible* (Chicago: Moody, 1995), 1323, note on Ezekiel 38:2. See also Mark Rooker, *Ezekiel*, Holman Old Testament Commentary, gen. ed. Max Anders (Nashville: B&H, 2005), 271.

8. Arnold G. Fruchtenbaum, *The Footsteps of the Messiah: A Study of the Sequence of Prophetic Events*, rev. ed. (Tustin, CA: Ariel Ministries, 2003), 107.

9. John MacArthur Jr., *The Future of Israel: Study Notes, Daniel 9:20–12:13* (Panorama City, CA: Word of Grace Communications, 1985), 78.

10. C. I. Scofield, ed., *The Scofield Reference Bible: The Holy Bible, Containing the Old and New Testaments* (New York: Oxford University Press, 1909), 883.

11. C. F. Keil, *Ezekiel, Daniel, Commentary on the Old Testament*, trans. James Martin, repr. (Grand Rapids, MI: Eerdmans, 1982), 159. Wilhelm Gesenius, *Gesenius' Hebrew and Chaldee Lexicon to the Old Testament Scriptures*, repr. (Grand Rapids, MI: Eerdmans, 1949), 752.

12. G. A. Cooke, *A Critical and Exegetical Commentary on the Book of Ezekiel*, ed. S. R. Driver, A. Plummer, and C. A. Briggs, The International Critical Commentary (Edinburgh: T & T Clark, 1936), 408–9.

13. John B. Taylor, *Ezekiel: An Introduction & Commentary*, Tyndale Old Testament Commentaries, gen. ed. D. J. Wiseman (Downers Grove, IL: InterVarsity, 1969), 244. For a comprehensive look at the evidence for Rosh as a place-name, see James D. Price "Rosh: An Ancient Land Known to Ezekiel," *Grace Theological Journal* 6 (1985): 67–89.

14. The mistranslation of *rosh* in many modern translations as an adjective can be traced to the Latin Vulgate of Jerome. Clyde E. Billington Jr., "The Rosh People in History and Prophecy (Part Two)" *Michigan Theological Journal* 3, no. 2 (Fall 1992): 54–61.

15. Block, *Book of Ezekiel*, 434.

16. Keil, *Ezekiel, Daniel*, 159.

17. Gesenius, *Gesenius' Hebrew and Chaldee Lexicon*, 752.

18. Joel C. Rosenberg, *Epicenter: Why the Current Rumblings in the Middle East Will Change Your Future*, rev. ed. (Carol Stream, IL: Tyndale, 2008), 86.

19. Billington, "The Rosh People (Part Two)," 145–46; Clyde E. Billington Jr., "The Rosh People in History and Prophecy (Part Three)," *Michigan Theological Journal* 4, no. 1 (Spring 1993): 59, 61; James D. Price, "Rosh: An Ancient Land Known to Ezekiel," *Grace Theological Journal* 6, no. 1 (1985): 71–73; Jon Mark Ruthven, *The Prophecy That Is Shaping History: New Research on Ezekiel's Vision of the End* (Fairfax,

VA: Xulon Press, 2003). Thomas Ice writes, "It is very likely that the name Rosh is actually derived from the name Tiras in Genesis 10:2 in the Table of Nations. Billington notes the Akkadian tendency to drop or to change an initial 't' sound in a name especially if the initial 't' was followed by an 'r' sound. If you drop the initial 'T' from Tiras you are left with 'ras.'" Thomas Ice, "Ezekiel 38 and 39: Part IV," Pre-Trib Research Center, accessed May 25, 2017, http://www.pre-trib.org/data/pdf /Ice-(Part4)Ezekiel38&39.pdf. See also Billington, "The Rosh People (Part Two)," 166–67.

20. Billington, "The Rosh People (Part Two)," 145–46.

21. It is found three times in the Septuagint (LXX), ten times in Sargon's inscriptions, once in Assurbanipal's cylinder, once in Sennacherib's annals, and five times in Ugaritic tablets. See Price, "Rosh: An Ancient Land," 71–73.

22. Billington, "The Rosh People (Part Three)," 48, 59, 61.

23. Fruchtenbaum, *Footsteps of the Messiah*, 108–9.

24. Daniel 11:40 mentions an end-time figure called the "king of the north" who will contest and challenge the authority of the final Antichrist. Because of the focus on the north in Daniel 11:40 and Ezekiel 38, John MacArthur holds that the king of the north in Daniel 11:40 is a reference to Russia and is a parallel passage to Ezekiel 38. MacArthur, *Future of Israel*, 78–79. Leon Wood also identifies the king of the north in Daniel 11:40 as Russia. See Leon Wood, *A Commentary on Daniel* (Eugene, OR: Wipf and Stock, 1998), 308–10. David Jeremiah similarly believes Daniel 11:40 "meshes perfectly" with Ezekiel's prophecy. David Jeremiah, *Is This the End? Signs of God's Providence in a Disturbing New World* (Nashville: W Publishing Group, 2016), 213.

25. John F. Walvoord, *The Nations in Prophecy* (Grand Rapids, MI: Zondervan, 1967), 106.

26. Paul P. Enns, ed., *Shepherd's Notes: Ezekiel* (Nashville: B&H, 1998), 92.

27. Walter C. Kaiser Jr., *Preaching and Teaching the Last Things: Old Testament Eschatology for the Life of the Church* (Grand Rapids, MI: Baker Academic, 2011), 92. Kaiser also believes Russia will lead the alliance of nations, referring to it as the "Russian-Iranian horde" and "Russian-Iranian coalition" (93, 95).

28. Charles Dyer and Mark Tobey, *Clash of Kingdoms: What the Bible Says about Russia, ISIS, Iran, and the End Times* (Nashville: Nelson Books, 2017), 16.

29. Charles H. Dyer, "Ezekiel," in *The Bible Knowledge Commentary*, ed. John F. Walvoord and Roy B. Zuck (Wheaton, IL: Victor Books, 1985), 1300.

30. Lamar Eugene Cooper, Sr., *Ezekiel*, The New American Commentary, vol. 17 (Nashville: B&H, 1994), 331.

31. Charles C. Ryrie, *The Best Is Yet to Come* (Chicago: Moody, 1981), 55.

32. Jeremiah, *Is This the End?*, 211.

33. J. Vernon McGee, *How Russia Will Be Destroyed: Ezekiel 38–39* (Pasadena, CA: Thru the Bible Radio Network, n.d.), 3.

34. J. Dwight Pentecost, *Things to Come: A Study in Biblical Eschatology* (Grand Rapids, MI: Zondervan, 1964), 328.

35. Rosenberg, *Epicenter*, 82, 87.

36. See, for example, Hank Hanegraaff, *Has God Spoken? Memorable Proofs of the Bible's Divine Inspiration* (Nashville: Thomas Nelson, 2011), 236.

37. Matthew Henry, "Complete Commentary on Ezekiel 38:4," *Matthew Henry's Complete Commentary on the Whole Bible* (1706), StudyLight.org, accessed June 8, 2017, http://www.studylight.org/commentaries/mhm/ezekiel-38.html.

38. Patrick Fairbairn, "The Assault of Gog and His Destruction" in *Ezekiel and the Book of His Prophecy: An Exposition* (Edinburgh: T & T Clark, 1855), 415, http://archive .org/stream/ezekielbookofhis00fairrich#page/415/mode/1up.

39. Robert Jamieson, A. R. Fausset, and David Brown, *Jamieson, Fausset & Brown's Commentary on the Whole Bible*, Zondervan Classic Reference Series (originally published as *Commentary Critical and Explanatory on the Whole Bible*, 1871), repr. (Grand Rapids, MI: Zondervan, 1961), 721.

40. William Kelly, *Notes on Ezekiel* (London: George Morrish, 1876), 195.

41. Ibid., 191, 194.

42. Arno Clemens Gaebelein, "Commentary on Ezekiel 38:4," *Gaebelein's Annotated Bible*, StudyLight.org, accessed June 8, 2017, http://www.studylight.org /commentaries/gab/ezekiel-38.html.

CHAPTER 4: EZEKIEL'S PROPHETIC INTELLIGENCE BRIEFING

1. Joel C. Rosenberg, *Epicenter: Why the Current Rumblings in the Middle East Will Change Your Future*, rev. ed. (Carol Stream, IL: Tyndale, 2008), 104.

2. Christopher J. H. Wright, *The Message of Ezekiel: A New Heart and a New Spirit*, The Bible Speaks Today, ed. J. A. Motyer (Downers Grove, IL: InterVarsity, 2001), 324–26. Eckhard Schnabel rejects a literal interpretation of Ezekiel 38–39 and cautions against pressing the details too far. He believes Ezekiel 38 is "a symbolic vision of God's ultimate victory over the enemies of his people." He adds, "It seems plausible . . . to interpret the Gog prophecy as Ezekiel's vision of the radicalized conflict between Yahweh and the nations in which Yahweh wins the final victory over the cosmic forces of chaos (represented by Gog and his allies)." Eckhard Schnabel, *40 Questions about the End Times*, ed. Benjamin L. Merkle (Grand Rapids, MI: Kregel, 2011), 224. If this view is correct, why does Ezekiel list ten specific names and give all the details he provides? I believe a symbolic interpretation fails to give due weight to all the intricate details of Ezekiel's prophecy. The symbolic view also goes against the literal fulfillment of hundreds of Old Testament prophecies (see, for example, Isaiah 7:14; 44:28–45:7; Micah 5:2). Biblical prophecies have been literally fulfilled, and this is true even in the book of Ezekiel. The prophecies in Ezekiel 4–24 concerning the coming destruction of Jerusalem were literally fulfilled. The regathering of the Jewish people in Ezekiel 37 is in the process of being fulfilled. It began in 1948. If the prophecies in Ezekiel 4–37 have been literally fulfilled, why should we interpret Ezekiel 38–39 symbolically?

3. Charles Lee Feinberg, *The Prophecy of Ezekiel: The Glory of the Lord* (Eugene, OR: Wipf and Stock, 2003), 219.

4. Charles Dyer and Mark Tobey, *Clash of Kingdoms: What the Bible Says about Russia, ISIS, Iran, and the End Times* (Nashville: Nelson Books, 2017), 21.

5. Paul P. Enns, ed., *Shepherd's Notes: Ezekiel* (Nashville: B&H, 1998), 92.

6. Charles C. Ryrie, *Ryrie Study Bible* (Chicago: Moody, 1995), 1323, note on Ezekiel

38:2. See also Mark Rooker, *Ezekiel*, Holman Old Testament Commentary, gen. ed. Max Anders (Nashville: B&H, 2005), 271.

7. C. I. Scofield, *Scofield Reference Notes* (1917 edition), note to Ezekiel 38:2, Bible Study Tools, accessed June 8, 2017, http://www.biblestudytools.com/commentaries/scofield-reference-notes/ezekiel/ezekiel-38.html.

8. Arnold G. Fruchtenbaum, *The Footsteps of the Messiah: A Study of the Sequence of Prophetic Events*, rev. ed. (Tustin, CA: Ariel Ministries, 2003), 108.

9. John Phillips, *Exploring the Future: A Comprehensive Guide to Bible Prophecy*, 3rd ed. (Grand Rapids, MI: Kregel, 2003), 327.

10. Josephus, *Antiquities*, 1.6.1.

11. Walter C. Kaiser Jr., *Preaching and Teaching the Last Things: Old Testament Eschatology for the Life of the Church* (Grand Rapids, MI: Baker Academic, 2011), 92.

12. Lamine Ghanmi, "Russia Enlarges Military Footprint in Libya," UPI, March 20, 2017, http://www.upi.com/Top_News/Voices/2017/03/20/Russia-enlarges-military-footprint-in-Libya/6031490019941/.

13. Darius Shahtahmasebi, "Russia Eyes Libya," *Anti-Media*, March 27, 2017, http://theantimedia.org/russia-libya-putin-middle-east/.

14. Thomas Constable, "Commentary on Ezekiel 38:4: Expository Notes of Dr. Thomas Constable," StudyLight.org, accessed June 8, 2017, http://www.studylight.org/commentaries/dcc/ezekiel-38.html#1.

15. See the New American Standard Bible.

16. See the discussion on the timing of the War of Gog and Magog in chapter 8.

17. Kaiser, *Preaching and Teaching*, 92.

18. Rosenberg, *Epicenter*, 130.

19. Not all commentators agree that Daniel 11:40 and Ezekiel 38–39 are parallel. John Walvoord rejects equating these two texts. He believes Daniel describes a war that occurs "possibly several years after the battle described in Ezekiel." John F. Walvoord, *Daniel*, ed. Philip E. Rawley and Charles H. Dyer, rev. ed. (Chicago: Moody, 2012), 355. Some Bible translations—the New Living Translation among them—seem closed to this possibility, but others (like the New American Standard Bible) seem to invite the comparison. The best defense I've seen for equating Daniel 11:40 and Ezekiel 38–39 is from Leon Wood in his commentary on Daniel. He provides five excellent arguments in support of his position. See Leon Wood, *A Commentary on Daniel* (Eugene, OR: Wipf and Stock, 1998), 309–10. See also Mark Hitchcock, "The King of the North in Daniel 11:40" (ThM thesis, Dallas Theological Seminary, 1991).

20. The full quote is "No war without Egypt, no peace without Syria." Quoted in Michael J. Totten, "No Peace without Syria," *Commentary*, August 31, 2009, https://www.commentarymagazine.com/foreign-policy/middle-east/no-peace-without-syria/.

21. Kaiser, *Preaching and Teaching*, 92. Joel Rosenberg supports this view. See Rosenberg, *Epicenter*, 130.

22. Saudi Arabia does harbor some terrorist elements but is vehemently opposed to Iran. Yemen is engrossed in a vicious civil war pitting the government against Houthi rebels backed by Iran.

23. Fruchtenbaum, *Footsteps of the Messiah*, 111.

24. Ibid., 112.

25. Rosenberg, *Epicenter*, 138.

CHAPTER 5: TRIPLE THREAT: RUSSIA, IRAN, AND TURKEY

1. "Kremlin: U.S. Has 'Emotional Obsession' with Russia," CNN, May 12, 2017, http://www.cnn.com/videos/tv/2017/05/12/lead-chance-kremlin-accuses-u-s-of -being-obsessed-with-russia-live.cnn, 2:59.
2. Abedin Taherkenareh, "Why Russia, Turkey and Iran Are Natural Allies," *The Conversation*, January 5, 2017, http://theconversation.com/why-russia-turkey-and -iran-are-natural-allies-70819.
3. Christian Caryl, "Sorry, but Putin's Still Winning," *Washington Post*, May 12, 2017, https://www.washingtonpost.com/news/democracy-post/wp/2017/05/12/sorry-but -putins-still-winning/?utm_term=.44f169d699a4.
4. Neil MacFarquhar and David E. Sanger, "Russia Sends Bombers to Syria Using Base in Iran," *New York Times*, August 16, 2016, https://www.nytimes.com/2016/08/17 /world/middleeast/russia-iran-base-syria.html.
5. John Bacon, "Putin Meets with Iranian Leader, Touts 'Reliable and Stable Partner,'" *USA Today*, March 28, 2017, http://www.usatoday.com/story/news/world/2017/03 /28/putin-meets-iranian-leader-touts-reliable-and-stable-partner/99723886/.
6. Ibid.
7. Douglas E. Schoen with Evan Roth Smith, *Putin's Master Plan: To Destroy Europe, Divide NATO, and Restore Russian Power and Global Influence* (New York: Encounter Books, 2016), 84.
8. Ahmad Majidyar, "Iran-Controlled Militant Group Says Regional Alliance Will Create 'Shiite Full Moon,'" Middle East Institute, May 11, 2017, http://www.mideasti .org/content/io/iran-controlled-militant-group-says-regional-alliance-will-create-shiite -full-moon.
9. Martin Chulov, "Amid Syrian Chaos, Iran's Game Plan Emerges: A Path to the Mediterranean," *Guardian*, October 8, 2016, https://www.theguardian.com/world /2016/oct/08/iran-iraq-syria-isis-land-corridor.
10. Majidyar, "Iran-Controlled Militant Group."
11. Chulov, "Iran's Game Plan Emerges."
12. Karim El-Bar, "Proxies and Politics: Why Iran Funds Foreign Militias," *Middle East Eye*, October 6, 2016, http://www.middleeasteye.net/essays/proxies-and-politics-why -iran-funds-foreign-militias-2124504867.
13. Alireza Nader, "Iran at Putin's Mercy," *National Interest*, January 12, 2017, http://nationalinterest.org/blog/the-buzz/iran-putins-mercy-19035.
14. "Iran Threatens 'Death to Israel' at Military Parade," *Tower*, April 19, 2017, http://www.thetower.org/4878oc-iran-threatens-death-to-israel-at-military-parade/.
15. Joel C. Rosenberg, "Why Iran's Top Leaders Believe That the End of Days Has Come," *Fox News*, November 7, 2011, http://www.foxnews.com/opinion/2011 /11/07/why-irans-top-leaders-believe-that-end-days-has-come.html.
16. Joel C. Rosenberg, "Understanding Egypt: The Twelfth Imam, and the End of Days," *The Blaze*, February 9, 2011, http://www.theblaze.com/news/2011/02/09 /understanding-egypt-the-twelfth-iman-and-the-end-of-days/.

17. Rosenberg, "Iran's Top Leaders."

18. Ben Hubbard, "Dialogue with Iran Is Impossible, Saudi Arabia's Defense Minister Says," *New York Times*, May 2, 2017, https://www.nytimes.com/2017/05/02/world /middleeast/saudi-arabia-iran-defense-minister.html.

19. Ariel Ben Solomon, "Erdogan's Regime Becoming More Dictatorship Than Democracy," *Jerusalem Post*, December 17, 2014, http://www.jpost.com/Middle-East /Analysis-Erdogans-regime-becoming-more-dictatorship-than-democracy-384895.

20. Patrick Kingsley, "Erdogan Claims Vast Powers in Turkey after Narrow Victory in Referendum," *New York Times*, April 16, 2017, https://www.nytimes.com/2017 /04/16/world/europe/turkey-referendum-polls-erdogan.html.

21. Eldad Beck, "Erdoğan: 'Liberate Jerusalem' from the Jews," *Ynetnews*, January 6, 2015, http://www.ynetnews.com/articles/0,7340,L-4663579,00.html.

22. Ibid.

23. Burak Bekdil, "Turkey's 'Jerusalem Fetish,'" Middle East Forum, May 30, 2015, http://www.meforum.org/5279/turkey-jerusalem-fetish.

24. "Turkey's President Rips into Israel, Tells Muslims to Swarm Temple Mount," *World Israel News*, May 8, 2017, https://worldisraelnews.com/erdogan-rips-into-israel -warns-trump-against-embassy-move/.

25. Amir Tsarfati, "Erdogan Calls on Muslims to 'Join Forces to Protect Jerusalem from Israel's Judaization Attempts,'" *Kehila News Israel*, May 10, 2017, http://kehilanews .com/2017/05/10/erdogan-calls-on-muslims-to-join-forces-to-protect-jerusalem -from-israels-judaization-attempts/.

26. Charles C. Ryrie, *The Best Is Yet to Come* (Chicago: Moody, 1981), 61.

CHAPTER 6: VLADIMIR PUTIN, RISING CZAR

1. Garry Kasparov with Mig Greengard, *Winter Is Coming: Why Vladimir Putin and the Enemies of the Free World Must Be Stopped* (New York: Public Affairs, 2015), xi.

2. David M. Ewalt, "The World's Most Powerful People 2016," *Forbes*, December 14, 2016, http://www.forbes.com/sites/davidewalt/2016/12/14/the-worlds-most -powerful-people-2016/#2ba85d7e368d.

3. Andrew Marszal, "Vladimir Putin Named Russia's 'Man of the Year'—for the 15th Time in a Row," *Telegraph*, December 17, 2014, http://www.telegraph.co.uk/news /worldnews/vladimir-putin/11298571/Vladimir-Putin-named-Russias-Man-of-the -Year-for-the-15th-time-in-a-row.html.

4. Fareed Zakaria, "Why Putin Is World's Most Powerful Man," *CNN*, March 14, 2017, http://www.cnn.com/2017/03/13/opinions/putin-most-powerful-man-world -zakaria/index.html.

5. Marszal, "Vladimir Putin Named Russia's 'Man of the Year.'"

6. Steven Lee Myers, *The New Tsar: The Rise and Reign of Vladimir Putin* (New York: Vintage Books, 2015), 290–91.

7. Ibid. See also Masha Gessen, *The Man without a Face: The Unlikely Rise of Vladimir Putin* (New York: Riverhead Books, 2012), 229.

8. Kasparov, *Winter Is Coming*, 245.

9. Douglas E. Schoen with Evan Roth Smith, *Putin's Master Plan: To Destroy Europe, Divide NATO, and Restore Russian Power and Global Influence* (New York: Encounter Books, 2016), 43.

10. Evan Osnos, David Remnick, and Joshua Yaffa, "Trump, Putin, and the New Cold War," *New Yorker*, March 6, 2017, http://www.newyorker.com/magazine/2017/03/06/trump-putin-and-the-new-cold-war.

11. Schoen, *Putin's Master Plan*, 34, 45.

12. Ibid., 34, 46.

13. Ibid., 45.

14. Ibid., 47.

15. Gessen, *Man without a Face*, 229.

16. Osnos, Remnick, and Yaffa, "Trump, Putin, and the New Cold War."

17. Zakaria, "Why Putin Is World's Most Powerful Man."

18. Associated Press, "Putin: Soviet Collapse a 'Genuine Tragedy,'" NBC News, April 25, 2005, http://www.nbcnews.com/id/7632057/ns/world_news/t/putin-soviet-collapse-genuine-tragedy/#.WRyOF2jys2w.

19. Areg Galstyan, "Is the Eurasian Economic Union Slowly Coming Apart?" *National Interest*, March 29, 2017, http://nationalinterest.org/feature/the-eurasian-economic-union-slowing-coming-apart-19947.

20. Emily Tillett, "Condoleezza Rice: Vladimir Putin Trying to Re-establish 'Russian Greatness,'" *CBS News*, May 7, 2017, http://www.cbsnews.com/news/condoleezza-rice-vladimir-putin-trying-to-re-establish-russian-greatness/.

21. For a more complete list of key dates, see "Vladimir Putin Fast Facts," CNN Library, February 6, 2017, http://www.cnn.com/2013/01/03/world/europe/vladimir-putin---fast-facts/.

22. For an excellent examination of Putin's business dealings, see Myers, *The New Tsar*, 281–303.

23. Rob Wile, "Is Vladimir Putin Secretly the Richest Man in the World?" *Time*, January 23, 2017, http://time.com/money/4641093/vladimir-putin-net-worth/. See also Emma Burrows, "Vladimir Putin's Inner Circle: Who's Who, and How Are They Connected?" *CNN*, March 28, 2017, http://www.cnn.com/2017/03/28/europe/vladimir-putins-inner-circle/index.html.

24. Schoen, *Putin's Master Plan*, vi.

25. Ibid.

26. Ibid., 13.

27. Ibid., 71.

28. Massimo Calabressi, "Inside Russia's Social Media War on America," *Time*, May 18, 2017, http://time.com/4783932/inside-russia-social-media-war-america/.

29. Joel C. Rosenberg, "Putin Rising: But Is He 'Gog'?" Joel C. Rosenberg's Blog, August 17, 2011, https://flashtrafficblog.wordpress.com/2011/08/17/putin-rising-but-is-he-gog/.

CHAPTER 7: RED DAWN: THE WAR OF GOG AND MAGOG

1. David Jeremiah, *Is This the End? Signs of God's Providence in a Disturbing New World* (Nashville: W Publishing Group, 2016), 211.

2. Randall Price, *The Temple and Bible Prophecy: A Definitive Look at Its Past, Present, and Future* (Eugene, OR: Harvest House, 2005), 459.

3. Ibid., 457.

4. Thomas Ice, "Ezekiel 38 & 39 (part 6)," Pre-Trib Research Center, accessed June 10, 2017, http://www.pre-trib.org/articles/view/ezekiel-38-39-part-6.

5. Charles H. Dyer, "Ezekiel," in *The Bible Knowledge Commentary*, ed. John F. Walvoord and Roy B. Zuck (Wheaton, IL: Victor Books, 1985), 1301.

6. Ibid.

7. Walter C. Kaiser Jr., *Preaching and Teaching the Last Things: Old Testament Eschatology for the Life of the Church* (Grand Rapids, MI: Baker Academic, 2011), 89–90.

8. Ibid., 94.

9. See Arnold G. Fruchtenbaum, *The Footsteps of the Messiah: A Study of the Sequence of Prophetic Events*, rev. ed. (Tustin, CA: Ariel Ministries, 2003), 115.

10. Dyer, "Ezekiel," 1301.

11. Fruchtenbaum, *Footsteps of the Messiah*, 115.

12. Randall Price, *Unholy War* (Eugene, OR: Harvest House, 2001), 310.

13. Dyer, "Ezekiel," 1302.

14. Kaiser, *Preaching and Teaching the Last Things*, 97.

CHAPTER 8: HOW CLOSE ARE WE?

1. John F. Walvoord, *The Nations in Prophecy* (Grand Rapids, MI: Zondervan, 1967), 116. Charles Dyer also believes "a reversion to more primitive methods of warfare might be possible." Charles H. Dyer, "Ezekiel," in *The Bible Knowledge Commentary*, ed. John F. Walvoord and Roy B. Zuck (Wheaton, IL: Victor Books, 1985), 1302.

2. Paul P. Enns, ed., *Shepherd's Notes: Ezekiel* (Nashville: B&H, 1998), 92. See also Charles Lee Feinberg, *The Prophecy of Ezekiel: The Glory of the Lord* (Eugene, OR: Wipf and Stock, 2003), 221.

3. Walter C. Kaiser Jr., *Preaching and Teaching the Last Things: Old Testament Eschatology for the Life of the Church* (Grand Rapids, MI: Baker Academic, 2011), 93.

4. Preterists, who view most biblical prophecy as already fulfilled, hold that the events in Ezekiel 38–39 have already occurred. Gary DeMar, a partial preterist, believes Ezekiel 38–39 was fulfilled in Esther 9. Citing various parallels between the battles in Ezekiel 38–39 and Esther, he claims the two events are "unmistakable" in their similarities. Gary DeMar, *End Times Fiction: A Biblical Consideration of the Left Behind Theology* (Nashville: Thomas Nelson, 2001), 12–14. A side-by-side comparison of the two passages, however, reveals substantial inconsistencies, demonstrating that they cannot be describing the same event. But more than this, if Ezekiel 38–39 was fulfilled in the events of Esther 9, why does the book of Esther make no mention of the fulfillment of this prophecy? The omission is telling. Moreover, the Jewish feast of Purim developed out of the Esther event according to Esther 9:20-32. The celebration at Purim includes the public reading of the book of Esther. If Esther 9 were a fulfillment of Ezekiel 38–39, one would expect the Jewish tradition to make some mention of this, yet there is nothing.

5. Walvoord, *Nations in Prophecy*, 105.

6. Randall Price, *The Temple and Bible Prophecy: A Definitive Look at Its Past, Present, and Future* (Eugene, OR: Harvest House, 1999), 458–59.

7. F. F. Bruce, "Eschatology: Understanding the End of Days," *Bible Review* 5 (December 1989): 43.

8. Harold Hoehner maintains that Ezekiel 38–39 will be fulfilled in two phases. Ezekiel 38 (phase 1) will be fulfilled early in the Tribulation, while Ezekiel 39 (phase 2) will be fulfilled at the end of the Tribulation. (Dr. Hoehner presented this view in a PhD seminar I attended.) Likewise, Ralph Alexander sees a double fulfillment with Ezekiel 38 and 39 fulfilled in Revelation 19:17-21 and Revelation 20:8. "The former, in one sense, prefigures the latter." Ralph H. Alexander, *Ezekiel*, Everyman's Bible Commentary (Chicago: Moody, 1976), 128. Charles Ryrie says, "Perhaps the first thrust will begin just before the middle of the Tribulation, with successive waves of the invasion continuing throughout the last part of that period and building up to Armageddon." Charles C. Ryrie, *The Ryrie Study Bible* (Chicago: Moody, 1995), 1323.

9. Ron Rhodes provides an excellent, evenhanded presentation and evaluation of each of these views in *Northern Storm Rising* (Eugene, OR: Harvest House, 2008), 179–95.

10. John Phillips, *Exploring the Future: A Comprehensive Guide to Bible Prophecy*, 3rd ed. (Grand Rapids, MI: Kregel, 2003), 343.

11. Mike Opelka, "John Kerry: Israel's 'Prosperity' May Be Blocking Peace Process with Palestinians," *The Blaze*, May 28, 2013, http://www.theblaze.com/news/2013/05/28/john-kerry-israels-prosperity-may-be-blocking-peace-process-with-palestinians/.

12. Charles Dyer gives several reasons why identifying Ezekiel 38 with Revelation 20:8 is flawed. He asks, "Why would the people remain on earth after the battle to burn the weapons of war for seven years (Ezek. 38:9-10) instead of entering immediately into eternity?" This kind of dissimilarity between these two passages precludes placing the war of Ezekiel 38–39 at the end of the Millennium. Dyer, "Ezekiel," 1300.

13. Kaiser, *Preaching and Teaching*, 76.

14. Price, *The Temple and Bible Prophecy*, 454.

15. Joel C. Rosenberg, *Epicenter: Why the Current Rumblings in the Middle East Will Change Your Future*, rev. ed. (Carol Stream, IL: Tyndale, 2008), 79.

16. Ibid., 80.

17. David Jeremiah, *Is This the End? Signs of God's Providence in a Disturbing New World* (Nashville: W Publishing Group, 2016), 225–26.

18. Another point against locating this invasion before the Tribulation is that Ezekiel places it in the "last days" or "latter years" of the Jewish people (see Ezekiel 38:8, 16). I don't believe the time period before the Tribulation qualifies as Israel's last days. The "last days" or "latter years" for Israel seem to begin with the Tribulation and continue on into the messianic kingdom; therefore, placing this invasion before the Tribulation is not the strongest view. Also, the language in Ezekiel 38:18-19 of God's fury, wrath, zeal, and anger being poured out on Gog and his armies fits a Tribulation setting for the events of Ezekiel 38 much better than a time period before its onset.

19. Charles Dyer and Mark Tobey, *Clash of Kingdoms: What the Bible Says about Russia, ISIS, Iran, and the End Times* (Nashville: Nelson Books, 2017), 68.

20. The main objection to placing the Battle of Gog and Magog during the first half of the Tribulation or near its midpoint is Ezekiel 39:9, which says that in the wake of the battle the inhabitants of Israel will make fires with the weapons for a period of seven years. This would mean that if this invasion occurs during the first half of the Tribulation, the weapons would be burned throughout the last half of the Tribulation and even on into the first years of the Millennium. While this is admittedly a problem for the view, it is not fatal. As long as some Jews continue to burn the weapons during the final half of the Tribulation, and briefly into the first three and a half years of the Millennium, the requirements of Ezekiel 39:9 can be fulfilled. John Whitcomb offers a solution to this objection: "I would suggest that this activity of massive cleansing takes place immediately after the second coming of Christ, just after the additional devastation in the holy land called Armageddon. By then, the bodies of Gog's soldiers are nothing but bones (v. 15)." John C. Whitcomb, "Gog from Magog: A Study in Prophetic Chronology," Whitcomb Ministries, 2010, http://media.sermonaudio.com/mediapdf/121110111401.pdf.

21. John Phillips, *Exploring the Future*, 347–48.

22. Jeremiah, *Is This the End?*, 226.

23. John F. Walvoord with Mark Hitchcock, *Armageddon, Oil, and Terror: What the Bible Says about the Future*, rev. ed. (Carol Stream, IL: Tyndale, 2007), 207.

CHAPTER 9: WHAT DOES THE FUTURE HOLD?

1. David Jeremiah, *Is This the End? Signs of God's Providence in a Disturbing New World* (Nashville: W Publishing Group, 2016), 210.

2. Charles Dyer and Mark Tobey, *Clash of Kingdoms: What the Bible Says about Russia, ISIS, Iran, and the End Times* (Nashville: Nelson Books, 2017), 20.

3. Joel C. Rosenberg, *Epicenter: Why the Current Rumblings in the Middle East Will Change Your Future*, rev. ed. (Carol Stream, IL: Tyndale, 2008), 285.

4. J. Vernon McGee, *How Russia Will Be Destroyed* (Pasadena, CA: Thru the Bible Radio Network, n. d.), 10–11, http://www.ttb.org/docs/default-source/Booklets/how-russia-will-be-destroyed.pdf.

5. This list is adapted from a book I coauthored. John F. Walvoord with Mark Hitchcock, *Armageddon, Oil, and Terror: What the Bible Says about the Future*, rev. ed. (Carol Stream, IL: Tyndale, 2007), 203–4.

6. A. W. Tozer, *Preparing for Jesus' Return*, comp. and ed. James L. Snyder (Ventura, CA: Regal, 2012), 21, 191.

7. Ed Hindson, *Final Signs: Amazing Prophecies of the End Times* (Eugene, OR: Harvest House, 1996), 196.

CHAPTER 10: IT'S ALWAYS SOON

1. C. S. Lewis, *The Voyage of the* Dawn Treader (New York: Harper Trophy, 2000), 162.

2. Warren Wiersbe, *Be Ready: Living in Light of Christ's Return, 1 & 2 Thessalonians*

(Wheaton, IL: Victor Books, 1979), 137, quoted on Bible.org, accessed June 12, 2017, https://bible.org/seriespage/4-correction-concerning-day-lord-part-1-2-thes-21-5.
3. A. W. Tozer, *Preparing for Jesus' Return*, comp. and ed. James L. Snyder (Ventura, CA: Regal, 2012), 15.
4. Paul N. Benware, *Understanding End Times Prophecy: A Comprehensive Approach*, rev. ed. (Chicago: Moody, 2006), 16.
5. Edward K. Rowell, ed., *Fresh Illustrations for Preaching and Teaching* (Grand Rapids, MI: Baker Books, 1997), 64.
6. Charles Spurgeon, "Watch for Christ's Coming" (sermon #2302), https://www.ccel.org/ccel/spurgeon/sermons39.xiv.html.
7. Ibid.
8. J. Dwight Pentecost, *Prophecy for Today: God's Purpose and Plan for Our Future*, rev. ed. (Grand Rapids, MI: Discovery House, 1989), 22.
9. David Jeremiah, *Is This the End? Signs of God's Providence in a Disturbing New World* (Nashville: W Publishing Group, 2016), 265.

APPENDIX 2: THE KING OF THE NORTH: THE NORTHERN CONFEDERACY
1. John Walvoord's original chapter on the king of the north goes on to describe "The Emergence of a World Religion," but it does not pertain to the subject of this book, so I've ended the chapter here.

APPENDIX 3: COMMON QUESTIONS RELATED TO RUSSIA, THE MIDDLE EAST, AND THE END OF DAYS
1. Arnold G. Fruchtenbaum, *The Footsteps of the Messiah: A Study of the Sequence of Prophetic Events*, rev. ed. (Tustin, CA: Ariel Ministries, 2003), 111.
2. Ibid., 112.
3. Max Abrahms, Denis Sullivan, and Charles Simpson, "Five Myths about Syrian Refugees," *Foreign Affairs*, March 22, 2017, https://www.foreignaffairs.com/articles/europe/2017-03-22/five-myths-about-syrian-refugees.
4. "ISIS Fast Facts," CNN Library, April 17, 2017, http://edition.cnn.com/2014/08/08/world/isis-fast-facts/.
5. The main points I've used are taken from Robert Harvey and Philip H. Towner, *2 Peter and Jude*, The IVP New Testament Commentary Series, ed. Grant R. Osborne (Downers Grove, IL: IVP Academic, 2009), 118–19.
6. Ibid., 118.
7. Ibid.
8. D. Edmond Hiebert, *Second Peter and Jude: An Expositional Commentary* (Greenville, SC: BJU Press, 1989) 153.
9. Harvey and Towner, *2 Peter and Jude*, 119.
10. Ibid.
11. Michael Green, *The Second Epistle General of Peter and the General Epistle of Jude*, The Tyndale New Testament Commentaries, gen. ed. Leon Morris, rev. ed. (Grand Rapids, MI: Eerdmans, 1989), 148.

ABOUT MARK HITCHCOCK

Attorney **MARK HITCHCOCK** thought his career was set after graduating from law school. But after what Mark calls a "clear call to full-time ministry," he changed course and went to Dallas Theological Seminary, completing a master's and PhD. Since 1991, Mark has authored numerous books, serves as senior pastor of Faith Bible Church in Edmond, Oklahoma, and is associate professor of Bible exposition at Dallas Theological Seminary. Mark and his wife, Cheryl, live in Edmond with their children and grandchildren.

ABOUT JEFF KINLEY

(COAUTHOR OF *THE COMING APOSTASY*)

JEFF KINLEY empowers people with God's vintage truth through writing and speaking. A bestselling author, Jeff has written twenty-five books. He is a graduate of Dallas Theological Seminary (ThM) and is a current doctoral student. He and his wife live in Arkansas and have three grown sons. See jeffkinley.com for more information about his ministry.